Communalism *in* MODERN INDIA

BY THE SAME AUTHOR

Essays on Indian Nationalism

Essays on Contemporary India

Ideology and Politics in Modern India

Indian National Movement: The Long-Term Dynamics

The Rise and Growth of Economic Nationalism

Communalism *in* MODERN INDIA

Bipan Chandra

Published by Ashok Gosain and Ashish Gosain for:
HAR-ANAND PUBLICATIONS PVT LTD
E-49/3, Okhla Industrial Area, Phase-II, New Delhi-110020
Tel: 41603490
E-mail: info@haranandbooks.com/haranand@rediffmail.com
Shop online at: www.haranandbooks.com

Third Revised Edition, 2008

Reprint, 2025

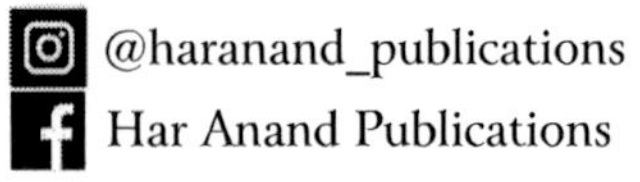

Printed in India at Royal Press

To
Lou and Bill Wake, Frieda Reed,
Monro Merrick and the late Dick Cecil,
my American friends with whom
I shared some very exciting years in my youth

Preface

This Work is an historical overview and analysis of the essential features of communalism and of the reasons for its growth in modern India. The concrete details of communal politics, demands and propaganda, of communal riots, and of negotiations and efforts to solve the communal problem have been brought in only to the extent that they serve to illustrate or illuminate the analysis.

I have sought to understand and interpret and expose communalism for what it is, to know what its roots and social functions were during the period of its birth and growth in the colonial period, and why it developed to the extent of resulting in the partition of the land. I have tried to understand which aspects of India's social, economic, political and cultural life were responsible for the growth of communalism, from where it drew its social support, which sections of society were 'represented' by it, whose interests it served, and which sections promoted and organized communal politics.

Rejecting the notion that communalism was the logical and inevitable product of Indian historical development, I have posited that it is capable of being explained historically and was not a mere historical accident or product of a diabolical conspiracy. Nor was its success ensured beforehand; it could have been curbed and controlled and even eradicated if certain social, political and ideological conditions had been met.

Social phenomena are usually complex and contradictory and are to be grasped by looking at all their contradictory aspects at the same time. My effort has been to bring out and analyse, in all their complexity, the multiplicity of forces which were responsible for the growth of communalism. I do not believe that a complex phenomenon like communalism can have a simple, mono-causal explanation or solution. At the same time, mere detailing of its many causes is not enough; a hierarchy of causes must also be established, for not all the causes of a social phenomenon are of equal weight. Some play a greater guiding, 'determining' role than others. This hierarchy of determination has also to be brought out. This has been doubly necessary as my objective has been not merely to study and analyse communalism but also to help in eradicating it from our life. One of my underlying concerns has been to examine the complex integration of communal ideology and politics with colonialism and colonial policy; another concern focuses on the failure of the national movement to deal effectively with the communal problem despite its commitment to secularism, national unity and anti-imperialism. I am of course fully aware that despite one's best efforts any social phenomenon is grasped and understood imperfectly, that is, not wholly correctly. A social scientist can but try to be 'as correct as possible'. This is particularly so when he or she tries to go beyond empirical details to generalizations and wider synthesis. But till the latter effort is made, it is not possible to understand or deal with specific events and developments.

This study deals with communalism and not with communal riots which, given the prevalence of communal feelings, can be explained and studied in specific, conjunctural terms. Similarly, the instruments and mechanisms through which communal ideology and politics were propagated have not been discussed here.

I have dealt with both Hindu and Muslim communalisms or rather with communalism which has both Hindu and Muslim faces and not just with Muslim communalism as has often been done in the past. Moreover, I have not treated communalism as equivalent to separatism. Separatism was only the last phase of Muslim communalism. To equate communalism with separatism would also imply that there was or could be no Hindu communalism since Hindus, as a religious majority, could not be 'separatist'. This would then also suggest that only Muslims had the propensity to be communal, that Hindus not being separatist were always nationalist even if there were weaknesses in their nationalist ideology. This is precisely what Hindu communalists have always argued before as well as after 1947. This has also led many to adopt a softer attitude towards Hindu communalism. Sometimes the word 'separatist' is defined to mean the effort at treating Muslims as a 'distinct and separate group or community' and thus at separating Muslims from Hindus. It is then argued that 'Muslim separatism' existed. But Hindu communalists too declared that Hindus were a separate and distinct community, that is, distinct from Muslims, and tried to separate Hindus from Muslims. One should then also talk of Hindu separatism which would be absurd. In fact, until 1937-38, both Hindu and Muslim communalists stood for Hindu-Muslim unity and a united Indian nation.

Even secular writers have tended to see communalism as a conflict between Hindus and Muslims. That is the case only so far as communal riots are concerned. Politically, the conflict was not between Hindus and Muslims—which is what communal ideologues asserted—but between Hindu and Muslim communalisms on one side and the secular nationalist forces on the other.

I hope that my analysis of communalism will have a certain wider application to and validity for other similar divisive phenomena such as casteism, regionalism and linguism which have developed in India since the middle of the nineteenth century.[1] Though the latter have certain distinct and separate aspects, they share many common characteristics and structural features as well as social roots and functions with communalism; they often reflect the same social tendencies. Moreover, quite often these isms tend to replace each other as if in a game of musical chairs. We have taken up

[1]I Would like to make it very clear that for me regionalism and linguism are very different from the democratic notion of linguistic cultural regions or linguistic states whose cultural and economic interests are to be protected and promoted within the overall perspective of the development of the Indian people or Indian nation. This conception and the concrete historical movements for its realisation have not in the past stood in the way of national unity or the formation of all-India classes. In fact, they have contributed to the formation of wider loyalties and the process of the nation-in-the-making. Linguism and regionalism have, on the other hand, set one state or region against another and have therefore been basically divisive ideologies.

communalism for separate study for several reasons. In certain crucial social, cultural and political aspects it was different. Moreover, during the period of this study, though the colonial state made consistent attempts to use all actual or potential antagonisms within Indian society, in the end they banked heavily only on the communal antagonism. Similarly, the national movement did succeed in overcoming or making passive, at least for the time being, all other antagonisms but the communal one. Moreover, among all such divisive ideologies and movements, communalism was the only one that was all-India in its scope. But by studying communalism I am certainly not denying or missing the significance of other communal-type phenomena. In fact, their existence and their tendency to emerge and grow wherever and whenever communalism is brought under check challenge the view that communalism was inherent in Indian society or was and is the special or unique product of its history of the medieval period.

In fact, even where I have not explicitly argued this, I have not viewed communalism as a unique social phenomenon not only in the Indian context, where other communal-type phenomena have prevailed, but also on a world scale. I am fully aware of its resemblance to the contemporary ideologies and movements of fascism. Similar resemblance can also be easily traced to racist ideologies and ideologies promoting Catholic-Protestant conflict in Northern Ireland or Canada or Belgium, or the Tamil-Sinhala division in Sri Lanka, or the Malay-Chinese-Indian division in Malaysia and Singapore, or Christian-Muslim conflict in Lebanon, and so on. Communalism was thus not an inevitable or inherent product of the Indian national character or of India's peculiar historical and social development. It was the result of conditions which have in other climates produced similar phenomena, especially where middle classes were involved. Of course, India's specific historical and socio-economic development imparted certain specific characteristics to communalism in India.

This study is confined to the pre-1947 period because certain breaks occurred in 1947. Several basic dissimilarities between the pre-

and post-1947 periods developed so far as the communal problem was concerned as the socio-political context of communalism changed in certain basic aspects. As I have tried to bring out these changes related to (*i*) the entirely different role of the state, (*ii*) the social and class character of communalism and social and political environment within which it operated, and (*iii*) the relative roles of Hindu and Muslim communalisms. But, at the same time, there are strong elements of similarity and continuity so that, I hope, the analysis will prove useful in understanding and fighting communalism today. In the last chapter, I have tried to suggest the 'way out' of the communal morass in which our country is still mired.

I have, of course, assumed both secularism and national unity to be valid and desirable values and goals for which we as a people have to strive. Not only the national movement but any nation-wide movement would require wider unity and suppression of communal and other divisive tendencies. Communalism has therefore been studied in the context of the struggle against it. At the same time, I have accepted that secularism and national unity and our struggle around them must have an objective basis rooted in scientific and factual analysis. Effort has therefore been made to understand communalism even while criticizing and deploring it. In the words of Lucio Colletti: "Value judgements are inevitably present in scientific research itself, but as judgements whose ultimate significance depends on the degree to which they stand up to historical-practical verification or experiment, and hence on their capacity to be converted ultimately into factual judgements. This is precisely the link between science and politics, between knowledge and transformation of the world...."[2]

This is basically a work of synthesis; and the ideas and analytical insights of a large number of authors have influenced it or, as in many cases, have been incorporated within it. It has not been possible to acknowledge in the footnotes, unless directly quoted, my deep debt to them. This is in particular true of the pioneering work of Jawaharlal

[2]Lucio Colletti, *From Rousseau to Lenin*, p. 76.

Nehru, K.B. Krishna, Beni Prasad, W.C. Smith, A.R. Desai, K.M. Ashraf, Tufail Ahmed Mangalori, Abid Hussain, C.G. Shah and the Kanpur Riots Enquiry Committee appointed by the Congress in 1931. Many of the other authors whose detailed research and insights I have drawn upon have been cited in the select bibliography. The footnotes have been kept to the minimum; they are given only when persons are quoted and figures cited, or when supplementary comments are made. I have relied in the main or monographic literature; primary sources are used only in the case of the thought of prominent communal leaders or to fill in lacunae in the existing literature.

I am grateful to my colleagues Romila Thapar, S. Gopal, K.N. Panikkar, Satish Saberwal, Madhavan K. Palat, Mridula Mukherjee, Aditya Mukherjee and Bhagwan Josh for having gone through the draft of this work and suggesting important changes. I have also benefited from many discussions with Professor Moonis Raza and Kewal Varma. A large number of my students, who have by now matured into scholaris in their own right, have helped in the making of this book. I am particularly in thankful to Sashi Joshi, D.N. Gupta, Lajpat Jagga, S.K. Raut, Harjot Oberoi, Anthony Thomas, Sucheta Mahajan, Salil Misra, Vishalakshi Menon, Rakesh Batabyal, Bodh Prakash, Bhupinder Yadav and Neerja Singh. I would like to express my gratitude to the late Dr. Devanesan and to Professors Sita Ram Singh, Ashin Das Gupta, J.S. Grewal and M.G.S. Narayanan for inviting me to their departments and universities to deliver the UGC lectures on the theme and thus enabling me to exchange ideas with a wider body of teachers and students. And, of course, this book would not have been written but for the opportunity provided by the UGC to think and speak and write about its theme.

Usha has as before acted as a sounding board, critic, advisor, and editor. What more can an author ask from his wife?

BIPAN CHANDRA

Contents

CHAPTER 1

What is Communalism?

Simply put, communalism is the belief that because a group of people follow a particular religion they have, as a result, common social, political and economic interests. It is the belief that in India Hindus, Muslims, Christians and Sikhs form different and distinct communities which are independently and separately structured or consolidated; that all the followers of a religion share not only a community of religious interests but also common secular interests, that is, common economic, political, social and cultural interests; that Indians inevitably perceive such interests through the spectacles of the religious grouping and are bound to possess a sense of identity based on religion, i.e., religion has to become the basis of their basic social identity and the determinant of their basic social relationships; that they possess the inherent tendency to act and function as a separate group or entity or unit in these fields; that they constitute separate 'organic wholes' or homogeneous and cohesive communities, especially in the political field; that each such religious 'community' has its own separate history; that communal identity and division have always pervaded Indian society, though they may have been reinforced in modern times; that the religious 'community' has become the basis of the organization of modern politics in India and of the perception of economic, political and cultural issues by the Indian people; that a 'real' Hindu or Muslim can belong only to a party of the community and cannot differ politically from other Hindus or Muslims; that all Hindus or Muslims must think alike in politics because they are Hindus or Muslims; that, in fact, each religious 'community' constitutes a homogeneous entity and even a distinct 'society' in itself;

that there is and can be no such thing as an Indian nation—India has been, is, and has to be, a mere 'confederation of religious communities.'

The communalist assumes that the most meaningful distinction among the Indian people on social, cultural, economic and political issues is to be made on the basis of such units of religious communities. The Indian people can exist and act socially and protect their collective or corporate or non-individual interests only as members of religion-based communities. They never think, want, feel or act in any other manner or category except as members of such homogeneous communities whose interests, outlook, way of life, etc., are the same.[1] All their choices are made and all their benefits are enjoyed as members of these communities. The different communities have their own leaders. Those who talk of being national, regional, or class leaders are merely masquerading; beneath the mask they are also only leaders of their own communities. Some writers go further and talk of the existence of the Hindu mind, the Muslim mind, etc.

Thus, the communal view asserts that the religious distinction is among Indians, the most important or fundamental distinction or cleavage or distinguishing mark. This distinction overrides all other distinctions. On the other hand, all other social identities and distinctions are either denied or, when accepted in theory, either negated in practice or subordinated to the religious identity. Not nation, nationalities, linguistic groups, or classes, but religious communities are seen as the fundamental social units of the Indian milieu. For the same reason, in communal politics, as also in communal historical writing, it is only the aspect of religious community that is emphasized, all other issues—political, economic, social, linguistic, cultural, and even purely religious—are ignored, confused and even suppressed.

Inherent in communalism is the second notion that the social, cultural, economic and political interests of Hiudus and Muslims and

[1]In this sense, a communal riot represents the concentrated essence of this notion when the killing of any stray individual represents an attack upon his 'community' and defence of the killer's 'community.'

Christians and Sikhs are dissimilar and divergent. Interestingly, this divergence and dissimilarity, as also the notion of common secular interests on the basis of religion, are never sought to be demonstrated empirically or logically in any of the fields. They are always either assumed as self-evident truths or are blandly asserted needing no proof.

Furthermore, the communalist usually starts from difference and divergence, but invariably ends up with the notion that the interests of the people following different religions stand juxtaposed to one another and in fact, are, and must be, antagonistic and mutually exclusive and incompatible because of the fact of their following different religions. Here again, difference and divergence are equated with, or transformed into, dissonance, incompatibility and antagonism by a sleight of hand, without concrete demonstration. It follows that mutual hostility and even hatred between the 'communities' is, and has always been, the normal and perpetual element, while tolerance, peaceful living side-by-side, cooperation and integration are temporary and contingent. A further consequence follows: in any election and in democratic institutions, followers of a religion, that is, members of a 'community,' were bound to vote for each other and, when elected, to work only for the interests of their co-religionists and to try to dominate the other 'communities.' Thus any democratic rule would, in the eyes of the Muslim communalist, mean the rule of the majority 'community' and also, therefore, its domination over, and suppression of, the minority 'community.' Consequently, he further believes that nationalism and democracy pose a threat to his 'community.' Interestingly, the Hindu communalist accepts this view and hails nationalism and democracy for that very reason. But he does so only on an all-India scale. In provinces and states where Hindus are in a minority, both democracy and secular nationalism are unwelcome to him also.[2]

Another consequence of the rigid division of society into 'communities' was that instead of analysing the social condition or

[2]Similarly, more Hindus in jobs are seen as equivalent to Hindu 'domination' which the Muslim communalist bemoans and attacks and the Hindu communalist gloats over and defends.

situation and its impact on, or relationship to, the individual's fate, the communalist blamed any personal failure to achieve an objective on the other 'community.' Thus Muslim 'backwardness' or a Muslim's failure to get employment became the product of Hindu 'progress' or 'animosity' or 'domination,' while 'Hindus' progress was declared to be constantly thwarted or frustrated by Muslim 'hostility.'

II

We have to distinguish between communal tension and communal politics.[3] The first, that is, communal tension, was spasmodic and usually directly involved the lower classes only. During the period when, and in the area where, communal tension prevailed, all mutual relations between the followers of different religions were snapped following the arousal of religious and communal passions through vicious propaganda, oral as well as written, inflammatory accusations, and wild rumours often involving some religious issue such as cow-killing or music before mosques. An atmosphere and climate of excitement and frenzy were generated and often actual violence also took place. The communal riot was a typical example of communal tension. The participants in and the victims of a communal riot—though not necessarily its instigators—were usually the urban poor and lumpen and *goonda* elements, though in a few cases the peasants were also involved. There was seldom any physical participation by the middle and upper classes, though they often lent material and moral support to the lumpen and *goonda* participants. However, once the frenzy abated and the excitement disappeared and the climate of immediate fear no longer existed, tension rapidly disappeared and normal relations were restored among the persons involved. Though each episode left behind a certain legacy, in general the tensions involving or generated by a communal riot rapidly and on the whole disappeared. The significance of communal riots should also not be exaggerated. Communal tension and riots began to occur only

[3]This distinction was first brought out by K.B. Krishna in *The Problem of Minorities.* See pp. 277-79. Also see W.C. Smith, *Modern Islam in India,* pp. 194, 196-97.

from the last quarter of the nineteenth century. Moreover, they did not prevail in India on a significant scale till 1946-47. The overwhelming majority of Indians, especially in the rural areas, were unaffected by communal tensions. Thus, during 1923-26, the four-year period of maximum communal tension in India before 1946, there were 72 major communal riots, which gives an average figure of one riot every 20 days for the vast continent-sized and heavily populated country.

Communal politics, on the other hand, were long-term, persistent and continuous. They involved, in the main, the middle classes, landlords and bureaucratic elements. They represented communal ideology in its political form and found expression in the political field and not in overt physical acts against the members of the 'other community' on a personal or even communal basis, even when their basis was mere personal political rivalry or promotion of personal interest. On the personal plane, friendly relations could prevail among the communal politicians as well as their middle and upper class supporters. In fact, the communal leaders quite often cooperated with each other in municipal committees, district boards and provincial cabinets, after having been elected to these bodies through communal politics and rivalry. Quite often, at least till 1945, they also maintained friendly social and economic relations.[4]

In this work we will be mainly concerned with communal politics and ideology, for communal riots are not the main form or content of communalism. They were, in the main, its reflection, its active episodic expression, its bitter and virulent manifestation and consequence, and one of the instruments and agencies for its spread.

[4]Cf. Tufail Ahmed Mangalori in his *Musalmanon Ka Roshan Mustaqbil:* "This system (i.e., of separate electorates) of elections does enable persons from the upper classes to have the convenience that they become members by getting votes from their own community and then after becoming members they become very friendly with Hindus. In the riots in the city the poor Hindus and Muslims have their heads split and in the civil lines [the upper class section of a city] Hindus and Muslims live in a friendly manner side by side. They dine and drink with each other. Their women have a great deal of love and unity in common. All this because they can vote for each other in the Boards and Councils. They help each other. On the other hand, a Hindu member has no way of reaching out to a poor Muslim. Consequently, a poor Muslim remains in every way oppressed and deprived." Pp. 419-20. (Translated from Urdu.)

The communal riot was sudden and spasmodic, was an aspect of social pathology, and its causation lay either in the prevalence of a communal atmosphere generated by communal politics and communal ideology or in conjunctural causes, involving religious feelings alone or combined with some particular local interests, which could be effectively handled by efficient administrative or police action and secular public opinion. It is communalism as politics and ideology which can be and perhaps should be the subject of analysis as also of ideological-political struggle.

Both types of communalism were of course integrally linked—both contributed to each other—though in a religiously plural society, communal riots could sometimes occur without the simultaneous development of communal politics. Communal riots had a tendency to force even basically secular persons to temporarily think in communal terms in order to provide for the safety of person and property and thus to generate a vicious circle. Moreover, a communal riot left a certain emotional residue or legacy which could be used later by the communal ideologue or politician. On the other hand, the ultimate power of communal politics came from this capacity, potential or actual, to involve the lower classes and to produce communal tension. This is one reason why, because the masses remained on the whole uninvolved in communal politics, communalism did not become till 1937-39 a basic political force or a widespread and all-pervasive phenomenon and remained confined on the whole to the middle classes. On the other hand, once the communal forces had succeeded in generating communal tensions on a large, national scale and in initiating a communal holocaust in large parts of the country, their political success became assured under the circumstances. It is to be noted that a direct relation between communal riots and politics was established for the first time as late as 1946 when the Muslim League gave the direct action call on 16 August.

III

Let us at this stage clarify certain points regarding our basic approach to communalism in modern India.

Communalism was not a remnant of the past—a hangover from the medieval period, a 'language of the past.' It was a *modern ideology* that incorporated some aspects and elements of the *past ideologies and institutions and historical background* to form anew ideological and political discourse or mix. Because it used many elements inherited from the past, it has been wrongly described as a revival or continuation of a medieval ideology or theory or at least as having 'roots' in the medieval period. Communalism is also often falsely equated with revivalism because the communalists are also often revivalists. That is however not always so. Furthermore, the use of earlier elements to fashion new theories and ideologies is a well-known historical phenomenon; and many a modern ideology claims to be reviving the past. The modern ideology of Meiji authoritarianism and later militarism in Japan was based on medieval Shintoism and emperor worship. The fascist New Life Movement of Chiang Kai-shek in the 1930s was based on Confucianism.

Hitler and Mussolini made appeals to old and conservative elements of the past ideologies and drew upon the most distant past for ideological sustenance. Anti-Semitism certainly dated back to the medieval period; but in Nazi Germany, it was not a revival but a structured part of one of the most modern of ideologies. The modern Catholic Church, the basis of much of the ruling party ideologies in Germany and Italy after the Second World War and in Spain and Portugual from the 1930s till recently, borrowed almost its entire theology from the medieval past. Yet, no one will think of describing Christian Democracy as a remnant of the past or of being 'rooted' in the past. It is as modern as the IBM or the multi-nationals. Nationalism was used as a basic component of imperialist ideology by France and other imperialist powers from the middle of the nineteenth century, yet it would be sheer nonsense to ascribe the origins of imperialism to the French Revolution, which first generated the ideology of nationalism.

One last example which is of course different from the examples cited so far because it pertains to an ideology which did not claim to be resurrecting the past but boldly claimed to be a new, revolutionary worldview of a new class. It is well known that Marxism was new and critically different, yet it drew heavily upon German classical philosophy, French political philisophy and British political economy. Thus, a large number of movements and institutions claim the sanction of tradition and therefore incorporate its symbols and elements. Numerous other examples can be cited: British parliamentary democracy traced itself to the Magna Carta; Stalin created Leninism to validate all his departures from Marx and Lenin; in India the backward and middle castes have overthrown the basic *varna* category of *shudra* as applying to themselves and then have used the caste system to keep the scheduled castes down; and, more crassly, the Shah of Iran simply declared that he was re-creating the Achamaenid Empire and then went through the ancient coronation rituals. Thus, a new system, institution or ideology has the capacity to incorporate less or more of past structures, but these past structures do not define the 'origins' or causation of the new institution or ideology. A social scientist has, of course, to study and bring out these older elements and structures, but without assigning them the role of 'origins' and 'causation.' For example, to revert to the example of Marxism, the many previous elements which went into its making do not become its 'origins' and 'causation,' which lie embedded in the contemporary social structure as a whole and in the development of capitalism in particular.

In India, the basis of communal politics, that is, the notion of religion serving as the basis for the new political process based on popular participation, was something new, though religious distinction and religion as one principle for social grouping had previously existed. But medieval politics were not communal, though religious suppression and oppression occurred during the medieval as also the ancient period. Communalism was a modern phenomenon that arose as a result of British colonial impact and the response of different Indian social classes, strata and groups. Communalism was a modern ideology that used the popular traditional consciousness of Hindus and Muslims forming separate groups for religious, marriage and interdining purposes in its effort to base modern politics of popular sovereignty on a religious identity.[5] To grasp the new, modern character of the basic features of communalism, it is necessary to realize that in history, as in all fields, there are continuities but there are breaks and innovations as well—and usually the breaks and innovations are the more important aspects of social development whether positive or negative in their consequences.

Communalism emerged as a consequence of the emergence of modern politics which marked a sharp break with the politics of the medieval or ancient or pre-1857 period. Communalism, as also nationalism and socialism, could emerge as politics and as ideology only after a structural break had occurred in the nature of politics, that is, after politics based on the people, politics of popular sovereignty, politics of popular participation and mobilization, politics based on the creation and mobilization of public opinion had been introduced, even if the term people was defined narrowly. In the previous politics, which were based entirely on the upper ruling classes in which the people either played the role of cannon-fodder or were compelled to rebel outside the political system with successful rebel leaders being incorporated into the old ruling classes, there was no need to take politics to the people and to unite and mobilize the people as a people. Thus the notion of Hindus or Muslims uniting as Hindus or Muslims for politics—or Indians uniting as Indians for politics—could come only with the entry of people as a constitutive element of politics, with politics based on the doctrine of popular sovereignty. It was for this reason that, as will be brought out in Chapter 8, the colonial authorities tried to keep Muslims apolitical as Muslims till 1905, and encouraged their political mobilization, though on a rather narrow social base, only after 1905 when popular politics could no longer be avoided.[6] Similarly, communalism could take an

[5]Thus, as brought out in Chapter 7, it was not medieval history which bequeathed communalism to modern India but a particular view of medieval history which was itself communal ideology as also a product of this ideology.

[6]Similarly, as brought out in Chapter 4, Syed Ahmed Khan and Raja Shiva Prasad tried during the 1880s to oppose the National Congress by mobilizing the upper classes on grounds of race, birth, status and caste. It was only after the failure of this attempt that the wider ideology of communalism was resorted to.

extreme or fascist form only when the people had to be appealed to and mobilized on a larger scale after 1937 because of the spread of democratic feelings, extension of the franchise and the rapid advance of the national movement.

Similarly, it is wrong to look upon communalism as a revival of traditional ideology or as an aspect of traditional India that has now to be discarded. The communal view was not present in our tradition; it was not a primordial feeling. Communal antagonism was not a problem inherited from the past. It was not an inevitable product of our history. Communalism is not only *in* the present; it is of the present. It did not serve, nor does it now serve, the past or decaying social groups and formations. It did not try to restore the past. It did not represent 'antiquated social and cultural forces which would rather bring back the social institutions and culture which date back to a couple of millennia.' It responded to and expressed the social urges and served the social needs and purposes of certain contemporary social groups, strata or classes. Above all, it became a cog in the politics of colonialism which can by no stretch of imagination be described as a remnant of the past. Thus the social roots of communalism as also its social, economic and political objectives were modern, in the present and of the present.[7]

It is the present, contemporary social structure which sustained communalism. To say this is, of course, not yet to explain its rise and spread. To do so is the task of the historian and other social scientists.

There exists one particular difficulty in the scientific study of communalism (and communal ideology). The very tools of analysis

[7]Cf. Jawaharlal Nehru (in 1936): "One must never forget that communalism in India is a latter-day phenomenon which has grown up before our eyes." *Selected Works* (hereafter *SW*), Vol. 7, p. 69. Humayun Kabir: "There is the talk about the 'rising tide of communalism.' That I think is not historically true.... As a matter of fact, communal differences have been there as a canker in Indian polity only from the beginnings of the modern period." *Muslim Politics 1906-47 and Other Essays,* p. 86. And *Kanpur Riots Enquiry Committee Report* in 1931: "Our retrospect of the Muslim period shows that the Hindu-Muslim problem in its present form is really of recent birth." Published as *Roots of Communal Politics,* edited by N.G. Barrier, p. 161. Also see Imtiaz Ahmad, "Perspectives on the Communal Problem'," pp. 36-37.

have been contaminated by it as a result of the ideological conditioning of the last 100 years, when the middle classes and the intelligentsia were perpetually surrounded by a communal outlook in politics, in the Press, in literature, and particularly in the educational system. Consequently, communalism has often been viewed in the social sciences, as in real life, through conscious or unconscious communal assumptions.[8] This is particularly so in the disciplines of political science and history where, traditionally, emphasis has been laid on ideas and ideologies and not on their social soil.' Moreover, many social scientists echo the communal ideology, though unconsciously and with secular intentions, because of lack of theoretical and conceptual clarity or a fuller historical study. This is also often due to an empiricist approach, where ideological and political statements are uncritically treated as empirical data. "But clearly, where phenomenal forms are deceptive, merely to describe them will not yield adequate concepts of the essential relations at issue. For here, categories grounded in observation alone will reproduce precisely the misleading features of the forms they describe."[9] Consequently, a great deal of present-day sociological and political science writing on the subject becomes an unconscious reproduction of the old liberal communal outlook. As a result, the effort to provide a secular and scientific analysis becomes infructuous. Several recent studies of communalism, both in India and abroad, act as examples of the dangers of well-meaning persons writing on this question when

[8]The full extent of the deep, subtle, and often unconscious penetration of the consciousness of most Indians by aspects of communal ideology is seldom realized by most of us.

[9]P. Corrigan *et al.*, *Socialist Construction and Marxist Theory*, p. 14. The authors add that according to Marx "the roots of ideology are to be found not in men's inaccurate perceptions of the world, 'manipulated' or otherwise, but in their *accurate* perceptions of the world as it 'represents *itself* to experience. Ideology derives specifically from the phenomenal forms of essentia! relations... Phenomenal forms ... can for Marx be misleading. If experience is the foundation of consciousness, as Marx contends, then where they are misleading, experience *itself* becomes the major 'means of ideological production.'" P. 21. Pointing out that those who, set out to analyse ideology or reality must go beyond observation, they quote Marx: "To resolve the visible, merely external movement into the true intrinsic movement is a work of *science*." P. 14. (K. Marx, *Capital*, Vol. Ill, p. 313.)

their grasp of the social origins and role of ideology, both in theory and its historical communal form in India, is, to say the least, inadequate. Many of them start with the assumption that communal interests and structured communities based on religion exist, whereas these assumptions have themselves to be examined and proved or disproved before one can seriously proceed with the discussion of the problem.[10]

[10]This weakness is brought out in two recent writings on the subject. In an otherwise sound, and even brilliant, study of Muslim communalism in UP in its liberal phase, Francis Robinson is not able to avoid this confusion, thus illustrating the hazards of writing on communalism. Starting out with a clear grasp of communal assumptions and throughout revealing a full understanding of the fact that Muslims did not constitute a community and therefore the growth of communalism has to be explained by some other historical factors and forces (pp. 3-4, 24-33, 345ff.), he slides down step by step because of the very inadequacy of his intellectual tools, and starts talking, in the introduction itself, of "Muslim interest in Indian politics," "Muslims interests," "Muslim political activity," "Government's recognition of Muslim claim to separate representation," "Muslim claims," "the politics of UP Muslims," "Muslims lost the power to dictate Congress policy," "how UP Muslims were able to assume leadership of all Indian Muslims." *Separatism among Indian Muslims,* pp. 4-6. Similarly, in his study *Nationalism and Communal Politics in India, 1916-1928,* Mushirul Hasan starts out by pointing out that Indian Muslims cannot be treated as a single entity or homogeneous community (pp. 3, 11, passim) and then more often discusses them as such and within communal digits in the main parts of his work and fails therefore to understand fully either communalism or nationalism. He thus soon starts writing about "Muslim leadership," "Muslims" in UP being more advanced than "Muslims" in other parts of India ("The UP Muslims were also in the forefront of politics ... because of their influence in government service and professions"), "Muslim civilization," "UP Muslims had enjoyed a unique position in the political, economic, and cultural life of medieval India," "the region was the seat of Muslim power," "in the UP ... Muslims retained their important position in the services; here they were relatively better placed in government service than were the Hindus," "this brief sketch of the economic and educational standing of the Muslims," "the size of a particular community was not necessarily reflected in its political influence," "the concern for maintaining the unity and identity of the Muslim community." All this within the space covered by the introduction and the first chapter! The later chapters are also basically written within this confused, partly secular, partly communal framework, though the author is certainly secular in his consciousness. We may give just one other quotation as an illustration: "The Bengali and Punjabi Muslims ... favoured recruitment to the Civil Service by a system of nomination because it served *their* interests better." P. 46. (Emphasis added.) The list of authors who make this particular error can be multiplied. See, for example, Prabha Dixit, *Communalism—A Struggle for* Power, pp. 1-3, 8-9, 83, 88-89, 138-43, 152-55, 158-59, 165, 197-98; Mushirul Haq, "The Background of Muslim Communalism in Indian Politics," pp. 2-3, 13, 15; Rasheeduddin Khan, "The Development of Muslim National Consciousness in India: A Political Analysis," pp. 1-2, 15.

Similarly, many secular writers today, following in the footsteps of many of the earlier nationalist leaders, adopt or adapt the basic communal digits and assumptions and then proceed to reject the communal argument. This is to analyse communalism in terms of its own political practice and to fight it on its own terrain, to be its hostage.[11] Instead both the communal ideology and the Ideology of its investigator have to be investigated thoroughly and critically before the communal question can be scientifically studied. Here the concept of the 'educator who must himself be educated' has to apply.[12] Similarly, the communal terminologies current during the last 100 years, especially from 1922 to 1947, must be rejected or at least examined critically before use. Otherwise one is going to be led, willy-nilly, up the communal path. For example, if one's analysis starts by accepting the communal leaders as leaders and representatives of their communities—and if one refers to the Hindu, Muslim or Sikh communalists as Hindu leaders, Muslim leaders or Sikh leaders—or if one accepts that communal political activity is the political activity of their 'communities,' one is already accepting the basic communal framework of thought and analysis. On the other hand, if no communal economic, political and social interests exist, the communalists cannot be representing such interests and are not therefore 'representatives' of their 'communities.' They are then clearly serving some other interests; their politics arise to serve interests other than those of their 'communities.' In other words, there is need to distinguish between Hindu or Muslim communal

[11]A new conceptual framework and new questions and not merely new answers to the'old questions and within the old framework were needed. The latter was what the nationalists and nationalist intelligentsia have provided. Once the inner logic of communalism was accepted, communal answers followed. For example, if Hindus and Muslims were separate communities and had separate interests, then it followed that under a democratic system Muslims and Sikhs would either suffer or fight for separate political existence.

[12]Before a person is permitted to qualify as a practising psychoanalyst, he or she has to undergo thoroughgoing psychoanalysis for the discovery of hidden psychological disorders. It may be suggseted that before a person undertakes the study of the communal problem, he or she should undertake thorough analysis of his or her hidden communal bias.

definition of Hindu and Muslim interests and the interests of Hindus and Muslims as parts of Indian people: and Hindu or Muslim communal politics and the political activity of Hindus and Muslims. Similarly, those who talk of Hindu mind or Muslim mind are already assuming the full structuring of Hindus and Muslims as communities.

Let me clarify my approach to the problem, even at the cost of some repetition. Not only did Hindus or Muslims or Sikhs or Christians *not* form a nation or a nationality, they did not even form a distinct and homogeneous 'community' except for religious purposes. That is, they did not separately form 'a monolithic social structure' or a cohesive unit on a religious basis with common economic, political, social and cultural interests, or bonds or outlook. The religious coordinates did not coincide with the class, ethnic, linguistic, or cultural coordinates. There were no sharply etched or articulated interests of Hindus and Muslims 'standing in juxtaposition to one another'; in particular, the condition of Hindu and Muslim peasants and workers was the same. While a communalist talked of, or believed in, defending his community's interests, in real life no such interests existed outside the religious field.[13] For Hindus or Muslims, no such separate interests existed on an all-India or even regional basis.[14] Socially, culturally and economically, Hindus and Muslims equally and in common belonged to whatever and any national,

[13]For example, in the election manifesto of the Muslim League in 1937, only two items were relevant to Muslims as a community, excluding the rights affecting the middle classes. One demanded protection of the religious rights of Muslims and the other asked for the amelioration of the general condition of Muslims. Other demands were equally relevant to other Indians, as, in fact, was the latter of the two. Z.H. Zaidi, "Aspects of the Development of Muslim League Policy, 1937-47," p. 252. The same was the case with the main resolution passed at the 1937 session of the League. S.S. Pirzada (ed), *Foundations of Pakistan, All-India Muslim League Documents,* Vol. 11, 1924-1947, p. 280. Also see M. Noman, *Muslim India,* pp. 356-57; Abid Husain, *The Destiny of Indian Muslims,* p. 102.

[14]Communal leaders and writers at no stage tried to show empirically what the common interests of their communities were, except in terms of fear of domination, etc., by the other community or general assertions of such common economic, cultural, social and political interests.

linguistic-regional, or local society and to all-India social classes, strata and groups.[15] On the other hand, Hindus and Muslims as such were divided among themselves by economic interests, class, caste, social status, language, culture and social practices, and even in religion.[16] Whatever the followers of a religion had in common by way of language, culture, customs, food habits, etc., was within a linguistic zone and often even that within a narrower locality or region within it. In fact, an upper class Muslim had far more in common culturally with an upper class Hindu than with a lower class Muslim. And a Panjabi Hindu stood closer culturally to a Panjabi Muslim than to a Bengali Hindu; and, of course, the same was true of a Bengali Muslim in relation to a Bengali Hindu and a Panjabi Muslim.[17]

[15]For example, in Northern India, at the village level, the social entities were formed not on a religious but a caste basis with Muslims serving in practice as just another caste. The village people viewed themselves as divided as Brahmins, Jats, Chamars, Ahirs, Rajputs, Muslims, etc. There was no separate integration of Hindus as Hindus and Muslims as Muslims *vis-a-vis* each other. Thus, to say that 'to their Hindu neighbours, they were Muslims' is to impose from outside the concept of 'Hindu neighbours.' To a Muslim, his neighbour was not a Hindu, except in a limited religious sense, but a Jat, Brahmin, Khatri, Baniya, Chamar, etc. Similarly, to the latter a Muslim appeared as belonging to another caste-religion and not to a community or nation. Cf. The Deputy Commissioner. Rohtak, to the Commissioner of Delhi Division in 1900 (27 December): "The Hindu and Muslim Jats and Hindu Goojars and Muslim Goojars think more of the common ancestors from whom they have descended than the fact that he is a Hindu or the other is a Mohammedan, and live in the same village with as much peace and good feeling towards one another as if they were members of the same race and religion." Quoted in Prem Choudhry, *Role of Sir Chhotu Ram in Panjab Politics,* p. 123. Also see, Dezil Ibbetson, *Panjab Castes,* pp. 13-14.

[16]For details regarding UP, see Francis Robinson, *op. cit.,* pp. 24-25, 28-33 and 345-46. After discussing the divisions among Muslims on ethnic, caste, status, religious and economic grounds, Robinson writes: "The Muslims were more a multiplicity of interests than a community. Hindus were no less divided than Muslims.... It should be clear that Muslim government servants and landlords were just a part, though a large part, of this (Urdu-speaking) elite, and that their connections with Hindus who belonged to the elite were far stronger than their connections with Muslims who did not, such as the butchers of the towns or the bigoted weavers of the villages ..., Muslims had little in common with each other apart from their religion; Hindus were fundamentally divided even by their faith," pp. 28, 32-33. Also p. 345. Also see Imtiaz Ahmad, *op. cit.,* pp. 36-37; Peter Hardy, *The Muslims of British India,* pp. 1-2, 8; Kamruddin Ahmed, *A Social History of Bengal,* pp. 12-13.

[17]AI1 this became evident after the formation of Pakistan when Bengali Muslims asserted that they had no linguistic, cultural, social, economic, or political affinity with the West Pakistani Muslims.

If Hindus or Muslims had any such common interests on a wider, all-India plane, these could only be in common against imperialism and for social development and, therefore, as Indians and along with other Indians; or on the basis of language and culture along with others of the same language or culture; or on the basis of class, stratum or group, along with others of the same class, stratum or group.[18] The unreal communal division thus obscured the *real* division of the Indian people into linguistic-cultural regions and social classes as well as their real, emerging and growing unity into a nation. Interestingly, as a nationalist organization, the National Congress also preached harmony among all Indians and emphasized their common, all-India interests. But, at the same time, it accepted the existence of linguistic regions and social classes. It only asked for their cooperation and collaboration in the fight against imperialism and in the task of nation-formation and nation-building.

If they had no common interests objectively, then did Hindus or Muslims constitute communities in real sense of the term? Certain religious systems and locally variegated agglomerations of certain religious beliefs and social customs were the only bonds between members of these so-called religion-based communities.[19]

They can at the most be described as communities of fellow-worshippers. Even partial or loose use of the term community must mean having some secular interests in common as Hindus or Muslims.

The issue can be put in another way. The difference between a communalist and a non-communal secular person was not that the former was narrow-minded and looked to, defended, and fought for his own community's interests while the latter looked to the wider

[18]Nationalism is the political-ideological reflex of the objective common interests of society as a whole. All Hindus, Muslims, etc., were divided into linguistic and cultural groups; or classes and strata and united into a nation against imperialism.

[19]As Rasheeduddin Khan has pointed ont, even the bond of religion existed "merely at the sentimental level rather than in specific terms, if one is to remember particularly the local variations of social customs, personal laws and historic myths and symbols among the Muslim *communities* (plural added deliberately)." Except for this bond, the writer continues, "there is no other binding force to coalesce a so-called Muslim identity." "Self-View of Minorities: The Muslims in India," p. 19.

national or class interests or the interests of all communities. Nor was it that the communalist had a partial view of the social reality. This is often said by many secular writers and political leaders. Thus, K.P. Karunakaran has written recently: "Communalism in India meant that philosophy which stood for the promotion of the interests of a particular religious community or the members of a particular caste." "In the Hindu Mahasabha," he says, the Hindu communalists "had a separate organization which was completely devoted to the promotion of Hindu interests."[20] Similarly, S.R. Mehrotra writes: "The Congress stood for democracy, secularism and a common Indian nationality. The Muslim League existed primarily to safeguard and promote the interests of the Indian Muslims as a separate political entity." He goes on to describe the League "as the champion of Muslim interests."[21] Louis Dumont has said: "As if the allegiance that should normally go to the nation were given by the communalist to his community instead."[22] Similarly, many secular nationalists quite often advised the communalists to subordinate their group or communal interests to the larger national interests. Because these writers and leaders have no theoretical grasp of what communalism is, in their analysis or empirical treatment they often accept the communalists at face value.

The real difference between the two approaches was that the secular nationalist denied that any such thing as communal interests—Hindu or Muslim interests in the secular realm—existed. Communalism was not a partial or sectional view of the social reality; it was its wrong or unscientific view. Communalism was not narrow

[20]K.P. Karunakaran, "Political Philosophy and Practice of the Hindu Mahasabha," pp. 2 and 19.

[21]"The Congress and the Partition of India," pp. 192 and 193. Francis Robinson also seems to have fallen prey to this error: "This change in the government's attitude divided the UP Muslims into two main groups: those who were prepared to defend Muslim interests at all costs, and those who were not." *Op. cit.*, p. 175. Also see Prabha Dixit, *op. cit.*, pp. 2, 165. Even E.M.S. Namboodripad tends to accept this view of communalism so far as minorities are concerned. Thus he refers to "communal-political organizations and parties formed to serve the Muslims, the Sikhs and Christians as communal groups." *Economics and Politics of India's Socialist Pattern*, p. 294. Also sec Rasheeduddin Khan, *loc. cit.*, pp. 18-19.

[22]Louis Dumont, "Religion/Politics and History in India," p. 90.

or false because it represented only one community but because it did not do that either. The communalist not only failed to represent national interests, he did not represent even the interests of the 'community' he claimed to represent. The political activities of the Hindu and Muslim communalists were detrimental to the interests of the country in general as also to the interests of Hindus and Muslims.[23] On the other hand, secularism did not mean the subordination of communal interests to the larger national or class interests but the denial of the existence of such communal interests. To accept the communalists as the representatives of minorities whether Hindu, Muslim or Sikh, was to accept communalism.

In other words, in one respect, communalism involved 'either conscious deception or unconscious self-deception'; the communalist was either deceiving others or, more likely, he was deceiving himself as well. He was deceiving himself and others because the interests he claimed to represent did not exist in real life and the demands he undertook to fulfil were incapable of being fulfilled in the way he had posed them and in the way he proposed to fulfil them.

Consequently, to revert to an earlier point, the use of the word community with reference to Hindus or Muslims or Sikhs in India was, and is, entirely misplaced. To agree to do so was to accept one of the basic premises of communalism. Prolonged usage of the term community to form a social grouping as an analytical or political category and for the identification and articulation of certain group interests was itself to become a vehicle for the spread of communalism even when the users did not intend to imply or create a wedge between Hindus and Muslims. If India consisted of structured communities, then communal interests existed, a community had its communal representatives, communities had contradictions with each other and communities were liable to be dominated by one another. To avoid such domination, either a neutral third-party administration was needed or, in case of democracy, separation was the efficacious

[23]It is in this sense that Jawaharlal Nehru's statement that the communal question was a "bogus question" acquires a profound meaning. See *SW*, Vol. 6, p. 107.

remedy. In any case, communities had to be constantly unified and mobilized to protect and promote their communal interests. The majority community also had to do so lest a strong, unified minority came to dominate through methods of force and fascism.

IV

The concept of false consciousness can play a crucial role in our understanding of communalism. All objective reality is grasped through its cognition by the human mind. But not all human thought, consciousness, or ideology are equally valid 'reflections' or cognition of reality. Certain ideas and ideologies are objectively more valid than others to the extent that they reflect the objective reality more truly, that they are more deeply and truly rooted in social reality, that social and political action can be organized around them more 'non-arbitrarily,' i.e., with a more long-term effect and a more lasting conviction. Nothing comes into politics without subjective cognition or consciousness; but not all politics or political understanding are on par; the differences between them are not mere questions of psychology or personal preference. The politics of men and women are guided by and ultimately based on objective social factors, but these factors can find reflection in politics in numerous symbols and ideologies. It then becomes necessary to distinguish between these factors and the ideologies in which they are represented.

Because objective reality exists, therefore the possibility of its correct cognition or consciousness and of political organization based on this correct consciousness also exists. Bat where correct consciousness does not develop adequately, false consciousness does so to fill in the gap. The origins of false consciousness often lie in the efforts of men and women to grasp and change reality. Many false consciousnesses emerge in the process, partially because men and women try to grasp the *new* reality in the context of, with the aid of, and in terms of inherited social ideas and institutions and more familiar traditional identities which were the product of an older, different social reality and which might be to a lesser or greater extent unsuitable for understanding the new social situation. There is often a lag between the emergence of new social relations and the birth and spread of new social ideas and identities with the aid of which these relations have to be grasped. Also objective relations do not necessarily get transformed into subjective consciousness. The new kinds of consciousness correctly representing reality develop inadequately and often lag behind reality, leading to the rise and spread of many false consciousnesses.[24] But not all false consciousnesses grow and prosper. Their staying power often depends not on their inherent strength or closeness to reality but on the working of other social forces and structures. Most of the false consciousnesses that emerge because of this lag are rapidly displaced unless they serve the urges and needs of some social groups, classes and interests. On the other hand, the spread of the more valid consciousness may be checked because powerful vested interests oppose it for their own reasons.

In other words, a false consciousness does not act as its own causation, and its growth and prevalence have, in turn, to be explained. Furthermore, the concept of the falsity of a consciousness only means its lack of correspondence to reality; it does not decide the question of its political effectivity which depends on other socio-economic and political factors. Also, if believed in widely and long enough, a false consciousness can get internalized within a large number of people, can be very effective and can become a major motive force for historical events. Such was, for example, the case with the success of racism in Germany in 1933 and communalism in the partition of India in 1947. It is wrong to argue that a consciousness, ideology or social movement having no objective basis cannot be sustained for long; or the converse that if it is popular over a sufficiently long period, it must be valid or

[24] *Cf.* Beni Prasad, *The Hindi-Muslim Questions,* p. 17: "It takes time to rebuild new habits in individual life and new traditions in social life to replace those which are breaking down. The process calls for a vast effort of re-orientation and is primarily the province of reason. The psychological difficulty consists in obtaining a corresponding change in those feelings which represent subjective valuations of activities and in which, therefore, customs and institutions are embedded."

true or a correct reflection of reality.[25] Otherwise racism or anti-Semitism or doctrines of the inferiority of women would have, by now, been proved true or valid many times over. They have certainly shown a greater degree of 'success' than communalism. Of course, a study of the reasons for the growth of a false consciousness—for example, a study of the actual communal movements, of the communal social process— is imperative. But such a study would not help prove its correctness, or 'truth,' or correspondence to reality. The purpose of describing a consciousness as false is not to 'foreclose the possibility of understanding the social process,' but only to create an opening for such understanding, to create conditions for a scientific study of this process and to avoid falling into the empiricist error of accepting the social process as its own causation and its own truth.[26]

In India, both nationalism and communalism were recent, i.e., modern, phenomena. Both of them were the products of social change, of the same historical process—the transformation of India under the impact of colonialism. They are reflections of a new widening reality that was being born out of the ashes of the pre-colonial social structure. The growing economic, political and administrative unification of the country and the people, the process of the making of India into a nation, the developing basic contradiction between colonialism and the Indian people and the formation of modern social classes and strata made it imperative to have wider links and loyalties among the people and to look for wider unities and identities. This also followed from the very newness of the modern politics that arose in India in the nineteenth century. Modern politics were the politics of mass participation, of the emergence of

[25]We would also then have to say that the success of the Muslim League in partitioning India validates communalism, while the failure to keep Pakistan united invalidates it.

[26]I am of course fully aware of the fact that the relationship between men's and women's social being and social consciousness is much more complex and needs far more elaboration than brought out in my rather simplified treatment. But, then, this is not an essay in political philosophy or the theory of ideology and therefore a certain simplification became inevitable.

public opinion and of the revolutionary and unprecedented notion of popular sovereignty. The new political life and loyalities had to be based on new uniting principles, new political identities.[27] The process of cognition of the new reality and the need to operate with it and upon it produced different kinds of consciousness, for the Indian people and the modern intelligentsia had no precedents, except those from Europe, to guide them and no clear conception of the socio-political order which was being born before their eyes.[28] It was inevitable that they would use pre-modern categories of self identity such as caste *(jati),* locality, region, 'race,' religion, sect and occupation to make wider connections and that some of the new identities and ideologies would be based on them. Nationalism and communalism or even casteism, as distinguished from religion and caste, were new kinds of consciousness, new ideologies, new organizing principles of politics. They were essentially modern, post-eighteenth century phenomena. Nationalism as well as communalism might try to appeal to the past and to establish links with the ideologies, movements and history of the past. But that does not mean that either of them existed in the past. Nationalism in the colonial situation and as the consciousness of the new identity of the Indian people or nation was the valid or legitimate consciousness of the objective reality, that is, of the developing identity in real life of the common interests of the Indian people for modern social, economic, political and cultural development and, in particular, against the common enemy, foreign imperialism, and the need to unite against it in struggle. Nationalism represented the struggle for national liberation from the colonial state

[27]Moreover, the very electoral process which made it necessary to appeal to voters in constituencies spread over hundreds of villages and towns, sometimes encompassing several districts, made it necessary to form and appeal to wider identities which went beyond the traditional village-level or local identities.

[28]Thus, for example, nineteenth-century Indians like B.G. Tilak and Surendranath Banerjee used the word nation for all Indians, for Hindus and for Maharashtrians, Bengalis, etc. The word race was used in a similar manner to describe all types of social groupings.

and for the formation of an independent state.[29] It was historically valid at the moment as it provided a real solution to a real problem—national liberation as against colonial domination.[30]

The demand for linguistic states reflected the valid consciousness of a common cultural heritage and the needs of common cultural development—and it is interesting that it was easily accommodated within nationalism. Similarly, modern class consciousness reflected correctly the common interests of the modern social classes and strata on the all-India plane. It is, however, to be noted that in all three cases, the growth and spread of the consciousness would be a difficult and prolonged process since the consciousness was entirely new, based on new concepts and new modes of thought. On the other hand, one reason why communalism developed in certain areas and sections of Indian society was because of their failure to adequately develop the new national consciousness, linguistic-cultural homogeneity and class identities.[31] This failure was also related to the high degree of opaqueness of the very complex emerging social structure and the historical process, and therefore its imperfect understanding by

[29]A colonial nation is very much like a class in one respect—it is constituted as a unity mainly because of the existence of and the struggle against a common enemy. A long quotation from an article I wrote a few years earlier may not be out of place here: "The national movement was based on the phenomenon of the nation-in-the making while it was itself a powerful factor contributing to this phenomenon. Its growing strength depended in part on the extent to which the people became conscious of their being part of a nation whose essential interests required a struggle for the overthrow of imperialism. This consciousness of nationhood—of being a people—did not, however, flow automatically from the objective reality. It had to be a hard, painstaking process in self-discovery in which the anti-imperialist struggle itself would play a crucial role."

[30]It is to be noted that in particular social situations, nationalism itself can become a false consciousness and an instrument of class domination when it has no objective basis left in terms of unification and development of the economy and society or the struggle against colonialism. This is the case with the resurgence of nationalism– chauvinism in Western Europe, USA and Japan since the last quarter of the nineteenth century.

[31]Once nation, linguistic-cultural zone, and class do not form—or are weakly formed—as the basis for the formation of collective identities, communalism, casteism, regionalism and other similar identities emerge to fill the gap and surge forth as the basis for such identification. For more detailed treatment of this aspect, see Chapter 5, Section I.

sections of the early intelligentsia.[32] Communalism was the false consciousness of the historical process of the last 150 years because, objectively, no real conflict between the interests of Hindus and Muslims existed.[33] Of course, religion as a social diversity or differentiation existed in real life; but making this diversity the basis of political organization, mobilization, and action or seeing it as the main inner contradiction in social, economic and political life was certainly an aspect of false consciousness. Communalism was not, like anti-imperialism or class consciousness, based on real conflict but on a distorted reflection of real conflict or 'replacement' of real conflict. Nor was there any objective basis for the other aspect of communalism, that is, the myth of the solidarity of interests of all members of a religious community or the myth of the existence of a religion-based community.[34] What were called Hindu and Muslim interests or

[32]This also emphasizes the aspect of active and conscious political and ideological struggle for the acquisition of the more valid new identities. This acquisition would have to be a conscious process and would not occur simply because of the objective reality or necessity. Social reality and social relations are not perceived directly through our senses. Their awareness is the result of political and ideological processes. As E.P. Thompson has put it regarding class consciousness: 'The class experience is largely determined by the productive relations into which men are born—or enter involuntarily. Class consciousness is the way in which these experiences are handled in cultural terms: embodied in traditions, value systems, ideas, and institutional forms. If the experience appears as determined, class-consciousness does not." *The Making of the English Working Class,* p. 10. I have found Adam Przeworski's unpublished paper, "The Process of Class Formation: From Karl Kautsky's *Class Struggle* to Recent Controversies," very useful in the discussion of this entire problem.

[33]Without grasping the full meaning of what he has written, K.K. Aziz, a major interpreter of modern Indian history from a communal point of view, has seen this basic difference between nationalism and communalism when he has written: "The Muslims felt that they were a nation, and by so doing they underlined the subjective factor. The Hindus claimed that India was a nation, and in this they emphasized the objective factor." And again: "In the final analysis, the idea of Muslim nationalism was more subjective than territorial, more psychological than political; while 'Indian' or Hindu nationalism was more territorial than cultural, more historical than religious." *The Making of Pakistan,* pp. 210 and 209, respectively.

[34]An objective basis for certain common interests on the basis of religion (or caste) could exist for a time only if suppression on religious (or caste) grounds was practised in the society. This was not the case in colonial India. This aspect was, however, seen clearly by the communal political leader or ideologue; that was why appeal to fear and

Hindu and Muslim minds or Hindu and Muslim communities represented either crystallized communal false consciousness or the failure of the writer or commentator to penetrate the veil of this false consciousness.[35] It is important here to reiterate that communalism was not a partial view of reality, which saw the communal side of the reality but missed its national side, for no communal side of the reality existed; it was a false view of the reality. Thus, the objective contradiction between colonialism and the Indian people was the efficient (or 'real') causation of the national movement; but the Hindu-Muslim contradiction, having no basis in reality, was not an efficient (or 'real') causation of communalism.

It may also be noted that communalism or identity formation around religion was not the only false consciousness to arise in modern India. Caste identity was another; and there were many others. An interesting example of the emergence of false consciousness in response to the need for wider unity and links among the Indians is to be found in the first version of the song *Bande Matram* in the novel *Anand Math* by Bankim Chandra Chatterjee. The author invoked the image of seven crore voices singing in unison and fourteen crore hands rising is unison. What principle of unity, loyalty and patriotism was being invoked? Seven crores was not the population of India, nor that of Hindus, nor even that of Bengalis. It was the population of the British-created contemporary Presidency of Bengal which included Oriyas, Assamese and Biharis as well! Similarly, the birth and spread of communalism in India were not due to the exceptional nature of the Indian character or Indian historical development. In other societies, similar conditions have produced communalism or communal-type ideologies and politics on a significant scale, though

potential suppression was his stock-in-trade whether he was a Hindu, Muslim or Sikh communalist. See Chapter 5, Section II. This was also why communal riots and the accompanying loss of life and property played a crucial role in creating an atmosphere of fear and in the success of the notion of communal solidarity.

[35]It was not religious differentiation that led to communalism but communal politics and ideological practices which transformed religious differentiation into communal cleavage.

with variations and characteristic features specific to those societies; for example, Ireland, Malaysia, Philippines, Lebanon and Sri Lanka.

Another way of viewing the lack of historical validity of communalism is to see that communalism was not its own inherent truth, that it was not the 'logical and inevitable product of India's historical development.' It had historical and social roots and causation, but it was not historically or socially inevitable. It was not a natural or an inevitable social phenomenon, given the existence of different religions, in the same way as nationalism and class struggle were, given the existence of colonialism and social classes. In other words, communalism was not a conceptualization of social reality but its false consciousness.

As an aside, we may unravel a baffling mystery: Why do many of the imperialist school of historians and writers even today take a communal view of recent history? How can a British, American or French writer be a communalist? This approach is a continuation of the earlier official approach and shares common historiographic or ideological roots with the latter. Once these writers deny, as did the earlier officials, the legitimacy of nationalism because of their approach towards colonialism and their refusal to see the central contradiction of modern Indian society between colonialism and the interests of Indian social development, they are left only with the play of the community, caste, language, region, province, or individual ambition and connections to explain the existence of the national movement. If the growing Indian political activity and movement were not directed against colonialism—for, according to the imperialist view, an objective basis for such activity does not exist—then they must have been directed against some other Indian social groups, for which, it is believed, Indian history and social development provide an objective basis, the most readily available basis being religion. If the Indian national movement could not have been a national, anti-imperialist movement, it must have been a movement for Hindu, or Brahmin, or Arya Samajist, or Bengali domination. Many early imperialist statesmen and writers used communalism to deny the legitimacy of Indian nationalism or even its capacity to come into existence. The most famous pronouncement in this respect was that of Lord Minto in his reply to the 'Muslim delegation' of 1906:

> The pith of your address ... (is that) the Mohammedan community should be represented as a community. You point out that in many cases electoral bodies, as now constituted, cannot be expected to return a Mohammedan candidate, and that if by chance they did so it could only be at the sacrifice of such a candidate's view to those of a *majority opposed to his own community* whom he would in no way represent.... I am entirely in accord with you.... I am as firmly convinced as I believe you to be that any electoral representation in India would be doomed to mischievous failure which aimed at granting *a personal enfranchisement* regardless of the beliefs and traditions of the *communities composing the population of this continent.* (Emphasis added.)[36]

These twin themes of India not being or becoming an Indian nation but of the prior as well as current division of Indian society into well-formed religious communities were to be reproduced *ad infinitum* by colonial administrators and writers. In 1888, Lord Dufferin, the Viceroy, wrote: "The most patent characteristic of our Indian cosmos is its division into two mighty political communities as distant from each other as the poles as under...."[37] The *Economist* of 27 February 1909 asserted: "Whatever may be the political atom in India, it is certainly not the individual of Western democratic theory, but the community of some sort."[38] C.H. Tyne wrote in 1923 that in India religions were a substitute for nationalities and Muslims in particular were "to all intent a nation, and the Government has to regard them as such."[39] To Lord Irwin, in 1927, Indian leaders were

[36]Reproduced in Ram Gopal, *Indian Muslims,* p. 338.

[37]Quoted in *Report on Indian Constitutional Reforms,* 1918, p. 91, para 141. He also referred to Muslims as "a nation of 50 millions with ... their rememberance of the days when, enthroned at Delhi, they reigned supreme from the Himalayas to Cape Comorin."

[38]Quoled in K.K. Aziz, *op. cit.,* pp. 171-72.

[39]Quoted in *ibid.*, p. 167.

leaders "of the great communities."[40] The Indian Statutory Commission ascribed communalism to the struggle for power among the two rival communities.[41]

Thus, the general pro-communal approach of the imperialist statesmen, officials and writers was, and is, not the result only of their 'insincerity' or subjective desire to be pro-Hindu or pro-Muslim. It is also the inevitable result of their failure, itself the necessary consequence of their commitment to colonialism, to acquire a correct understanding of the most important aspects of the colonial historical process—the developing contradiction between colonialism and the Indian people and the process of the nation-in-the-making.

In historical writing, the communal view was an extension of the colonial view of the historical process. Similarly, the communalist of those times missed the main contradiction of colonial India—the ascendancy or domination or exploitation he feared was not that of colonialism but of Hindus or Muslims or Sikhs; the enemy was not colonialism but Hindus or Muslims. This shared view, as also common interests, made possible political and ideological cooperation and alliance between the communalists and imperialism, particularly against the secular nationalist movement; it was not a question of the communalists being conscious agents of imperialism. Nor was it that imperialism was pro-Hindu at one time and pro-Muslim at another; or that it was pro-communalism in principle. The alliance between communalism and imperialism became inevitable because imperialism tried to ally with all those forces which did not emphasize the basic contradiction of colonial society leading to anti-imperialism.[42] At the same time, the ideological and political space provided for communalism by colonial ideology and colonial policy led to its

[40]Quoted in C. Manshardt, *The Hindu-Muslim Problem in India,* p. 76.

[41]*Report of Indian Statutory Commission,* Vol. I, pp. 29-30. For more views on similar lines see K.K. Aziz, *op. cit.* pp. 50 ff. and 167 ff., and Chapter 8 of this work.

[42]Similarly, imperialism has allied with all non-nationalist forces and ideologies in Africa and Asia, and its ideologues have been willing to accept as legitimate all sorts of ideologies and movements in the colonial and ex-colonial countries, even 'leftist' ones, but not those which are nationalist or anti-imperialist.

formation and growth. It was for this reason that in a profound and subtle sense communalism became, in the twentieth century, and especially after 1937, the chief political and ideological base of imperialism.[43]

We may now come back to the main point of this section: There is no inherent and inevitable historical or social reason why communalism must arise and prevail where different religions exist, any more than racialism must flourish in an ethnically plural society or casteism in a multi-caste society. Quite often what are believed to be the 'inherent' causes of communalism,—e.g., a basic incompatibility or 'schism which nothing could heal' between Hindus and Muslims, an age-long and continuous clash of interests or centuries-old cultural, religious and national antagonism between them, a basic clash of distinct cultures or civilizations which 'stood side by side and met only on the field of battle,' irreconcilability of the 'two social systems,' historical memories of being rulers and the ruled, possession of separate 'histories' and their bitter memories—are not causes at all but the basic constituents and creations of communal ideology. Indeed, these as well as other similar 'inherent' causes can be shown to have had no real existence in India in the past or in the present. Their acceptance is more an index of the citizen's, or political worker's or historian's inability to successfully cope with the prevailing communal ideology, for they are not the causes of communalism but the products of communal ideology. In this context, we may once again reiterate that in the study of communalism, not only are the right answers to be sought but the very questions are to be formulated in the right way. Once one agrees to ask the questions in terms that are formulated by the communalist, the answers would tend to remain within the communal framework. Thus, if one does not differentiate between objective reality and its false communal consciousness, one is likely to be swamped by communal ideology and would start asking and answering wrong questions even when one is subjectively secular.

[43]For a detailed discussion of this aspect, see Chapters 4 and 8.

V

Perhaps, the real question regarding communalism is not why did it arise? That is, as we have seen, to some extent at least, inherent in the processes of the cognition of the new reality and of new identity formations. Everywhere in history, given similar processes, such false consciousnesses and ideologies have arisen, but not all of them have survived or spread and flourished. Many prospered for a certain period and then receded as more valid new concepts and identities developed. Even in India communalism was not the only false consciousness to be born. For a certain period and in some regions, casteism and provincialism appeared even more powerful and 'inherent.'[44] But these were on the whole rapidly overcome in the 1920s and 1930s—to be revived again in recent years. Even communalism was confined to minor proportions until 1937. The false consciousness of Presidency-patriotism embodied in the first version of *Bande Matram* did not survive even Bankim's lifetime. The novelist himself revised the seven crore voices to twenty crores—though again leaving the princely states out of the ambit of Indian nationalism. The latter were to be incorporated among the Indian people only during the 1930s after the states' peoples' movement had been born.

The real questions then are: Why and how did communalism grow, spread and thrive? How did it become such a pervasive part of the social reality? Why did millions of people begin to feel that they had a community of interests with their co-religionists all over the country simply because of their common religion? If there was no real clash of interests between Hindus and Muslims, how could they be set at each other's throats by 1946? In other words, the real task of the historian is not, in the main, to trace *the origins of communalism* but to look for *causes or factors in Indian society* responsible for its growth and for the stage-by-stage enlargement of its social base. As pointed out earlier, differences based on caste, language and province, or between *bhadra*

[44]For example, the powerful anti-Brahmin movements in Western India at the end of the nineteenth century, the non-Brahmin movement in South India in the 1920s and early 1930s, the anti-Bengali provincial movements in Bihar and Orissa.

and *abhadra,* Arya Samajists and Sanatnists, reformers and revivalists, existed in real life and could have served as the 'origins' of separatist or communal-type movements, just as religious differences were there and could be seen as the 'origins' of communalism.[45]

And these causes or factors did exist and can be analysed. It is not enough to say that communalism was not inherent or inevitable in the situation in the same way in which nationalism or class struggles were or that it was a false consciousness, for it was not a mere conspiracy by clever, power-hungry politicians and administrators either.[46] There *was* something in the social, political and economic situation of colonial India which favoured its emergence and growth. It did not arise from nowhere; nor did it hang in a void. It had socio-economic, historical and political, that is, structural, roots. It responded to some urges of the people, and to some features in their life situation. True, communalism was adroit propaganda and clever manipulation of religious identities, for no real communal interests or religion-based communities existed, but only under certain concrete and specific socio-historical circumstances, and because of difficulties born out of certain socio-economic and political conditions, could such propaganda and manipulation have been a success among large sections of the Indian people.[47] In other words, while communalism had no objective basis in reality, it was a false consciousness of a concrete social situation, and there was a relation between communalism and reality 'which corresponded to each other through

[45]Beni Prasad, for example, wrote in 1941: "The idea of separatism propagates itself naturally by seizing on existing differences and magnifying them into fundamentals." *Op. cit.,* p. 90. The search for 'origins' of phenomena like communalism and racism inevitably leads to such reductionism. The 'original' cause invariably turns out to be the difference which is used by the communalist or the racist to define his ideology.

[46]While some writers see communalism as inherent, others see it just as a success of clever propaganda. Some others see it simultaneously as benefiting religious groups and as the result of political manipulation.

[47]Not to see this meant not to be able to evolve a viable strategy to fight communalism. While the capacity of a few to mislead the many should not be underestimated, we should still try to find out what enabled the few to succeed in doing so. Also see W.C. Smith, *op. cit.,* pp. 290 ff.

a whole series of mediations.' We may put this aspect in another way. Communalism represented a *distorted or perverse reflection of reality;* that is, it reflected reality in a wrong, distorted way. It did reflect, especially in its later phase, the aspirations, fears and sentiments of sections of the Indian people, but in a distorted, 'false' way. It was a distorted way because even if the solutions offered by it were accepted, they would not solve the problem originally set to be solved; they were no real solutions. Discontent among the people was an objective aspect, but to turn Hindus against Muslims as a means of allaying it was a false step. For example, Muslims were suffering in colonial India, not as Muslims, but as Indian workers, peasants, unemployed youth, merchants, etc. And Hindus were also suffering in the same way. Nor were their sufferings being caused by each other. The situation was in this respect similar to that of Fascism, the other major contemporary false consciousness. Fascism too had social roots and reflected a reality crying out for a solution; but it was a distorted reflection or false consciousness of that reality, and not the logical and inevitable product of the social and historical roots. On the other hand, nationalism was basically a true consciousness in the colonial countries precisely because the overthrow of colonialism was the first necessary condition for opening the path to social development. For the same reason, nationalism in the imperialist countries was a false consciousness because it papered over class divisions but did not help solve any of the problems of the people. At the same time, if the social situation calls for new solidarities and new identities and the struggle for social change requires new principles of organization and mobilization, and if in certain areas and segments of society national and class consciousnesses do not emerge as a response to the situation, communal and other similar identities and forms of politics are likely to emerge and move in to fill the vacuum.

In other words, if reality is not reflected and represented correctly, it will get reflected and represented through a distortion.

The distorted reflection may, however, serve the interests of some social groups whose interests would not be served or might even be ill-served if the real problems of society led to politics and ideologies that were relevant to their solution. These interests 'demanded' the rise and spread of the distorted reflection of the reality, that is, false consciousness, which stood for representation in their case and manipulation in the case of the masses. Such, for example, was the case with the needs of colonialism in India and of the semi-feudal classes and strata.[48] Then there were the middle classes whose interests did not require communalism or other similar distortions, but which could use them to promote their interests in the short run.[49] Moreover, many of the middle class groups believed that they could obtain material resources and social and political power more easily through communalism. Lastly, there were sections of society such as peasants and workers who perceived their social condition in a distorted form, who could not establish a correct identity between their social interests and their ideological reflection and who, therefore, saw their own social struggles in the communal (or casteist) mirror.[50]

Herein lies the analytical value of seeing communalism as false consciousness. On the one hand, one can see the objective falsity of communalism and therefore not accept its surface view; on the other hand, one can see that false consciousness does not grow unless it reflects, though perversely, some aspects of social reality and serves a social function for some social groups, classes and interests.[51] It is the social scientist's, as also the citizen's, task to study and analyse what

[48]See Chapters 4 and S. Also sec Francis Robinson, *op. cit.*, p. 348.

[49]See Chapter 2.

[50]See Chapter 3.

[51]Thus, one does not accept communal leaders and legislators as 'representatives' of their 'community's' interests since no such interests exist, but, at the same time, they are to be seen as representing or serving some interests other than those they claim to be serving. This entire aspect can be summed up in E.P. Thompson's comment, even though he does not like the use of the concept of false consciousness: "I am not happy with the notion of 'false consciousness,' since while such ideological consciousness certainly falsifies universals and mystifies rationality, it can be a very forcible and 'true' consciousness of the particular interests who espouse it, a necessary mask, a necessary set of concepts for their own systematized exploitation of other groups, and a powerful source of self-delusion and rhetoric which is, in its own right, a potent social force." "An Open Letter to Leszek Kolakowski," *The Socialist Register 1973*, p. 87.

concrete and specific circumstances enabled this particular false consciousness to grow.[52] What social forces lay at its back? Why did it appeal to some? What urges did it satisfy? What was it in the social situation of its followers to which it responded? What anxieties did it try to allay? Whose interests did it represent or serve? Who were its beneficiaries? In the past, some people failed to ask these questions and fell prey to communalism; others failed to answer them adequately and therefore could not succeed in their struggle against communalism through appeals to nationalism, morality, and humanitarianism and through protest fasts and political pacts. For example, many nationalists like Gandhi, most of the National Congress leaders and the Liberals did not understand communalism in terms of its historical basis or as a part of reality, though in a distorted form, with the result that they failed to evolve a clear or effective strategy to fight it.

Moreover, it may be pointed out, parenthetically, it was not enough to see or prove the false character of the communal

[52]The following remarks of Renzo de Felice in the context of Fascism are very relevant here: "First, no one can seriously maintain that Fascism is not subject to historical explanation or that it should be considered an irrational occurrence. There is no doubt that in the nineteenth-century history of countries such as Italy and Germany one can isolate 'certain themes that later expand under Fascism and see in them the seeds that later bore fruit' (Chabod). Second, this does not mean, however, that Fascism was inevitable and the logical historical result of prior events in those countries. On the contrary, it was avoidable to the very end. If Fascism triumphed, it was not so much because of the pre-existence of these'motifs' and 'seeds'—which in the nineteenth century had neither a decisive nor a primary role —as it was because of the change brought about by World War I and the 'massification' of society. Only in this new situation, and because of the faults and errors of the existing ruling class, did these 'motifs' and 'seeds' that had been secondary become primary. Other quite new and decisive factors were added to them; and from their sum Fascism ensued. Gerhard Ritter summarized this twofold criticism better than anyone else when, in his book on Carl Goerdeler and the anti-Nazi opposition, he stated: '... None the less, it is fundamentally untrue ... to say that National Socialism was the result of earlier German history, the last consequence, the fulfilment of German tradition.... National Socialism is at bottom not an original German phenomenon, but only the German form of a European one—the phenomenon of the one-party state—and that is to be explained not as arising from an old tradition, but as arising from a specific contemporary crisis, the crisis of the liberal society...'." *Interpretations of Fascism,* pp. 27-28.

consciousness. Colonial society, as also capitalist society today, tended to be in perpetual disequilibrium and was therefore constantly producing all kinds of false consciousness. As in the case of the mythological buffalo, Asura, the killing of one would soon produce another. Mere exposure of these false consciousnesses would not lead to their disappearance; the social condition, which was 'trying' to get solved though in a distorted fashion, and which provided a soil for the false consciousness, had to be transformed. Often, not only are the interpretations of the social reality wrong, but the reality itself is 'wrong' or 'topsyturvy' or 'standing on its own head.' One has not only to understand it right and criticize its wrong or distorted interpretation but one also has to change it and make it 'right' to 'put it back on its feet.' At the same time, the critique and exposure of false consciousness as false comprehension or as a distorted reflection of the social condition is a necessary part of the struggle to understand and change the social condition. (See Appendix for a discussion of forms of communalism in modern India.)

CHAPTER 2

Social Roots of Communalism: I

Basically, communalism was one of the byproducts of colonialism, of the colonial character of the Indian economy, of colonial under-development. Colonialism provided the social structure which produced communalism and in which it could grow. Historically, the rise of modern politics and social classes occurred in the same period in which the full impact of the colonialization of the Indian economy began to be more completely felt and the crisis of the colonial economy began to emerge. Colonial economy, underdevelopment and economic stagnation produced conditions which favoured internal division and antagonism within society as also its radical transformation. This was particularly true of the impact of colonialism on the middle classes, which were, in particular, torn by fears, jealousies and frustration.

I

First of all, I would like to draw attention to the middle class or petty bourgeois base of communalism under conditions of relative economic stagnation.

Throughout the twentieth century, in the absence of the development of modern industries and modern social and cultural services, such as education, health services, the Press, libraries, music, dance, drama, radio and films, and because of shrinking governmental expenditure, there existed extremely poor and worsening economic opportunities and increasing unemployment, especially for the educated middle and lower middle classes who could not fall back on land and who found government jobs to be getting scarce and the professions overcrowded. Even youngmen with a sound academic record found that the possibilities of economic achievement and success were getting narrowed down. This aspect was further heightened during the years of Depression and recession from 1929 to 1941 and the years after World War II. The period of World War II witnessed a massive rise in prices and filled the middle classes with anxiety and fear as to what would happen after the War. Furthermore, the distorted pattern of the colonial economy, which continues in some aspects till this day, produced a large middle or service or tertiary sector which was neither integrated with the productive sectors nor capable of being productively absorbed by the colonial economy or by underdeveloped capitalism. In other words, the growth of the middle classes constantly outpaced economic development. There was, moreover, an acute shortage of superior jobs carrying high salaries and social status, most of these being reserved for the Europeans till the 1920s. This led to intense competition for the remaining.

Consequently, the middle classes in general and the lower middle classes and the newly educated in particular suffered constant deterioration in their socio-economic conditions and prospects and were continually haunted by the spectre of unemployment. Moreover, the lower middle class was oppressed by all, including the indigenous merchants, money-lenders and capitalists. Above all, after 1929, during the Depression years, its members underwent a serious crisis and were filled with disappointment, despair, insecurity and vague fears and anxieties. Social development was breaking down the existing class identities and status system. Many lower middle class individuals faced becoming déclassé while others found their hard won upward mobility checked too soon. Existing opportunities and traditional sources of livelihood were disappearing. There arose new opportunities for some, but they were often immediately threatened, sometimes within one or two generations. There was a lack of correlation between status and new position for some and a complete breakdown of status position for others. There was a constant contradiction between expectation and aspiration and opportunities.

In other words, the lower middle classes were increasingly placed in a position of economic misery, lack of opportunity, constant threat to their existing position and increasing breakdown of their class position and social status and value systems. A certain edge and urgency were imparted to their wordly struggle to maintain their class position and identity. In fact, this struggle became increasingly sharp and even bitter though often also frustrating.

This frustration, a sense of social deprivation and a constant fear of loss of identity and status often created an atmosphere of violence and brutality which when triggered off by a religious issue led to communal riots. The petty bourgeois identity and ego got tied up with the cow or *peepal* tree protection and music before a mosque; protection of such supposed rights—a cow must not be sacrificed, a music procession before a mosque must become silent—was seen as a life-and-death question because it came to represent symbolically the preservation or destruction of the petty bourgeois ego.

In this social situation of the potential or actual loss of their old world by the middle classes, the far-sighted intelligentsia, the national movement, the left-wing groups and parties, and other popular movements worked for the long-term radical solution of the social condition by the overthrow of colonialism and the restructuring of the social system and the national economy. They held up the perspective of social transformation leading to the building of a brand new world. They used the very conditions of unemployment, economic stagnation, underdevelopment and the atmosphere of frustration and unrest to arouse anti-imperialist sentiments among the people, including the middle and lower middle classes. In fact, these latter social strata formed the backbone both of the militant national movements from 1905 to 1947 and the left-wing movements, parties and groups since the 1920s.

But those individuals and sections of the middle classes who lacked a wider social vision or faith in the capacity of the national and social movements to transform the reality within a reasonable span of time, when faced with an immediate social and personal condition, looked to their narrow immediate interests and sought short-term solutions to their individual problems. In fact, this was true even of some of those whose views extended to the overthrow of imperialism in the long run but who felt it necessary to safeguard their position in the short run as well. These individuals and sections acted on the assumption that given the *status quo* it was better 'to fight for the little that there is' or that 'while the antidote is being fetched all the way from Iraq the snake-bitten person may be dead.'

Because of economic stagnation, the middle class Indians were compelled to compete with each other for the scarce opportunities and resources. There existed a perpetual and increasingly intense, tough and unhealthy competition among individuals for jobs, in professions, and among traders and shopkeepers for customers.[1] Nor did the problem end with the entry into a job or profession or trade; for then came the lifelong individual quest and competition for promotion, betterment and success. Every available means was used in this competition, and no weapon was too lowly if it could bring success within one's grasp. There was the individual struggle through educational qualification and personal merit—and middle class parents, and sometimes other relations, would make tremendous sacrifices to provide educational opportunities to their children. Nepotism, corruption and familism were used on a large scale. The net of extended family connections could stretch over a wide territory and sometimes involve hundreds of government servants.[2] The acceptance and payment of bribes in return for appointments to jobs and offices became increasingly common. To private business, family connection was the chief mode of recruitment.

[1]This competition also took the symbolic form of competition in protecting the alleged putative rights in religious practices which led to communal riots usually organized and financed by professional men, shopkeepers and traders.

[2]Much of what came to be later seen as Hindu or Muslim domination of jobs or professions was not to begin with the result of Hindu or Muslim communal effort but of the devotion to the family or village or marriage and kin connections. See, for example, R.E. Frykenberg, *Guntur District, 1788-1848,* and Francis Robinson, *Separatism among Indian Muslims,* p. 40, fn 3. Later such preponderance became a cause of the spread of communalism.

But to give their struggle a wider fighting ground, the middle classes also used other group identities, such as caste, province, region and religion, to enhance the individual's capacity to compete through a group. This latter aspect may be explained further rather briefly. If an individual had to compete with 100 others for a job or in a profession, the odds in his favour would improve perceptibly, and sometimes drastically, where the total number of qualified competitors was small, if by legal or other means the job or profession could be 'reserved' for members of the particular group to which he belonged. Quite often, in his hunt for a job or professional position a young man would use several group identities simultaneously, along with the weapons of nepotism, family and village connection and 'recommendation.'

Thus, the crisis of the colonial economy and society constantly generated two opposing sets of ideologies and political tendencies among the petty bourgeoisie. On the one hand, when social change and revolution appeared as immediate possibilities—for example, the slogan of Swaraj in one year or Quit India—the petty bourgeoisie enthusiastically joined the struggle for the radical transformation of their existing social condition and therefore also of society. It then took up the cause and demands of the entire society from the capitalists to the peasants and workers. It was propelled forward towards the anti-imperialist struggle and the movements towards social transformation when all individual strivings were ignored or transcended and individual ambitions were sunk in the wider social vision. On the other hand, when revolutionary change receded into the background, when the real social solutions seemed once again to be 'a pie in the sky,' when the anti-imperialist movement subsided and lost its immediate reality and could no longer inspire the petty bourgeoisie, when the days of hope were over, when it appeared that things would not change, when there was a decline of faith in the capacity of the united national movement to liberate and transform society, the petty bourgeoisie shifted to short-term considerations and advantages, to the struggle for individual survival, to egoistic and selfish politics, that is, to the strategy of trying to recover or maintain the existing social position. Imperialism and the social situation were now seen as a 'given' or 'fixed' factor and there was keen competition for a share of the shrinking national cake. The struggle for economic opportunities was now internalized; and any means were found good enough in this struggle to save one's class position and identity and to get out of a 'situation with no exit.'

Grouping around religion leading to communalism, and other similar groupings and ideologies, could and did play an important role in this struggle. The enemy was a group which could be collectively dislodged to improve one's personal position as a member of an alternative group. Or one promoted a group whose membership would enable one to maintain a situation with a better opportunity and opposed a group whose entry would reduce one's own opportunity. Moreover, whenever a petty bourgeois individual finds his position shaky, insecure and endangered and recovery blocked, he starts looking for some group which can be declared hostile to his position and held responsible for his own precarious situation. But while all other groupings such as caste and region or province had a narrow territorial and social spread and had therefore a self-limiting effect,[3] communalism centred around all-India religions and was therefore all-India in scope. It was, as we shall see, also able to get massive official backing. Consequently, in colonial India, the struggle of the individuals within the middle classes and their desire to find scapegoats acquired mainly a communal form in the end.

Under the existing circumstances, the middle class Muslims could feel that if the share of Muslims in government services and professions was increased, everyone of them would stand a better chance in the job or in professional competition. For the same reason, the middle

[3]Such middle class, job-oriented groupings did emerge strongly around province and caste, for example, anti-Bengali ideology in Bihar and Orissa and caste in Bihar, Madras and Bombay, but no all-India coalition could emerge. In 1960s and 1970s, the Bharatiya Kranti Dal (BKD) or Bharatiya Lok Dal (BLD) or Lok Dal succeeded in building a caste coalition around the Jats, Ahirs and Kurmis from Haryana to Bihar, but it failed to convince the Reddis and Kammas of Andhra Pradesh, Marathas of Maharashtra, Patels of Gujarat, and Lingayais of Karnataka that they belong to the same caste configuration as the Jats of northern India. However, such a caste combine has now been built around backward caste issue or reservations. But that is another story or has wider causes or consequences.

class Hindus could feel that any increase in the Muslim share would reduce the chances of each one of them. Thus, the two could be made to feel to be each other's rivals who were keen to take away jobs from each other. The competition for jobs among individuals could be given the turn of being a struggle between two 'communities,' even though the colonial underdevelopment which had led to and intensified this competition was affecting both Hindus and Muslims equally and simultaneously. The larger proportion of Hindus in jobs in an area could be declared to be "Hindu economic domination," while the larger share of Muslims in the same jobs could be pronounced a 'Muslim threat' to the 'Hindu position.'

In particular, because of the scarcity of jobs, any and every appointment to a government job was seen as communal and unjust and fed communalism. Soon a vicious circle operating within a cast iron framework came into existence where every appointment, usually well publicized by the Press, proved the 'truth' of communalism. For example, a non-appointment would convince the communalist that the 'others' would not let his 'community' go ahead and an appointment would show that communalism paid. Communalism thus operated through a built-in accelerator.

Moreover, the number of families suffering from personal frustration either because of being outcompeted on grounds of merit or because of being denied merit appointments and promotions or seats in medical, engineering, and other technical colleges due to reservation, nepotism, etc., was very large. Due to strong family and kinship relationships and emotional ties, a large number of people were materially or psychologically affected by a single appointment or promotion. The very family solidarity widened the communal impact of personal rivalry. In fact, personal frustration and the consequent resentment against the other 'community' tended to engulf virtually the entire petty bourgeoisie.

Looked at in this way, the wonder is not that so many persons of the middle classes were involved in communalism but that so many others succeeded in remaining outside its influence. And it is important to remember that a large number of middle class individuals remained, on the whole, free of communalism even in the 1930s and 1940s. This was in particular true of most of the intellectuals, whether Hindu or Muslim. In fact, the typical Indian intellectual of the 1920s tended to be both secular and broadly left-wing.

The middle classes suffering from an internal contradiction based on individual interest constantly oscillated between anti-imperialism and communalism or communal-type politics. With the same social causation, the middle classes took to militant nationalism and social radicalism as also to communalism, casteism, regionalism, etc. In a broad sense, they were in both cases moved by the need to defend and extend their social interests. But there was a crucial difference in the two cases. When their sectional interest was mediated through a nationalist ideology, this interest merged with the interests of general social development and their politics merged with the broader anti-imperialist movement. But when the middle classes functioned as an interest group, they operated through a communal or a communal-type ideology which was invariably based on the acceptance of the social, economic and political *status quo* and was, in the specific political conditions of colonial India, either pro-colonialism or at best neutral towards it; but it was invariably opposed to the movements opposed to colonialism or the existing social system.

Thus, in one of its main aspects, communalism was an expression of and deeply rooted in the interests, aspirations, outlook and attitudes and psychology and point of view of the middle classes in a social situation characterized by economic stagnation and the absence of a vigorous struggle to transform society—the communal question was a petty bourgeois question *par excellence.* At the same time, while communalism was able to draw supporters from all classes of people, its main social base was to be found in the middle classes or the petty bourgeoisie. It drew its main social support from, and made its main emotional appeal to, these social strata.

II

The colonial economy had one other particular aspect that favoured communal politics. In the absence of openings in industrial and commercial establishments, social services, and the fields of culture and entertainment, government or municipal bodies' service was the main avenue of employment, especially for the educated middle and lower middle classes who possessed little capital or land. Much of the employment for teachers, doctors and engineers was also under government control. Thus, as late as 1951, while 1.2 million persons were covered by the Factory Act, 3.3 million were employed in government service. This explains the keenness of competition for the major economic opportunity for the middle classes. Moreover, government services accounted for almost all the available well-paid jobs. The European firms' higher cadre were invariably foreigners, while few Indian firms of the period recruited outsiders to their higher cadre.

Sectional groupings around individual interests became particularly important when competition over government jobs, educational opportunities, contracts, etc., occurred, for they involved administrative action and therefore politics directly. Political power could not, however, be thrown into the scale till some wider group was formed. But once formed, communalism could be most 'fruitful' in this sphere, especially when encouraged by the government. For this reason, constitutional reforms increased the rivalry among upper and middle classes. Even the petty political and administrative power devolved under them could now be used as a counter in the struggle. It is therefore not accidental that the communal struggle occurred mostly over government jobs, educational concessions, etc., and the political positions in the legislative councils and municipal bodies which enabled control over them.[4]

Almost all the basic guarantees that the communal leaders demanded for their 'communities' referred to these two aspects.

[4]The legislators spent a great deal of their time and energy on the question of appointments to public services. This enabled them to both feed communalism and appease communal sentiments among their communal-minded middle and upper class supporters. Within this strange twilight world, once the common digits were accepted, the fight over each post from that of a chaprasi to that of a High Court judge acquired a queer validity, and, in turn, strengthened the validity of communal politics.

Moreover, the dependence of the middle classes on government services, educational facilities, contracts, etc., placed the crucial levers of patronage in the hands of the colonial state and the communal leaders capable of influencing appointments from within or without the administration. This patronage could be used to encourage communalism and discourage nationalism among the job-hungry middle classes. Once initiated, the system of communal patronage became a powerful external factor compelling middle class youth to conform to the patterns of communal behaviour and thinking, very much in the manner of the Pavlovian dog. The scramble for jobs could also be extended to other sectional groupings and Indian society could be fragmented *ad infinitum* once the reservation of jobs became an ideal. To involve political power in the struggle for jobs, etc., caste and provincial identities could be and were mobilized. But this could be done successfully only on a local plane. For the all-India plane, as pointed out earlier, the communal identity alone was viable. Quite often, therefore, the same social groups mobilized around caste or region on the local plane and around communalism on the all-India plane. Thus, in the late 1930s, the Muslim section of the Unionist Party leadership was organized around caste in Panjab and therefore united with Sikh and Hindu casteists, while it was affiliated to the Muslim League at the all-India level. In a different class and caste context, similar was the case in Bengal in the 1930s and early 1940s.

Similarly, because of the involvement of the government and the possibility of influencing employment and promotion decisions through politics, even railway workers, especially in the petty bourgeois positions of clerks, guards, TTs, drivers, etc., tended to veer towards communalism in the 1920s.[5]

It may be noted that where private enterprise was involved, sectional identities were not influential and tended to break down. The capitalist class, for example, was not divided on a communal basis during the period when communalism mainly raised issues of divisions of places in administration and seats in legislatures. Muslim

[5] I owe this point to Lajpat Jagga.

capitalists started taking up communal positions only when communalism advanced to separatism. Capitalists could now use the state power of the separate 'Muslim' state to strengthen themselves by measures such as exclusion of the Hindu capitalists.

III

Some individuals from the middle classes did, in the short run, benefit from communalism, especially in a relatively stagnant economy and in the field of government employment. This gave a certain 'validity' to communal politics which enabled one to improve one's chances in government service. This partly explains why communal propaganda succeeded among the middle classes. This is the opposite of the nationalist or integrationist belief regarding the 'futility of self-seeking' through communalism or that communalism had no basis at all in the social reality. Communalism did have a basis, however partial and perverted in the social existence of the petty bourgeoisie. Communal propaganda was not utterly disconnected with social reality. The communalist could impose his interpretation of the reality on the middle class individuals because it seemed to conform to their experience or reality as they were then living it. Of course, the extent of benefit from communalism was larger the higher one went up in the social scale and the fewer became the competitors; the upper middle class individuals benefited far more than the lower middle class individuals. Communalism was likely to benefit the aspirants for the High Court judgeship, the university chair or vice-chancellorship, or the directorship of a hospital much more than those trying to become chaprasis or clerks, though the latter would also improve their life opportunities to a certain extent, even if marginally. Of course, in the long run, the latter were more likely not to be beneficiaries but victims of communalism. In any case, it is clear that the role of the individual interest in middle class politics may not be underrated.

In time, the spread of education to the middle and rich peasants and small landlords extended the boundaries of the petty bourgeoisie to the rural areas. The newly educated rural youth, denied opportunities on land whether as landlords or peasants because of colonial underdevelopment, flocked to the towns in large numbers in search of jobs. Moreover, the landed or jagirdari upper classes were also threatened by economic crisis and slow disintegration which they tried to overcome by entering the urban job market and fighting for or against the system of reservations and nominations. This development gradually widened the social base of communalism to cover the rural areas. While before 1947, this development affected largely the landlords and rich peasants, it has proceeded much faster among all sections of the peasantry in post-independence India, Pakistan and Bangladesh, creating a vast potential field for communal and communal-type movements which burst out every now and then with immense fury and sweep.

In the situation described above, not only the Muslim but also the Hindu, Christian and Sikh middle classes were inclined, to some degree or the other, towards communalism.

As has been repeatedly pointed out, communalism was only one of the weapons used by the middle classes in their effort to bolster their individual opportunities. Simultaneously, other similar weapons such as caste, religious sect, language, locality, province and region were also freely used. In fact, having successfully used communalism to improve one's chances, one's 'community' was quickly forgotten and other weapons such as nepotism, familism and corruption and communal-type ideologies of casteism, regionalism, etc., were used freely and with no holds barred against members of one's own 'community.' Often the struggle for jobs or promotions within one's own 'community' was no less sharp, ruthless and virulent. Witness, for example, the struggle between Shias and Sunnis, Arya Samajists and Sanatanists, urbanites and ruralites, Jat and non-Jat, Brahmin and Kayasiha, Brahmin and non-Brahmin, Baniya and Jat. Bhumihar and Kayastha, Reddy and Kamma, Jat or Kurmi and Rajput, residents of eastern and western UP, North and South Indians, Bengali and Bihari, Maharashtrian and Gujarati, Sindhi and Gujarati, Sindhis and Punjabis and ex-U.P. *wallas* in Pakistan, Bengalis and Biharis in

Bangladesh, northern and southern Biharis. The most recent example is the struggle between the 'forwards' and 'backwards' in Bihar and reservation of virtually all jobs, including those of teachers and doctors, in Kerala, on the basis of caste-communal quotas.

As shall be brought out in Chapters 3 and 4, communalism and communal politics also served the interests of the landlords, bureaucratic elements and colonialism. But the landlords and the colonial authorities were too distanced from the lower middle classes and the masses to be in a position to politically organize and mobilize them. Nor could the *Ulama* be the leaders or creators of communal politics organized and developed on modern lines. Their main role was to arouse religious fanaticism in support of communal politics and movements. They could act in the main as the mobilizers of the masses and the lower middle classes. The tasks of organizing and leading a communal movement and of incorporating the lower middle classes and sections of the peasantry in it had to be performed by the modern educated sections of the middle classes, including the intellectuals. As will be brought out later in Chapter 6, the relative weakness of Hindu communalism in drawing intellectuals to itself and the relative backwardness of the Muslim middle classes and intellectuals and therefore their greater absorption into communal groups and parties were to be important reasons for the different fates and degrees of success of the two communalisms in modern India.

IV

Communalism was not, as many writers have argued, basically the consequence of a backward (Muslim) middle class trying to catch up with an advanced (Hindu) middle class. It was the consequence of the *individuals* of the middle classes competing among themselves in a tight economic situation and forming 'sections' and 'groups' to enhance their capacity to do so successfully or to improve their chances in the competition. If in Bengal Muslim middle classes were backward, they were not so in UP or Bombay. In Panjab Hindu middle classes were more advanced but no less communal. In fact, almost till 1947, Muslim communalism was stronger in UP than anywhere else and Hindu communalism in Panjab than in any other province. Similarly, in post-Independence India, not only the backward middle classes of Telangana but the advanced middle classes of coastal Andhra Pradesh have produced separatist movements. In Maharashtra, the social base of the Shiva Sena was educationally one of the most advanced petty bourgeoisies. In Kerala, both the backward Ezava middle classes and the advanced Nair middle classes have produced caste-communalism. In Panjab, there is both Hindu and Sikh communalism. In Bihar both the 'backward' and the forward' caste petty bourgeoisies have fought furious battles.

The fact was that competition would occur among middle class individuals in any case. The question was of putting some labels on the competitors and of finding or forming some sectional grouping to aid in the competition. Thus, when one form of sectional grouping for this competition recedes, another immediately comes forth to take its place. In recent history, in India as a whole as also in states such as Maharashtra, Panjab, UP, and Bihar, communal regional, and caste groupings have tended to rotate as in a game of musical chairs.

Moreover, such competition would occur whether some 'sections' or 'groups' of the middle classes were more or less developed educationally or economically. The less developed or the backward would fight for more opportunities and the more developed or the forward to preserve the existing ones. The fact is that the more educated are no less keen to get employment; nor are the economically advantaged less eager to maintain their advantage. Similarly the knowledge that Hindus or Brahmins have a higher percentage of existing jobs does not make unemployment more bearable to the individual Hindu or Brahmin. Hence, most of the middle class individuals, however advanced or backward, have shown a readiness to use sectional groupings for enhancing their individual capacity to compete in the job market.

So, under conditions of relative economic stagnation and limited opportunities for employment and advancement, some amount of communal-type groupings of the petty bourgeoisie and their mutual political struggles were perhaps inevitable—the question was whether in the wider political contest these or other more meaningful nationalist or social struggles would predominate.

It should be noted that, for various historical reasons,[6] economic and educational disparities between groups formed around religion, caste, language or region did develop on a local or national plane. It was also necessary that these disparities be removed. But communalism went further and tried to make these disparities the very basis of politics. On the other hand, the removal of these disparities was often neglected by the nationalists in the name of nationalism and national integration. The price of this neglect was the growth of communalism and communal-type ideologies and movements.

V

The middle class tendency to think and act communally combined with the greater weight of the middle classes in Indian politics in general and in the national movement in particular tended to weaken the nationalist struggle for secularism and against communalism. Despite its ever-widening social support after 1905, the national movement was up to the end crucially dependent on the lower middle classes whose urges and ethos shaped its general political and ideological outlook. This dependence was there even during the phases of active campaigns against imperialism, but the Congress leadership could to a certain extent ignore the middle classes by relying on the masses and the enthusiasm generated among the people during these campaigns. This dependence was, however, significant and even total during the phases of Parliamentarian politics when elections to the legislatures or to local bodies had to be fought. Under the restricted franchise of the Acts of 1919 and 1935, electoral politics were confined to the middle classes who had the right to vote, the masses being more or less without this right. Every widening of the electorate since 1892

[6]Sec Chapter 6. For example, the lower-level employees in administration were largely Hindus even during the medieval period. This was also true of Bengal where the widest disparity in government employment between Hindus and Muslims occurred in the nineteenth century.

brought in more petty bourgeois voters and thus extended the potential electoral base of communalism. Few parties and candidates had the political courage to wholly ignore the communal and other prejudices of the middle classes. The separate electorates made this dependence doubly binding on Muslim candidates. The nationalist leaders were on the whole secular, but they dared not wage a resolute struggle against the communalism of the prestigious communal leaders, whether Hindu or Muslim, who shared with the National Congress leaders the support of large sections of the middle classes.[7] A vigorous and simultaneous struggle against both Hindu and Muslim communalisms would have meant initial loss of support and seats and even perhaps electoral wilderness. So the Congress followed till 1936 a policy of trying to conciliate both communalisms.

Consequently, the nationalist leaders' efforts to solve the communal problem mainly took the form of negotiating at the top with the recognized communal leaders. But, as we have seen, the communal demands pertained above all to the division of shares in government jobs and seats in municipal and legislative bodies. Generosity in this respect by the Hindu middle classes would have been one effective answer. Concessions in this field also perhaps bore the lowest social cost to the people and the nationalist struggle. But the Hindu middle classes, especially in Panjab, Sind and Bengal, were equally communal. Consequently, precisely here the nationalist leaders dragged their feet and dared not compromise in a generous spirit, lest their middle class followers desert them. Every time they got ready to make concessions to the Muslim communalists, the Hindu communalists organized strong counter-campaigns. In almost all high-level Hindu-Muslim unity conferences and constitutional discussions, the leadership of the Indian National Congress would not override the Hindu communal opinion. In all such discussions, the Hindu and Muslim communal

[7]Cf. *Report of the Kanpur Riots Enquiry Committee:* "The programme of Council entry made them susceptible to the influence of popular mood. Consequently, the power of the Congress collectively and whole-heartedly to fight communalism was altogether undermined ... the exigencies of electoral campaigns, all made it almost impossible for the Congress openly and directly to come to grips with communalism." Pp. 222-23, 225.

leaders enjoyed an unspoken veto. Similarly, the nationalist Muslim leaders often found it difficult to defy such demands of the Muslim middle classes as reservation of jobs and educational facilities.

Nor were the nationalist leaders wrong in their political judgment in the short run. The electoral and political cost of openly flouting the communal opinion of the middle classes could be quite high. Thus, when the Congress leadership headed by the fully secular Motilal Nehru ignored the strong current of middle class communal opinion in 1926, the price was the loss of the Central Legislative Assembly seats on a large scale all over the country and a virtual rout in Panjab and Bengal. The victors were the communal nationalists and liberal communalists who had publicly accused Motilal Nehru of being 'pro-Muslim,' 'beef-eater,' etc. The Congress also lost important party men to the Hindu and Muslim communal parties and groups. Similarly, the Congress lost a large number of general seats to the Hindu communalists in 1937 in Bengal and Panjab, even though it had accommodated the communal nationalists in its own ranks. The Congress also failed to make a large dent among the middle class Muslims. A similar result was produced by the democratization of the Congress constitution after 1920. From then on, to the extent inner party democracy functioned within the Congress, a Congress leader had to pay heed to the views and prejudices of the overwhelmingly petty bourgeois membership of the party.

Jawaharlal Nehru was in this sense quite right in suggesting that communalism was an inherent weakness of a national movement largely based on the middle classes.[8] In other words, the Congress would have found it easier to engage in a resolute struggle against communalism if the centre of gravity of its social and ideological base had been shifted from the petty bourgeoisie to the mass of the peasantry and the working class; or if it had possessed control over the social condition so that the petty bourgeoisie could be rescued from the socio-economic dead-end which led it to take to communal

[8]"We have to admit that, under present circumstances, and so long as our policies are dominated by middle class elements, we cannot do away with communalism altogether." Presidential address to the Lucknow Congress in 1936, *SW*, Vol. 7, p. 189.

politics. The third alternative was to undertake an intense educative ideological and political campaign among the petty bourgeois strata.

It was also perhaps politically counter-productive to carry on negotiations with communal leaders on the question of communal reservations in government services, educational institutions, etc. These negotiations enabled the communal leaders to emerge in the public eyes as the champions of the 'interests' of their respective 'communities.' Moreover, they led even secular leaders to get contaminated with communalism and to think in terms of their 'communities.' Any debate or discussion with the communalists in these terms meant playing into the hands of the communal leaders and the colonial rulers who were practising the policy of reservations. The failure to fight communalism and communal-type movements in post-independence India, Pakistan and Bangladesh can also perhaps be best explained on a similar basis. Even political parties which have been fully free of the communal-type outlook, ideologies and politics have failed to do so effectively because of the fear of alienating their petty bourgeois base. Instead they have tended either to compromise with communal-type movements or to keep quiet, preferring to let the whirlwind blow over.

VI

The middle classes formed the main mass social base of communalism for one other reason. The middle class individuals alone had the capacity to move up or down socially as individuals; in their case alone could personal motives and social questions be integrated. Other numerically significant social classes could do so only on the basis of class. Thus, workers and peasants could not benefit from communalism in any way. Communalism could not be an inherent property of these social classes. In fact, Hindu and Muslim workers, peasants, artisans, craftsmen and even sections of the lower middle class were able on the whole to see that there was no rivalry among themselves on a communal basis. Therefore, except for rare communal tension or riots organized entirely on the basis of religious prejudices, communalism could not spread to these classes till 1937-39. On the other hand, they could be, and were, successfully mobilized against imperialism in the two non-cooperation movements and in the trade union and peasant movements of the 1920s and 1930s.

However, as a result of colonial stagnation and social oppression, these classes were also increasingly affected by general though vague social discontent and unrest. In the absence of vigorous organization of anti-imperialist and class struggles, the diversion of this discontent and unrest into some other channels was quite possible and in the end inevitable. Moreover, the Depression led to such sharp increases in unemployment that all sections of society were now open to appeals by communalists as also by the left. The communal appeal found special favour with the growing class of lumpen individuals in the towns and cities.

It is interesting that the leading communal organizations, speaking in the name of their communities, did not take up any issues other than those pertaining to the middle classes or defined communal interests in any other manner. In the discussions of the minorities problem, the religious, cultural or social rights of the minorities seldom came up for discussion. References to them were at the most of a ritualistic nature and vague in character. The 'protection' and 'safeguards' demanded for religious minorities at the Centre and in the provinces were invariably defined in terms of shares in public services, higher education providing training for such services and the professions and political and administrative power. It was not therefore accidental that it was the middle classes that saw competition to be between 'communities.' For example, the Muslim communal demand was for reserving a majority of seats in the Muslim majority provinces for Muslims and not for adult franchise which would even according to communal logic automatically guarantee a larger number of Muslim legislators in these provinces. Similarly, the demand made on the government was for the promotion of education among Muslims and not education among all. In fact, Muhammad Shafi and other communalists opposed Gokhale's Primary Education Bill in 1911. The question of protecting the economic, social or cultural rights of the Muslim or Hindu peasants and workers did not arise at any stage, for even the communalists realized that these rights were not separated by communal boundaries.[9] The masses were brought within the sphere of communal politics not through their demands, as was done in the case of the middle classes, but through the arousal of their passions via religion (though, as we shall see later, the communal question had 'no reference to religious issues even'), or by diverting their class struggles into communal channels.

Our discussion so far has led us to conclude that in a sense communalism was, and is, basically a petty bourgeois ideology. At the same time, this stratum does not have an independent or homogeneous economic or social position. It is not 'a real social class imbued with its own functions and forces.' Its social position does not contain any possibility of its own 'class system' or of the domination of society in its own 'class' interests; it can form part of a political ruling class bloc but, unlike the landlords, or the bourgeoisie or the working class, it cannot create a social system which functions predominantly in its interests and in which property relations are dominated by it. It cannot have 'independent, clear and relevant policies.' It cannot project or put forward 'a viable alternative of its own.' In other words, there is no 'middle class' solution of social problems as there is a capitalist or a socialist solution. Even in the narrower sense of fuller employment and greater economic opportunities for the middle classes, communal politics of reservations and safeguards could not create more jobs or economic opportunities; that could be done only if economic development was opened up and the social reality, of which communalism was a perverted reflection, was set right. In other words, the communal programme could not provide a solution even to the problems of the petty bourgeoisie as a whole; at the most, it could lead to some individuals of the petty bourgeoisie getting jobs,

[9]For example, weavers, many of them Muslims, were being continuously ruined by colonialism and the rise of the modern textile industry in India. Their cause was not taken up by Hindu or Muslim communalists at any stage. It was the nationalists who, from the last half of the nineteenth century, championed their interests vigorously. The same was the case with the interests of the Hindu or Muslim tenants and land-owning peasants in most parts of the country.

contracts, etc., through the reallocation of the existing, extremely narrow job, professional, educational and other opportunities.[10]

From this point of view, the essential point is not whether when the communalist argued that the social problems of his 'community' could be solved through communal reservations, safeguards, etc., or communal politics, he was 'honest' in his beliefs or not whether he was consciously misleading the masses in his own or in the middle classes' interest. Often, he was deceiving himself as well as the middle classes.

Above all, whatever benefits petty bourgeois individuals might derive in the short run, the politics of the petty bourgeoisie could, in the long run, only serve the interests and politics of some other social class or classes. In other contexts, the petty bourgeoisie had played and was playing a positive and active role in the anti-imperialist struggle and in the initiation of the socialist, trade union, peasant and social reform movements. However, as brought out in Chapters 4 and 8, through the mediation of communalism, its politics were placed at the service of colonialism and the colonial state and the reactionary 'feudal' or jagirdari classes and strata. In this sense, it is incorrect to see communalism as a 'middle class movement' even though the middle classes constituted its main social base.

VII

The real question always was, and is, as to what type of struggle would prevail? The national and social struggle which reflected the correct consciousness of the reality and therefore provided real, meaningful social solutions for the restructuring of society; or the individual and sectional struggle which reflected the false consciousness of the reality, and was therefore incapable of solving the social problem, but which did serve the short-term interests of the middle classes, or, at least, of

[10]This is where the large size of the university-educated among Hindus and the small size of the university-educated among Muslims till 1920s became relevant. The educated Hindu youth could see that "there were far too many of them and not enough jobs to go round, and so they became déclassé intellectuals who are the backbone of national revolutionary movements." Communalism was much more relevant to the existential situation of the educated Muslim youth. Jawaharlal Nehru, *An Autobiography*, p. 464.

some of the individuals belonging to them, and catered to their psychology of trying to find scapegoats or hostile groups on whom to put the blame for their social situation?

In the absence of a correct social struggle and a correct comprehension of reality, it was not only the remedy that was false but also the cause of the disease was seen wrongly. Not colonialism or the social system but some other individuals or religious (or caste or regional) groups were seen as the cause of one's joblessness or economic insecurity. A Hindu, who was successful in competition, or a Muslim, who got in through reservation, did seem to be the reason for one's own unemployment. Communal diagnosis seemed compatible with the life experience of the middle class individual. After all, to a particular job only one person, a Hindu or a Muslim, could get appointed. In other contexts, other similar seemingly correct diagnoses were made. For example, parents were likely to blame their children's 'fault' in not doing well in the examinations for their failure to get any employment, forgetting completely that even in the most 'honest' of all societies the examination results can at best allocate 'rationally' the existing jobs and not create new ones, if all students were to work hard and get first classes, some would still remain unemployed. Similarly, communalism, even when successful, can reallocate jobs among the middle class individuals, it cannot create fresh job opportunities. Unemployment was an objective fact, but giving it the twist of a Hindu versus Muslim problem was a false step. Similarly, Muslims and Hindus were suffering economically, but not because they were Muslims or Hindus: nor did the communal programme provide a remedy to this suffering. In fact, there were no communal interests, only individual interests masquerading as such. This is what we mean when we say that communalism neither comprehended the problem correctly nor provided a correct solution—it represented a false consciousness of the reality.

VIII

To sum up: Firstly, communalism was (and is), thus, in one of its basic aspects, under conditions of underdevelopment and limited opportunities for individual advancement, one of the forms through which individuals of the middle and lower middle classes, including the fresh entrants into these strata from the landlords, peasantry and the working class, could group and struggle to maintain and improve their individual positions.

Secondly, communalism, or some other communal-type movement, was, in a sense, inevitable in a stagnant economy and in the absence of alternative rallying points in the form of adequate anti-imperialist and class movements. If the activity of the middle classes, and even the masses, was not turned against imperialism and into movements of social transformation, their desperate urges, passions and longings and political energy would find expression in other, socially regressive and tragic channels. In a social situation which is ripe for social revolution and transformation, if revolution and transformation would not occur, some other form of social division and struggle would.

Thirdly, if the middle class scramble for jobs created communalism, middle class base and domination of politics made it difficult and even impossible to fight it successfully.

Lastly, it follows that there could be no final solution to the communal problem within the colonial situation and the existing social order. This does not mean that communalism and such other social phenomena should not be opposed. They should be and can be opposed successfully but with a clear recognition that they will not totally disappear from the social scene so long as the social soil for them remains fertile. Till the economy starts developing and the petty bourgeoisie loses its predominance over the political and social ethos, such phenomena and ideologies would continue to appear and grow, and, when not vigorously opposed politically and ideologically, even prevail.[11]

[11]On the other hand, that rapid economic development can help unify even the most diverse people is brought out by the experience of the United States of America where, despite tensions, the volatile Irish, the garrulous Russians, the excitable Italians, the chauvinist Germans, the stolid English, the persecuted Jews of all lands, the ex-slave Blacks, the culturally different Japanese, Chinese and non-resident Indians and numerous people from other lands were welded into a strong and intensely self-conscious nation.

CHAPTER 3

Social Roots of Communalism: II

If communal politics masked the struggle within the middle classes for individual positions and posts, at the popular plane of the masses and lower classes, communalism often distorted or misinterpreted social tension and class conflict between the exploiters and the exploited into communal conflict. Popular discontent was usually due to non-religious or non-communal factors, and, in fact, often economic factors. But under conditions of backward social and political consciousness, it found a distorted expression in communal tension. The struggle between different classes belonging to different religions acquired or was directed into or was given communal forms or interpreted as a communal struggle. Class oppression was seen as or declared to be communal oppression.

And this in two senses: Sometimes the distortion occurred in the popular mind spontaneously or as a result of the growth of communal feelings and propaganda. The discontent was real; it had an objective basis in the economic and social suffering of the masses under the existing social system. But it found expression through the false consciousness of communalism (and casteism). The broad context and motivation of their social action was economic, but in the consciousness of the participants it took a religious or communal outer form. As C.G. Shah has put it: "Under the pressure of communal propaganda, *the masses are unable to locate the real causes of their exploitation, oppression, and suffering and imagine a fictitious communal source of their origin.*"[1]

[1]C.G. Shah, *Marxism Gandhism Stalinism,* p. 185. We may also note that the mobilization of the peasantry around religious symbols, slogans and ideologies in its struggle against agrarian oppression is a common occurrence in pre-modern sccieties.

But often a communal form is given to the social conflict not by the participants but by the observer, the official, the journalist, the politician, and, in the end, the historian, all of whom provide a *post-facto* communal explanation for the conflict because of their own conscious or unconscious communal outlook. For example, many a writer sees the 1921 Mappila agrarian uprising in Malabar as anti-Hindu but the Deccan riots of the 1870s as anti-money-lender and not as anti-Marwari. Similarly, the anti-Mughal struggles of the Satnamis, Jats, Sikhs or Maratha chieftains are seen as anti-Muslim but the anti-Peshwa struggles of the other Maratha rulers are not seen as anti-Brahmin.[2] An extreme example of this distortion was the depiction of the relative failure of the Congress ministries from 1937- 39 to fully satisfy the urges of the rural and urban poor as the Congress betrayal of the Muslim masses. It is to be noted that the Congress record was in most cases superior to that of the Muslim League-supported or led ministries so far as the Muslim workers and tenants were concerned.

What made possible such communal (or casteist) distortion and the giving to socio-economic contradictions and conflicts a communal colour was the peculiar feature of Indian social development that in several parts of the country the religious distinction coincided with social and class distinctions: the zamindars, landlords, money-lenders, lawyers, or merchants on the one side, and the tenants, share-croppers, agricultural labourers, debtors or artisans on the other, often followed different religions or belonged to different sects or castes. This social feature favoured both communal and caste tensions. Moreover, most often the propertied and exploiting sections were upper caste Hindus while the poor and the exploited were Muslims or lower caste Hindus so that the propaganda by the Muslim communalists that Hindus were exploiting Muslims or by the Hindu communalists that Muslims were threatening Hindu property or

[2]M.E. Grant-Duff and other British historians were more consistent though not, for that reason, more correct. They described the Maratha struggle as anti-Muslim and the anti-Peshwa struggles of other Maratha chiefs as anti-Brahmin.

economic interest could succeed, even when wholly incorrect. Political mobilization of both the exploiters and the exploited could thereby proceed on communal lines. Consequently, as W. C. Smith noted in the early 1940s, often "communal riots have been isolated instances of class struggles fought in communal guise."[3]

In large parts of East Bengal, for example, the tenants and debtors were mostly Muslim while the zamindars and money-lenders and traders were largely Hindu. Moreover, the mostly absentee or non-managing zamindars managed their estates through *naibs* (deputies) or agents who were very largely Hindu even in the case of Muslim zamindars. The ryots often felt direct oppression in the person of these Hindu *naibs*.[4] Of course, the problems of the Muslim tenants and debtors were not peculiarly 'Muslim.' The Hindu tenants and debtors suffered no less than the Muslim tenants and debtors from

[3]W.C. Smith, *Modern Islam in India*, p. 194.

[4]Humayun Kabir, *Muslim Politics 1906-47 and Other Essays*, p. 23; Sufia Ahmed, *Muslim Community in Bengal 1884-1912*, pp. 102-03; Sumit Sarkar, *The Swadeshi Movement in Bengal 1903-1908*, pp. 443-44 ; Kamruddin Ahmad, *A Social History of Bengal*, p. 43; *Report of the Bengal Provincial Banking Enquiry Committee 1929-30, p.* 195; Ramakrishna Mukherjea, "The Social Background of Bangladesh," p. 403. At the same time it is to be noted that Hindus were not oppressors as a 'community'; Hindus were no less oppressed. Nor were all Muslims tenants. The number of Muslim rent receivers, mostly as sub infeudatories was quite large. In East Bengal, in 1911 the number of Hindu rent receivers was 71, 154 and of Muslim rent receivers 54, 059. *Census of India*. 1911, Vol. V, Part II (tables), p. 379. On the other hand the number of agents, managers of landed estates, clerks, rent-collectors and so on who were Hindu or Muslim was 28,318 and 7,471, respectively. *Ibid.*, p. 380. (I am thankful to my student, A.Y.S. Alam, for providing me with these figures.) In rural Bengal as a whole, the social profile of the population was as follows (Ramakrishna Mukherjea. op. cit., p. 405) :

Category	*Percentage of total households*	
	Hindus	*Muslims*
Petty zamindar, *Jotedar*, rich farmer	5	3
Self-sufficient cultivator	37	44
Sharecropper, agricultural labourer	58	53
Total	100	100

rack renting, high rates of interest and other forms of agrarian oppression. But when both tenant and landlord belonged to the same religion, the class conflicts could not take a communal form. It should also be noted that the conflict between tenants and zamindars and the debtors and money-lenders did not assume a communal colour until the twentieth century and the rise of communal politics. In the Pabna agrarian riots of 1873 both Hindu and Muslim tenants fought zamindars together, just as the Bengal Rent Bill of 1885 was opposed both by the Hindu and Muslim zamindars. On the other hand, the Mymensingh agrarian riots of 1906 assumed a communal form. In the 1920s and 1930s, the Muslim peasants' discontent against money-lenders and zamindars increasingly took on a communal colour,[5] just as the Hindu zamindars and money-lenders put increasing pressure on the Bengal Congress to defend 'Hindu' interests.

In western Panjab and Sind, while the small cultivators as well as the big landlords were Muslim, their creditors and the buyers of their products were Hindu or Sikh. The Muslim peasantry was moreover heavily indebted to the latter, "and all the feeling of the impoverished debtors against the creditor, out for his pound of flesh, went to swell the communal tide."[6] One aspect of the growth of communalism in Panjab was the effort of the big Muslim landlords to protect their economic and social position by using communalism to turn the

[5]For a detailed and perceptive study of this aspect in three communal riots in East Bengal during 1930-31, see Tanika Sarkar, "Communal Riots in Bengal." Tanika Sarkar's conclusion is: "Thus what were fundamentally agrarian Jacqueries or the fury of the urban poor against a social system reinforced by an alien imperialism turned into communal fighting due to imperfect politicization." P. 298. Also see Sumit Sarkar, *op. cit.*, pp. 80-81, 87, 443 ff.: J. H. Broomfield, *Elite Conflict in a Plural Society: Twentieth-Century Bengal*, p. 328.

[6]Jawaharlal Nehru, *An Autobiography*, p. 140. Also see, Urmila Sharma, *"Social and Economic Aspects of Separatism in the Panjab 1849-1947,"* pp. 11ff.; Satya Rai, *Partition of the Panjab*, pp. 20ff. For south-eastern Panjab, see Prem Choudhry's article, based on district level data, "Hindu-Muslim Relations in South-East Panjab." Here the communal conflict in one case involved Hindu landlords and Muslim tenants and in two other cases Muslim landlords and Hindu tenants. In a few cases the parties to the conflict were Hindu peasant debtors and Muslim money-lenders.

anger of their Muslim tenants against Hindu traders and money-lenders and the use of communalism by the latter to protect their threatened class interests by raising the cry of Hindu interests in danger. Repeatedly, as in 1915 and 1922 in Multan division, in 1926 in Rawalpindi district and in 1930 in Ferozepur and Multan districts, the Muslim peasants arose under the communal banner, directing their anger against the money-lender and his *bahis* (account books), where the evidence of their indebtedness was recorded.[7] On the other hand, the enactment of the Panjab Alienation of Land Act in 1901, which debarred the traditional money-lender-merchant Hindu castes from buying up peasants' and landlords' land, led many of them to turn to communalism. Thus, the Hindu Sabhas came into existence in Panjab during 1903-09. to agitate against the Act, since the National Congress refused to lead such an agitation because of its secular character and pro-peasant stance. Later too, the Hindu traders and money-lenders provided a solid base for Hindu communalism, especially during periods when agrarian legislation was debated or enforced. In turn, the Hindu Mahasabha stoutly opposed all measures for the reduction of the burden of rural debt and restriction on land transfers.[8]

The Mappila peasant uprising of 1921 against landlords and colonial authorities could be given a terrible communal twist by the *mullas* primarily because the class cleavage and antagonism in Malabarran along religious lines—the rebellious (Muslim) Mappilas were tenants and their landlords and money-lenders Hindu.[9]

Even in other parts of the country, where Muslims were a minority, the Muslim peasants invariably faced Hindu money-lenders and merchants as appropriators of a large part of their social product.

[7]Urmila Sharma, *op. cit.*, Chapter II and pp. 44-45, 104-06.

[8]See, for example, V. D. Savarkar's Presidential address to the Hindu Mahasabha in 1938: "In the Panjab and some other provinces measures like Land Alienation Act seek to crush the Hindus economically...." *Hindu Rashtra Darshan*, pp. 34-35.

[9]K.N. Panikkar, "Peasant Revolts in Malabar in the Nineteenth and Twentieth Centuries," pp. 601 ff. Also see W.C. Smith, *op. cit.*, pp. 226-27; and K.B. Krishna, *The Problem of Minorities*, pp. 265-67.

The Bombay City communal riot of 1929 had features of a class war by proxy, a conflict between strikers and blacklegs. To break a strike in two oil companies, the owners brought in Pathan strike breakers, leading to a fight between the blacklegs and the strikers and their worker supporters. Additionally, in Bombay City the workers were in many cases indebted to Pathan money-lenders who charged usurious rates of interest. The struggle between the striking workers and the Pathan blacklegs, however, soon acquired a communal character.[10]

In UP and Bihar, both Hindu and Muslim communalisms were encouraged by landlords and money-lenders-merchants during the 1920s and 1930s to divert the rapidly growing peasant movements. In many of the northern Indian towns the weavers and other craftsmen were quite often Muslims while the middlemen, controllers of their products and of the overall conditions of production, were Hindus. Similarly, Muslim litigants (as also Hindu litigants) were often fleeced by Hindu lawyers and other professional men. In Maharashtra and South India, anti-Brahmin and anti-upper caste movements tended to weaken Hindu communalism, At the same time, particularly in Maharashtra, the upper caste Hindu communalists tried to promote communalism as a method of providing an alternative to the anti-Brahmin and anti-upper caste movements.

In general, in many parts of India the peasants and agricultural labourers and the landlords and money-lenders belonged to different religions, creating a fertile ground for communal propaganda. As an American observer noted in 1936: "There is scarcely a grave communal disturbance in the rural areas in which the thread of economic oppression cannot be distinguished in the tangled skein of causes."[11]

[10]Sse K.B. Krishna, *op. cit.*, pp. 268-69; W.C. Smith, *op. cit.*, p. 195; C. Manshardt, *The Hindu-Muslim Problem in India*, pp. 57-59, Chapter 6.

[11]C. Manshardt, *op. cit.*, p. 54. Also sec, Sumit Sarkar, *op. cit.*, pp. 455 ff. On the other hand, the Government of India noted in 1928 that "in the villages where their horizon is bounded by the same agricultural interests the two communities ordinarily live amicably enough together." Quoted in Anita Singh, "Nehru and the Communal Problem 1936-1939," p. 48.

In the type of social situations discussed above, where the exploiters and the exploited, the oppressor and the oppressed followed different religions, the social content of social tension and conflicts was primarily of a struggle between classes. The question was what type of ideological-political reflex would they acquire. In many cases, in the absence of modern class and political consciousness, they were easily given a communal (and later a casteist) turn. The social oppression was then seen not as that of one class by another but as that of Muslims by Hindus or vice versa. The oppressors were defined not by their class or social character but by their religion. The communalists freely talked of Hindu oppressors and Muslim oppressors. Both the communalists and the colonial administrators stressed the communal as against the class aspects of agrarian exploitation and oppression. Thus, it was held that the Muslim peasants and debtors were being exploited not as peasants and debtors but because they happened to be Muslim.[12] And if agrarian or debt-relief legislation was passed, it was portrayed by the Hindu communalists, as in Panjab and Bengal, as an attack upon Hindus and not upon landlords and money-lenders.[13] The Muslim League in particular implanted and widely propagated after 1938 the notion of community-based economic oppression of Muslims by Hindus, thus copying verbatim the Nazi anti-Semitic propaganda regarding economic oppression of the German and other peoples by the Jews.[14]

[12]For example, a communal leaflet brought out in Lahore in 1936 declared that "day by day the immovable property of the Mussulmans is passing out into the hands of the Hindus, and whatever they earn by the sweat of their brow goes in some shape or other to strengthen the other community." Quoted in C. Manshardt, *op. cit.*, p. 56.

[13]For example, a Hindu communal gathering at Amritsar passed a resolution in 1924 declaring that the money-lenders' Registration Bill "is fatal to the Hindu interests. It will ruin the legitimate transactions of the Hindu and Sikh communities." Quoted in Urmila Sharma, *op. cit.*, p. 45.

[14]Today the rich peasant-capitalist farmers' conflict with the agricultural labourer is sought to be given a caste form. The rich peasants do so to mobilize the poor and middle peasants of their own castes behind themselves. Certain radical-sounding political leaders do so in order to win over the lower castes without antagonizing or having to criticize the rural upper classes. Many upper class leaders of the lower castes do so to hide the increasing class differentiation within the ranks of the lower castes and thus to use their social and economic oppression for their own class ends. Similarly, today we hear a great deal of false propaganda regarding oppression of tribal people by Assamese or Bengalis, or of Assamese by Bengalis, and so on.

The socio-economic struggles were not, of course, always or even most often distorted into communal channels. The peasants and workers and the radical intelligentsia did create powerful secular class movements and organizations especially after 1918.[15] Moreover, quite often, the rural and urban discontent got linked with the anti-imperialist struggle. However, the transformation or misdirection of actual or potential class struggles into communal politics also occurred in other cases in the same period. The partial failure of the nationalist leadership to integrate the urges and demands of the oppressed classes with the national movement and of the left to organize the working people, including the lower middle classes, often enabled the communal leadership to succeed.[16] It should be noted at the same time that while giving a communal colour to class struggles, the communalists did not take up, even in a distorted form, any of the basic class demands of the masses. For example, while complaining of Hindu or Muslim oppression, no demands for the abolition of landlordism, moratorium on debts, and higher wages for agricultural labourers or urban workers were taken up. Similarly, it was the National Congress and not the Muslim communal leaders from Syed Ahmed Khan to Jinnah which took up the cause of the Muslim weavers undergoing continuous ruin and suffering under the impact of colonialism. Nor did the communal leadership promote class struggle even in its distorted communal form or mobilize the masses behind communal-oriented class demands.[17] In this respect, communalism and communal movements differed dramatically from the earlier, pro-modern religious or religion-inspired movements, from the Satnamis and Sikhs to Ferrazis in India or early Christianity to Taipings abroad, which had represented and promoted class

[15]In modern India, most of the peasant struggles from the Indigo Rebellion and Pabna agrarian unrest to peasant movements in UP in the early 1920s and the early 1930s and in Bihar in the 1930s to the Tebhaga struggle in Bengal, Telangana in Andhra Pradesh and Muzara movement in Patiala took secular forms.

[16]Communal ideology here played the same role as the imperialist, racist and chauvinist ideologies did in the West, namely, to distort and replace the class struggle.

[17]On the other hand, when faced with the struggles of the rural poor, the upper class Hindu and Muslim communal leaders tended to unite against them.

struggles in a religious ideological garb, or the spontaneous rural communal riots in which the emphasis was on attack on the zamindars, money-lenders and other men of property.[18] The communalists, on the other hand, merely used the existing class feelings to promote the interests of the middle and upper classes and of colonialism. While the politics of the earlier religious movements had arisen within the sphere of the lives of the oppressed classes and represented their interests, though in a distorted form with religion serving as a mobilizing factor, the politics of communalism arose outside this sphere and represented the interests of the upper and middle classes and of colonialism. Communal politics placed the social urges of the exploited at the command of upper class politics and the colonial state. For example, after a detailed discussion of the communal riots of 1906-07 in Bengal, Sumit Sarkar comes to the conclusion:

> But if the social distress and discontent were genuine enough, it must also be emphasized that their distorted expression through communal riots and plunder robbed the outburst of all permanent value from the point of view of the peasant ... in fact the Muslim communal leaders seem to have used the peasants as so much cannon-fodder in their fight with the Hindus for jobs and council scats.[19]

It is also important to note that the coincidence of religious division with class division which we have noted earlier was entirely the result of the specific historical development of Indian society and of the

[18]Sumit Sarkar says, regarding the communal riots of 1907 in Bengal: "At Dewangunj and Phulpur the contagion spread to the lowest ranks of rural society, and the official record spoke of something like a general 'plunder of the rich by the poor,' with Hindu cultivators joining in the loot at some places and Mussalmans and Marwaris being robbed 'nearly as much as Bengalis.'" *Op. cit.*, p. 459. Also K.N. Panikkar, *op. cit.*, for Malabar; Urmila Sharma, *op. cit.*, Chapter V and p. 44, for Panjab; and Tanika Sarkar, "Communal Riots in Bengal," for Bengal.

[19]Sumit Sarkar, *op. cit.*, p. 460. Also pp. 462-64. Also see Chapters 4 and 8 of this volume.

pattern of the development of colonialism and capitalism. If in many areas the Hindu propertied classes exploited the Muslim masses, this was not because of their being Hindu or the existence of a Hindu conspiracy or design or desire to dominate or exploit Muslims. Their being dominant did not represent Hindu domination.

For example, Hindu zamindars had acquired control over land in Bengal not because they were Hindus but as a result of the historical factor that it was the lower castes and classes which had been converted to Islam, not the higher caste and upper class Hindus. Even under the Muslim rulers of Bengal, the upper rural strata were largely Hindu. Hindu zamindars and merchants and bankers flourished under Murshid Quli Khan, religiously the most devout of Aurangzeb's officials and followers. Under his rule, more than 75 per cent of the zamindars and most of the *talukdars* were Hindus.[20] Moreover, the Permanent Settlement and early colonial impact gradually ruined and expropriated a large number of old zamindars, both Hindu and Muslim and, in fact, because of their earlier high proportion, more of the former. But land now fell into the hands of the new commercial groups who were almost wholly Hindu. The commercial groups were overwhelmingly Hindu even under Muslim rulers;[21] the new feature was the nature of colonial rule and colonial policies which enabled men of commerce to control land. A subsidiary reason for the gradual decline of Muslim zamindars was the subdivision of their estates under the principle of female inheritance. How little 'Hindu' designs had to do with all this is also brought out by the fact noted earlier that even in the twentieth century most of the Muslim zamindars employed Hindu *naibs* or deputies to manage their estates. Also it is interesting that during the discussions on the Bengal Rent Bill from 1880 to 1885, most of the younger nationalist leaders—all Hindus—supported the cause of cultivating tenants, most of whom were

[20]N.K. Sinha, *The Economic History of Bengal*, Vol. I, p. 4. In his second volume, Sinha points out that at the time 90 per cent of the zamindaris were held by Hindus, while most of the lower ryots were Muslims. Hindus also manned the Qanungos' department almost exclusively, p. 229.

[21]*Ibid.*, Vol. II, p. 229.

Muslims, against the predominantly Hindu zamindars, while most of the upper class Muslims, claiming at the time to be Muslim leaders and many of whom later became initiators of Muslim communal politics, either opposed the Bill or remained indifferent to it. Most of the Hindu and Muslim zamindars of Bengal and Bihar of course united in opposing the pro-tenant provisions of the Bill. Similar groupings prevailed in the discussions on the Bengal Tenancy (Amendment) Bill of 1928.

The Hindu preponderance in trade and money-lending in northern India, particularly in Bengal and Panjab, was also a phenomenon that dated back to medieval times. This was so partially because the Turks, Persians and other Central Asian nobles and soldiers of fortune, who constituted, along with the Indian Muslim upper classes, the dominant section of the then ruling elite, could not possibly see into the colonial or capitalist future. They occupied the current dominant surplus extracting positions linked to administration and land control. They did not, therefore, go into commerce and banking on a significant scale, nor did they develop the traditions of a merchant bourgeoisie. They concentrated instead on getting control of land and positions in the administration and the army. It was the same with the Sikh ruling elite in Panjab in the eighteenth and nineteenth centuries. Once again, it was not as Hindus that the merchants and money-lenders threatened the economic position of the old zamindars of all types and of the peasant cultivators and tended to become the dominant rural and urban strata; they did so because of colonial revenue and judicial policies, the colonialization of the Indian economy and the crucial role that merchants and money-lenders played in the colonial structure of surplus extraction and appropriation. Colonialism by its very economic character encouraged circulation more than production. If by some chance, by another social process, the money-lender and trader had been weakened or eliminated, 'Hindu' economic domination would not have occurred.[22]

[22]Today, increasingly the 'Baniya' domination of the countryside is giving way to rich peasant domination, leading also to a change in the character of the 'dominant' castes. But the change cannot be seen primarily in caste terms.

Similarly, the impact of the colonial integration of India with the world economy leading to the free imports of machine products and exports of raw materials gradually ruined the urban and rural craftsmen. Even those who struggled for survival tended to lose their independent economic position and become increasingly subordinated to exploitation by the merchant middlemen who advanced them cash and raw materials and marketed their products. That Muslims constituted a large section of the craftsmen while the merchants were mostly Hindu was again a given fact of the medieval period, the period of the so-called Muslim domination.

To sum up: It is not true that "the Muslim upper classes steadily lost ground to the Hindus." They lost ground to men of trade and finance who happened to be Hindu but who did not acquire this ground as Hindus and who did so because of the socio-economic outcome of colonialism. Similarly, it was the colonial economy which led to the peasantry's indebtedness and loss of land to the predominantly Hindu money-lenders. It was forced commercialization that put the agricultural producer at the mercy of the Hindu merchant. It was the colonial economy and legal structure that forced landlords and peasants to resort to courts and Hindu lawyers, and delivered the artisans into the clutches of Hindu merchants. In other words, *while colonial history guaranteed the growth and economic domination of the merchants and money-lenders, medieval history had guaranteed that they would be mostly Hindus.*

This historically given situation was taken advantage of by the Muslim communalists. In the absence of a correct social and historical understanding, the Muslim tenants, debtors, craftsmen and producers in general could see only the Hindu landlords or money-lenders or merchants or lawyers as their exploiters and oppressors. Taking a surface or external view of the social reality, they were not able to see either the colonial reality or their class oppressors as products and agents of colonialism. Consequently, when the communalists emphasized the Hinduness of the exploiters, they were not able to dissent.

The overlapping of class division and religious division led to a few other consequences in so far as communalism was concerned. Firstly, it explains why the lower class communalism often led to violence in contrast to the middle and upper class communalism where the two sides maintained friendly social and political relations. For the masses, communalism was sometimes a 'substitute' for class struggle. Moreover, a large number of the urban poor, victims and products of colonial underdevelopment, were declassed, rootless, lumpen social strata and persons whose social anger and acute sense of deprivation invariably found expression in senseless violence or in a tendency to loot and plunder. A communal riot was tailor-made to serve as an outlet for their social and psychological urges, as also economic needs. A communal riot was to them both an economic and psychological opportunity and an occasion to lodge their blind protest against society and their social condition. This is one reason why communal riots were mostly an urban phenomenon and why they tended to break out on the pettiest of grounds. Interestingly, in these distorted class struggles, especially in the countryside, the main sufferers were men of property; the lower class individuals of the 'attacked community' or their meagre property were seldom attacked.[23]

Secondly, it partially explains why communalism could become so strong and dangerous. As the ideology of the petty bourgeoisie it would always lack 'teeth.' But it could become a ferocious force when it acquired a mass base and the energy and commitment that class conflict could impart to it even in its distorted form.

Thirdly, it partially explains why Hindu communalism could not become, outside a communal riot, a mass or popular movement or why anti-Muslim sentiments could not be aroused among Hindus on a sufficiently large scale, or why Hindu communalism on the whole remained weak, for Hindus were seldom in the oppressed class

[23]See, for example, Tanika Sarkar, "Communal Riots in Bengal." She also points out that the targets of the rioters were debt bonds and other legal documents pertaining to debt or land; the family members, especially women and children, were seldom attacked. Also see references in Footnote 18 to this Chapter.

position *vis a vis* Muslim exploiters. Even in Panjab, where Hindu communalism was rather strong, its strength lay among the middle classes and not among the Hindu peasants who could not see the 'enemy' among Muslims but saw him in the Hindu money-lenders. For this reason, Chhotu Ram, an ardent Arya Samajist and even a communalist to a certain extent, organized the Haryana Jats against the 'non-agriculturist' Hindus and not against Muslims. Hindu communalism, in Panjab as elsewhere, could seldom appeal to the class feelings of workers, peasants and artisans; it could only arouse feelings of petty bourgeois jealousy and deprivation, on the one hand, and the upper classes' fear of loss of property and class position, on the other. In fact, one reason why even after the partition of India on communal lines and with vast resources at its command Hindu communalism has found it difficult to arouse anti-Muslim sentiments on a large scale lies in the fact that Muslims do not occupy any positions of class dominance *vis a vis* Hindus in today's India. It is therefore difficult to cast them in the role of the 'Jews' of the Nazi movement. There is hardly any section of the Indian people which can be made to see Muslims as exploiters or even rivals, except in isolated spots where commercial rivalry may develop. This is of course not an insurmountable barrier as the growth of communalism and the increase in communal riots show.

Fourthly, this analysis does highlight the need for struggle against landlordism, usury, etc., if communalism was to be successfully opposed. This struggle by the secular forces remained weak all over India, but especially so in the two crucial provinces of Panjab and Bengal where this weakness was to prove fatal to nationalism and secularism. In these two provinces, the provincial-level Congress leadership, at least partly because of the large influence wielded by the landlords and money-lenders on the leadership, not only failed to fight for agrarian reform and to organize the peasantry, but sometimes opposed or vacillated over even the hesitant and paltry pro-peasant legislation initiated by the colonial authorities or the non-nationalist parties during the 1920s and 1930s.[24] Nor did any left alternative to Congress inactivity on the agrarian front in the Muslim majority areas emerge.[25] Not that there did not exist the awareness of this need: the contemporary writings of Nehru, communists and socialists constantly emphasize it; the failure lay in the realm of action or implementation. This was seen clearly even by middle-level political workers as is brought out by the following letter written by Mangal Singh, MLA, to Jawaharlal Nehru, the Congress President, on 9 April 1937:

> As I submitted to you at Wardha, the only way by which we can get in Muslims in the Panjab and defeat the Unionists is to adopt the same agrarian programme in the Panjab which you are carrying on in U.P. and Bihar. I have had lengthy discussions with Doctor Satyapal and others and we may be able to find out a satisfactory way but as you know the Panjab Congress leaders have to work in peculiar circumstances. It seems it is difficult for some of our prominent leaders to get away from the influence of the money-lending classes.... If we adopt a pro-agriculturist programme I am sure Muslims would join us and we would be able to defeat or even to disrupt the present Unionist Party in the Panjab.[26]

II

At another level, communalism represented the struggle between two exploiting classes or strata for as large a share as possible of economic

[24]Gautam Chattopadhyay, *Role of Bengal Legislature in the Freedom Struggle;* Satya Rai, *Role of Punjab Legislature in the Freedom Struggle.* According to Gautam Chattopadhyay, the Swarajist support, including that of Subhash Chandra Bose, to the pro-landlord Bengal Tenancy (Amendment) Bill of 1928, led to the alienation of Congress, pro- Congress and pro-peasant Muslim leaders and opinion from the National Congress. (See Chapter VI of his book.) The Congress did carry out some pro-peasant activities in some areas of Panjab and Bengal; but their scale was inadequate and their organization faulty.

[25]In Panjab, for example, the left-led peasant movement was largely confined to the Sikh peasantry of central Panjab. It failed to penetrate western Panjab.

[26]*AICC Papers,* P. 17/1937, Nehru's correspondence with the Panjab Provincial Congress Committee. Also see Humayun, Kabir, *op. cit.,* p. 22.

power and privileges. Belonging to different religions (or castes), these classes or strata used communalism to mobilize the popular support of their co-religionists behind themselves in their mutual struggles. The people were mere pawns in this struggle which was fought in a communal guise. These classes did not, however, create communalism as a conscious act and out of nowhere. They usually used religion and communalism because they were already available as a part of socio-political development. In other parts of India, as also at other times, they used caste, language and region for the same purposes.

One example of such communal struggles was that of Muslim landlords' struggle against Hindu money-lenders and merchants in West Panjab. In South Panjab (or now Haryana), a similar struggle occurred along caste lines between rich Jat peasants and landlords and Brahmin and Baniya money-lenders. The former used 'Jatism' to win their battle, the latter repaid by arousing on a caste basis the Harijan agricultural labourers and tenants against the rich Jats. Another example was that of the struggle of the Muslim rich peasant-cum-landlords *(jotedars)* against the Hindu zamindars in East Bengal.

To a certain extent, communalism in its early phase also disguised a struggle between the 'semi-feudal' social forces of landlordism and the forces of bourgeois social development represented by the modern intelligentsia. Later it masked the landlords' fear of agrarian reform. These aspects have, however, been discussed at greater length in Chapter 4.

III

A struggle *within* an exploiting class taking some other guise is also a well-known social phenomenon, especially under conditions of economic underdevelopment and stagnation. This is particularly so where new entrants fight against the older, entrenched persons for control over non-expanding or stagnant economic opportunities. In this struggle, both the new entrants and the entrenched persons find it necessary to form some groupings so that wider social and political forces can be mobilized in their support. Such groupings can take many forms, the communal form being one of them. Unfortunately, this aspect of the communal problem has not been studied adequately as yet. The following remarks are therefore tentative in character. Communalism quite often represented a struggle between the new landlords and the dispossessed landlords as in Bengal, Bihar, UP and Panjab. In Panjab, it also expressed the rivalry between the older Khatri and Baniya Hindu money-lenders and the newly emerging rich peasant and landlord Muslim and Jat money-lenders. This was also to some extent the case in Bengal where the Muslim jotedar-cum money-lender was entering the field against the Hindu money-lender.

Similarly, communal politics as also communal riots often disguised commercial rivalry among merchants and shopkeepers. This factor became quite important during the great Depression from 1929 to 1939 and during the Second World War when rival merchants promoted the view that customers should patronize shopkeepers of their own religion. The organized communal riots were often financed by rival merchants who would raise funds to hire the lumpen and *goonda* elements to do the actual fighting. The Kanpur riot of 1931, for example, originated in the commercial jealousy among Kanpur merchants. Earlier still, one of the roots of communal animosity in Bengal during the anti-partition agitation after 1905 lay in the struggle between the sellers of foreign goods and the proponents of the Swadeshi products. Similarly, it has been suggested that the communal turn given to Bengal's agrarian radicalism in the 1930s was the result of rivalry between the Hindu and Muslim traders.[27] In South Panjab, rural communal conflict during the 1920s and 1930s often disguised a struggle over appropriation of communal land or between cattle-owning peasants and butchers, who encouraged cattle theft.[28]

After 1932 and particularly after 1936 the new entrants to the Indian capitalist class constantly looked around for new counters or weights to politically bolster their competitive strength. Some used religion and communalism, others were to use casteism and linguistic

[27]Kamruddin Ahmad, *op. cit.,* pp. 43, 58-59.

[28]See Prem Choudhry, "Hindu-Muslim Relations in South-East Panjab."

and provincial identities; the choice often depended on what was available and could be made serviceable.

Sometimes, it has been said that communalism also represented the struggle between the Hindu bourgeoisie and the Muslim bourgeoisie. Hindus and Hindu castes, it is said, had acquired a monopoly in the field of modern capitalist enterprise and they would not let others enter. The Hindu capitalist class wanted to dominate the country and curb the Muslim capitalist class. Consequently, the Muslim bourgeoisie had to struggle against the Hindu bourgeoisie's domination in the same manner as the latter had to struggle against the British bourgeoisie. This so-called Marxist explanation or justification of Muslim communalism was articulated most clearly by W.C. Smith in 1943 at a time when the Communist Party of India was arguing that the demand for Pakistan represented bourgeois nationalism of the Muslim nationalities. Let us quote Smith in full:

> Their [Indian capitalists'] aim is to expand and to exploit with as little opposition as may be.... Being a bourgeoisie, they must crush any upstart and rival bourgeoisie that seeks to develop within their sphere of influence. They must treat any nascent Muslim or other separatist nationalism in much the same manner as the British bourgeoisie has treated them. In this context, then, the 1942 Hindu Mahasabha resolution to fight Pakistan is understandable.... the middle class of Muslims, driven by the same inexorable law of capitalist development, emerge, gain some strength ... and seek freedom from this domination. They seek freedom just as this more developed group desperately seeks freedom from the British.... The Muslim bourgeoisie is indeed determined to resist economic suppression or subordination at the hands of the "Hindu" monopoly capitalist group.[29]

Apart from the fact that this line of argument fails to see the difference between the anti-colonial struggle and the struggle within a

[29]W.C. Smith, *op. cit.*, pp. 211-12.

colonialized capitalist class, it is misleading because the Indian capitalist class cannot be looked at in this way. It implies that there was something 'Hindu' about the capitalists who were Hindu by religion, or that their being Hindu was relevant to their class position economically or politically, or that they used Hinduism objectively or subjectively as a method of grouping themselves. All this is utterly incorrect. The Indian capitalist class was not Hindu in any sense other than that its majority followed the Hindu religion. At no stage did any section of the Indian bourgeoisie think of itself or act objectively or subjectively as a Hindu (or Parsi) bourgeoisie or in communal terms.[30] The Indian bourgeoisie, including its Hindu and Muslim members, did not act communally in its business activities and industrial companies or in its business organizations such as chambers of commerce and industries. In their economic activities, there was integration, including at the level of company directorships, between capitalists of different religious persuasions. No doubt there existed an element of exclusiveness on the plane of managerial cadre; but that was because of the familial base of business organization and higher employment. This led, however, to caste and regional narrowness and not to communal narrowness. K.M. Ashraf, therefore, rightly described the capitalists, who were branded as Hindu by the Muslim communalists, as Indian. He contrasted the behaviour of the Muslim capitalists with that of the Indian capitalists and not that of the 'Hindu' capitalists.[31] Even W.C. Smith had some doubts on the matter and put the term Hindu capitalists within quotation marks.

The major interest of the Indian bourgeoisie as a class was to preserve and develop further the all-India market and to expel imperialism and not to suppress the 'rival' 'Muslim' bourgeoisie. It opposed communalism mainly because, as C.G. Shah has put it, "the carrying through of any programme (even bourgeois) of economic and

[30]Individual capitalists apart. Individuals, including individual capitalists, may have had strong religious or communal beliefs and behaviour patterns. A few Jewish capitalists supported Nazism; that does not mean that the Jewish capitalists as a section were Nazis or that a 'Jewish' bourgeoisie as such existed as a unity.

[31]K.M. Ashraf, *Hindustani Muslim Siyasat Par Ek Nazar*, p. 67.

social reconstruction is incompatible with the continuation of communal warfare."[32] As a propertied class the bourgeoisie might support communalism when threatened by working people's movements with a view to disrupting them. But it was faced with no such strong movements. On the other hand, only a united anti-imperialist movement could overthrow imperialism, a task in which it was also interested along with other sections of the Indian people.

In fact, to the extent that there was a sectional struggle within the Indian capitalist class, it was not along Hindu and Muslim lines. Certainly, some capitalists 'ate' others up. But that is a basic feature of capitalism. There is no proof that any individual capitalist or capitalist group was curbed or suppressed for being Muslim. Similarly, there were barriers in the way of fresh entrants, the most important being their weak financial position. But, once again, these barriers were not specific to Muslims; they affected all would-be capitalists equally, especially if they were outside the kin-and-caste circles of the entrenched capitalist families. All this explains why Muslim capitalists did not actively support Muslim communalism or create separate Muslim chambers of commerce etc., till the late 1930s and early 1940s. Instead, they participated fully in the secular all-India or regional business organizations.

W.C. Smith seems to suggest that the Hindu Mahasabha was the spokesman of the 'Hindu' bourgoisie.[33] But we know that not more than a small number of Hindu capitalists supported the Mahasabha. The vast majority of Indian capitalists supported the politics of the National Congress or the Liberal Federation. And at no stage does Smith deny the secular nationalist character of the Congress. To see the dominant section of the Indian capitalist class as Hindu, one would also have to declare the National Congress as a Hindu body, as the Muslim communalists did.

Once again, therefore, a 'false consciousness' was involved since, in real life, no Hindu or Muslim bourgeoisie existed. But, then,

[32]C.G. Shah, *op. cit.,* p. 188. Jawaharlal Nehru too saw this clearly. See his *An Autobiography,* p. 477.

[33]W.C. Smith, *op. cit.* p. 211.

from where does this categorization come if not from life? It comes from the fact that late comers or fresh entrants to a class always find it difficult, and sometimes even impossible, to compete with those already entrenched. Consequently, they as well as the existing competitors, constantly look for extra-economic 'counters' to push forward against those already well entrenched in the world of trade, banking and industry.

In the specific historical context of twentieth-century India, some of the capitalists who were Muslim, and who were, except in Bombay, late comers, once again, for specific historical reasons, saw the objective possibility of using Muslim communalism, which was already there, *which they did not create,* which was getting whole-hearted support from the colonial state, and which was beginning to grow rapidly, for advancing their own interests.[34] It was they who at that time came out and declared themselves 'Muslim capitalists' and branded others, the stronger ones, as Hindu capitalists and as anti-Muslim.

Several aspects of this development need to be noted very carefully. That a very large majority of Indian capitalists were Hindu in social composition was entirely because of certain historical factors and not because of the working of Hindu communalism or 'Hindu' planning. They were treated as 'rivals' by some of the Muslim capitalists who also began to deploy communalism against them not because they were Hindu but because they were stronger and well entrenched. Of course, the possibility of using communalism as a 'counter' arose because of the historical 'accident' of these stronger capitalists being Hindu. But if the entrenched capitalists had also been Muslim, the late-entering and weaker Muslim capitalists might well have raised Shia-Sunni, Qadiani-true-Muslim, regional or some other similar cries. In recent times, other late comers who could not appeal to communalism have, according to the exigencies of the specific

[34]This once again shows that communalism, once started, is a self-perpetuating evil. It starts pouring in wherever there is a political vacuum or social conditions exist for its growth.

competitive situation, tended to describe their well entrenched rivals as Bengalis, Assamese, Gujaratis, Marwaris, Panjabis, Tamilians, northerners, non-mulkis and so on. In Pakistan itself, the weaker capitalists have branded their rivals in terms of region and sect. The late comers have, both in India and Pakistan, used such other 'counters' as corruption, caste, linguism, and support to different political groups and factions, sometimes even radical ones.

The Parsi capitalists also belonged to a religious minority, but because they were firmly established they did not raise the bogey of Hindu domination—nor, for that matter, till the early 1940s, did the successful Muslim capitalists of Bombay. For the same reason the weaker Muslim capitalists at no stage thought of joining hands with the Parsi capitalists on grounds of both 'representing' religious minorities. It is to be noted that when the communal section of the Muslim capitalists decided to help mobilize the Muslim masses behind Muslim communalism, this was done to weaken not Hindu communalism or the Hindu bourgeoisie but the national movement, including its undoubtedly secular sections represented by Gandhi, Nehru, communists and socialists, and the national bourgeoisie as a whole. Also, simply because a group of capitalists described themselves as Muslim capitalists does not mean that the remaining capitalists were Hindu. The identity of the others has to be objectively established and not by such a process of elimination. An analogy may be useful here. Simply because some capitalists in Assam or Panjab or Maharashtra or Tamil Nadu may declare themselves to be Assamese, Panjabis, Maharastrians or Tamilians, this does not mean that the other capitalists are anti-Assamese, anti-Panjabi, anti-Maharashtrian or anti-Tamilian. Similarly, because some workers of Bombay see themselves as Scheduled Caste workers, this does not mean that the identity of the other workers is defined by their being upper caste or that they are anti-Scheduled Caste workers.[35]

[35]In fact, in the early 1930s, a section of the railway workers declared themselves to be Muslim and branded the others as Hindu. That did not mean that the railway working class was divided into two distinct categories: Muslim and Hindu working classes.

Thus, to sum up the discussion so far, the grouping of Indian capitalists as Hindu or Muslim had, till the late 1930s, no objective validity, not even as much as is represented by the regional groupings in the USA, Britain, Italy or India, since there was no common interest which could unite the Muslim bourgeoisie as Muslim, unlike the middle classes which could use communalism to improve their opportunities in government services. The Muslim bourgeoisie had little to gain from communalism and the accompanying reservations, safeguards, etc., and everything to lose if the Hindu and Parsi capitalists turned communal.

The position, however, changed in the late 1930s once the Muslim League moved towards the adoption of the goal of a separate Muslim state. Muslim capitalists could acquire common interests or cohesion only if an exclusively Muslim state was created and its entire weight thrown behind Muslim capitalists to the exclusion of Hindu capitalists. And Muslim capitalists could acquire a separate group identity and as such support the Muslim League only when the perspective of exclusive and discriminatory state support appeared. Communalism thus acquired features of bourgeois ideology only after the demand for a separate independent state was raised. Until then it had been primarily the ideological reflex of the petty bourgeois and jagirdari interests. The Muslim capitalists at that stage declared themselves to be 'Muslim' and separate from other Indian capitalists. Even though Muslim Chambers of Commerce which were more or less paper organizations had come up in Bombay in 1931 and in Calcutta in 1932 in order to claim additional seats in the forthcoming constitutional rearrangements, real moves towards creating separate Muslim business organizations came only in the late 1930s. Until then Muslim capitalists remained active as individual constituents of the capitalist class in the Federation of Indian Chambers of Commerce and Industry and its regional or trade-wise affiliates. Despite constant prodding by Jinnah, the first All-India Federation of Muslim Chambers of Commerce was founded only at the end of 1944 and its first meeting took place on 24 April 1945 when the creation of Pakistan as an independent state or at least as an autonomous part of a federation had become a near certainty.

This development also imparted certain inevitable fascist characteristics to the movement for Pakistan as well as to the newly founded state of Pakistan. Unlike India, the new state and its ideology had to be based on the exclusion of Hindus from Pakistan. Otherwise, how could the Muslim capitalists benefit? They would still have had to compete with the financially and otherwise stronger Hindu capitalists. Either Hindus had to be legally made second-class citizens or they had to be physically pushed out. That Jinnah could seriously think of establishing a modern secular state once Pakistan was created[36] only goes to show that he did not fully realize the character of the socio-economic and political forces he had unleashed and led. (Of course, a similar pressure for communal monopoly also came from the weakly developed Muslim traders, shopkeepers, money-lenders, professionals and other sections of the middle and lower middle classes. Moreover, the fascist features were also otherwise inherent in communal ideology.)

In a sense, the situation was truly dialectical. Without a genuinely separatist programme and ideology, as distinguished from safeguards, reservations in services, etc., from which the capitalists had little to gain, the Muslim League could not hope to get large-scale capitalist support; at the same time, once Muslim capitalists supported the League, its march towards separatism was inevitable. It could no longer compromise on the demand for a separate, sovereign state even if it only meant getting a moth-eaten version of it.

[36]Addressing the people of Pakistan, Jinnah said in his Presidential address to the Constituent Assembly of Pakistan on 11 August 1947: "You may belong to any religion or caste or creed—that has nothing to do with the business of the State.... We are starting with this fundamental principle that we are all citizens and equal citizens of one State.... Now, I think we should keep that in front of us as our idea), and you will find that in course of time Hindus would cease to be Hindus and Muslims would cease to be Muslims, not in the religious sense, because that is the personal faith of each individual, but in the political sense as citizens of the State." *Speeches and Writings,* Vol. II, pp. 403-04.

CHAPTER 4

Communalism as Reaction

In the wider historical perspective, communalism was an extreme form of reaction, as is also brought out by the role of the Muslim League and the Hindu Mahasabha in politics. Communalism was a major weapon of political, social and economic reaction in the modern period that had to be 'fought on all fronts and given no quarter.' Communal leaders and parties were in general opposed to political and social change and represented, or were allied with, the most reactionary social and political forces in the country. This inevitably led them to join hands with the foreign rulers who too were interested in maintaining the existing colonial, political and economic structure.

The social, economic and political vested interests deliberately encouraged or unconsciously adopted communalism because of its capacity to distort popular struggles, to prevent the masses from understanding the social and economic factors responsible for their social condition and to turn them away from their real national and socio-economic interests and issues and mass movements around them. Communalism also enabled them to disguise their own privileged sectional, economic and political interests in the garb of communal ideology and religious identity and instead to secure for their interests not only a moral and ideological cover but also popular mass support, inspired by religious passions.[1] And where class identity was submerged in communal identity and class struggle was represented as communal struggle, the upper classes were able to use

[1]In the post-World War I period, it became increasingly difficult to keep the masses out of politics. Reactionary social forces could therefore no longer take a visibly socially reactionary form; nor could they exclude the masses from their consideration. Communalism enabled them to achieve both objectives; it provided them a mask as well as a mass base.

even the class struggles of the oppressed to serve their own purposes and class interests. Thus, landlords hid from their tenants and money-lenders from the indebted artisans and peasants the reality of their exploitation and emphasized instead 'communal' (or 'caste') unity between the exploiters and the exploited. They were able to meet the threat to their class interests by substituting communal solidarity for class conflict.

Communalism also enabled the upper classes and the colonial rulers to unite with sections of the new middle classes and to utilize the latter's politics to serve their own ends.[2]

Apart from the petty bourgeoisie—the middle classes—the main social base of communalism was provided by what K.M. Ashraf has described as the jagirdari elements—the landlords, zamindars and aristocracy in general—and money-lenders, the bureaucratic elite (the serving or retired higher officials) and, in some areas, the merchants. Moreover, the leadership of the communal parties and groups was drawn chiefly from these segments of the population. Most of the leading communal leaders were ex-government officials, big landlords, title-holders and big merchants. Even during the 1930s and 1940s, when middle class politicians had come to the fore in communal politics, the jagirdari and bureaucratic elements tended to predominate.[3] These were also the social classes, strata and groups whose position was dependent on imperialism and who were therefore loyal to British rule. As will be brought out in a later chapter, the colonial authorities, for their own reasons, supported communalism, apart from the fact that even otherwise most of these social strata served as the main social base of colonialism.

For decades after 1885, communalism served as the second line of defence of both imperialism and the reactionary social forces.

[2]This was facilitated by the fact that the landlords, faced with actual or threatened ruin, and higher bureaucracy were also vitally interested along with the middle classes in communal reservation of jobs, etc.

[3]For example, in 1942, of the 503 members of the Muslim League Central Council, 163 were landlords. K.F. Sayeed, *Pakistan—The Formative Phase 1857-1948,* p. 207. The same was true of the Hindu Mahasabha.

But with the passage of time it increasingly became their chief political and ideological instrument. In a non-expanding economy, the struggle for existence was fierce and tended to take radical class and anti-imperialist forms. Both the alien rulers and the Indian vested interests used communalism to divert popular movements, to prevent unity on both national and class lines and to widen their own socio-political base in the era of electoral and other political mobilization. There was thus a crucial difference between the active participants—the foot-soldiers—in the communal movements and those who mobilized and organized them and benefited from communal politics. In a very basic sense, *communalism was the ideology of the petty bourgeoisie at the command of imperialism and the jagirdari elements.*[4]

While communalism originated and wallowed in the needs and outlook of the petty bourgeoisie, its rapid 'growth is explained in part by the willingness of the colonial authorities and the vested interests to use it to mobilize popular support for their own politics. Without that, communalism might not have grown to such monstrous proportions. This was particularly so in the 1930s, as a result of the radicalization of the National Congress, especially in its agrarian programme, its growing popularity as attested to by the Civil Disobedience Movement from 1930 to 1934 and the results of the 1937 elections, the growth of the left wing and the rise of powerful peasant and trade union movements. The British rulers and the Indian jagirdari elements were at that stage thoroughly alarmed and opted for support to communalism as the one viable and strong political force through which the radical nationalist forces could be disrupted and the threat of land reforms averted. Faced with their own

[4]Moreover, the actual mobilization had to be undertaken by petty bourgeois individuals since the life-style of the jagirdari and bureaucratic elements distanced them socially from the masses and middle classes which had to be politically mobilized. It may also be kept in view that many from the petty bourgeoisie were socially and economically linked to the jagirdari elements. On the other hand, the slowly disintegrating landed strata increasingly looked to government jobs to bolster their economic position and thus entered the ranks of the petty bourgeoisie.

waning popularity and the rising tide of the nationalist and left forces, the communal leadership, in turn, became even more dependent on the landed, jagirdari elements and sections of the trading classes.

II

In the United Provinces, for example, the Muslim League was, from the beginning, dominated by the Nawabs, zamindars and ex bureaucrats. In the 1870s and 1880s, the Hindu and Muslim landlords and government servants had tried to develop in common conservative politics to protect and promote their socio-economic interests. In the late 1880s, Syed Ahmed Khan had, with the help of Shiva Prasad, Raja of Bhinga, Raja of Benares and others, tried to organize along secular and class lines the UP jagirdari and bureaucratic elements, whose economic and social power was weakening and who were feeling threatened by the rising modern middle classes and the democratic national movement, into an anti-Congress front. The Congress demanded open competition for government jobs and elections to the legislatures as against the jagirdari elements' demand for the retention of nominations in both fields.[5] This attempt at secular and class mobilization of the jagirdari elements in the name of traditional leadership and the principle of superiority by birth and land-holding failed to get off the ground.

The jagirdari elements now needed an ideology which would enable them to acquire a wider social base and a social and political appeal in defence of their declining social and economic power and position. Despite the fact that the decline in their fortunes was the result of the colonialization of Indian society, economy and polity, they could not take recourse to anti-colonial politics since they could retain even their existing social and economic position only with the help of the colonial government, which was coming under growing attack from the nationalist intelligentsia and the modern middle classes. Syed Ahmed then set out to organize the jagirdari elements

[5]See, for example, Syed Ahmed Khan, *Writings and Speeches*, pp. 209-10.

among Muslims as Muslims so that their class interests as landlords and bureaucrats could be defended and promoted in the name of religion and 'community' *(qaum)*. The conservative jagirdari opposition to the emerging national movement was declared to be Muslim opposition. Muslim communalism thus developed as the politics of the jagirdari and bureaucratic social classes and strata. The foundation of the All-India Muslim League in 1907 was a further effort in this direction. From then on the jagirdari elements fought for communal power, for communal reservations in jobs and for separate electorates to safeguard their interests which they could not have done in an open, class form even under the limited franchise of 1909, 1919 and 1935.

At the same time, till 1937, the UP jagirdari elements were also organized on political and class lines irrespective of religion both inside and outside the legislature. The Hindu and Muslim landlords and *talukdars* worked together in the two landlords' associations, namely the Oudh Association and the British India Association of UP, in the Aman Sabhas organized by the British to counter the First Non-Cooperation Movement, and later in the 1920s and 1930s in the landlords' parties in the legislature, where, operating as landlords, they were successfully able to protect their class interests, especially in relation to tenancy and rent legislation.

But they switched over almost wholly to communal politics after 1937 when they found that the open defence of landlords' interests was no longer feasible and the landlord political parties, having been roundly defeated in the provincial elections, were no longer capable of defending their interests.[6] At the same time, the Congress programme of agrarian reform, including the reduction of rent, the enhancement of tenants' security and the abolition of zamindari,

[6]While of the total number of seats in the UP Legislative Assembly, the Congress won 134, the National Agricultural Parties of Agra and Oudh—the landlord parties—won only 25, of which 6 were from special seats reserved for landlords. The Muslim League won 30 and the independents 38. The Liberals won only one seat while the Hindu Mahasabha drew a blank. P.D. Reeves, "Changing Patterns of Political Alignment in the General Elections to the United Provinces Legislative Assembly, 1937 and 1946," pp. 114-15.

threatened their basic interests. The threat was intensified by the Congress efforts to organize the Muslim masses through a mass contact programme around radical economic agitation. To meet this anticipated threat, they decided to seek other political channels of protection. The Muslim landlords of UP disbanded the National Agricultural Parties and went over *en masse* to the Muslim League and made it an active organization to be able to resist the agrarian threat to their vested interests. It was at this stage that the Muslim League took off as a political force in UP though, in the process, it became even more of an upper class, jagirdari organization.[7] It offered stubborn opposition to the Congress-sponsored land reform measures from 1937 onwards, even though these were quite mild by any standards.[8] This opposition also enabled the League to acquire a degree of popularity among Muslim middle classes and government servants, many of whom had a share in smaller or larger zamindaris.

Similarly, a large number of Hindu zamindars and *tahikdars* of UP joined the Hindu Mahasabha after the 1937 elections. To attract them further towards the Mahasabha, its President, V.D. Savarkar, condemned any 'selfish' class tussle between landlords and tenants.[9] Even earlier, i.e., from the end of the nineteenth century, Hindu zamindars and merchant-money-lenders of UP had started supporting Hindu communalism though there did not yet exist a formal Hindu communal party.

In Panjab too the Muslim League mainly relied on the big landlords. But the landlords on the whole supported the Unionist Party, which united the Muslim landlords of West and Central Panjab, Sikh landlords of Central Panjab, Hindu landlords of South Panjab (or Haryana) and Kangra and the large landed proprietors and bureaucratic elite from all over Panjab, and which successfully protected their interests both against Hindu, Sikh or Muslim tenants

[7]Simultaneously, sections of the Muslim peasantry, working class and younger intelligentsia were shifting to the Congress and to the left parties and groups.

[8]One of the reasons why the left Congressmen opposed any alliance with the Muslim League in UP in 1937 was the fear that this would jeopardize agrarian reforms.

[9]V.D. Savarkar, *Hindu Rashtra Darshan*, pp. 141-42.

and the Hindu money-lender-merchants. The Unionist Party, on the one hand, was a class party of the landed elite and therefore semi-secular and, on the other hand, it articulated the semi-communal outlook of the Muslim landlords of West Panjab and the casteist outlook of the Jat landlords and rich peasants of South Panjab. The result was that till 1937 the Muslim League remained quite weak in Panjab. From 1937 to 1943, under the impact of the nation-wide growth of communalism, the links between the League and the Unionist Party grew. These links were facilitated by the League support to Muslim landlords. Moreover, the landlords and the bureaucratic elite increasingly felt that the Unionist Party, being a provincial party, could no longer protect them from Congress radicalism. The Muslims among them gradually switched over to the League, both in West Panjab and in the canal colonies of Central Panjab. By 1944-45, the League had won over from the Unionists the influential landlord families such as the Hayats, Noons, Daultanas and Mamdots as well as the leading *Pirs* and *Sajjada Nashins,* who had large holdings attached to their shrines. It was in part the large-scale support of landlords and religious heads that enabled the League to overwhelm the Unionist Party in the elections of 1946.

Similarly, from the mid-1920s, the Hindu Mahasabha and other Hindu communal groups became the spokesmen for the Panjab Hindu urban merchants and money-lenders who strenuously opposed agrarian legislation meant to curb their exploitation of the peasants and landlords by raising the cry of Hindu interests in danger. Even though the Panjab Congress was socially quite conservative and sensitive to the interests of the merchant-money-lender combine, it would not and could not defend their interests because of the pressures from left-wing elements within its ranks and from the all-India Congress leadership. These classes and strata, therefore, turned to the Hindu communalists, providing the latter with a very large and stable social base.

In Bengal, the Hindu and Muslim zamindars initially joined hands in the British India Association to defend the Permanent Settlement and their zamindari rights which were threatened by legislation. In the beginning of the twentieth century, the Muslim zamindars and other aristocratic or jagirdari elements joined the newly founded Muslim League. They had earlier supported the colonial authorities on the question of the partition of Bengal. The Muslim League was weakened when, after 1915 and during the 1920s, the Muslim *jotedars* and other 'dependent' intermediaries between the largely Hindu zamindars and the Muslim tenants formed the Praja Samity. The Samity adopted an anti-zamindari stance, including the defence of certain tenant interests, though, the social strata supporting it were opposed to the interests of all tenants and claimed, because of their alleged non-Bengali descent, to be standing socially above Muslim tenants and artisans. (For that reason, many of them tried to teach Arabic, Persian or at least Urdu to their children as a mark of social distinction.) Even though the Samity's activities were directed against Hindu zamindars and it indulged in semi-communal propaganda, it did not represent a basically communal movement. In 1935, under pressure from its left wing, its name was changed to Krishak Praja Party (KPP). Its left wing also pressed for the adoption of a more concrete and radical agrarian programme including the abolition of zamindari. This led to most of the zamindars and other jagirdari elements leaving the party and joining the Muslim League. The landlord-dominated Muslim League and the KPP clashed in the elections of 1937. The two joined hands to form a League ministry with Fazlul Huq as the Prime Minister. The Huq ministry enacted several pro-tenant laws, though its agrarian radicalism gradually petered out as it was overwhelmed by the landlord-ridden all-India Muslim League leadership. The more the influence of the zamindars over Fazlul Huq increased, the more communal he became. Huq unleashed an aggressive communal attack against the pro-peasant members of his own party, accusing them of playing into the hands of the 'Hindu' Congress. Still, unlike the League in other parts of India, the Bengal Muslim League contained till the very end a vigorous left wing which opposed the jagirdari elements but which could not be fully effective and was repeatedly outmanoeuvered organizationally by the right wing because of its being chained by its own communalism. It is also interesting to note that in the organizational tussle, Jinnah and the Central League leadership invariably backed the pro-zamindar Nizamuddin and not the pro-*jotedar* Huq, or the pro-tenant Abul Hashim, or even the liberal Suhrawardy, the spokesman of the middle classes.

Even though the Hindu Mahasabha did not become a major force in Bengal, because of zamindari influence large sections of the Bengal nationalists tended to oppose agrarian reform. They also tended to accommodate aspects of communal ideology. Though under left-wing influence the Bengal Congress adopted a radical agrarian programme, it always dragged its feet when it came to its implementation. One reason why the Congress and the KPP could not come together in 1937 was the Congress leadership's reluctance to support the latter's agrarian legislation. In any case, the Hindu zamindars made every effort to oppose the KPP's agrarian legislation by portraying it as an attack upon Hindu interests. They also did not support the Congress in the 1937 elections.

In the end, we may note that one reason why the Hindu Mahasabha and other Hindu communal groups were politically weaker than the Muslim League was that a section of the Hindu landlords followed a strategy of class defence which was different from that followed by the Muslim landlords. While nearly all the Muslim landlords and most of the Hindu landlords supported communal parties because of their policy of non-conflict with the alien rulers and defence of the landlords' class interests, a section of the Hindu landlords, mostly the smaller ones, supported the Congress, banking upon its right wing to defend its interests. By the 1920s, the Congress had gained such vast support among the Hindu masses that any support to anti-Congress parties would have been counter-productive from their point of view. It could only make the Congress more radical. Thus, for example, while the Muslim zamindars of Bihar went over to the League, a section of the Hindu zamindars supported the right wing of the Congress.

As shall be brought out later, another reason for the relative weakness of the Hindu Mahasabha was the lesser weight of the jagirdari elements among Hindus, among whom the modern intelligentsia and the bourgeois elements rapidly rose to positions of social, economic, political and ideological hegemony. Among Muslims, the jagirdari and bureaucratic elements still predominated. In this sense, the backwardness or weakness of the 'Muslim' middle class contributed to the growth of Muslim communalism.

III

As pointed out at the beginning of this chapter, communalism represented reactionary and backward looking forces in nearly every area of life, and, in general, communal parties and individuals took reactionary positions in political, economic, social and cultural affairs.

The communalists opposed all radical forces in the fields of social and cultural change and religious reform. While the Indian people faced the real problems of adoption of and adaptation to the modern scientific culture, the communalists invariably opposed them under the banner of revivalism. They were actively opposed to the contemporary upsurge among women and the lower castes. The Hindu communalists upheld the upper caste domination while the Muslim communalists tended to support the social domination of the *ashraf* over the *ajlaf*. While the religious elite among Hindus, Muslims and Sikhs openly fought for religious and social orthodoxy and conservatism, communalism had a dampening effect on the reforming zeal of its more modern adherents, for any effort at socio-religious reform would have tended to divide its supporters. For example, communalism blunted the edges of Syed Ahmed Khan's earlier efforts at religious reform and women's uplift. Similarly, in the 1930s, various Muslim educational and reform societies were atrophied. The religious and social enthusiasm of those Arya Samajists who entered active communal politics became muted. Even the socio-religious radicalism of V.D. Savarkar was tamed by communalism.

As pointed out in Chapter 1 and later in Chapter 6, communalist organizations and leaders were seldom concerned with the socio-economic issues that affected the masses, who formed the bulk of their 'community,' or pertained to economic development. They lacked any social or economic programme which would help solve the problems even of their co-religionists; in fact, they shied away from raising or discussing any material question relating to the masses. Their programmes or the demands they put forward, except in a purely ritualistic manner, were seldom relevant to the needs of the workers, peasants, artisans or even the lower middle classes except the demand for reservations in government jobs, which, while benefiting a small number of individuals, could not solve the problem of even middle class unemployment and whose real benefit was reaped by the upper class individuals. Instead, the communalists concealed the absence of any such social, economic or political programme behind the smoke-screen of communal demagogy.

The communalists also invariably opposed any meaningful changes in the economic structure which would have adversely affected the vested interests. The Hindu Mahasabha, for example, actively opposed land reforms as well as anti-landlord, anti-capitalist movements. It also opposed all anti-money-lender legislation designed to give relief to the peasants and small landlords. Similarly, the Muslim League generally opposed anti-landlord measures. For example, it opposed, along with the landlords, the Tenancy Bill introduced by the Congress in UP in 1938. In Bengal, it opposed the agrarian reform programme of the Krishak Praja Party before 1937, and after the latter's merger with it in 1937 it curbed the radical, pro-peasant section of its new ally. Once the radicalism represented by the *jotedar* elements was satiated, the Bengal Muslim League became quite conservative in its agrarian approach and, in the end, it virtually purged its pro-tenant sections. We may also note that the efforts of the pro-tenant sections of the Krishak Praja Party and the League to give to the class situation in East Bengal a communal colouring led, in the end, to the landlord-*jotedar* domination of their own politics. In practice, it was found impossible to harness communalism to agarian radicalism. Rather, the reverse happened. In Panjab, the Muslim League supported landlord domination of the agrarian social structure. It vigorously defended landlord interests against the tenants. Even when supporting anti-money-lender legislation, the interests of the peasants against landlord-turned-money-lenders were ignored. As noted in an earlier chapter, the demands put forward by the Muslim communalists for safeguarding Muslim interests did not, till 1937, include a single demand pertaining to the Muslim poor.

In general, the communal leaders catered to the conservative instincts of the upper classes and opposed social and economic change. Jinnah repeatedly frightened the upper classes by predicting that Congress policy would lead to "class bitterness." He warned that "all the talk of hunger and poverty is intended to lead the people towards socialistic and communistic ideas." He accused Nehru of wielding a "red pen."[10] The Hindu Mahasabha was no less a defender of 'society' against notions of 'class war.'[11]

Many of the League leaders were, of course, willing to adopt radical rhetoric as demagogy after 1944; but this was done after the landlord base of the League as also the landlord domination over its organization had been secured and there was, therefore, no danger of landlords being scared away.

Two other aspects of the communalists' defence of vested interests and the existing economic structure, specially the agrarian structure, may be noted. First, it often led to mutual cooperation among the Hindu, Sikh and Muslim communalists. Secondly, it provided an important point of convergence between their politics and the interests and policies of the colonial rulers.

[10]M.A. Jinnah, *Speeches and Writings,* Vol. I, pp. 28, 32 and 42. The red-baiting of the Congress and Nehru was more extreme at the level of popular propaganda by the League publicists. See W.C. Smith, *Modern Islam in India,* p. 322.

[11]Bhai Parmanand in Indra Prakash, A Review..., p. 204. Similarly, B.S. Moonje declared in 1938 that while some of the most prominent leaders of the Congress stood for communism, "in view of the fact that demolition of Religion forms the very foundation of the Russian Communism, ... the Hindu Mahasabha regards Communism ... as 'the greatest danger, socially and morally, that faces the world today.'" He argued that the Hindu Mahasabha "will always prove a handy organization to act as a buffer between the Congress and the Muslim League on one side and an effective weapon with which to strike at and subdue the demon of Communism on the other." *Ibid.,* pp. xvii-xix.

IV

The communalists were, even apart from the communal question, political reactionaries, though, of course, communalism was only one of the forms that political and conservative reaction took in India.[12]

Both the Hindu and Muslim communalists adopted political positions which were basically opposed to democracy and social equality. A basic assumption in this respect was that democracy and social equality were Western concepts which did not suit the Indian social structure and the Indian people's traditions as evolved over time.

The argument regarding social equality was frankly put forward by Syed Ahmed Khan and others before the politics of mass mobilization came into being and drove the argument underground. Combining the communal and aristocratic points of view, Syed Ahmed argued against the nationalist demand for representation in legislative councils through democratic elections and pleaded for a system of nomination of members of the upper classes on account of their social position. Thus, he said at the end of 1887:

> It is very necessary that for the Viceroy's Council the members should be of high social position. I ask you—would our aristocracy like that a man of low caste or insignificant origin, though he be a B.A. or M.A., and have the requisite ability, should be in a position of authority above them and have power in making the laws that affect their lives and property? Never! Nobody would like it. A seat in Council of the Viceroy is a position of great honour and prestige. None but a man of good breeding can the Viceroy take as his colleague, treat as his brother, and invite to entertainments at which he may have to dine with Dukes and Earls.[13]

[12]As Jawaharlal Nehru put it in 1933: "It is this political reaction which has stalked the land under cover of communalism and taken advantage of the fear of each community of the other." *SW,* Vol. 6, p. 164.

[13]Syed Ahmed Khan, *op. cit.,* p. 204.

The same social snobbery was combined with an appeal to communal and anti-Bengali provincial feelings when he argued against entry into higher government services through competitive examinations. "Men of good family," he asserted, "would never like to trust their lives and property to people of low rank with whose humble origin they are well acquainted." The country was even otherwise not ready for competitive examinations:

> Now, I ask you, have Mohammedans attained to such a position as regards higher English education, which is necessary for higher appointments, as to put them on a level with Hindus or not? Most certainly not. Now, I take Mohammedans and the Hindus of our Province together, and ask whether they are able to compete with the Bengalis or not? Most certainly not.... Think for a moment what would be the result if all appointments were given by competitive examinations. Over all races, not only over Mohammedans but over Rajas of high position and the brave Rajputs who have not forgotten the swords of their ancestors, would be placed as ruler a Bengali who at sight of a table knife would crawl under his chair.... Therefore if any of you—men of good position, Raises, men of the middle classes, men of noble family to whom God has given sentiments of honour—if you accept that the country should groan under the yoke of Bengali rule and its people lick the Bengali shoes, then, in the name of God jump into the train, sit down, and be off to Madras....[14]

Reverting to the question of elections to the Imperial Legislative Council, Syed Ahmed said:

[14] *Ibid.*, pp. 208-09. The reference to Madras is to the coming National Congress session there. Syed Ahmed recognized that in the Civil Service examination conducted in Britain "men of all social positions, sons of Dukes and Earls, of *darzies* (tailors) and people of low rank, are equally allowed to pass this examination." But there was a saving factor: "Those who come from England, come from a country so far removed from our eyes that we do not know whether they are the sons of Lords and Dukes or of *darzies....*" *Ibid.*, pp. 207-08.

> In the normal case no single Mohammedan will secure a seat in the Viceroy's Council. The whole Council will consist of Babu So-and-so Chuckerbutty. Again, what will be the result for the Hindus of our Province, though their condition be better than that of the Mohammedans? What will be the result for those Rajputs the swords of whose ancestors are still wet with blood?[15]

Syed Ahmed Khan, Muhammad Shafi and others criticized those Muslims who joined the National Congress as being men of no substance and belonging to lower or poor classes. On the other hand, the "Raises" who "are counted the leaders of the nation" were opposed to the Congress.[16]

The main communal argument against democracy was that it would lead to majority rule which would in effect mean the majority 'community's' domination over the minority. Muslim communalists put forward this argument on an all-India scale in the name of preventing Hindus from exercising effective power and permanent domination over Muslims, who would remain a permanent minority, while Hindu communalists repeated it almost verbatim in the provinces where Muslims constituted the majority.

Once again, the argument was initiated by Syed Ahmed Khan, though in this case it was carried to the end by the later communal leaders. Starting with the basic communal assumption that Hindus and Muslims had separate economic, political and social interests because of their following different religions and therefore constituting separate communities *(quam,* which is also translated as nation), he argued, first in 1883 while speaking in the Imperial Legislative Council on the Central Provinces Local Self-Government Bill, that while the principle of self-government by means of representative institutions, which means "the representation of the views and interests of the majority," could work well in England, where "for

[15] *Ibid., p.* 210.

[16] *Ibid.,* pp. 181, 244; Anita Singh, "Nehru and the Communal Problem 1936-1939," pp. 19-20. Also see Anil Seal, *The Emergence of Indian Nationalism,* p. 327.

[17] Syed Ahmed Khan, *op. cit.,* pp. 156-57.

socio-political purposes it may be said that the whole of the population of England forms but one community," it could not work at all in India "where caste distinctions still flourish, where there is no fusion of the various races, where religious distinctions are still violent...." Here, "the larger community would totally override the interests of the smaller community."[17] He picked up the theme of the non-suitability of democracy to India again in 1887 during his campaign against the National Congress. Once again making the basic communal assumption that in an election "all the Mohammedan electors vote for a Mohammedan member and all Hindu electors for a Hindu member," he concluded that there would be four times as many Hindu members as Muslim members. Assuming further that Hindu members would serve 'Hindu' interests only and use their power to dominate non-Hindus, he concluded: "And now how can the Mohammedan guard his interests? It would be like a game of dice in which one man had four dice and the other only one."[18] Repeating the argument in 1888, he said that any system of elections would put the power of legislation into the hands of "Bengalis or of Hindus of the Bengali type" which would lead to Muslims falling into "a condition of utmost degradation" and "the ring of slavery" being put on them by Hindus.[19] This argument was to be a major strand in communal ideology and politics from 1906 onwards. Thus, the Agha Khan-led deputation's memorandum to Minto in 1906 emphasized the need to adapt democratic representative institutions to Indian social, religious and political conditions, otherwise their adoption was likely to place Muslim interests "at the mercy of an unsympathetic majority."[20]

The logic of this position was to lead inexorably to separation and secession, for if self-government and democracy led to permanent

[18] *Ibid.*, p. 210. Another communal assumption underpinned this thinking: Not only were the interests of Hindus and Muslims divergent but mutually hostile and therefore they could not live peacefully side by side, "equal in power." "It is necessary," said Syed Ahmed, "that one of them should conquer the other and thrust it down." *Ibid.*, pp. 184-85.

[19] *Ibid.*, p. 242.

[20] Ram Gopal, *Indian Muslims: A Political History (1858-1947)*, p. 20.

Hindu domination and perpetual 'maltreatment' of Muslims, the only viable denouement could be dependence on British power and its perpetuation to protect the minorities or creation of two religion-based nation-states.[21] The latter being out of question at the turn of the century, the Muslim communalists of the time preferred and supported British rule. When in the 1930s and 1940s, the end of British rule became inevitable as a result of the anti-imperialist struggle of the Indian people, the Muslim communalists were driven to adopt the Pakistan ideal.

M.A. Jinnah was to pick up and elaborate Syed Ahmed Khan's argument repeatedly and at length and in nearly all his major speeches after 1937. It was, in fact, to become the corner-stone of his separatist communal ideology and propaganda. Thus, at Aligarh in February 1938: British parliamentary democracy was not suited to India because of essential differences between the bodies-politic of the two countries; in India, "we have a permanent Hindu majority and the rest are minorities which cannot within any conceivable period of time hope to become majorities." The answer was not representative democracy with safeguards for minorities, for the majority was bound to act communally. The only answer was for minorities to claim "a definite share in power," that is, outside the system of representative government.[22] In November 1939, in a statement on "The Question of Democracy in India," he asserted: "Democracy can only mean Hindu Raj all over India." Even the existing constitutional structure had led to "the domination and supremacy of the majority communal rule over the minorities." He also widened the scope of the argument by incorporating the traditional conservative view: "Having regard to the 35 millions of voters, the bulk of whom are totally ignorant, illiterate and untutored, living in centuries-old superstitions of the worst type, thoroughly antagonistic to each other, culturally and socially, the working of this Constitution has clearly brought out that it is impossible to work a democratic parliamentary government in

[21]For even if the National Congress accepted all the Muslim communal demands what was the guarantee of their fulfilment or preservation after the transfer of power?

[22]M.A. Jinnah, *op. cit.*, Vol. I, p. 42.

India."[23] By 1940, the minority community argument had been transformed into the two-nation theory. Asserting that "Western democracy is totally unsuited for India and its imposition on India is the disease in the body politic," he said: "If, therefore, it is accepted that there are in India a major and a minor nation, it follows that parliamentary system based on the majority principle must inevitably mean the rule of the major nation." This was the reason why the Congress, "mainly a Hindu body," had from the beginning bent all its effort towards securing for India "a completely democratic form of government."[24] Repeating all this, Jinnah developed the argument in a separatist direction during 1940 and after. Democracy meant, he repeatedly asserted, expression of the national will. Where there were two nations with nothing in common, it was not possible to have democracy. The only answer was partition and Pakistan.[25]

The Hindu Mahasabha and other Hindu communalists repeated the Muslim communal argument in respect of provinces and areas where Muslims were a majority. Maintaining that Muslim majority in legislatures would mean Muslim domination and a perpetual state of Hindu inferiority, they tried their very best to reduce Muslim representation in the legislatures of Muslim majority provinces. They opposed the creation of Sind as a separate province because that would reduce Hindus there to a small minority and lead to 'loss' of their 'power.' Aping the Muslim communalists on the all-India plane, the Hindu (and Sikh) communalists of Panjab, Sind, and the North-West Frontier Province (NWFP) put forward the theory that simple democracy was dangerous for minorities and that better reliance for the defence of minority rights could be placed on the colonial

[23] *Ibid.*, p. 89.

[24] *Ibid.*, pp. 117-18. Also see p. 123.

[25] *Ibid.*, pp. 116-18, 123-24, 139-40, 151-52, 161-62, 217-19, 239-40, 253, *passim*. This constant denigration of democracy was to produce fateful results for Pakistan. This socialization of leaders, cadre and people in an anti-democratic ideology was an important reason for the easy submergence of democracy in Pakistan after 1947. In contrast, the Indian national movement from its very foundation in 1885 fought for and internalized the values of democracy and civil liberties among its leaders and cadre and people.

authorities. Consequently, they opposed the introduction and extension of democratic constitutional features in the NWFP. Both in Sind and the NWFP, they supported the increase in the constitutional and administrative powers of the Governors in the name of providing safeguards to the minorities. They did support joint electorate and democracy for the country as a whole. But that was the result of their *communal* belief that democracy would lead to Hindu domination. Even at the cost of some repetition it may be pointed out that two basic communal assumptions lay at the base of this argument: (*i*) that Hindus and Muslims had separate economic and political interests; and *(ii)* that Hindus (or Muslims) would always act together as a solid communal group in politics—that all Hindu (or Muslim) members of legislatures would act as Hindus (or Muslims) as a solid parliamentary bloc irrespective of political, social, ideological or programmatic considerations—and that their being Hindus (or Muslims) would constitute the heart of their politics.

Till the middle 1930s, both the Hindu and Muslim communalists opposed the extension of franchise to cover all adults, partly because it would bring to the fore issues which interested the mass of the people. Their attitude towards civil liberties was also ambiguous. At a time when Moderate nationalists were fighting whole-heartedly for civil liberties, including freedom of speech and the Press, Syed Ahmed Khan openly supported Lytton's attack on the freedom of the Press. The later communalists were much more circumspect in this respect, but, unlike the nationalists, they waged no campaigns for civil liberties and fought no battles against their repeated abridgement by the colonial authorities. Most often, they used the periods of such abridgement to bargain with the colonial authorities.

The anti-democratic character of the communal parties, groups and individuals also found expression in their support to the rulers of the princely states. In his Presidential address to the 1940 session of the Hindu Mahashabha, V.D. Savarkar strongly supported the cause of Hindu princes and declared that they were realizing "that their duty required them not only to sympathize with but to lead the Hindu movement" and that "their present and future interests as well are, in fact, identified with the Pan-Hindu movement." If the Hindu princes had failed to "lead the Hindu movement," the fault was not altogether theirs; the "Congress Hindus" had not only failed to extend them support but "looked down on the Hindu states as an impediment in the path of India's progress, which the sooner it was removed the better it would be for the Nation." Savarkar urged Hindus to emulate the example of Muslims (i.e., Muslim communalists) who were "intensely proud of the few Moslem States in India" and who "looked upon them as organized centres of Moslem strength and even tried to augment the power and prestige of their Nizams and Nababs."[26]

Similarly, Bhai Parmanand demanded in 1938 that the states' representatives in the federal legislature should be decided by the princes. He also declared: "The princes are the flesh of our flesh and the most essential part of our body politic."[27] The Hindu communalists also adopted Nepal as a Hindu state whose ruler was destined to fulfil "the great and glorious destiny" of being the leader and saviour—"the Hope"—of Hindus, the "defender of the Hindu Faith" and "the commander of Hindu forces."[28]

The Muslim communalists did not lag behind in this respect. Even M.A. Jinnah "built up alliances with Muslim native rulers against the federation and against the demand that states' representatives at the federal centre be elected by their subjects."[29] B. Shiva Rao has recorded how princes, including Hindu princes, became sympathetic towards

[26]V.D. Savarkar, *Hindu Rashtra Darshan,* pp. 171-72. Savarkar added: "The Hindu states are, in fact, nearly the only centres of the organized military administrative and political Hindu strength and are bound to play a more active and more decisive part in the near future in moulding the destiny of the Hindu Nation than any other factor within our present reach." P. 172. Also: "As defenders of Hindu faith and Hindu honour they form the reserve forces of Hindudom, organized centres of Hindu strength...." *Hindu Sanghtan,* p. 214.

[27]Indra Prakash, *op. cit.,* p. xxiv. At its Nagpur session, the Hindu Mahasabha passed a resolution condemning Congress interference and its instigating trouble in the Indian states, particularly the Hindu states. *Indian Annual Register,* 1938, Part II, p. 340.

[28]V.D. Savarkar, *Hindu Rashtra Darshan,* pp. 2-3, 173, 231; *Hindu Sanghtan,* pp. 215-16.

[29]B.R. Tomlinson, *The Indian National Congress and the Raj, 1929-1942,* p. 139.

the Muslim League in the late 1930s because of the Congress-supported popular agitations against them. As Jam Saheb of Nawanagar, the Chancellor of the Chamber of Princes, told him while discussing an alliance between the Muslim League and the Chamber for the federal elections: "Why should I not support the League? Mr. Jinnah is willing to tolerate our existence, but Mr. Nehru wants the extinction of the Princes."[30] Interestingly enough, all the different schemes for Pakistan postulated leaving the princely states as they were.

One of the favourite manners of, and excuses for, supporting the princes was to accuse the Congress of fighting the princes of only one religious denomination. The Hindu communalists accused the Congress of leading popular agitations only against the 'Hindu' states such as Kashmir and Rajkot to the exclusion of the 'Muslim' states and refusing to support popular agitations for democratic rights in the 'Muslim' states such as Hyderabad and Bhopal.[31] On the other hand, the Muslim League accused the Congress of attacking the Nizam and Hyderabad state while keeping silent about the affairs of Kashmir whose ruler was a Hindu.[32]

An interesting feature of the anti-democratic political outlook of the communal groups and parties was the adoption of V.D. Savarkar, M.A. Jinnah and M.S. Golwalkar as permanent presidents or heads by the Hindu Mahasabha, the Muslim League and the RSS, respectively. These organizations functioned more or less on the contemporary 'leader' or Fuhrer principle.

V

Political reaction lay, above all, in the pro-colonial role of communal individuals, groups and parties. In relation to the primary contradiction of Indian society at the time, that is, the contradiction between colonialism and the Indian people, the communalists often took up basically pro-colonial and loyalist positions and developed a relationship of mutual dependence *vis-a-vis* the colonial authorities. In

[30]B. Shiva Rao, *India, 1935-47,* p. 420.
[31]V.D. Savarkar, *Hindu Rashtra Darshan,* pp. 78, 91-92.
[32]M.A. Jinnah, *op, cit.*, Vol. I, pp. 75-76.

no case did they adopt active anti-colonial political positions. At worst, they cooperated with colonialism, at best, they avoided conflict with it. As pointed out at the beginning of this chapter, communalism was the vehicle through which petty bourgeois politics was placed at the command of colonialism.

(*i*) Negatively, the communalists, unlike the nationalists even in their most moderate phase during 1880-1905, developed or made no critique or analysis of colonialism.[33] The communal leaders did, of course, sometimes criticize the British rulers, but at no stage did they make a basic anti-colonial analysis of British rule or put forward any demands which would basically undermine colonial domination.

Similarly, the communalists organized no agitation or struggle against colonialism or for independence even of their own conception. Once the country was widely politicized during the 1930s, a general anti-imperialist air filled the country, especially among the intelligentsia, and it became clear that the days of British rule were numbered, the communalists were forced to talk against British rule. Even this they did most feebly. But in no case did they make any effort to oppose British rule, not to speak of taking any steps to end it. They neither organized nor participated in any mass or direct action for the achievement of freedom. In fact, they did not do so even for their own communal demands.[34] They were always feeding, as political parasites,

[33]Many writers, including, surprisingly enough, W.C. Smith *(op. cit.,* p. 204), readily assume that the political approach of the Muslim League in 1907 and that of the Moderate nationalists after 1885 were similar—that both were moderates and that the League was repeating the politics of the Moderates after a lag of 20 years. In fact, the two politics were basically different. The Moderates made and popularized a fundamental economic critique of colonialism and put forward democratic nationalist political demands and were, therefore, despite their protestations of loyalty, anti-colonial. All such anti-colonialism was missing from the politics of the Muslim League in 1907. Its politics were directed, however mildly, not against colonialism but against the Congress and Hindus.

[34]A few instances may be cited. (*i*) When, on several occasions, the Hindu communalists agitated against cow-killing the edge of their agitation was against the slaughter of cows by Muslims and not against their slaughter in the cantonments for British soldiers. In fact, it was not cow slaughter and cow protection societies that gave birth to communalism, but communalism which led to the sudden spurt in cow protection. (*ii*) In 1911, the Muslim communalists refused to agitate against the decision to annul the partition of Bengal. (*iii*) The language the commualists opposed was Persian or Urdu or Hindi and not English.

on the political work and struggles of the anti-imperialist forces. When on rare occasions mass actions were organized, they were directed not against the British but the nationalists or the followers of other religions. For example, the first mass action of the Muslim League in the form of 'the Day of Deliverance' in December 1939 was directed against the Congress. The main 'mass action' of the communalists took the form of communal riots, especially during 1946-47, and these riots were directed against the followers of other religions. Similarly, the RSS carefully 'preserved' its strength and militancy during the War so as to be able to use it later against Muslims.

In the 1930s and 1940s communal politics assumed that the British would give political concessions to Indians and perhaps even depart in the end, but the communal parties and groups made no contribution to these processes. Even the final creation of Pakistan was not the result of an anti-imperialist struggle carried on by the Muslim League but a by-product of the nationalist struggle against imperialism and the Muslim League struggle against the nationalist forces. "Others forced open the doors through which Jinnah walked to his goal." In general, the communalist politician was not concerned with fighting for concessions from the colonial rulers; he was concerned primarily with whatever could be got from the concessions the nationalists had secured through struggle. He was not concerned with how or when these concessions were secured by the nationalists. He had the patience—and politics—to wait forever.[35]

For this reason, it is important to note that communalism could not be treated as communal anti-imperialism or as *Hindu nationalism, Muslim nationalism,* and so on, as some recent writers have tried to

[35]Inevitably, the communalist denied that nationalist politics were responsible for the concessions that colonial authorities gave. He gave the credit to the colonial authorities instead. For example, after ascribing the proclamation of 16 August 1917 to the influence of President Wilson and his declaration of the right of self-determination for nations on the British, Bhai Permanand wrote in 1938: "It is in the fulfilment of this proclamation that the British Government has been taking steps to extend self-goverment by easy stages to the Indian people." Hence, "we do not owe this constitutional progress, restricted as it is, to the Congress." Foreword to Indra Prakash, *op. cit.*, pp. xxxv-xxxvii.

maintain. Communalism was not religion-based nationalism or anti-imperialism as it was in Indonesia or Iran or some Arab countries. In these countries, political struggle was defined in religious terms but was directed against colonialism. In India, communalism defined politics in religious terms but their politics were directed against fellow Indians and not against colonialism; their fight was against the other 'community.' The protection they sought was from the followers of other religions and the exploitation they denounced was also by them. Even the struggle for jobs, economic and political safeguards, and seats in legislatures, was directed not against the foreign rulers but against fellow Indians belonging to other religions. Their demands were made on the nationalists and the edge of their politics was turned against the national movement; on the other hand, they usually looked to the colonial regime for support and favours and cooperated with it. Communalism did not, therefore, belong to the genre nationalism, which dealt, in however conservative a form, with the contradiction between colonialism and the colonialized people, but to the genre loyalism, because it divided the colonial people, prevented the growth of national unity and disrupted the united anti-imperialist struggle and thus objectively served the interests of colonialism and provided it with the only justification it could put forward for holding on to the colonies, namely, preservation of peace among 'the warring communities.'

(ii) As Jawaharlal Nehru put it, "one of the best tests of its (communalism's) true nature is what relation it bears to the national struggle,"[36] that is, the actual, historically specific, struggle against foreign domination that was going on at the time. And there is no doubt that this relation was highly negative, as G.K. Gokhale was able to see as early as 1909. Referring to the formation of the Hindu Sabha in Panjab, he wrote to Wedderburn: "The movement is frankly anti Mohammedan, as the Moslem League is frankly anti-Hindu, and both are anti-national."[37]

[36]Jawaharlal Nehru, *SW,* Vol. 6, p. 165.
[37]Quoted in B.N. Pandey, *The Break-up of British India,* p. 72.

Even when the communalists were the beneficiaries of the political consequences of the ongoing national struggle, they played no role in it, especially after 1934. More importantly, apart from not fighting against colonialism, they often opposed the actual anti-colonial movement and its leading organ, the National Congress. This was particularly so during the 1930s and 1940s, when they spread dislike and hatred against the Congress and made it the main target of their attack. Depending on their own brand of communalism, they condemned it as pro-Hindu or pro-Muslim whose political objective was to subjugate the Muslims or to sacrifice the Hindus. This attack upon the Congress and the consequent weakening of anti-British sentiments, especially among the youth and their diversion into anti-Muslim or anti-Hindu channels, was, in fact, a major service that communalism performed for colonialism.

(iii) In many cases, especially before 1937, communal parties, groups and individuals gave active support and loyalty to the foreign regime.

(*iv*) In one major respect, communalism served colonialism by its very existence. Once the national movement in India and the anti-imperialist sentiments in Britain had grown sufficiently strong, which was the case by 1918 and in particular after 1937, the British rulers had to justify their continued existence in India both to the Indian people and to the British people, and, perhaps, even to themselves, as this was necessary in terms of their hegemony over Indian and British minds. The earlier colonial ideology of India not being a nation, its people being incapable of governing themselves and the civilizing and developmental mission of colonialism had lost its force and credibility by the end of the First World War. Increasingly, thereafter, colonial ideologues justified foreign rule by asserting that an honest 'umpire' or third force was needed to keep peace among Indian communities which would otherwise tear each other apart, and, in particular, to protect the minority 'communities' from domination and exploitation by the majority 'community.' The activity of the communalists thus increasingly became the major, and, in the end, the only, element in the ideological and political defence of colonialism. Moreover, the communalists both accepted and reinforced the official ideology in this respect.

(*v*) Overt or covert support to colonialism also resulted from the social base of communalism and its basic ideological and political position. The privileged social position of the landlords and other jagirdari elements and that of the bureaucrats could be preserved only with the support of the colonial administration. Facing and fearing social change, they needed colonial state support. Their politics were therefore inevitably loyalist whether they functioned openly as landlords and bureaucrats or covertly as communalists.

Similarly, as brought out earlier in Chapter 2, individuals and sections of the middle classes used communalism to improve their position in the struggle for jobs, educational opportunities, etc., and this needed the cooperation of the government. In fact, because of its capacity through nomination and reservation to influence employment, contracts, educational facilities, share in administrative power and so on, the colonial state possessed an immense capacity to win over, that is, to coopt and buy, large sections of the petty bourgeoisie; and it was willing to use this capacity to offer better terms to different communal groups in return for their collaboration and willingness to oppose the national movements and, in particular, to divert the young people from the nationalist path by encouraging and promoting an alternative stream of emotional politics.

All these social groups could get better terms in the short run by cooperating with the government than by joining the nationalist stream. The communalists could function effectively only at the pleasure or at least tolerance of the colonial authorities, and in no case could they come into a basic conflict or antagonistic relationship with them.

Siding with the colonial regime lay also in the very logic of the basic communal ideological and political position and strategy which stressed that the basic socio-economic, political and cultural interests of Hindus and Muslims were separate and incompatible and even antagonistic, that the main enemy was the other 'community,' that the threat of domination and subjugation came not from colonialism but from the other 'community,' and that, therefore, the need for political organization of the 'community' also arose in order to compete with and confront the other 'community' and not colonialism. If Indian politics were triangular among Hindus, Muslims and British rulers and the main enemy was Hindus or Muslims as the case may be, it was inevitable that the communalists would try to join forces with the British, the third party. Moreover, if the main threat came from the other 'community,' then the third party, which was also the ruling party, would have to remain in India to maintain the balance and to protect the threatened 'community.' The politics of safeguards and reservations also needed the presence of a third party which could guarantee their implementation and continuity. Even if an eventual future free of colonial rule was envisaged, the communalists believed that they should seek favours of the foreign rulers in order to strengthen their 'community's' position for the eventual struggle for power in free India.[38]

The Muslim communal position in this respect has been summed up rather well by K.K. Aziz:

> It (i.e., a loyalist political position) was the safest course of action for a minority which was backward and helpless. Either it could cooperate with the Hindus, which it would not, or it could keep on good terms with the rulers. To alienate both the present and the future rulers would have been folly without any mitigation.... Most Muslims appreciated the fairness with which they had been, or were being, treated by the British. Between the Hindus and the British they chose to trust the latter, and on the whole found that this policy paid dividends.... The British ruled the country and held power and patronage in their hands. The

[38]We have shown in a later chapter that the colonial authorities, in turn, actively encouraged and fostered communal forces. The relations between the two were of mutual dependence, assistance and accommodation. This also therefore meant that sometimes hard bargaining between the two occurred.

> Muslims, as a minority, wanted safeguards, and the British alone could grant them.[39]

Many Hindu communalists turned this argument around and said that Hindus should appease the government so that Muslims might not gain from the politics of loyalty and Hindus suffer because of their nationalism. This argument did not go down very well with the more politically conscious section of the people. Most of the Hindu communalists therefore tended to use another of its variant. Since Hindus faced two enemies and the British were bound to leave, Hindus should not waste their energy in the anti-British fight; they should let the Congress carry that on. Hindus should conserve their strength for the eventual and final struggle against Muslims.

The communalists also opposed any serious political struggle against colonial rule for other reasons; it would lead to an emphasis on the common interests of all Indians, bring about Hindu-Muslim unity and seriously undermine communal ideology. This was what had happened during 1919-22 when the Khilafat issue had led many Muslim communalists to oppose imperialism and unite with other Indians with the consequent near disintegration of communal groups and their influence over Muslims. The powerful Akali agitation against the government during 1922-26 had a similar disastrous impact on the fortunes of the Sikh communalists. Later, several sections of the Akali Dal took to communal politics; but it is of interest to note that the colonial authorities could not, because of their patronage to Muslim communalism, adequately appease Sikh communalism and it had to often take anti-imperialist positions with the result that Sikh communalism could not flourish fully in Panjab and large sections of the Akali Dal tended to remain within the nationalist stream. Sikh communalism could flower fully only after 1947. For the same reasons, the communalists also opposed trade union and peasant struggles which tended to cut across religious barriers and thus subverted communal ideology.

[39] K.K. Aziz, *op. cit.*, pp. 73-75.

At this stage, it perhaps needs to be re-emphasized that the pro-colonial politics of the communalists were not a matter of their private feelings but of their public politics; privately many of them shared in the sense of humiliation of belonging to a subject people from which most politicized Indians suffered.[40] As M.A. Jinnah put it in his Presidential address to the Muslim League in December 1938 while denying that the League was an ally of imperialism: "I say the Muslim League is not going to be an ally of anyone, but would be the ally of even the devil if need be in the interests of Muslims. It is not because we are in love with imperialism; but in politics one had to play one's game as on the chess board."[41] Similarly, presiding over the Hindu Mahasabha session in 1933, Bhai Parmanand told the delegates:

> There is an open alliance between the British Government and the Muslims .... we have reached a stage where the Congress with its theory of Swaraj through Hindu-Muslim unity and Civil Disobedience goes entirely out of the field ... the future is very gloomy and dark for the Hindus.... I feel an impulse in me that the Hindus would willingly cooperate with Great Britain if their status and responsible position as the premier community in India is recognized in the political institutions of new India.[42]

Thus, to sum up the discussion so far, it was, above all, in its aspect of being an ally or instrument of colonialism against the anti-imperialist movement that communalism emerged as an instrument of reaction, even when a communalist might not be subjectively pro-imperialist.

[40]This dichotomy was not confined to the Indian communalists. We have the famous example of Chiang Kai-shek, who possessed fierce anti-foreign feelings which even found expression in his book, *China's Destiny*, and who still played a comprador or agent's role to imperialism for major periods of his life. In fact, some of the Indian communal leaders had a strong nationalist past; for example, V.D. Savarkar, Bhai Parmanand, K.B. Hedgewar, M.A. Jinnah, Khaliquzzaman, Maulana Shaukat Ali and Hasrat Mohani.

[41]M.A. Jinnah, *op. tit.*, Vol. I, p. 78.

[42]*Indian Annual Register*, 1933, Vol. II, pp. 204-06.

VI

With the greater weight of jagirdari-feudal and bureaucratic elements among the Muslim upper classes and intelligentsia, Muslim communalism, from the beginning, adopted openly pro-colonial politics. Throughout his political life, Syed Ahmed Khan made it a point to support the colonial regime and preach loyalty to it. In 1878, he welcomed Lytton's repressive Vernacular Press Act as a liberal measure. In 1883, he asked Muslims not to agitate for the Ubert Bill since it was being actively opposed by the Europeans. He actively opposed the Congress from the beginning, first on the basis of an upper class alliance of Hindus and Muslims and later on the basis of Muslim communalism. Throughout, he preached that the British rulers were the best guardians of Muslim interests. He declared the British to be *Khilafatullah* or God's representative on earth, who would reward Muslims for their loyalty.[43]

In this early phase Muslim communalism was not organized politically. Rather, Syed Ahmed and others held that all political agitations at that stage would tend to become seditious and anti-government or at least create suspicions of disloyalty in the official mind. They therefore asked Muslims to shun all politics and remain non-political and non-agitational, that is, politically passive, in their approach.[44] At no stage did Syed Ahmed try to organize Muslims into a political association. Later, under the pressure of younger men, an attempt was made in 1903 on the question of the UP Governor's order regarding the use of Hindi in government offices to create a non-agitational Muslim political organization; but the attempt was foiled by the upper class successors of Syed Ahmed. Other early communalists were also actively loyalist and opposed to the Congress

[43]See his *Writting and Speeeches,* especially pp. 102ff., 180ff., 202ff., 21 Off., 243. Of course, he also took positive steps outside this loyalist framework to uplift Muslims, particularly by promoting modern education and culture, though even the educational effort had its loyalist aspect.

[44]Cf. Syed Ahmed's letter to Badruddin Tyabji: "I will state briefly that as a general rule all political questions which can be discussed are dangerous and prejudicial to the interests of Mohammedans, and that they should take part in no political Congress." *Ibid., p.* 243. Also see Abid Husain, *The Destiny of Indian Muslims,* pp. 38-39.

and the national movement from 1888 onwards. The Muslim communalists openly sided with the government in the course of the Swadeshi Movement and condemned the Muslim supporters of the movement as 'vile traitors' and 'Congress touts.'

After the partition of Bengal and Swadeshi agitation and the Morley-Minto Reforms, when it became impossible to keep Muslims totally passive politically, the Muslim League was founded in 1907 by a group of landed magnates, ex-bureaucrats and other upper class Muslims as a loyalist and conservative political organization. One of its objectives was to keep the emerging modern intelligentsia among Muslims and Muslim students from joining the Congress and the national movement. It raised the slogan of special Muslim interests, especially in government services and legislatures, which could be promoted only through cooperation with the colonial authorities. It was in the nature of a joint enterprise by the communalists and the government—it was a 'government party.'

After 1911, the Muslim League increasingly came under the influence of younger men oriented towards nationalism and the Congress and opposed to the loyalist and slavish mentality. The result was an intense struggle between the upper class loyalists and the younger, more middle class nationalists. In 1916 came the Lucknow Pact between the Congress and the Muslim League. These young Muslim nationalists also joined the Congress in condemning the Montagu-Chelmsford Reforms in 1918. The years between 1918 and 1922 were years of Hindu-Muslim unity and intense nationalist struggle. The landlord-communalists and ex-bureaucrats increasingly dissociated themselves from the Muslim League, the Khilafat movement and the Congress, while the League itself was overshadowed by the Khilafat Committee as the League leaders—as also many of the old Congress leaders—found it difficult to keep pace with the new militant mass politics of jail-going and sacrifice. However, after the withdrawal of the Non-Cooperation Movement in 1922, the Muslim League was revived and cleansed of radical and nationalist elements. Once again, the upper class leaders with their policy of strengthening the British connection came to the fore. Even so, the

League split on the question of the boycott of the Simon Commission. One section led by M.A. Jinnah boycotted it while another section led by Muhammad Shafi cooperated with it. The League, however, commanded little public support at that time; the nationalist Muslims still represented a major political force.

The Muslim communalists also opposed the Civil Disobedience Movement of 1930-31. The All-India Muslim Conference declared it to be an attempt by Hindus to impose their domination over the minorities. This phase of the national struggle, however, pushed the communalists, as a whole, into the background, and young Muslim intellectuals, peasants and workers, and others increasingly joined the mainstreams of nationalism and socialism in the early 1930s. In the Civil Disobedience Movement itself, led by the Congress, Jamiat-ul-Ulama-i-Hind, Khudai Khidmatgars and other organizations, thousands of Muslims went to jail. The communalists were largely isolated and weakened.[45]

Most of the Muslim communalists cooperated fully with the British Government during the Round Table Conferences in the early 1930s. This spirit of loyalty to colonial rule was exemplified by the article written for the *Empire Review* in 1931 by Maulana Shaukat Ali, one of the two famous Ali brothers known for their anti-British oratory during the Khilafat Movement. Rejecting any possibility of Hindu-Muslim cooperation, he appealed for Muslim-British friendship: "We both need each other. We would grasp that hand and Islam would stand with Britian, a good and honourable friend, a brave fighter and a staunch ally .... should Hindus and Muslims live together for a thousand years, there is no chance of the two cultures merging into one."[46]

At the Second Round Table Conference, the Muslim communalists joined hands with the most reactionary sections of the British ruling classes. They foiled all attempts by Gandhi to solve the communal

[45]K.K. Aziz, *op. cit.,'p.* 90. Also see M.N. Islam, *Bengal Muslim Public Opinion as Reflected in the Bengal Press 1901-1930,* pp. 98-99.

[46]Quoted in K.K. Aziz, *op. cit.*, p. 73.

problem so that the issue of independence could be brought to the front.[47] In this they rendered invaluable service to the colonial rulers. During the Third Round Table Conference, at a meeting in the House or Commons, the Aga Khan, the poet Mohammad Iqbal and the historian Shafaat Ahmad Khan stressed "the inherent impossibility of securing any merger of Hindu and Muslim, political or indeed social, interests" and "the impracticability of ever governing India through anything but a British agency."[48]

By 1935, the Muslim League had sunk into relative insignificance. Most of the younger Muslim intellectuals were attracted by the Congress, the Congress Socialist Party or the Communist Party. In Bengal, many joined the secular and radical Krishak Praja Party. The League was, however, reorganized after 1936 under the leadership of M.A. Jinnah. It also tried to widen its social base among the lower middle classes and the youth. Consequently, it could no longer follow openly loyalist politics or refuse to put forward the demand for independence. The communalists now had to adopt a more independent stance vis-a-vis colonialism. Jinnah now repeatedly declared, as in 1937, that "the Muslim League stands for full national democratic self-government of India"; or, in 1940, that "we stand unequivocally for the freedom of India."[49] But the policy of collaboration with colonialism continued in more indirect forms.[50] Above all, the edge of communal politics was now directed entirely against the Congress and the national movement; the main criticism

[47]According to Nehru: "Gandhiji offered personally to accept every single one of their communal demands, however illogical and exaggerated they might be, on condition that they assured him of their full support in the political struggle for independence. That condition and offer was not accepted and it became clear that what stood in the way was not even communalism but political reaction." *SW,* Vol. 6, p. 164.

[48]Report in *The Statesman,* 31 December 1932, quoted in Nehru, *SW,* Vol. 6, p. 163.

[49]M.A. Jinnah, *op. cit.,* Vol. I, pp. 26 and 146.

[50]Communalists' loyalism could, however, still sometimes take a direct form. For example, while trying to frighten the British of the danger of large-scale Muslim support to the Congress, Jinnah told Linlithgow, the Viceroy, in September 1937, that the British should keep the power at the Centre as it was and that if the British 'protected' the Muslims in Congress provinces, Muslims would 'protect' the British at [the Centre. S. Gopal, *Jawaharlal Nehru—A Biography,* Vol. I, p. 240.

of colonial authorities made by the League leadership was that they were willing to negotiate with the Congress. Jinnah and the League carried on a large-scale vilification campaign against the Congress and tried to identify it as a Hindu organization before Muslims and British opinion. It did, of course, achieve a certain success in this campaign, especially because of the unemployment generated among the petty bourgeoisie by the Depression. Moreover, while formally self-government was demanded, in practice it was suggested that the British must not leave India so that Muslims were not left "at the mercy of Hindus."[51] In 1937, the Muslim League supported the colonial authorities in the controversy on governors' powers on the ground that these powers were needed to protect the minorities from Hindu domination.

In any case, the League did not carry out any political work or movement for the achievement of self-government and in no way undermined or attacked colonial rule or came into open conflict with it. In time, a small anti-colonial and radical section did develop in the League, but, at no stage, did it exercise much influence on the League's leadership. Instead, it was the conservative, pro-colonial dominant leadership of the League which used the presence of the small anti-colonial group to give some credibility to its otherwise reactionary politics. Above all, as pointed out earlier, the League provided the British with their main, and in the end the only, justification for staying on in India. The colonial authorities held that they could not discuss the question of independence till the Congress and the League came to an agreement. Jinnah would not negotiate with the Congress unless its leadership accepted before hand that the Congress was a Hindu body, that the League represented all Muslims and that Muslims in the Congress represented nobody. These were conditions that no nationalist organization could ever accept. And so the colonial authorities could coolly declare that the Congress did not represent the

[51]Jinnah told Linlithgow in February 1939 rather 'coyly' that to maintain the balance between Hindus and Muslims the British would have to stay in India. Report of Jinnah's talk with Linlithgow in Linlithgow to Zetland, 28 February 1939, *Zetland Papers,* Vol. 15, Reel No. 5.

entire Indian people and that disagreement among the Indian 'communities' was responsible for India's non-advancement towards independence.[52]

During the Second World War, when the Congress came into confrontation with the government, the Muslim League leadership permitted its members to support the war effort. In any case the League did nothing to obstruct it. Jinnah exploited Congress- government conflict, and, at the very outset of the War, hinted to the Viceroy that (in the words of the Viceroy) "a firm hand with the Congress" would receive his support.[53] The Congress was demanding an immediate declaration of independence. The League put forward the demand that no declaration regarding constitutional advance be made without the prior approval of "the two-major communities."[54] Later, it made the acceptance of Pakistan as such a precondition. These conditions were to become the sheet-anchor of British defence against Indian nationalism. The British Government neither wanted to accept transfer of power to Indians nor did it want to appear before British, Indian and world opinion as refusing to accept the Indian demand at a time when it was supposed to be engaged in a war for the defence of freedom and democracy. The League leadership enabled it to escape the dilemma by hiding behind the facade of communal disagreement.[55] At the same time, the Muslim League leadership denounced the Quit India Movement of 1942 as being directed not so much against the British as against Muslims because it sidetracked the demand for

[52]See Chapter 8 for a fuller discussion of colonial policy in this respect.

[53]Linlithgow's notes of an interview with Jinnah on 12 January 1940, annexure to Linlithgow's letter to the Secretary of State, 16 January 1940, *Linlithgow Papers,* Reel No. 9.

[54]*Ibid.*

[55]Nor was Jinnah unaware of the service the League was performing for the colonial regime. He told the Viceroy in his January meeting that his condition would at the most mean that the Congress would not settle with the League. In that case, he said, the British would lose nothing, i.e., they would have to make no concession regarding transfer of power. *Ibid:* In his address to the 1941 session of the League, he said: "The British Government ought to be grateful to the Muslim League for saving them the maximum amount of trouble the Congress was determined to give them." He added, "in their heart of hearts the British people were grateful to the Muslim League." M.A. Jinnah, *op. cit.,* Vol. I, p. 262.

Pakistan. The League also took the support of colonial rulers to install League ministries in Bengal, Sind and the MWFP.

Throughout the period 1937-47, the Muslim League did not organize a single agitation or political movement against the colonial authorities, even in favour of its own demands. It carried out several propaganda campaigns after 1937, but all were directed against the Congress governments on such issues as the singing of *Bande Matram* in schools, hoisting of the Congress flag on public buildings and the Wardha education scheme. Its first major agitation was in December 1939 when it observed a Deliverance Day to celebrate the resignation of the Congress ministries. The British administration gave almost open support to the League on this occasion. Its only political movement was organized on 16 August 1946 when it observed Direct Action Day to achieve Pakistan. The British having declared their decision to transfer power, the League leadership could now indulge in heroic action without displeasing the rulers. The Council of the League then declared that as "Muslim India has exhausted, without success, all efforts to find a peaceful solution of the Indian problem by compromise and constitutional means" and as "the Congress is bent upon setting up Caste-Hindu Raj in India with the connivance of the British ... the time has come for the Muslim nation to resort to Direct Action to achieve Pakistan...." Explaining the decision, Jinnah said: "We have taken a most heroic decision. Never before in the whole life-history of the Muslim League did we do anything except by constitutional methods and constitutional talks.... Today we have said good-bye to constitutions and constitutional methods."[56] But far from being a call for anti-imperialist action, this was a declaration of communal civil war. It was to result in the bloodiest of communal riots in Calcutta—with the death toll reaching 5000 in the first two days—and to initiate a chain reaction of communal massacres in the subcontinent.

Hindu communalism too was loyalist from the beginning. Its proponents too advocated cooperation with the colonial regime with a view to get "concessions" for the 'Hindus.' It was of course less open

[56]Quoted in S.S. Pirzada, *Foundations of Pakistan...*, Vol. II, pp. 557-58 and 560.

and more circumspect in its loyalist politics because it was more open to the nationalist pressure on its ranks since the social weight and influence of the middle classes and the nationalist intelligentsia were much greater among Hindus. Also, the British Government gave Hindu communalism few concessions and little support, for it banked heavily on Muslim communalism and could not easily simultaneously placate both communalisms.

Hindu communalism made an indirect beginning in the 1880s and 1890s with a vigorous cow protection movement in Panjab which soon spread to UP and Bihar. This movement was mainly directed against Muslims; on the other hand, the British cantonments were left relatively free to carry on cow slaughter on a large scale.

The pro-colonial and anti-Congress line of Hindu communal politics was laid down in 1909 by one of the first theoreticians of Hindu communalism. Founder of the Panjab Hindu Sabha in 1909, Rai Bahadur Lal Chand attacked the Congress frontally in a series of articles which were gathered in the booklet, *Self-Abnegation in Politics,* reprinted in 1938. He described the Congress as the "self-inflicted misfortune" of Hindus and as "a veritable source of weakness for purely Hindu interests." He also accused the Press of refusing to take up "the pure Hindu cause" because of the Congress influence over it. His main charge against the Congress was that it appeased Muslims and refused to protect "Hindu interests" out of the fear that it would annoy Muslims and prevent the creation of a united nation, an objective which the Congress was willing to promote "even by self-immolation." Hindus, Lal Chand wrote, were moving towards extinction because of "the poison imbibed for the last twenty-five years." The Hindus could be saved only if they were willing to "purge" the poison and get rid of the "evil." If the government favoured Muslims, as it did, the fault lay with the Congress which had sacrificed Hindu interests "at the altar of unification." "If from the very first the Hindus had assisted their own interests separately and independently and claimed their special class privileges," said Lal Chand, "the result would have been different...." The government could not be blamed for joining hands with

Muslims; "why not go deep to the root of the evil? Why not acknowledge that Government has joined hands with the Mohammedans *because the Congress began to make impossible demands.* As Lord Dufferin said, it wanted 'to sit in the seat of Phaeton and guide the chariot of the Sun,' and as Lord Morley says it wanted 'to have the moon.'" In fact, said Lal Chand, from the beginning in 1885, the Congress put forward political demands such as the abolition of the India Council, the repeal of the Arms Act, a decrease in the military expenditure, and non-official majority in the legislative councils, which alarmed the government. "It was a case of mad arrogance ... leading its votaries to insensate attitude, and the result was doubly disastrous." The government's retaliation led to the "crippling" of the Congress and "a repulse to the Hindu community." Thus, wrote Lal Chand, "the real cause" of the Hindus' disastrous condition was "the Congress, which for the time completely dominated Hindu politics and by reason of its impossible demands and defiant attitude alienated the Government sympathy from the Hindu cause and actually converted it into sullen hostility." The Congress had, after 1905, compounded the error by demanding self-government as in the colonies. Describing this demand as an "insensate" cry, he said that the result was "to needlessly array the Government in opposition and to irritate it against the community which practically is responsible for agitating for the demand." The correct course, advised Lal Chand, should have been different. While in an independent democracy, the leadership of a people might "be discourteous, unaccommodating and wholly selfish" in relation to the government, the situation was different under an alien government. "The object in view is to secure greater privileges for and safeguard the interests of the democracy behind (sic), and in order to achieve it, it is absolutely essential to move with a conciliatory attitude. The leader ... must be willing and ready to accommodate the Government in some matters." The correct policy for the Hindus at that stage was to reconsider their past politics and make necessary changes so as to neutralize and if possible win over the third party—the government—involved in the Hindu-Muslim fight. This objective could not be achieved by mending the Congress. It would neither become a Hindu Congress nor would it give up the self-government goal. Since it was necessary to give up the "insensate cries for Indian ideals and colonial forms of Government," it was essential to abandon, to *"end"* the Congress.[57]

Hindu communalism failed to consolidate itself before 1918, suffered a setback during 1918-22 and took off in an organized form only in 1923 when the all-India session of the Hindu Mahasabha led to a minor revival. The Hindu Mahasabha was, however, still a weak organization in which many nationalists were also involved. The more active communalists took up the tasks of *Shuddhi* and *Sangathan*. Their propaganda and activity were directed not against the government but against Muslims. The anti-Simon Commission and the Civil Disobedience Movements seriously weakened the Hindu Mahasabha. Earlier, the semi-communalist moderate elements of the Swarajist Party had split away from it and offered responsive cooperation to the government. Consequently, a new group of leaders came to the fore in the Hindu Mahasabha in the years after 1928. They officially dissociated themselves from the anti-imperialist politics of the Congress. The Panjab Hindu communalists had cooperated with the Simon Commission, defying the decision of the All-India Hindu Mahasabha to boycott it. In his presidential address to the 1933 session of the Mahasabha, Bhai Parmanand lauded this action and declared the boycott to have been unfortunate from the 'Hindu' point of view.[58] He argued in several statements that Hindus should not lose official favours by opposing the government, especially as it was strongly entrenched and the power to grant favours still resided in it.[59] As pointed out earlier, he made a plea at Ajmer for cooperation between Hindus and the British Government.[60] In 1938, in his foreword to a new edition of Lal Chand's booklet, he wrote:

[57]Emphasis added.
[58]*Indian Annual Register*, 1933, Vol. II, p. 204.
[59]Quoted in Nehru, *SW*, Vol. 6, pp. 165-66.
[60]See footnote 42 of this Chapter.

> There is not a word in them (Lal Chand's letters) which does not apply to the existing situation.... To me these letters are of special importance. For I have in my humble way preached the philosophy with a certain dauntless stubbornness.... In one or two letters he condemned the indifference of the Congress towards public services and expressed the belief that the Congress ideal of a colonial form of government was impracticable ... his remarks about a colonial form of government would apply to the present method and ideals of the Congress, i.e., non-cooperation and complete independence.[61]

N.C. Kelkar, with his long nationalist past, articulated similar sentiments in a milder form. In his presidential address to the Hindu Mahasabha in 1932, he said that "Hindus as Hindus should only go as far as the major minority communities will be prepared to go by way of actual non-cooperation."[62] B.S. Moonje, another major Mahasabha leader at the time, pleaded in May 1933 for "responsive cooperation" with the government.[63] He had also attended the First Round Table Conference, boycotted by all nationalist elements, though in his individual capacity.

Loyalism was expressed more openly by the lower echelons of communalism. For example, the Panjab Hindu Youth League of Lahore stated in May 1933: "We feel that time has now come for unity not so much between Muslims and Hindus as between the British and Indians."[64]

After 1937, the Hindu Mahasabha came under V.D. Savarkar's leadership; the Rashtriya Swayamsewak Sangh (RSS) also began to emerge as a major communal force. Neither of the two was now openly loyalist and even professed a certain nationalism and the desire to make India free. Apart from the fact that communalism of the majority could masquerade as nationalism, these organizations remained basically within the loyalist or at least non-nationalist framework. They

[61]Lal Chand, *Self-Abnegation in Politics,* pp. ii, v-vi.

[62]*Indian Annual Register,* 1932, Vol. II, p. 326.

[63]*Ibid.,* 1933, Vol. I, p. 425.

[64]Quoted in Nehru, *SW,* Vol. 6, p. 168.

carried out no political agitation or other struggle against colonialism except on the allegedly pro-Muslim bias of the government, and they vigorously attacked the Congress and Congress-led movements. For example, in the presidential address to the Mahasabha in 1938, Savarkar accused the Congress of being anti-Hindu and said that Congressmen "betray Hindu interests at every turn but keep dancing attendance on the Muslim League." He asked Hindus to boycott the Congress which had become "an anti-Hindu and anti-National organization."[65] In 1940, in his presidential address to the Mahasabha, Savarkar made an appeal to Hindus "to participate in all war efforts of the British Government" and not to listen to "some fools" who "condemn" this policy "as cooperation with imperialism."[66] Other Hindu Mahasabha leaders also extended "responsive cooperation" to the government during the Second World War period.[67]

The relationship of the RSS to colonial rule was more complex and subtle. It was being built up as a militant organization of young volunteers belonging to the middle class. It had perforce to adopt a radical nationalist stance, but its politics were no less at the command of colonialism than those of the Muslim League. For one, its leadership also treated the Congress as its enemy number one which had to be weakened and destroyed by all available means. In 1939, indirectly referring to the Congress leaders as traitors, M.S. Golwalkar said: "Strange, very strange, that traitors should be enthroned as national heroes and patriots heaped with ignominy."[68] In the second instance, Golwalkar was referring to the Congress treatment of the communalists. The Congress, he said, was created by Hume, Wedderburn, and Cotton

[65]V.D. Savarkar, *Hindu Rashtra Darshan,* pp. 71 ff. He repeated this accusation several times; for example, in 1942. *Ibid.,* p. 298.

[66]*Ibid.,* pp. 203ff. He also claimed that "the Government has in fact met the demands put forward by the Hindu Mahasabha at the outbreak of the war in a substantial measure." *Ibid.,* p. 217 In private, Savarkar told the Viceroy in October 1939 that Hindus and the British should be friends and made an offer that the Hindu Mahasabha would replace the Congress if the Congress ministries resigned from office. Linlithgow to Zetland, 7 October 1939, *Zetland Papers,* Vol. 18, Reel No. 6. Also see Prabha Dixit, *Communalism—A Struggle for Power, pp.* 184-85.

[67]Prabha Dixit, *op. cit.,* p. 186.

[68]M.S. Golwalkar, *We,* p. 6.

as "an instrument to destroy National consciousness" and it "has been, as far as they are concerned, a success. Our own 'denationalization' under the name of Nationality is nearing its consummation."[69] Golwalkar repeatedly referred to the Congress leaders as "these creatures (who) took upon themselves the burden of 'leading' the people" and as men of the stamp of the traitors Jaychand, Mansingh, Chandrarao Morey with "the same pettiness, selfishness" and working like them for "our ruin" and "playing false to the Nation merely to maintain themselves in the public eye." He referred to the "degeneration of these self-styled 'regenerators of the Nation'" and condemned the frittering away of national energy in "anti-national work."[70]

During 1947, the anti-Congress venom of Golwalkar scaled new heights: Its leaders were accused of asking the 'Hindu,'

> to ignore, even submit meekly to the vandalism and atrocities of the Muslims. In effect, he was told: "Forget all that the Muslims have done in the past and all that they are now doing to you. If your worshipping in the temple, your taking out gods in procession in the streets irritates the Muslims, then don't do it. *If they carry away your wives and daughters, let them. Do not obstruct them. That would be violence.*"[71] (Emphasis added.)

The reference to violence in the end makes it clear that Golwalkar's finger was pointing at Gandhi. The attack on Gandhi and the Congress leaders was even more explicit and vicious in another passage of the same speech: "Those who declared 'No *swaraj* without Hindu Muslim unity' have thus perpetrated the greatest treason on our society. They have committed the most heinous sin of killing the life-spirit of a great and ancient people."[72]

[69] *Ibid.*, p. 20.

[70] *Ibid.*, pp. 70-72.

[71] M.S. Golwalkar, *Bunch of Thoughts*, p. 150.

[72] *Ibid.*, p. 152. Continuing the reference to Gandhi, Golwalkar said: "Once, a notable Hindu personality of those days, in a largely attended public meeting, declared: 'There is no *swaraj* without Hindu-Muslim unity and the simplest way in which this unity can be achieved is for all Hindus to become Muslims'!" *Ibid.*, p. 151.

Secondly, the RSS not only carried out no anti-imperialist agitation or struggle on its own and practised instead utter political passivity, but, at crucial moments, held back the nationalist-minded youth under its influence from joining in the on-going nationalist struggles. In fact, this immobilization of its young nationalist-minded cadre and volunteers was a major service to colonial authorities, especially during the crucial 1942 struggle, and then again during 1945-46. The young men were told that the RSS was conserving its strength for future use against Muslims when the real struggle would be fought. This entire aspect has been well brought out by a writer who was a RSS volunteer during 1942, though he is one of its major critics today:

> Whatever the attitude of the leadership, the youth who came into the RSS did occasionally feel restive, may be because of the general atmosphere of struggle prevailing in the country. They were told: "we have to bide our time. The opportunity will come. We should conserve our strength for that time." Catharsis of youthful militancy was brought about by the fiery tone of speeches and occasional clashes with the Muslims. Thus the anti-British sentiment was being channelled into anti-Muslim action.[73]

Goyal goes on to add that in view of this policy of "dulling the anti-British sentiment growing in the youth" and its diversion into anti-Muslim channels, the colonial authorities did not take any serious action against the RSS even though its leaders sometimes made anti-British speeches in their training camps, etc., though, even here, the verbal fire was mainly directed against Muslims.[74]

The role of the RSS during 1942-44 is well brought out by the Home Department's analysis of and attitude towards the RSS during

[73]D.R. Goyal, *Rashtriya Swayamsewak Sangh,* p. 87. As a fourteen-year-old volunteer in the RSS at the time, who was drawn into the Sangh because of nationalism and concocted stories of the Sangh's links with Gandhi, Nehru and Subhas Bose propagated by its higher cadre out on recruiting missions, I can testify to the accuracy of Goyal's description of the RSS attitude and propaganda of the time.

[74]*Ibid.*, p. 67.

these years.[75] A note by A.S. in the Home Department, dated 7 August 1942, stated that even though the RSS's activities were objectionable and rabid, they were really "old history" and so long as the civil disobedience threat was not supported by it, no serious note of its activities should be taken. According to another note giving a summary of the CID *Report on RSS's Officers Training Camp,* Golwalkar said on 3 May 1942 that "the Sangh had been started not only for combating Muslim aggression but for completely extirpating that disease." The Sangh wanted Swaraj, but "they would not waste their energy but would reserve it and would make use of it at the proper time."[76] Another Home Department note on the RSS stated: "At meetings of the Sangh during the Congress disturbances, speakers urged the members to keep aloof from the Congress movement and these instructions were generally observed."[77]

Earlier, i.e., on 2 December 1940, at the height of the Individual Satyagraha Campaign of the Congress, there had been discussion between Abhyankar and other leaders on behalf of the RSS and the Secretary, Home Department, Bombay. According to the Home Department note on it, Abhyankar had, on behalf of the RSS, given an assurance to obey government orders regarding restrictions on dress, drills, etc. "He also promised to encourage members of the Sangh to join the Civic Guards in greater numbers. It was understood that members of the Rashtriya Swayamsevak Sangh joining the Civic Guards accepted their obligations to Civic Guards as paramount." In a note to the Chief Secretary, the Central Provinces Government, dated 7 January 1944, R. Tottenham of the Intelligence Bureau noted that it had been suggested that Golwalkar be warned "to keep the

[75]In analysing the RSS's politics, one is forced to rely on evidence of its ex-members or on the CID reports because its activities were shrouded in secrecy. All its propaganda, including that in the *Shakhas* (branches) was oral. There were no pamphlets or booklets putting forward the RSS's political and ideological policies and programmes or its leaders' pronouncements in this respect.

[76]According to the *Report,* another speaker, P.C. Sahasrabudhe, praised dictatorship, the Fuhrer principle of Germany and the leader principle of Mussolini,

[77]*Home Department (Political) Proceedings,* F. 28/8/42-Poll (I).

activities of this organization in check, but it was noted that he himself appeared to be anxious not to offend and we decided not to pursue this suggestion." In a letter dated 21 January 1944, the Chief Secretary, Punjab, after pointing out to the Secretary, Home Department, Government of India, that "at present the militant side of its activities is not very strong," noted, very perceptively, that danger from the RSS lay in its communal activities which might threaten peace and tranquillity. On 16 February 1944, H.V.R. Iyengar, Home Secretary, Bombay, advised the Central Government that the Government of Bombay was of the view that no further restriction need be imposed and enforcement of the existing restrictions (on dress and drilling) would do "as the Sangh has scrupulously kept itself within the law and, in particular, has refrained from taking any part in the disturbances that broke out in August 1942." The Provincial administration of the Central Provinces was the only one to recommend, in March 1944, suppression of the RSS. This it did mainly on the grounds that its communalism might provoke Hindu-Muslim conflict and because its Muslim counterpart, the Khaksars, had been suppressed.[78] Another Home Department note, dated 19 June 1946, stated: "In a secret meeting held at Rohtak on 19.5.46, Dada Bhai of Nagpur is reported to have said that the Sangh's struggle was not against the British but against the Muslims...."

Sikh communalism was no less pro-colonialist. The Central Khalsa Diwan adopted openly loyalist politics. The Diwan, as also Sikh communalism, suffered a major setback during the anti-imperialist Akali movement in the early 1920s. But, after the disintegration of the Akali movement, gradually the Akali Dal itself began to get divided into several groups, some of which increasingly adopted communal positions, while others, the traditional Sikh communalists, led by leaders like Sunder Singh Majithia, were constant in their loyalism—they were so even at the height of the Akali struggle. The communal section of the Akalis led by Master Tara Singh was 'hampered' by the strong anti-imperialist traditions of the

[78] *Home Department (Political) Proceedings*, F. 28/3/43-Poll (I).

Panjab peasantry as also their own anti-imperialist past. However, over the years, they dithered in their anti-imperialism, joined hands with the loyalist communalists, adopted collaborationist positions and, in the end, went over to pro-princes and pro-government politics during the Second World War.

VII

A few other aspects of communalism as reaction also should be noted. Even though different communalisms were supposedly directed against each other, in political practice they quite often cooperated with one another in municipalities, district boards, legislatures and provincial governments, and in landlords' and professional associations on concrete legislative, administrative and financial measures along class and non-communal lines. Communal identity was seldom permitted to stand in the way of class or group interests. In particular, the communalists often joined hands in cooperating with the colonial authorities. In any case, their politics moved on parellel lines under the benevolent eye of the latter. They also often combined to oppose efforts at social, economic and political reform. Moreover, interestingly enough, the communal leaders and organizations seldom attacked their communal counterparts but reserved most of their venom for the Congress and its leaders. They did of course promote hatred between their Hindu and Muslim followers.

The Hindu and Muslim communalists had little hesitation in joining together in provincial cabinets under the benign guidance *of* the colonial bureaucracy. In the North-West Frontier Province, Sind and Bengal, the Hindu communalists helped the Muslim League and other communal or semi-communal groups to form ministries which opposed the Congress.

It may also be reiterated that communalism was only one of the forms reaction took. Sometimes, it also took casteist or regionalist forms; at other times it took open reactionary forms and openly defended imperialism and vested interests. For the same reason, the communalists, especially in the liberal communal phase, were willing to discard the communal identity and assume some other identity if their individual or class interests so required. What Francis Robinson says about the Muslim communalists was equally true of the Hindu communalists:

> They were concerned with a wide range of provincial, class and sectarian interests many of which knew no communal divisions. In their endeavours to promote these specific interests different Muslim politicians adopted the Muslim identity when it was useful, and discarded it when it had served their purpose. Being a Muslim was less an article of political faith then a useful weapon in their political armoury ... they have emphasized Islamic issues when convenient and ignored them when not.[79]

Furthermore, communal politics attracted, especially after 1937, particular types of persons, that is, those who were politically inclined but did not want to follow loyalist politics and yet were afraid of political and administrative authority. The peculiar militancy of the post-1937 Hindu and Muslim communal groups and parties enabled them to satisfy their politico-psychological urges without earning the hostility of the powerful alien authority.

The basically pro-colonial and reactionary character of communal parties and groups also provides the clue to the failure of the nationalist forces to conciliate them or adjust with them. It is usual to blame this or that national leader for missing a 'golden opportunity' of placating the communalists. But, in reality, the concrete safeguards, reservations and so on demanded by the communalists, at least till 1940, were never such that they could not be adjusted in the interests of national unity. The problem arose when the price demanded, and this price was inherent in the socio-political character of communalism, was the virtual abandonment of the goals of socio-economic change,

[79]Francis Robinson, *Separatism among Indian Muslims,* pp. 353-55.

national unity and independence or the abandonment of the secular character of the Congress and the national movement.

VIII

To sum up: in a social movement or political trend, there may be a difference among the participants, the activists, the leaders and the social classes and groups which stand to benefit from it. A movement's or an ideology's social roots lie in those strata and classes and political forces which would develop or support this movement or similar movements and ideologies in any case because their interests so require. For example, nationalist, peasant and trade union movements would have developed even if a Hume or middle class individuals or intellectuals in the first case, and lawyers, middle class radicals and intellectuals, or organized political parties, in the other two cases, were not there to initiate and lead them. Whosoever may initiate or lead them, so long as they take up real anti-imperialist or anti-landlord or anti-capitalist demands and causes, their social roots lie in the nation as a whole, peasantry or the working class, as the case may be. On the other hand, without the imperialist authorities, reactionary social classes and sections of the middle classes, communalism might have existed but would not have grown into a major political force in India, for it took up no real demands or causes of the workers, peasants and the mass of the middle classes. Of course, once the former social groups found communalism serviceable, they used the existing social condition and the backward consciousness of sections of the common people to mobilize social support behind communalism. Thus, while the mass of the communal followers were mobilized by fear, religion, etc., the communal leaders and the reactionary social classes and strata and the colonial authorities standing behind them used communalism to thwart the processes of democracy, social change and anti-imperialism. This is the full meaning of Nehru's statement: "And it is this political reaction which has stalked the land under cover of communalism Honest communalism is fear; false communalism is political reaction."[80]

[80] Jawaharlal Nehru, *SW,* Vol. 6, p. 164.

CHAPTER 5

The Role of Ideological, Social and Cultural Elements: I

A large number of ideological, social and cultural elements contributed to the rise and growth of communalism. They were often in the nature of mechanisms and supportive conditions which promoted it. Some of them also served as instruments and channels for the spread of communalism. Some were basic constituents of communal ideology. In fact, some of the psychological, social and historical explanations offered as causes of communalism by some authors amount to an acceptance of certain aspects of communal consciousness. Communal consciousness or its different constituents do not explain communalism; they are not its causes. They *constitute* communalism and have themselves to be explained. Their acceptance as causes in theories of interlinked causation is a sign of the wide, though mostly unconscious, acceptance of communal ideology even by those who arc otherwise non-communal or even anti-communal. An illustration may perhaps help make this point clear. Almost none of the ideological, social and cultural factors discussed in this chapter and in Chapter 6, or other similar factors often offered as causes, operated in Panjab after 1947. If anything, before 1947, Hindu and Sikh communalisms were united against Muslim communalism and sometimes also against Indian nationalism. Yet, the two communalisms grew in a rabid form—against each other in Panjab in the 1950s and 1960s. Clearly, the basic causation of communalism lies in its social roots.

To argue that these ideological, social and cultural factors are not causative in nature is not to suggest that they do not play an important role in the rise and growth of communalism. All that is meant is that in the absence of social causation they could not have brought communalism into being. For one, such factors have to be studied and clearly brought out and their wider linkages established even when the social causation of a political-ideological phenomenon is clearly visible as, for example, in the case of anti-imperialist movements or class struggles. This need is greater when, as in the case of communalism, the social causation itself is hazy and not easy to grasp. Secondly, while these factors could not have on their own 'caused' communalism, given its social roots they could even play a decisive or overdetermining role.

I. FAILURE OF NATIONAL CONSCIOUSNESS

A major factor in the growth of communal consciousness was the slow rate at, and the uneven and imperfect manner in, which the national, anti-imperialist consciousness developed and spread in the country. In the nineteenth century was initiated the prolonged historical process of welding the Indian people into a nation or a 'people.' The nationalist, anti-imperialist movement was based on this phenomenon of the nation-in-the-making, while it was itself a powerful factor contributing to this phenomenon. Its growing strength depended partially on the extent to which the people became conscious of their being a part of a nation whose essential interests required a struggle for the overthrow of imperialism. This consciousness of nationhood—of being a people—did not, however, flow automatically from the objective reality. It had to be a hard, painstaking process of political and ideological self-discovery. But, by its very nature, the process of the nation-in-the-making was, and is, a highly differential process. Moreover, the formation of new social classes and strata and the impact of colonialism on the people also occurred in a differential manner. This resulted in the extremely uneven development, both in time and space, of national and anti-imperialist consciousness among different social classes and strata as well as people belonging to different religions, castes, linguistic areas, etc. One of the major tasks facing the leadership of the national movement was to impart a common *national consciousness* to the Indian people and to unite them in the common struggle against imperialism.

There were certain weaknesses in the anti-colonial political, economic, social and cultural programme evolved by the Indian national leadership. What was more important, it was not able to propagate even this programme among the people intensively and widely to an extent which would enable them to realize subjectively, in their consciousness, the objective reality of the developing identity of their common interests and their becoming a nation in the struggle to overthrow colonialism and to clear the path to social development.

More particular and concrete was the failure to organize and politically educate the Muslim lower middle classes and masses, which could be done successfully only by showing them through a concrete programme that the communal identity was a false one while the national and class identities were real because they reflected and served their social interests. In general, the nationalists did not organize an active political and ideological struggle against communalism. This failure of the nationalist leadership was shared by the leadership of the newly arising trade unions, *kisan sabhas* and other mass organizations and left-wing parties and groups. Involved here was a certain mechanical and reductionist understanding that the development of a modern economy and the contradiction with colonialism would automatically lead to the development of national and class consciousness. But the acquisition of new identities and consciousness has to be a conscious process which is a part of wider and intense political and ideological processes. People do not grasp social reality directly through their senses. They become aware of objective social reality and social relations only in the realm of ideology. "What people come to believe and what they happen to do is an outcome of a long-term process of persuasion and organization by political and ideological forces engaged in numerous struggles for the realization of their goals. Social cleavages [as also national cleavages], the perception of social differentiation, arc never given directly to our consciousness. Social differences acquire the status of cleavages as an outcome of ideological and political struggles."[1] As modern economy and politics compel people to organize on the basis of wider collective identities, if such organization does not occur on the bases of nation and class, it would occur on some other bases such as religion, sect, language, region, 'race,' ethnicity, caste or even profession and type of work.

Similarly, the nationalists appealed to the people against communalism on the basis of its anti-national character. But because of the lack of a deeper penetration of nationalist ideology, that is, in the absence of the wide prevalence of a scientific nationalist outlook such nationalist appeals failed to make enough of an impact on the people. In the case of a large section of the people, there was no existing consciousness to which an appeal could be made, while communalism did seem relevant in view of the religious element with which they were familiar. It was therefore necessary not only to appeal to nationalism but also to generate and spread national consciousness.

Consequently, communalism developed in certain areas and sections of Indian society because of the failure to develop the new national consciousness and class consciousness. Thus, due to the vacuum created by the insufficiency of the old identities and social groupings in a situation of social change, the awareness of the need for wider grouping and rapid politicization was filled not by the true consciousness of nationalism (anti-imperialism) and class, but, in many cases, by the communal or caste identity, which based itself on the older, familiar and easily comprehensible religious or caste affiliation. The nationalist failure to provide adequate channels for the flow of newly awakening political awareness inevitably enabled communalism (and casteism) to create a diversion, especially among the politically backward sections of the people. New unities and identities of nation, nationality and class were needed by the people; but the real-life unities, collective identities or principles of organization of nation and class often failed to penetrate to the people in time. In their absence, the people, feeling the need for wider unities, links and identities with which to

[1]Adam Prezworski, "The Process of Class Formation," pp. 27-28.

understand and cope with the changing colonial world, inevitably took recourse to some aspects of the older consciousness, based on the older cultural terms, and to the pre-existing principles of compartmentalization and organization of social and cultural life, even for the newly emerging political life. Of course, this led not to the restoration of some older unity or identity but the flourishing of a new communal (or caste) consciousness which used the garb, and appealed to some aspects, of the older consciousness. Thus, where nationalism would not make headway, religion and caste—the old stand-bys—would. In this respect, communalism may be seen as the punishment for the failure to wage a correct and consistent ideological and political struggle for the spread of national and class consciousness.

It is interesting to note that communalism receded during the days of hope when the anti-imperialist struggle was at a high tide, while it surged forth when this struggle was at an ebb and the hope was lost. Thus, during the three major waves of nationalist struggle communalism lay dormant. The years from 1918 to 1922 were the halcyon days for both the anti-imperialist struggle and for Hindu-Muslim unity. The rise of the left after 1926, the growth of trade unions and the youth movement, and the anti-Simon Commission protest movement once again enthused the people and reduced communal tensions. During 1930-34 the Civil Disobedience Movement swept the entire country. Both Hindus and Muslims participated in it in large numbers. The communal parties and leaders went into virtual retirement or hesitatingly supported the national movement. The Civil Disobedience Movement engulfed for the first time two new major areas with a Muslim majority—the North-West Frontier Province and Kashmir. Moreover, increasingly, in the late 1920s and the 1930s, the Hindu, Sikh and Muslim youth and workers, and in many areas, the peasants, looked up to the communists, the socialists, the Naujavan Bharat Sabha, the National Revolutionaries, and Nehru and Subhash Chandra Bose for political leadership. The influence of the Muslim League, the Hindu Mahasabha, the RSS and other communal organizations was minimal. In fact, none of them possessed a mass base at the time even among the lower middle classes.

In 1942 too, there was no communal trouble in spite of the Muslim League's strong opposition to the Quit India Movement.

The communalists became active only when the anti-imperialist movement entered its passive phases. Despite work in the legislatures and the costructive programme, the national leadership could provide few outlets for the political energies of the people after 1922 and after 1934. Between 1942 and 1945, even such outlets were not there. In the post-1922 period, it was the disillusionment, frustration and discontent born out of the sudden petering out of the dream of Swaraj within one year—people found themselves, in the words of a historian, "all dressed up and nowhere to go"—that created favourable conditions for the rise of communal bitterness. The government, the propertied classes and the political reactionaries could at that stage succeed in giving a communal colour to the politics of the middle classes and in diverting the newly aroused political passions and the incipient and inherent struggles of the masses for the improvement of their lot into communal channels. Moreover, the parliamentary politics after 1922, based on a limited franchise, made the middle classes, which along with the landed elite enjoyed a virtual monopoly of electoral franchise, the virtual arbiters of the fate of parliamentary leaders.[2] It was now that a horde of 'Hindu,' 'Muslim,' 'Sikh' and 'Christian' leaders emerged from within and without the nationalist ranks. Even so, the after-glow of the Non-Cooperation Movement was strong enough to keep the social base of the communal leaders narrowly confined to sections of the middle and upper strata of society.

The suspension of the Civil Disobedience Movement in 1931 once again enabled the communal leaders to appear on the scene. It was at

[2]This dependence on the middle classes and the landed elite for parliamentary success also weakened the capaciiy of the Congress to struggle against communal politics. This was pointed out by the Kanpur Riots Enquiry Committee: "The programme of Council entry made them susceptible to the influences of popular mood. Consequently, the power of the Congress collectively and wholeheartedly to fight communalism was altogether undermined.... The complicated nature of the problem, the pre-occupations of the political leaders and the exigencies of electoral campaigns, all made it almost impossible for the Congress openly and directly to come to grips with communalism." *Report of the Kanpur Riots Enquiry Committee,* pp. 222-23, 225.

this stage that the colonial authorities declared communalism to be the major political issue which must be settled before constitutional advance could be made. They gave hand-picked communal leaders a free run of the Round Table Conferences; and the Congress leadership fell into the trap. The vigorous mass campaigns of Nehru and other leaders during 1936-37 once again aroused the people. The inevitably more passive period of parliamentary politics, unaccompanied by vigorous political ideological work, from 1937 to 1940, enabled the communal forces to grow to a certain extent. However, the actual leap forward of the Muslim League, as also of the RSS in the north, occurred only after 1942 when the Quit India Movement had been suppressed, the Congress leadership lay quiescent inside jails, the communists had failed to become the spearhead of the anti-imperialist and popular movements and to organize the anti-communal struggle under the mistaken notions of how to support the international anti-fascist war and of the character of Muslim communalism and the Indian upper, middle and lower middle classes had abandoned nationalist politics in order to reap the war time harvest of jobs, contracts and high profits.

Another important aspect of the effort to create and spread national consciousness has also to be noted. This was the need to impart a new, modern culture to the people and to promote modern scientific temper among them as a part of this effort, for the existing, traditional, religion- and caste-based culture and obscurantist outlook tended to encourage communal and other similar political ideologies and movements. For this reason, when some sections of the nationalists, for example, the Khilafatist Ulema, the militant Akalis and certain orthodox Hindus, opposed communalism by appealing to the older, non-communal religious consciousness, they could not succeed. Instead, they became hostages to communalism. They kept the way open to communalism via the old culture.

Moreover, the spread of modern secular culture and scientific outlook had to be based on an active effort. It would not occur automatically—in course of time—as was believed by certain mechanical materialists, as a result of 'modernizing forces' such as industrial development, education, trade union and peasant movements and electoral or non-electoral political activities. On the contrary, in the absence of a struggle for the spread of modern culture and scientific outlook, all these modernizing forces could themselves be 'blocked,' for cultural backwardness would then 'hit back.' It is important to note that while the Congress and left-wing leaders actively worked for Hindu-Muslim unity, they did not, at any stage, organize an active and mass political and ideological struggle or campaign against communalism. While they saw Hindu-Muslim unity as a basic political necessity, communalism was not seen as a formidable foe till 1945, when it was too late. They expected communalism to die out on its own as nationalism and class consciousness developed because of its inherent falsity and its narrow social base. Involved here was a deterministic version of the relation between the reality and its subjective cognition by the people. It was assumed that since communalism did not reflect the interests of the masses, the masses would not be affected by it to a serious extent, especially if economic issues came to the forefront.[3]

They also believed that class consciousness and the development of trade unions, *kisan sabhas,* etc., would automatically eliminate communalism. In practice, in the absence of a conscious effort to transform cultural, ideological and political consciousness, even active members of the trade unions and *kisan sabhas* retained traditional cultural-ideological traits such as religiosity and caste consciousness,

[3]Refer to, for example, Jawaharlal Nehru in 1931 and 1936: "The real thing to my mind is the economic factor. If we lay stress on this and divert public attention to it we shall find automatically that religious differences recede into the background and a common bond unites different groups. The economic bond is stronger than even the national one. Working among the kisans, among peasants, I have found very little difference when they have this economic bond." *(SW,* Vol. 5, p. 203.) "If the masses are fully represented, inevitably economic issues affecting them will come to the forefront and superficial problems, like the communal one, will lose importance." *(SW,* Vol. 6, p. 127.) "The obvious way to deal with the communal problem is to allow the fundamental economic issues to come forward, so that attention can be diverted from the communal issue. The latter will have to be faced and will inevitably be solved as the economic issues are allowed to come up." *(Ibid.,* p, 112.)

remained open to communal appeals and fell prey to communal passions during communal riots.

In fact, communal ideology, once initiated, would develop on its own steam unless actively opposed. Once developed, it could not be appeased, it had to be opposed. The policy of no concessions to the Muslim communalists then helped the Muslim communal groups grow, while any important concessions tended to produce a Hindu communal backlash. Furthermore, this only whetted the appetite of the Muslim communalists, so that the appeased groups and leaders constantly gave way to more extreme ones. A part of the weakness of the nationalist struggle against communalism was the failure of the Congress to demarcate itself strongly from Hindu and Muslim communal politics. Till 1938, it permitted the Hindu Mahasabha and the Muslim League leaders and members to join its ranks. Till 1930, instead of coming to grips with communalism, the Congress tried to become a mediator between different communal groups and parties, organizing negotiations with and among the communal leaders. As the Kanpur Riots Enquiry Committee pointed out:

> The position which the Congress occupied in these efforts was that of an intermediary, and by implication it accepted the extreme communalists of both sides as true representatives of the interests of their respective communities. The more it clung to them for settlement, the more it abdicated its own undoubted right to arrive at final conclusion on communal matters on behalf of the nation. The result was that the Congress, instead of crushing out communalism from the national life by giving direct and open fight for real leadership in communal matters, invested communalists with greater importance and prestige. This course was bound to be infructuous, as it left no chance for the saner elements in society to assert themselves and in an organized way to subdue the mischievous activities of the communalists on both sides.[4]

[4] *Report of the Kanpur Riots Enquiry Committee*, p. 227.

Even later, i.e., after 1936, when the policy of mediating between and appeasing the communal forces was given up, negotiations with the Muslim League continued, and few efforts were made to vigorously combat the League and its growth. In fact, the Congress failed to evolve a viable and effective strategy to combat communalism at the ideological and cultural level.

The cultural aspect of the communal problem had another dimension. Initially, nationalism in India spread among the intelligentsia and the middle classes belonging to the upper castes among Hindus, with the result that a major stream of nationalism got identified with elements of the traditional upper caste Hindu culture ('great tradition'). Other streams, of course, tended to break away from this tradition and to absorb elements of the modern democratic culture at the political and economic as also more strictly cultural levels. But Muslims, Sikhs, Christians, Buddhists, tribal people and lower caste Hindus awakened to different cultural traditions which were often local in character ('little traditions'), though Muslims also had their own 'great tradition.' Consequently, many of them found it difficult to adjust to the upper caste cultural terms of a large section of the national movement. Some of them turned to the left wing of the national movement or the left parties and groups. Many others rallied round communal, casteist and anti-upper caste political forces. It was therefore necessary for the national movement to transcend its upper caste Hindu cultural component and base itself entirely on a healthy integration of the democratic and humanistic aspects of its traditional culture and the modern scientific culture.

One result of this dichotomy between traditions was that, among Hindus, even the communalists soon found that any attempt to impose the 'great tradition' tended to tear apart their efforts to create a Hindu communal identity, and so they were increasingly compelled to define Hindu culture in the vaguest of terms, especially when the effort was to acquire a wider base for communal politics in terms of locality, region, caste and class.

Similarly, the religious and social reformers tended to dilute or even abandon their reformist zeal when they took to communal politics, for reform would invariably lead them to clash with the orthodox and narrow down their popular base. For example, in northern India, a large number of Hindu communalists came to politics and communalism via the Arya Samaj, but they soon abandoned the public advocacy of Arya Samaj religious and social tenets in order to placate the majority who were conservative, idol-worshipping Sanatanists. Today, a common sight in northern India is that of RSS leaders, who are Arya Samajists and therefore anti-idolatory in private, presiding over the all-night Bhagwati Jagran functions or participating or even leading Ram Janam Bhoomi agitation. Similarly, it is well known that Syed Ahmed Khan abandoned his religious reform activities and even championed socially reactionary practices such as the refusal to send girls to schools once he decided to emerge as a leader of Muslims. The poet Iqbal also gave up his radical social and ideological stance and began to champion orthodox causes once he took to open communal politics.

To sum up: The inadequacy of the nationalist effort to generate a new national consciousness on the basis of a new, modern culture led to the spread of communal and casteist ideologies and consciousness and therefore to the disruption of the united national movement. And a sort of dialectical relationship evolved between the imperfect, uneven and slow process of the nation-in-the-making (or national integration) and communalism. On the one hand, the imperfection of this process contributed to the growth of communalism, on the other hand, the growth of communalism was partially responsible for this imperfection.

II. FRUSTRATION, FEAR AND THE MINORITY COMPLEX

Frustration and Fear : The economic and social insecurity bred among several sections of Indian society—the zamindars, peasants, middle classes and artisans—by colonialism and capitalism was conducive to the growth of irrational ideologies. The people felt a vague sense of deprivation, economic misery, frustration, discontent and personal and social anger. They were filled with feelings of uncertainty and insecurity and of deepening anxiety about their present and future, and sometimes their very existence. These feelings were, in the 1930s and 1940s, accentuated and deepened by the Depression, World War II, runaway inflation and political uncertainty.

This was particularly true of the middle classes, which faced a constant threat to their economic position and social status and also the danger of the erosion and even loss of their identity. Their very world seemed to be crumbling around them. This result was also brought about in part by the partial breakdown of caste as a status-giving institution for the upper castes.

In this general atmosphere of frustration, insecurity and anxiety, it was easy for feelings of mistrust, fear and suppressed violence and hatred to flourish. In fact, violence lay very close to the surface in a society like this and in a situation like this. The solidarity promised by caste, religion, region and language made a certain appeal; it tended to allay the anxiety.[5]

Not only Muslims, Sikhs and Christians, who were religious minorities, but even Hindus suffered equally from this anxiety and felt the fear and the air of violence. Crucial in this respect was the role of the psychology of fear. The fear of being deprived, surpassed, 'losing out,' threatened, dominated, suppressed, beaten down and even exterminated—of losing one's very identity and even life—was widespread.

In a politically dynamic situation, all this—the discontent, the fear and the anger—had found expression in the national and other popular movements. The petty bourgeoisie was increasingly active in these movements and was often their chief organizer as well as their main striking force. The National Congress as well as the radical left-wing parties and groups such as the communists, the Congress Socialists, and the revolutionary terrorists could and did flourish on the frustrations of the lower middle classes.

However, the end of each of the three waves of nationalist struggle—1920-22, 1930-34, 1942-43—added a feeling of political

[5]In case of a communal (or caste or linguistic) riot, it seemed to provide actual, and in case of official apathy and inactivity, the only physical security.

frustration and helplessness to the already frustrated existence of the people, especially of the petty bourgeoisie.[6] The communalists and other reactionaries were able to use the real-life insecurity, anxiety, frustration and fears of the petty bourgeois and other social strata to attack other Indian groups, who were held responsible by the communalists for their deprivation, etc. The lower middle class individual, unable to get security or acquire identity as an individual or as a member of a class and with the recession of the national movement, sought security in the religious or caste group, hoping thereby to also acquire a new identity in the guise of maintaining an old one.

The communal leaders took full advantage of the anxieties and fears felt by the people. In fact, these anxieties and fears were their ultimate ideological and psychological stock-in-trade and their arousal and manipulation the main form of attack against the anti-imperialist struggle. They turned these vague anxieties and fears against the followers of other religions and propagated the moral that members of a particular 'community' must organize and act as a unity. The Muslim communalists constantly played up the theme of Hindu domination over Muslims and of the latter being suppressed, crushed and exterminated and their culture and religion undermined and overthrown by the overwhelming Hindu majority. This theme had, of course, been there for long. In 1907, Viqar-ul-Mulk had expressed the fears of "the possibility of the Muslims being reduced to slavery, and of the tyranny of the majority ... and of the danger of the minority

[6]This was recognized at the time by Jawaharlal Nehru. Writing later, in his *Autobiography*, about the withdrawal of the Non-Cooperation Movement and the consequent growth of communalism, he said: "It is possible, however, that this sudden bottling up of a great movement contributed to a tragic development in the country. The drift to sporadic and futile violence in the political struggle was stopped, but the suppressed violence had to find a way out, and in the following years this perhaps aggravated the communal trouble.... It is just possible that if civil resistance had not been stopped and the movement had been crushed by Government, there would have been less communal bitterness and less superfluous energy left for the subsequent communal riots." Pp. 86-87.

losing its identity."[7] In 1926, the *Moslem Darpan* of Bengal warned that without government help the 23 crores of Hindus would "completely wipe out the 7 crores of Muslims."[8] But this motif of domination and suppression became the dominant theme in the Muslim League propaganda after 1937 during its extremist or fascist phase. After 1937, M.A. Jinnah built up his political campaign to popularize the League around this theme. He used his presidential addresses and other speeches and statements to appeal to this fear and insecurity and to repeatedly drive home the theme that the Congress wanted not independence from British imperialism but Hindu raj in cooperation with the British and domination over Muslims and even their extermination. Thus, in his 1937 presidential address, he warned that by following the policy advocated by the Congress Muslims "the community will seal its doom," and that "there are forces which may bully you, tyrannize over you and intimidate you."[9] In his 1938 presidential address, Jinnah said:

> One thing has been demonstrated beyond doubt, namely, that the Congress High Command wanted the Musalmans to be a mere understudy of the Congress, mere foot-pages of the Congress leaders, to be used, governed and brought under the heels when they had served the purpose of the Congress. The Congress leaders wanted them to submit unconditionally to the Hindu raj ... the High Command of the Congress is determined, absolutely determined, to crush all other communities and cultures in this country and to establish Hindu raj .... His (Gandhi's) ideal is to revive Hindu religion and establish Hindu raj in this country ...

[7]Moin Shakir, *Khilafat to Partition,* p. 195.

[8]M.N.Islam, *Bengal Muslim Opinion as Reflected in the Bengal Press 1901-1930,* p. 127.

[9]M.A. Jinnah, *Speeches and Writings,* Vol. I, pp. 31, 36. At this session of the Muslim League, according to an observer, "out of the clouds of circumlocution and confusion arose the cry of Islam in danger. The Muslims were told that they were about to be crucified by the Hindus." Mahmudullah Jung in the *Pioneer,* 7 November 1937, quoted in B.R. Nanda, "Nehru and the Partition of India," p. 159.

> they (the Congress) will be in (the Federation) to pursue their nefarious scheme of destroying the Muslim culture and organization....[10]

In a statement on Independence Day, in 1940, Jinnah said that the Congress leadership was working for an "alliance with the British Government in order that Musalmans and minorities and other interests may be placed at their mercy, once more for them to begin their process of crushing them downright."[11] In March 1940, in a speech at the Muslim University Union, Aligarh: "Mr Gandhi's hope is to subjugate and vassalize the Muslims under a Hindu raj." And: "It is not that they want the British Government to go but only to cajole and coerce it to give them something which would enable them to dominate the Muslims under British protection."[12] In the presidential address in March 1940: "But it must be freedom for all India and not freedom of one section or, worse still, of the Congress caucus and slavery of Musalmans and other minorities."[13] In a speech in November 1940: "The Congress High Command had only one objective in view, namely, the establishment of a Hindu raj in India and domination of the Muslims and all the other minorities."[14] In a speech at the Muslim University Union, Aligarh, in March 1941: "Pakistan is not only a practicable goal but the only goal if you want to save Islam from complete annihilation in this country."[15] In his presidential address of April 1941, Jinnah declared that in a united India "the Muslims will be wiped out of existence."[16] In a statement on

[10]M.A. Jinnah, *op. cit.*, Vol. I, pp. 69-70, 72-73, 77. The Muslim League Working Committee in its resolution of 18 September 1939 declared that the Act of 1935 had resulted, in the provinces, "wholly in a permanent communal majority and the domination of the Hindus over the Muslim minorities whose life and liberty, property and honour are in danger and even their religious rights and culture are being assailed and annihilated every day under the Congress Government in various provinces." *Indian Annual Register*, 1939, Vol. II, p. 352.

[11]M.A. Jinnah, *op. cit.*, Vol. I, p. 127.

[12]*Ibid.*, pp. 139, 141.

[13]*Ibid.*, p. 146.

[14]*Ibid.*, p. 185.

[15]*Ibid*,, p. 243.

[16]*Ibid.*, p. 248.

13 April 1942, after the failure of the Cripps Mission, he asserted that "if the Congress demand [for a national government] had been accepted it would have been the death-knell to the Musalmans of India."[17] Regarding the interim government in 1946, on 18 August, Jinnah referred to "the caste Hindus Fascist Congress and their few individual henchmen of other communities who want to be installed in power and authority of the Government of India to dominate and rule over Musalmans and other minor communities of India with the aid of British bayonets."[18] The more popular propagandists of the League were, if anything, even more strident. Thus, for example, Z.A. Suleri wrote that in view of the Muslims being a permanent minority, Indian nationalism "meant perpetual slavery for the Musalmans," and warned Muslims against the dangers of "complete absorption into Hindudom" and "complete extinction."[19]

Similarly, the Hindu communalists tried to instil a sense of fear, the fear of suppression and domination by Muslims, among Hindus. The task was not easy since Hindus were a religious majority. It was sought to be performed by declaring that the danger arose because Hindus were a milder, weaker, unorganized and disunited people. Furthermore, the prospects of Indian Muslims being aided by Afghanistan, Iran and Arabia were seriously discussed. In 1909, Lieutenant-Colonel U.N. Mukerji published a book with the suggestive title "a dying race" applied to Hindus and concluded: "They [Muslims] are growing in number, growing in strength, growing in health, growing in solidarity, we are crumbling to pieces. They look forward to a united Mohammedan world—we are waiting for our extinction."[20] In the same year, in a series of articles, Lal Chand described the Congress politics as politics of "self-abnegation and self-

[17] *Ibid.*, p. 383.

[18] *Indian Annual Register*, 1946, Vol. II, p. 226.

[19] Z.A. Suleri, *My Leader*, pp. 11, 38, 88.

[20] Quoted in Indra Prakash, *A Review...*, p. 12. The phrase "a dying race" was repeatedly used later by Swami Shraddhanand. G.R. Thursby, *Hindu-Muslim Relations in British India*, p. 151.

[21] Lal Chand, *Self-Abnegation in Politics*, p. 13.

immolation" by Hindus.[21] In 1921, the editor of the Lahore daily, *Pratap,* warned: "If the Hindus do not wake up now, they will be finished."[22] In his address to the Hindu Mahasabha in 1924, Dr. Kurtakoti, the Shankracharya, declared that if Hindus did not take up in right earnest the work of *Shuddhi* or conversion, "within ten decades you shall find no Hindu on the surface of this earth."[23] In his presidential address to the Hindu Mahasabha in 1925, Lala Lajpat Rai expressed the apprehension that Hindus might get "obsessed by false ideas of Ahimsa," which might encourage others, i.e., Muslims, "to interfere with our rights and to humiliate and destroy us."[24] In the same year, he told the Hindu Conference at Bombay: "If the Hindu community does not wish to commit a political *harakiri,* they must move every nerve to be communally efficient." In fact, there was a danger of Hindus being "eaten up and devoured" by Muslims.[25] In 1926, the Chairman of the Reception Committee of the Mahasabha session at Gauhati warned that if Hindus did not take appropriate steps, "we are sure to perish at no distant time."[26] In his presidential address, Madan Mohan Malaviya talked of saving "the dying Hindu race from ruin."[27] In the presidential address to the Mahasabha in 1927, B.S. Moonje, after referring to the "proverbial mildness and docility of the Hindus," declared that Muslims with "their aggressiveness" were dreaming of giving "such a push to the mild Hindu as to send him down headlong along the inclined plane of extinction. Thus they were dreaming of absorbing the whole of Hindu

[22]Quoted in Prabha Dixit, *Communalism—A Struggle for Power,* p. 159.

[23]Indra Prakash, *op. cit.,* p. 90.

[24]*Ibid.,* p. 91. Earlier, in 1924, he had said that Hindus must be saved "from the death which threatened them." *Indian Annual Register,* 1924, Vol. II, p. 488.

[25]Lala Lajpat Rai, *Writings and Speeches,* Vol. II, pp. 246, 253.

[26]*Indian Annual Register,* 1926, Vol. II, p. 354.

[27]*Ibid.,* p. 355.

[28]Indra Prakash, *op. cit.,* pp. 104-05. He also conjured up the extremely provocative picture of "the daily occurrences of Hindoos' running away for life when attacked by Moslem ruffians, leaving behind their women-folk to be dealt with by them as they may please." The Hindu, he said, was living, "at that present moment, under the dual domination of the British machine-gun and the Moslem lathi." *Ibid.,* pp. 105, 107.

India into themselves."[28] Later, in 1938, Moonje wrote that the likelihood was that "by the time the Poorna Swaraj comes," Hindus would have been "swallowed and wiped out of existence."[29]

In his presidential addresses V.D. Savarkar repeatedly referred to the danger of Indian Muslims conspiring with Afghanistan and other Muslim countries to enable the latter to conquer India and establish Muslim rule.[30] Furthermore, he said in 1937, Muslims "want to brand the forehead of Hindudom and other non-Moslem sections in Hindusthan with a stamp of self-humiliation and Moslem domination" and "to reduce the Hindus to the position of helots in their own land."[31] In 1938, he said that these Hindu fears were already on the way to realization: "We Hindus arc reduced to be veritable helots throughout our land. In some cases as in Bengal and the Frontier our very life and property stand in hourly danger, the honour of womenhood insecure."[32]

In 1938, Bhai Parmanand warned that the "unavoidable result" of the Congress policy and programme "will be the racial and national self-immolation of the Hindus."[33] In 1939, M.S. Golwalkar declared that, if the minority demands were accepted, "Hindu National life runs the risk of being shattered." He condemned contemporary secular nationalism for "hugging to our bosom our most inveterate enemies and thus endangering our very existence."[34] The volatile communal atmosphere of 1947 brought out the full venom of Golwalkar in portraying the impending danger to Hindus and their present degraded condition in a highly provocative and inflammable language. Referring to the Congress leaders and their policies, he said:

[29] *Ibid.*, p. v.

[30] V.D. Savarkar, *Hindu Rashtra Darshan*, pp. 14, 26-27, 62, 113-14. Also see his *Hindu Sanghatan*, p. 215. This was a very common feature of Hindu communal propaganda. See, for example, N.C. Kelkar's presidential address to the Hindu Mahasabha, 1925, *Indian Annual Register*, 1925, Vol. II, p. 351.

[31] V.D. Savarkar, *Hindu Rashtra Darshan*, pp. 21-22.

[32] *Ibid.*, p. 77.

[33] Indra Prakash, *op. cit.*, p. xxi. In 1933, he told the Hindu Mahasabha session that if Hindus accept the Communal Award "they are doomed to undergo double slavery." *Indian Annual Register*, 1933, Vol. II, p. 204.

[34] M,S. Golwalkar, *We*, pp. 58, 73.

> As they dared not tell the Muslim to forget his separatism, they pitched upon the docile Hindu for all their preachings.... The Hindu was asked to ignore, even submit meekly to the vandalism and atrocities of the Muslims ... the Hindu was told that he was imbecile, that he had no spirit, no stamina to stand on his own legs and fight for the independence of his motherland and that all this had to be injected into him in the form of Muslim blood.... Those who declared "No Swaraj without Hindu-Muslim unity" have thus perpetrated the greatest treason on our society. They have committed the most heinous sin of killing the life-spirit of a great and ancient people.[35]

Communal riots were also often the result of the overall fear that the other side would wipe out or dominate 'us.'[36] Petty questions such as cow-killing, music before a mosque, throwing of coloured water during the Holi festival and cutting down of a *peepal* tree became the occasions for communal tension because they got tied up with the fears of the people, especially with the problems of petty bourgeois identity, ego and insecurity. They became 'symbols of dominance,' their abandonment or tolerance would show that 'we' were weak and ripe for being dominated. The petty bourgeoisie was constantly trying to build up its ego, which life was daily eroding. Consequently, it was constantly throwing and meeting challenges to prove its 'strength,' 'courage' and 'manliness.' The constant theme of communal propaganda was that of fall from greatness in the past, challenge of domination today, need for toughness and unity of the 'community' to provide security and to meet the threat from the other 'community' and the glorious future in store if only the threat was met successfully. Similarly, the petty bourgeoisie's cultural and psychological needs were responsible for the strong glorification of some historical periods

[35]M.S. Golwalkar, *Bunch of Thoughts*, pp. 150-52.

[36]And, of course, communal riots tended to become self-fulfilling prophecies for they did physically endanger, and that too at the hands of the other community, all residents of the localities involved.

or historical characters as heroes with whom one could identify. The only difference was that while the petty bourgeois Hindu looked for golden ages and heroes within Indian history, the petty bourgeois Muslim, for the same purpose, referred to 'historical Islam.'

Fear Complex of a Minority. Apart from other aspects, there is an understandable and perhaps even justified tendency among minorities, whether religious, linguistic or national, to mistrust the majority and to be afraid that their social, religious and cultural interests might suffer because of their weaker numerical position and that the majority might use the force of numbers to injure the minority or absorb it. While the fact is that it was not possible for a powerful minority like the Muslims to be dominated in a democratic India, still the apprehension, however unreasonable, was there.

As brought out above, the Muslim communalists constantly played upon this natural minority fear complex of Muslims and aroused and fed feelings of fear and hatred. In particular, they argued that the nationalist demand for self-government and democracy would bring into play the principle of majority rule which would inevitably lead to permanent Hindu domination and therefore to a bleak future for Muslims in a free and united India since they could not expect a fair and equal treatment from the permanent Hindu majority.[37] For years, the Muslim communalists, therefore, fought for all sorts of special safeguards and concessions. But the logic of their position inevitably led to the demand for a separate Muslim state; for no safeguards and concessions would ultimately protect Muslims if it was accepted that Hindus, who would be in a permanent majority, were bound to be inimical to Muslims. And who would guarantee that in a free and democratic India the safeguards and concessions themselves would be pre-served?

Herein lay the special responsibility of the majority. The best remedy in such a situation was for the majority to give proof by word and deed that these fears of the minority and its mistrust of the

[37]See Chapter 4. For example, Syed Ahmed Khan, *Writings and Speeches,* pp. 209-10 and M.A. Jinnah, *op. cit,,* Vol. I, p. 89.

majority were groundless. Wherever and whenever a majority has done so, the fears of the minorities have on the whole disappeared or have been marginalized. It was the task of the nationalist leadership to analyse concretely the genuine sources of the minority's anxiety, to expose concretely its false aspects and to help the minority grasp the real way of meeting the challenge of its situation through its own political experience. It also had to show to the people, both the majority and the minority, the real face of their anxiety, frustration and fears and to bring out the falsity of the communal analysis and solution. More concretely, the actions of the majority had to help the minority to realize that its religion and particular social and cultural traits would be safe, and that religion should not and would not be a factor in determining economic and political policies.

The Hindu communalists consistently played the very opposite role. Instead of allaying the minority's fears, they created a psychology of fear of, and hatred towards, Muslims among Hindus. They propagated the theory of Hindu weakness and the consequent dangers of Muslims dominating, converting and crushing them. They actively opposed the policy of giving adequate safeguards to the minorities so as to remove their fear of domination by the majority. Instead of persuading the minorities to become active constituents of the process of nation-in-the-making, they propagated theories of Hindutva, Hinduization of the minorities and India being a Hindu nation. They thus helped intensify the fear complex of Muslims and gave seeming legitimacy to Muslim communal ideology and politics.

In particular, it was the Hindu middle classes which had to show a certain magnanimity, for, as pointed out earlier in Chapter 2, it was, in the main, the competition for jobs and seats in the legislatures and municipal committees that produced fear and insecurity as well as communalism among the Muslim middle classes, and it was these that had to be allayed. But then the Hindu middle classes, especially in the north, were also imbued with communalism. They not only showed little magnanimity, they resisted, often in an organized way, all efforts of the nationalist leadership to give timely concessions to the Muslim middle classes so as to get rid of their mistrust, fears and insecurity.[38]

The political situation was further complicated by the fact that in some areas of the country Hindus were a minority and suffered from all the fear complexes of a minority. And here the Muslim communalists showed little consideration for their feelings and thus encouraged the growth of communalism among them.

Anyway, the result was that feelings of mistrust, fear and being dominated came to be shared by a large number of Hindus and Muslims.

III. THE HINDU TINGE IN INDIAN NATIONAL LEADERSHIP'S WORK AND THOUGHT

The strong Hindu tinge in much of the nationalist thought, propaganda and agitation and their permeation through ideas associated with Hindu religion, in spite of the basically secular approach and programme of the Congress, tended to repel and alienate Muslims instinctively. They tended to orientate Muslims towards a communal outlook with the feeling that the success of such a national movement would mean 'a Hindu supremacy in Indian polities.'

This was particularly true of the strong Hindu religious element in the Extremist thought and propaganda from 1905 to 1909. Many of the Extremists identified nationalism with the revival of Hinduism, talked of Indian culture in terms of ancient Indian culture to the exclusion of medieval Indian culture and of the unity of India in

[38]Gandhi and Jawaharlal Nehru were the great protagonists of the view that Hindus, as the religious majority, should adopt an unconditional generous approach towards the safeguards demanded by the communalists on behalf of Muslims. See, for example, Jawaharlal Nehru, *An Autobiography*, p. 136; and *SW*, Vol. 6, pp. 168-69 and Vol. 7, p. 190. This view has been recently criticized by S. Gopal in his biography of Nehru. This view, writes Gopal, "in itself, despite the call to magnanimity, assumes a communal approach, however subconscious. The argument is based on the belief that the majority community is a privileged one, and the minority community has reason to be communal ... the implication that there was something to choose between Hindu and Muslim communalism was dangerous in its possibilities." *Jawaharlal Nehru—A Biography*, Vol. One, p. 183.

terms of the unity of Hindus and saw nationalism as a religion — which was invariably, in the nature of things, Hinduism.[39] They tried to provide a Hindu ideological underpinning to Indian nationalism or at least a Hindu idiom to its day-to-day political agitation.

Also important in this respect was the role of a certain type of modern literature in Bengali, Hindi, Urdu and other Indian languages whose tone was partly communal. Representative of this literature were the later historical novels of Bankim Chandra Chatterjee, which became prototypes of much of the later Indian literature of this genre. Bankim treated Muslims as foreigners and identified nationalism or Indianhood or indigenousness with Hindus. In their historical fiction, poetry and drama, Bankim and other such writers usually cast Muslims in the role of oppressive and lecherous tyrants while portraying Hindus either as heroes struggling for positive values including freedom or as traitors and collaborators when they integrated with the Muslim rulers. This type of literature with its running theme of Muslim tyranny inevitably tended to produce resentment among literate Muslims and to alienate them from the emerging national movement.[40]

[39]Aurobindo Ghose, for example, wrote in 1908: "Nationalism is a religion that has come from God.... If you are going to be a Nationalist, if you are going to assent to this religion of Nationalism, you must do it in the religious spirit. You must remember that you are the instruments of God." *Speeches,* p. 6. And then again in the famous Uttarpara speech, delivered on 30 May 1909: "I say no longer that nationalism is a creed, a religion, a faith; I say that it is the Sanatan Dharma which for us is nationalism. This Hindu nation was born with the Sanatan Dharma; with it it moves and with it it grows." *Sri Aurobindo, Collected Works,* Vol. 2, p. 10. Similarly, Bipin Chandra Pal said in 1910: "Behind the new nationalism in India stands the old *Vedantism* of the Hindus." Quoted in K.P. Karunakaran, *Continuity and Change in Indian Politics,* pp. 97-98.

[40]Thus, for example, in 1917 the Bengali journal, *Al-Eslam,* criticized the absence of Muslims in the national song *Banga Amar* composed by D.L. Roy: "It mentions Asoka, Nimai, Rasumani, Pratapaditya—but contains no trace of Muslim heroes like Gyasuddin Khan, Isa Khan and so forh. The population of Bengal is seven crores—more than half of these are Muslims. Why then were Muslims excluded from a national song composed for this vast Bengali nation constituted of both Hindus and Muslims?" In 1918, the *Al-Eslam* wrote that a major ground for Hindu-Muslim friction was that "Hindus unjustly and unfairly attack Muslims in literature." Similarly, in 1926, the *Ahmadi* complained that Hindu cultural media still bred anti-Muslim feelings. Quoted in M. N. Islam, *op. cit.,* pp. 113, 123. For a recent treatment of this theme in late nineteenth-century Hindi literature, sec Sudhir Chandra, 'Communal Consciousness in Late 19th Century Hindi Literature."

Of course, an intellectual or a writer may adopt what may be described as Bankim's approach as part of a writer's licence, especially when the process of nation-in-the-making was in its initial stage; and Bankim and similar other writers had no strong national sentiment to guide them.[41] More important was the use to which Bankim, for example, was put later. He was hailed as a great nationalist writer precisely for the wrong reasons; his historical novels were proclaimed genuine historical novels based on a correct understanding of history. His role became reactionary and communal not so much in his own times and not so much in terms of his own writings, but because of the manner in which their 'communal' parts were hailed to serve chauvinism and communalism.

It is interesting that as a modern intelligentsia began lo arise among Bengali Muslims and national sentiment spread among it, it tended to accept Bankim as a great Bengali writer, despite his negative portrayal of Muslims. But the semi-communal Hindu writers insisted that he was great precisely because of this portrayal. Consequently, the nationalist Muslim intellectuals gradually yielded to the pressure of the loyalist and communal Muslim writers.

Tilak too encouraged the growth of the Hindu tinge in Indian nationalism with his propagation of Ganesh Puja and Shivaji Festival with their Hindu religious overtones. It is true that Tilak's basic political propaganda and agitations were organized around political and economic issues and contained little appeal to Hinduism, and certainly much less than in the case of Aurobindo Ghose and B.C. Pal, and that his primary motive in organizing the festivals was "to find opportunities of collecting and speaking to the masses."[42] Regarding his glorification of Shivaji, Tilak was to say later that he did so because

[41]Many of them simultaneously favoured Hindu-Muslim unity. Moreover, as the national movement arose and grew, many of them began to mute their critical treatment of Muslims and even reverse it to make it more favourable. Others became more openly communal. See, for example, Sudhir Chandra, *op. cit.*, pp. 181-82, as also pp. 172-75, 180.

[42]J. Dwarkadas, *Political Memoirs*, p. 27. Also see G.P. Pradhan and A.K. Bhagwat, *Lokamanya Tilak*, pp. 83-90.

Shivaji was a popular hero in Maharashtra. In northern India, he said, he would have adopted Akbar as the common hero of Hindus and Muslims.[43] But while Tilak's politics, ideology and agitational methods were not communal—and a large part of the 'communalism' imputed to him is the result of large-scale falsification of history by imperialist writers like V. Chirol and by the later Hindu and Muslim communalists—there is no doubt that because of the Hindu tinge they bred communalism among both Hindus and Muslims and tended to antagonize the latter.

As pointed out earlier, many Extremist leaders like Aurobindo Ghose, Bipin Chandra Pal and Lala Lajpat Rai used Hindu symbols, idioms, and myths in their political speeches and writings. India was often referred to as Mother Goddess, or compared with Kali, Durga and other Hindu goddesses. The early National Revolutionaries swore by the *Gita* and Kali and some even saw in the Hindu tinge a revolutionary feature. Many leaders of the anti-partition of Bengal agitation tried to give a religious colour to the boycott movement in order to popularize it among the masses.[44]

During the 1890s and the first decade of the twentieth century, this Hindu tinge was to prove particularly harmful because just during those years the newly formed educated Muslim stratum was tending to be attracted to nationalist ideas and movement. But the Hindu tinge simultaneously generated unease and apprehension in the minds of the educated and politically conscious Muslims who were suspicious of a movement whose nationalist message was couched in religious terms, and who, therefore, saw the National Congress as representing a Hindu movement. It tended to repel them ideologically and made it difficult for them to join the Congress and the national movement. As S. Abid Husain has pointed out, this

[43]Ram Gopal, *Indian Muslims,* p. 88.

[44]Cf. Sumit Sarkar, *The Swadeshi Movement in Bengal 1903-1908,* pp. 47-48: "The emphasis on self-reliance became identified increasingly with the revivalist approach to the Hindu religious tradition, the moderates were condemned as denationalized Anglicists, and an appeal to religious sentiment came to be regarded as the most effective technique for bridging the gulf between the educated and the common people, as well as an extremely useful morale-booster for political activists."

Hindu tinge created "general unrest, panic and doubt" and "an atmosphere of fear and suspicion" among them, especially in northern India. Till then, "the secular nationalism of the Congress had a great appeal" for the Muslims. But, at that stage, "circumstances became extremely unfavourable for secular nationalism among Muslims and it received a great setback."[45]

A contemporary Muslim intellectual, who was otherwise oriented towards vigorous nationalism, expressed these feelings in words which bear reproduction in full. In an article in the *Comrade* entitled "Communal Patriot," Mohammed Ali wrote in 1912:

> Whatever may be the inspiration of Hinduism as a religious creed, the educated Hindus made it a rallying symbol for political unity.... Past history was ransacked for new political formulas; and by a natural and inevitable process "nationality" and "patriotism" began to be associated with Hinduism. The Hindu "communal patriot" sprang into existence with "Swaraj" as his war cry.... He knows, of course, the use of the words like "India" and "territorial nationality"; and they form an important part of his vocabulary. But the Muslims weigh on his consciousness, all the same, as a troublesome irrelevance; and he would thank his stars if some great exodus or even a geological cataclysm could give him riddance.... The spectacle of a go-ahead Hinduism, dreaming of self-government and playing with its ancient gods clad in the vesture of democracy, dazed the conservative Muslim.... He felt as if he was being treated as an alien, as a meddlesome freak, who had wantonly interfered with the course of Indian history. Strange incidents were raked up from his long and eventful career, which he was called upon to justify.... With the loss of empire he felt as if he were to lose his self-respect as well. The "communal patriots" amongst the Hindus treated him as a prisoner in the dock, and loudly complained of him as an impossible factor in the scheme of India's future.[46]

[45]S. Abid Husain, *The Destiny of Indian Muslims,* pp. 50-53.
[46]Mohammed Ali, *Selected Writings and Speeches,* pp. 66-67.

In another article in the *Comrade* in August 1911, Mohammed Ali had written that Muslims had

> every ambition to live and act as patriotic Indians and work for a nationality of which they would be a yet conscious part. But they dread the position of the second fiddle which the new-fangled "Nationalism" of some Indian public men and newspapers assign to them: a nationalism which is avowedly Hindu in sympathies and aspirations, has developed Hindu symbolism and battle cries and formula of faith, and draws its energizing forces from Hindu religion and mythology.[47]

One result of the Hindu tinge was that a large number of educated Muslims remained aloof from the national movement or became hostile to it and fell easy prey to the propaganda of the imperialist publicists and communal politicians. Even so, many politically advanced Muslim intellectuals did join the national movement, and nationalist sentiment continued to spread among Muslims also.

Later, in the post-1909 period, the Hindu tinge was not so strongly etched and a basically secular national movement was being built up. Even so, apart from the fact that serious damage had already been done, a vague Hindu aura continued to pervade much of the Congress agitation or at least the idiom of Congress political expression.

Gandhi's use of religious terms and symbols made its own contribution in this respect. Gandhi's politics were of course fully secular and his basic appeal to the people was made on economic, political and moral grounds, *and never on religious grounds.* He really catered to the new secular national consciousness. Still, his political thought was couched in the language of religiosity. He often employed Hindu terms and symbols, even though their use by him was seldom offensive to the followers of other religions. But his secularism came to represent the confluence of several religiosities or what Mohammed Ali

[47]Quoted in Francis Robinson, *Separatism among Indian Muslims,* pp. 200-01.

described as a "federation of religions."[48] However, in later years Gandhi came to realise that his views and statements were being misrepresented and not only by communalists. He then often declared that religion and politics should be completely separated and that religion was an entirely private affair of an individual.[49]

Other leaders like Subhash Chandra Bose and the general run of Congress workers too freely used Hindu symbols, myths, imagery and idioms and found it difficult to bypass religion in their daily political practice. The only exceptions were Jawaharlal Nehru, the different Marxist parties, groups and individuals and a handful of liberal intellectuals and politicians. It is, therefore, not accidental that during the 1930s the young Muslim intellectuals were attracted by left nationalism and not by the conservative, Hindu-tinged nationalism.[50]

Inevitably, some of the Hindu tinge was carried into the functioning of the Congress ministries from 1937-39, especially at the level of the lower cadres. After 1937, the Muslim League was to use this Hindu tinge to mount a powerful political and ideological offensive against the Congress and the Congress ministries and to mobilize the Muslim masses and middle classes. The Congress leadership failed to meet this challenge adequately. For example, the League leadership made much of the Congress use of the song *Bande Matram.* They attacked it on the ground that it was idolatrous and that it had been composed in the *Anand Math* by Bankim Chandra Chatterjee in an anti-Muslim context. Many Congress leaders saw that while this attack was

[48]For the danger of this approach so far as secularism and nationalism were concerned, see the following comment of Beni Prasad: "It may be that all religions, if properly understood, would exert a unifying and a harmonious influence; but the crucial fact is that religions are not likely to be properly understood in a world where everything is likely to be misunderstood." *The Hindu-Muslim Questions,* pp. 50-51.

[49]See Bipan Chandra, "Gandhiji, Secularism and Communalism," *Social Scientist,* Vol. 32, No. 368-369, Jan. Feb., 2004.

[50]It may also be remembered that more young Muslim intellectuals moved into the nationalist (and the socialist and communist) stream during the 1930s than into the communal stream.

basically communal, there was also some substance in it.[51] Yet, they failed to rectify the situation fully; they did in 1939 drop all but the first two stanzas for Congress use, partially because of the pressure of a section of Congressmen. Interestingly, the rectification came, though rather late, in 1947 in independent India.

The secular aspects of the national movement were also distorted by several other features. A large number of nationalist leaders assumed a dual socio-political role: they were simultaneously religious-social reformers within the circle of their co-religionists and political leaders within the wider national political arena. This duality started with the very founders of the National Congress, or earlier still. Even Dadabhai Naoroji was, till the 1870s, both a vigorous, secular nationalist and a Parsi socio-religious reformer. This often led the nationalist leaders to talk of 'we' with different meanings in different contexts, sometimes meaning Hindu or Muslim and sometimes Indian. While in theory it could be maintained that there was nothing wrong in a person being a good Indian and a good Hindu or a good Muslim, in practice this could apply only to their personal lives. It was not possible nor therefore desirable to have such a dual public role in a multi-religious country where communal elements were active with the full backing of the government. This invariably spread confusion among the people, which was freely taken advantage of by the communal leaders.

At its best, this dual socio-political role produced individuals like Ranade, Gandhi and Maulana Azad. At its worst, it led many Congress leaders to participate in the downright communal movements of *Sangathan* and *Shuddhi* on one side and *Tabligh* and *Tanzim* on the other. In any case, it encouraged the 'good-Hindu—good-Muslim friendship' approach towards national integration.

[51]For example, Nehru wrote to Subhash Chandra Bose in October 1937 that after reading *Anand Math* it did seem to him that the background of the song was "likely to irritate the Muslims.... There is no doubt that the present out-cry against *Bande Matram* is to a large extent a manufactured one by the communalists. At the same time there does seem some substance in it and people who are communalistically inclined have been affected by it." *SW*, Vol. 8, p. 187. Also see pp. 38, 222, 236-37, 341-42, 435-36, 768.

Much more damaging was the presence of 'communal nationalists' or even plain communalists in the ranks of the National Congress. "Many a Congressman was a communalist under his nationalist cloak."[52] The Congress leadership permitted openly communal elements or those whose ideological and political make-up contained a large dose of communalism to join the Congress and even occupy positions of leadership in it from the local to the all-India plane. Such communal nationalists had little difficulty in shifting from one camp to the other. They often left the Congress and opposed it from communal platforms. But soon after they would be readmitted into the Congress fold and leadership without any disavowal of their recent politics or even current communal or semi-communal ideology. Till the early 1930s, several leaders were simultaneously members and leaders of the Congress and the Hindu Mahasabha or the Muslim League.[53] It was only in 1938 that the Congress barred its doors to the members of the communal organizations. Both in Panjab and Bengal, many a Congress leader had no difficulty in simultaneously with nationalism, championing the 'Hindu cause' in respect of jobs or constitutional discussions or communal riots, in being a secular nationalist on one platform and a defender of Hindu interests on another. But while a communal Muslim joined the Muslim communal organizations, only the very rabid Hindu communalist would join the Hindu Mahasabha or the RSS in the 1930s; the ordinary one tended to remain in the Congress, creating unease among Muslims, especially at the local level where the Hindu tinge was most visible, though it was not absent at the top.[54] A large number of newspapers such as the

[52]Nehru, *An Autobiography*, p. 136. Also see Maulana Abul Kalam Azad, *India Wins Freedom*, p. 197.

[53]The prominent role played by Madan Mohan Malaviya in the Congress during the 1920s and 1930s constantly baffled and annoyed Muslims. See, for example, Mohammed Ali to Jawaharlal Nehru, 15 June 1924, in Nehru, *A Bunch of Old Letters*, pp. 37-38. Also see Choudhry Khaliquzzaman, *Pathway to Pakistan*, p. 132.

[54]Thus, in 1937, Ambika Charan, a Congress worker complained to the central leadership that an Arya Samaj preacher had become President of the Tehsil Congress Committee at Balrampur and was advocating *Shuddhi* and Hindu-Muslim unity simultaneously. This, he warned, would produce "great conflict, collision and

Tribune, Amrita Bazar Patrika and the *Leader,* and a vast mass of Hindi, Urdu, Bengali and Marathi newspapers, known as nationalist newspapers and serving as the main printed vehicles for nationalist propaganda, simultaneously championed Hindu communal causes. They were spokesmen for all Indian people in one column and the protectors and champions of the interests of Hindus in the other. In case of communal riots, for example, their editorials, as also the speeches and writings of many other nationalists, roundly condemned the riots, preached Hindu-Muslim harmony, and usually blamed Muslims as the initiators of the riots![55] Their reportage and comments were invariably loaded on the side of the Hindu communalists. These newspapers (and leaders) preached nationalism in one breath and complained of Hindus losing government jobs to Muslims and of Hindus suffering loss of lives in communal riots in another. The very idea that a Hindu should be more concerned with the loss of a job or loss of a life of a Hindu than that of a Muslim bred a communal outlook. The average Muslim reader or listener could hardly be blamed for being suspicious of such nationalism, for failing to distinguish between the leaders' Jekyll-and-Hyde roles and for becoming embittered.

misrepresentation." Similarly, a Congress worker of Bulandshahar complained in a letter to the AICC in September 1937 that the Muslims looked upon the District Congress Committee with suspicion because its members "take prominent part in the communal affairs." Similar complaints were made by K.D. Malaviya, Organizing Secretary of the UPCC, in 1939 and Abdul Qauyum, Congress MLA from NWFP. Cited and quoted in Anita Singh, "Nehru and the Communal Problem 1936-1939," pp. 240 ff. In 1937, in Panjab, Abdul Majid Khan protested strongly against a major Congress leader of Panjab, Gopi Chand Bhargava, attending the Hindu Mahasabha Executive meeting. Lala Jagat Narain complained to the Secretary, Panjab PCC, that Pandit Amarnath of Mahabir Dal was given 100 forms to enroll members. Another Congressman, Mahmud Hasan, wrote to the PCC on 22 May 1937 criticizing the communalism of Panjab Congressmen and pointing out that a "communalist" and "rebel" like Malaviya was being shown favours. *All India Congress Committee Papers,* File No. P 17 of 1937. The file also contains a long critique by Duni Chand on the communal penetration of the Panjab Congress. Also see for Malabar complaints, *ibid.,* File No. 47 of 1937 and for a Bihar complaint, File No. G-22 of 1938.

[55]The Muslim communal newspapers took a similar approach, but then, they did not claim to be secular and nationalist.

The Congress leadership failed to take note of and struggle against the communal elements within the nationalist ranks especially at the local and middle level leadership. There was also the wider failure to wage any real, active, consistent and principled political struggle and to fight at the level of ideas against the Hindu, Muslim and Sikh communalisms.

It would, of course, be wrong to suggest that because of the Hindu tinge and other weaknesses discussed earlier the National Congress became a communal body and the national movement could be characterized as a Hindu national movement. Nor were these the 'causes' of the birth of communalism in modern India. They were rather a cause of the failure to check the rise and growth of communalism. They made it difficult to win over Muslims to the Congress. Moreover, they put a powerful weapon in the hands of the government and the communalists who used it effectively to keep large sections of the Muslim masses and middle classes away from the national movement and to instil the feeling among them that the success of this movement would mean Hindu domination.

The Hindu tinge also made it difficult to ideologically oppose the Hindu communalists; in fact, it encouraged not only Muslim communalism but also Hindu communalism. It also helped the spread of a Muslim tinge among the Muslim nationalists.

Before concluding this section, a few other relevant points may be clarified.

(i) The use of religion and the traditional religious-cultural idioms or the glorification of the past were not special features of the Indian national movement. They have been a very common feature of the nineteenth and twentieth-century national movements from those of the Greeks and Italians to those of the Irish and Indonesians. They have been used as an easy method both to reach the people with the new ideology of nationalism[56] and to restore among the oppressed and

[56]The defence of new institutions and the dissemination of new ideologies and outlooks by appealing to the past and claiming to be restoring or reverting to the earlier ideologies and institutions are again very common. As Marx has put it: "The tradition of the dead generations weighs like a nightmare on the minds of the living. And, just when they appear

dominated peoples the feelings of self-respect and self-confidence. Even the Soviet leadership appealed to the past and used traditional (pre-1917) symbols and idioms to mobilize the people during the Second World War. In fact, in India, the process of appealing to the past was initiated by the entirely secular leadership of the Moderate period—Surendranath Banerjea was the first to glorify Shivaji and Guru Gobind Singh as national heroes during his 1877-78 speeches—and the more Hindu-tinged leadership of the Extremist period as a conscious imitation of the nationalist movements of the Greeks, the Italians and the Irish. The inculcation of self-respect and self-confidence and a certain cultural autonomy were even more necessary in India because their destruction was one of the basic features of the colonial culture and ideology.

Nevertheless, efforts should have been made to keep away from religious idioms and symbols and to actively oppose the association of nationalism with Hindu religion in any way. The Indian national movement had to be different in this respect from most other national movements because Indians were a different type of people. It was essential not to follow Italy and Greece here, as Tilak, Aurobindo Ghose and others did, because a multi-religion, multi-caste and multi-culture country like India could not afford to exalt, or claim to restore, any one religion, caste, culture or historical tradition; it could not afford to build the new by appealing to the past or by pretending to

to be engaged in the revolutionary transformation of themselves and their material surroundings, in the creation of something which does not yet exist, precisely in such epochs of revolutionary crisis they timidly conjure up the spirits of the past to help them; they borrow their names, slogans and costumes so as to stage the new world-historical scene in this venerable disguise and borrowed language. Luther put on the mask of the apostle Paul; the revolution of 1789-1814 draped itself alternately as the Roman republic and the Roman empire; and the revolution of 1848 knew no better than to parody at some points 1789 and at others the revolutionary traditions of 1793-5. In the same way, the beginner who has learned a new language always retranslates it into his mother tongue: he can only be said to have appropriated the spirit of the new language and to be able to express himself in it freely when he can manipulate it without reference to the old, and when he forgets his original language while using the new one." *The Eighteenth Brumaire of Louis Bonaparte,* pp. 146-47.

be restoring or reviving it.[57] Here, nationalism and the nation had to be projected as new historical phenomena; here, not the concept of the restoration of a past nationhood but that of the development of the new nation-in-the-making had to be stressed and propagated.

The task of the national leadership here was not only different but stiffer and more difficult, requiring immense patience, ideological clarity and boldness. Here, the new spirit of nationalism could not be inculcated by appealing to an old consciousness, the consciousness of religion; it could only be done by bringing out the link between the people's lives and concerns and anti-imperialism. Here, the appeal had to be entirely modern, secular and democratic. Here, nationalism required 'a fundamental change in the system of values.' Here, a national movement had to base itself on a correct understanding of the basic central contradiction between colonialism and the Indian people and on an entirely modern political, economic, social and cultural programme as the Moderates had done and Nehru and the left were doing and not on a programme of cultural revival or 'cultural nationalism' as the Extremists and the later conservatives did. The latter would invariably divide the people for it was basically and perhaps inevitably derived from the dominant 'great tradition' of the upper caste Hinduism of northern India. Nor was it a question merely of the division fostered by communalism. In time, it produced or would produce regionalism, casteism and tribalism. Upper caste Hindus, among whom nationalism first arose, could identify cultural consciousness based on the 'great tradition' with nationalism, but followers of other religions, members of the lower castes and tribal people would awaken, whenever cultural and political awakening came to them, to other cultural, social and religious traditions. They would rebel against any nationalism linked to the culture of caste hierarchy or reflecting the outlook of the upper castes. Then either nationalism would transform itself to respond to their social and cultural ethos or they would take to communal, casteist or other forms of divisive politics. Even women would not work actively for a

[57] Even Ireland got divided because of the Catholic religious base of its nationalism.

movement that glorified and aimed at the restoration of the culture of their utter degradation and domination.

(ii) A major dilemma faced by the Indian national movement, as any other movement, was that any 'massization' of politics would also tend to bring in the masses' backward cultural and social outlook and ideologies. As a recent author has pointed out, any nationalist attempt "to come closer to the mass of population was in the nature of things likely to adopt a Hindu (or Muslim or Sikh) idiom."[58]

The resurgence of religion-based culture and religious political idioms, terms, etc., were, in a way, an aspect of the democratization of the national movement. So long as the national movement was confined to the intellectuals, as in the Moderate phase in the nineteenth century, it could maintain a certain balance by keeping religion out of the political vocabulary and trying to build an entirely modern nationalist ideology. But as the social base of the movement shifted to the lower middle classes, most of whom were socially and culturally conservative and intellectually narrow and limited, its ideological modernity began to get compromised. The lower middle classes began to impose their own backwardness and narrowness on the ideological and political content of the movement.[59] As the movement reached down to the masses, religious idioms, myths and symbols entered its language, for in the language, culture, way of life, and worldview of the Indian people religion played an important part.

[58]Peter Hardy, *The Muslims of British India,* p. 227. A certain uncritical glorification of the masses and their culture led to lack of adequate emphasis on this aspect by most of the nationalist leaders after 1919, including the left-wing ones. In this respect, the earlier Moderate leaders showed a greater grasp over the processes of social and political change, as did Gandhi to a certain extent. Many leaders, including Nehru, wrongly expected mass participation in the national movement to automatically solve the communal problem.

[59]The fact is that if the leaders are not careful and in full command, their followers in a mass movement can gradually impose a content on the movement which its leaders might not have planned to impart to it. The logic of wanting to remain popular leaders can then have an inexorable quality of its own, unless the leadership is ideologically strong and clear and has the ability to go against popular opinion. One contemporary example of this has been the imposition of their cultural, ideological and political backwardness by the peasantries of the Soviet Union and China on their socialisms.

Here was, in fact, a classic dilemma or a dialectical situation. Mass-based anti-imperialism without adequate ideological foundations could be dangerous. On the other hand, how was an anti-imperialist movement to be built without struggles? How could struggles be organized without the masses? And could the masses be brought in without bringing in to a certain extent, their existing consciousness?

In India, therefore, simultaneously with modern mass politics, it was necessary and urgent to have a cultural revolution or complete modernization which would simultaneously incorporate the humanist and rational elements of the traditional culture.[60] India, more than any other country, needed all-round radicalism, based on a socially radical mass ideology and not merely on political radicalism. Otherwise, even mass politics, depending on the *existing* backward social and cultural consciousness of the masses, hid this reactionary aspect that they would tend to strengthen socially backward ideologies and outlook and, instead of uniting the people, further divide them.[61]

It was always easier to build up a movement on existing consciousness than to generate a new consciousness for this purpose. Finding the radical process more slow, tedious and difficult, and not having a ready-made consciousness to appeal to, certain sections of the nationalist leadership, especially during the Extremist phase, found it easier, and tended to some extent, to appeal to the existing religious consciousness, or rather to put the nationalist message in religious terms in order to immediately create and build a national movement which would gradually help make India a nation and, in time, create the more advanced and modern secular consciousness. But in the process, however unconsciously, this effort left space for

[60]A cultural revolution necessarily requires the incorporation of all healthy elements of the past cultural achievements of a people and society. This was also necessary in order to cut at the popular roots of revivalism, communalism and obscurantism.

[61]Similar was the case with the spread of literacy and the Press and other means of mass communication. In the absence of simultaneous cultural and ideological reorientation, the rise of the modern Press and pamphleteering led to the wider spread and reach cf communal propaganda.

communalism and casteism and even made their own thinking and writing hostages to communalism. This failure of the traditional leadership was in one respect shared by the rising left-wing leadership. The latter too, with some exceptions as in Kerala, did not actively propagate a modern culture and value system among the people, let alone initiate a cultural revolution. It also did not mobilize its followers actively against communal and casteist forces and ideology, perhaps in the expectation that class organization and struggles and the anti-imperialist struggle would directly result in their gradual elimination.

(iii) A sharp distinction has, however, to be made between religious consciousness and communalism. The use of religious myths, symbols, idioms, etc., was not communalism though, as pointed out earlier, it created space, or kept an opening, for communalism, and weakened defences against it. It was also not one of the causes of communalism. Communalism arose for other reasons, though, as we shall see in Chapter 6, it used religion for the purpose; and to that extent the intrusion of religious consciousness, etc., into nationalism contributed to the growth of communalism.

Not only Gandhi but even Tilak can not be placed in the communal camp, even though the latter's appeal to Hindu culture and an extremely narrow historical tradition antagonized Muslims and encouraged Hindu communal feeling and thus proved harmful in the Indian context. In particular, the entire criticism of the Hindu tinge should be put in its proper historical setting so far as the post-1918 nationalists are concerned. Their use of the Hindu political idiom was very different from that of Aurobindo Ghose and Bipin Chandra Pal. To brand Indian nationalism since the 1870s as Hindu nationalism is absurd. It is also wrong to say that in the Gandhian era one of the basic elements of nationalism has been the 'orthodox and revivalist varieties of Hinduism.' Gandhi, not to speak of Nehru and the left wing, was fully secular and free of religious narrow-mindedness. Even when couched in the language of religion—which was much less common than asserted by his critics—his appeal was to modern, secular economic, political and social principles.[62] None of the movements of the Gandhian era used Hindu religion or religious appeal in any manner. In no way was religion used after 1918 in the ideological definition of nationalism or of its programme. It is true that the leaders of the national movement and the intellectual generators of national consciousness were predominantly Hindu. It is also true that not all of them would measure up to the highest standards of secular nationalism. But it is equally true that in politics they did not act as Hindus; they produced a basically non-communal, secular national movement. The nationalist intelligentsia was limited by class but not by communalism or religion.[63] That with all its weaknesses Congress secularism was genuine and not Hindu communalism or Hindu 'nationalism' in disguise was amply proved later when, after 1947, under Congress leadership, India adopted a fully secular Constitution and set out to build a society and polity which was on the whole secular, despite serious shortcomings.

[62]Even the notion that Gandhi got his legitimacy and popularity because of religious symbolism and religious veneration is, to say the least, grossly exaggerated. To start with, Gandhi became a major Indian leader in South Africa where the question of religious veneration for the young lawyer of 24 did not arise, apart from the fact that a large number of his followers were Muslims who could not have interpreted his weapons of 'truth,' 'satyagraha' and 'non-violence' through Hindu eyes. In India, his first three public campaigns in Khera, Champaran and Ahmedabad were entirely non-religious. Nor was there any religious aspect to the anti-Rowlatt Bills agitation which pitch-forked Gandhi into national leadership. A great deal of the case regarding the religious legitimacy of Gandhi is based on his title of 'Mahatma.' But Mahatma was more a moral, cultural and social category than a religious one of the guru or maharishi or baba variety. Gandhi has never been worshipped as a religious man whose benediction could help in personal salvation or worldly success. Despite his vast popularity and eventual martyrdom, no temples have been erected around him. His busts and photographs are not worshipped in a religious manner. And no religious sect has claimed him or arisen around him. The non-political part of his appeal to the people was not to their religious sense but to their moral sense.

[63]On the other hand, the Muslim League, the Hindu Mahasabha and the RSS were not only communal, but they were not nationalist at all. They did not represent nationalism, whether Muslim or Hindu. They were just communal, and objectively allies of colonialism. Also see C.G. Shah, *Marxism Gandhism Stalinism,* pp. 173-74.

CHAPTER 6

The Role of Ideological, Social and Cultural Elements: II

I. THE ROLE OF RELIGION

Is the fact that there exist many religions in India the basis or the underlying cause or reason for the rise of communalism? Yes, say some. A recent writer has, for example, asserted: "The proposition that the root of political polarization in India was the religious antipathy between Hindus and Muslims command(s) greater-acceptance today...."[1] He goes so far as to describe the communal issue as "the communal-religious issue."[2] A more sophisticated form of saying the same thing is that communalism was, and is, inevitable in a plural society marked by the existence of different religions.[3] This also means that so long as religious differences remain, communalism in some form would also remain—'a plural society cannot escape from communalism.' The answer is to tolerate and civilize it, perhaps by integrating it as 'sub-nationalism' within broader nationalism.[4] Other

[1]Gopal Krishna, "Religion in Politics," p. 375. He also says: "In the political evolution of modern India no single element has been as pervasive as religion. It has governed in large measure the political cleavages, the competition for power and the coalition-building activities of the last hundred years."' *Ibid.*, p. 362.

[2]*Ibid.*, p. 380.

[3]*Ibid.*, pp. 376, 394; Rasheeduddin Khan, "Self-View of Minorities: The Muslims in India."

[4]Rasheeduddin Khan writes: "In a plural society, tensions and conflicts between viable segments—regional, linguistic, cultural, communal or political—are not only unavoidable, as is evident in any situation of dynamic change, but the significant point is that, if the tensions and conflicts are 'contained' within the legitimized political system and mediated through functional and not dysfunctional methods of pressure and bargaining, they arc capable of becoming creative catalyst of change itself." *Ibid.* Also see, A.R. Kamat, "National Integration and Sub-national Loyalties." In my view, it is wrong to put communalism and communal conflict in the same category as linguistic, cultural or political loyalties and conflicts.

answers could be the abolition of all religions (the rationalist answer) or the absorption by one religion of all other religions (the communal-fascist answer). The secular answer is different. It does not see religion as lying at the root of communalism.

While religious differences were real, they were not the cause of the communal division. Religious differences do explain a sense of separate religious and social identity; they cannot explain the genesis or persistence of a long-term socio-political phenomenon like communalism.[5] Communalism in modern times was not inspired by religion, nor was religion the end or object of communal politics.[6] In other words, religion was not the underlying or basic-cause, whose removal was basic to tackling or solving the communal problem.

It is necessary in this respect to distinguish between religion as an ideology or a belief system and the ideology of religious identity, which is communalism. The two are very different. Moreover, not only is consciousness of one's religion not communalism; the use of religion as a social or mobilizing ideology as in the case of Taipings in China, early Christianity, peasant wars of Germany or the Satnami and Sikh revolts of the eighteenth century is also not communalism. In fact, to understand communalism, or the ideology of religious identity, "one must go outside the sphere of religion and explore the spheres of economics and politics."[7]

What then was the role of religion in the genesis and growth of communalism? What is true is that communal cleavage was based on differences in religion and that the communalist defined his politics and political differences in terms of differences in religious identity and made it the crucial determinant of separate community or nationhood.

[5]Even to explain a communal riot—a sudden outburst of communal violence—we cannot take recourse to a factor which was always present, namely, religious difference. We have to search for a factor or a situation which leads to sudden hatred and violence among a people who were previously living harmoniously and were likely to do so again.

[6]This is quite obvious in the case of the rise of Sikh communalism in Panjab. Here it was communalism, both Hindu and Sikh, which produced the full-fledged identity of a separate religion.

[7]P.C, Joshi, "The Economic Background of Communalism in India—A Model of Analysis," p. 171.

In other words, religious difference was a basic element of communal ideology and politics and was used by the communalist as an organizing principle and to mobilize the masses, but it was not their cause; it does not explain why some Hindus and Muslims organized their politics around religious identities; for that the content of communal politics has to be analysed, because religion was neither the cause nor the end of communalism—it was only its vehicle.

The religious difference was used to 'mask' non-religious social needs, aspirations and conflicts which were the products of the interplay of forces released by the impact of colonialism on Indian society. That is, religion served politics arising in spheres other than religion and as a garb or rationalization,[8] even though the communalist believed to the contrary and had often internalized this belief. Communal politics had "no other reference to religious issues" than their use for this purpose. Or, as we have said in Chapter 1, using religious distinctions which were very real, and of which the Indian people were certainly fully conscious, the communalist created the false consciousness of religious identity and communal antagonism. We may here explain by recourse to a close analogy. The religious distinction between the Christian German and the Jewish German was real, but it was not responsible for the rise of—was not the cause of—Nazism or anti-Jewish politics or racial politics and theories. That is, Nazism did not *originate* in these differences. Similarly, the colour distinction between blacks and whites is real, but it is not the cause of racialism; that is, racialism does not originate in the difference in colour. The same was the case with religious distinction and the rise of communalism.

One of the ways of looking at the question is to note, as W.C. Smith does, that communalism was based upon religious differences, and a communalist firmly believed that it had a religious basis, but *it had no religious solution.* That is what I mean by false consciousness. What it

[8]K.M. Ashraf put this aspsct in an appropriate and picturesque phrase when he described communalism as *"Mazhab ki siyasi dukandari"*— a phrase which is nearly impossible to translate, but an approximation is: "political trade in religion." *Hindustani Muslim Siyasat par Ek Najar*, p. 73.

poses as the problem is not a problem and what it suggests as the solution is not a solution. By true consciousness I mean precisely that the solution indicated has a reference to the problem and also *is* a solution or at least part of the solution. For example, anti-imperialism was and is part of the solution of the colonial condition; without the overthrow of imperialism the colonial condition cannot be set right.

We may look at the problem from another angle. For decades, the only concrete demands the communalists raised related to government jobs (and educational opportunities related to them) and seats in councils and municipal bodies or to religious liberty and freedom of conscience. They could not define in concrete any other communal interests.[9] Of course, general assertions of Muslim cultural, economic, social and political interests were made, but they were left vague and undefined. Similarly there was a general talk of removing the economic backwardness of Muslims but no issues or remedies specific to Muslims were taken up. In fact, even religious demands were seldom raised, perhaps for the simple reason that it was difficult to suggest that the religious liberty of Muslims was or was likely to be in danger. When challenged, the communalists were hard put to suggest any fundamental rights other than religious freedom and freedom of language and culture, which could be demanded specifically for Muslims but which did not apply equally to Hindus and other Indians.[10] Religion could not, in other words, be the basis of the socio-economic demarcation or 'separation' between Indians. Interestingly, when the Muslim League leadership did, as a result of goading by younger men, frame a socio-economic programme during the late 1930s, it was no different from what 'Hindus' had framed: there was nothing specifically 'Muslim' about it.[11]

[9]For Resolutions of the All-India Muslim Conference, 1 January 1929 and M. A. Jinnah's Fourteen Points, 28 March 1929, see Gwyer, M. and Appadorai, A., *Speeches and Documents on the Indian Constitution 1921-47,* Vol. I, pp. 244-47.

[10]*Ibid.*

[11]The 1937 session of the League adopted the following "economic, social and education programme": "to fix working hours for factory workers and other labourers and to fix minimum wages: to improve the housing and hygienic condition of the labourers and make provision for slum clearance: to reduce rural and urban debts and abolish usury; to grant a moratorium with regard to all debts, whether decreed or otherwise, till proper

Religion was brought in actively during the mass, fascist phase of communalism when it was used to mobilize the common people. The middle classes were attracted to communalism during its liberal, elitist phase by the adoption of their communal demands for 'safeguards' regarding jobs, education, and council seats. These demands belonged to the secular or non-religious sphere of life, even though the community was formed by religion. The masses, on the other hand, were attracted by having their religious fervour excited, for, in their case, communalism involved or projected none of their real-life demands or interests. The fear complex could, in their case, be fully aroused not by propagating that their interests were in

legislation has been enacted; to secure legislation for exemption of houses from attachment or sale in execution of decrees; to obtain security of tenure and fixation of fair rents and revenue; to abolish forced labour; to undertake rural uplift work; to encourage cottage industries and small indigenous industries both in rural and urban areas; to encourage the use of Swadeshi articles, especially hand-woven cloth; to establish an industrial board for the development of industries and the prevention of exploitation by middlemen; to devise means for the relief of unemployment; to advance compulsory primary education; to reorganize secondary and university education, especially scientific and technical; to establish rifle clubs and a military college; to enforce prohibition; to abolish and remove unIslamic customs and usages from Muslim society; to organize a volunteer corps for social service; and to devise measures for the attainment of full independence and invite the cooperation of all political bodies working to that end." S.S. Pirzada, *Foundations of Pakistan...*, Vol. II, p. 280. The 1936 election manifesto of the League put forward the following programme: "1. To protect the religious rights of the Mussalmans. In all matters of purely religious character, due weight shall be given to the opinions of Jamait-ul-Ulema-i-Hind and the Mujtahids. 2. To make every effort to secure the repeal of all repressive laws. 3. To resist all measures which are detrimental to the interest of India, which encroach upon the fundamental liberties of the people and lead to economic exploitation of the country. 4. To reduce heavy cost of administrative machinery, central and provincial, and allocate substantial funds for nation-building departments. 5. To nationalize the Indian army and reduce the military expenditure. 6. To encourage development of industries, including cottage industries. 7. To regulate currency, exchange and prices in the interest of economic development of the country. 8. To stand for the social, educational and economic uplift of the rural population. 9. To sponsor measures for the relief of agricultural indebtedness. 10. To make elementary education free and compulsory. 11. To protect and promote Urdu language and script. 12. To devise measures for the amelioration of the general conditions of Muslims. 13. To take steps to reduce the heavy burden of taxation. 14. To create a healthy public opinion and general political consciousness throughout the country." Z.H. Zaidi, "Aspects of Development of Muslim League Policy, 1937-47," p. 252. Also see, Mohammad Noman, *Muslim India...*, pp. 356-57. For the 1920s, see Ram Gopal, *Indian Muslims...*, Chapters 17-27 and Prabha Dixit, *Communalism—A Struggle for Power*, Chapter 3.

danger, but by constantly suggesting that their religion itself was in danger. In fact, some such emotionalizing and inflammable factor was needed to raise communal politics to the level of a popular movement. In view of the pro-colonial and upper class character of the communal leadership, this factor could only be religion.

This was in particular true of Muslim communalism which had no real mass base till 1938 or even in 1945-46 and which became a popular movement from 1937 and particularly during 1945-47 only when it increasingly placed almost its entire emphasis on Islam and religious zeal, picked up the banner of 'the crescent and the Quran,' used religious appeal and religious symbols to mobilize support, aroused religious hysteria and took up vigorously the cry of Islam in danger.[12] Earlier, the Muslim interests were in danger, now Islam was in danger.[13] Earlier, Muslims faced oppression, domination, even extinction, now Islam faced extermination. Earlier, communal politics, and even Pakistan when first conceived, were to safeguard the interests of Muslims of India, now it was to enable the rule of Islam that Pakistan was demanded.[14] Earlier, Muslims had been asked to work for Pakistan, now, in the elections of 1945-46, they were asked to vote for

[12]The League leaders and the *Ulama* began to raise the cry in 1937 and after, when the Congress effort to appeal to the Muslim masses around a secular programme was widely portrayed as an attack on Islam; but it was taken up on a large scale only during ihe Second World War and the post-War period. M.A. Jinnah, for example, started apppealing to Islam in the late 1930s. See *Speeches and Writings*, Vol. I, pp. 73 and 86-88. Also see Ram Gopal, *op. cit.*, p. 260.

[13]The people could see for themselves whether Muslims or Hindus were in danger; or at least some proof would have to be offered by the leaders and publicists. But Islam or Hinduism in danger was a pure mystique which could rely on blind religious emotions accentuated by prejudice, fear and hatred.

[14]See M.A. Jinnah, *op. cit.*, and Z.A. Suleri, *My Leader.* Also see, for example, Jinnah's speech at the Aligarh Muslim University, 10 March 1941: "Pakistan is not only a practicable goal but the only goal if you want to save Islam from complete annihilation in the country." *Op. cit.*, Vol. I, p. 243. Suleri was even more blatant: "Congress is the name of Hindu cult, it works for it"; or "The post-Khilafat day Mussalmans were willing to liquidate the very existence of Islam"; or nationalist Muslims were "purchasable commodities"; or Jinnah was "determined to establish the supremacy of Islam in his own home-lands"; or Jinnah "symbolizes the stubborn nature of Islam in the face of invasions"; Gandhi was "an enemy of Islam" while Jinnah was "the greatest living architect of Islam." *Op. cit.*, pp. 54, 62, 74, 186, 189, respectively.

Pakistan because "a vote for the League and for Pakistan was a vote for Islam... (and) the mission of Islam in the world." Pakistan, it was promised, would be ruled under the *Sharia,* the divine law of Islam. Muslims needed a homeland in order to introduce the reign of Islam and to live their lives on the principles of Islam; Pakistan would embody "the renaissance of Islam." All nationalist Muslims were now denounced as "renegades from Islam" or "traitors to Islam" who were following the dictates of the enemies of Islam, in particular Gandhi. Freedom without Pakistan would mean "giving up of Islam." The mosques were used on a large scale to spread League propaganda; League meetings were often held in the mosques after Friday prayers. The pro-Muslim League Ulama, *pirs,* etc., were now brought forward as election propagandists and to issue *fatwas* backed by quotations from the Quran and *hadis* to prove that the two-nation theory was Islamic while the one-nation theory was unlslamic. Pakistan, it was said, would be the first step towards the establishment of the Quranic kingdom on earth. They asked Muslim voters to choose between a mosque and a temple. The Quran was widely used as the League's symbol, and League leaders often began their speeches with a text from the Quran; and pledges to vote for the League were made on it. The League's victory over the Congress was portrayed as the victory of Islam over *kufr.*[15] The Hindu communalists too tried to raise the cries of

[15]See Peter Hardy, *The Muslims of British India,* pp. 238-42; W.C. Smith. *Modem Islam in India,* pp. 298, 300; K.B. Sayeed, *Pakistan—the Formative Phase,* pp. 198-206, 211; Mushirul Haq, *Muslim Politics in Modern India, IS57-1947,* p. 148; Anita Singh, "Nehru and the Communal Problem 1936-1939," p. 70; I.A. Talbot, "The 1946 Punjab Elections"; Abid Husain, *The Destiny of Indian Muslims,* pp. 112-13. Asking Muslims to vote for the League, the tallest of the League leaders, Jinnah. said: "If we fail to realize our duty today you will be reduced to the status of Sudras and Islam will be vanquished from India." *Op. cit.,* Vol. II, pp. 240-41. Similarly, in his presidential address to the League in April 1943, he described Khan Abdul Ghaffar Khan as being "in charge of the Hinduizing influences and emasculation of the martial Pathans." *Ibid.,* p. 489. The political crisis in Pakistan since 1947 is in part due to the legacy of this agitation and its ideological underpinning. On the one hand, Islam and Islamic law found hardly any place in Pakistan's legal, constitutional and economic structure; on the other hand, ready agitation around a greater role for Islam has been available to political adventurers which the modern parties and rulers have found difficult to oppose successfully.

"Hinduism in danger," "Hindu faith in danger" and "Hindu culture or *sanskriti* in danger" and to warn Hindus against Muslims and their agent, Gandhi.[16] But for reasons discussed below, that is, primarily the heterodox and caste-ridden character of Hinduism and the consequent weakness of religiosity, it was not easy to popularize the first slogan. And the second slogan was neither emotive enough nor did it make much sense to the Hindu masses or even an average middle class Hindu across the country. Only in Panjab, where Hindus were a minority and the Arya Samaj a social force, could it get enough of a political response; that is, apart from the momentary frenzy of a communal riot. One reason why Hindu communalism could not dig deep roots among the masses was the failure to link up with religion. As a political movement, it remained at the level of 'Hindus in danger' and not 'Hindu religion in danger.' On the other hand, Hindus were as involved in communal riots as Muslims because the riots occurred around a religious issue.

It may be reiterated here that while the liberal communalists had been open to argument, the fascist or extreme communalists, relying on the irrational aspects of religious appeal, felt, as W.C. Smith puts it, that this "absolved them from rational thought and from meeting rational criticism. By saying that 'Islam is so different' (or that 'Hindu culture or civilization is so different') they released themselves from the duty of learning anything from history, from the West, from modern sociology." We can, therefore, readily agree with Smith's conclusion: "Whatever else it might be, Pakistanism [or Hindu Sanskritism] was unlovely."[17] Unlovely, that is, if communal fascism was no more than 'unlovely'!

How could religion be brought into politics so easily? Initially, because it encompassed a large part of the life of a pre-capitalist people. In the absence of nationalism and class feeling, it is the most

[16]M.S. Golwalkar, *We;* V.D. Savarkar, *Hindulva, Hindu Rashtra Darshan* and *Hindu Sanghtan,* pp. 214, 216; Indra Prakash, *A Review....*

[17]W.C. Smith, *op. cit.,* p. 300.

emotionalizing aspect in their life.[18] As K.B. Krishna puts it: "Causes do not operate in a void. They operate in life. Hence they reproduce all phases of life." And: "Religion comes into the fray because it is a part of the social order in which men live. It cannot be dissociated from the modes of thought that characterize a society."[19]

Religion always had, of course, explosive potentialities in promoting conflict and inspiring extreme and violent action. It has, in the past, led to violent conflict not only between followers of different religions as, for example, between Hindus and Muslims, Muslims and Christians and Hindus and Buddhists, but also between followers of the same religion as, for example, between Catholics and Protestants, Shias and Sunnis, Shaivites and Vaishnavites, Sanatanists and Arya Samajists (and today between Akalis and Nirankaris).

Moreover, differing religious practices were the immediate cause of situations of communal tension and riots which were produced by communalism as well as contributed to its growth. Before 1946, almost all the communal riots occurred around such religious issues as music before mosques, cow slaughter, cutting of a *peepal* tree, throwing of coloured water during Holi and the coincidence of Holi and Muharram or some other festivals and conversions and reconversions.

Similarly, followers of different religions were certainly conscious of their religious differences. But the religious grouping has to be placed alongside other traditional groupings, some of which since 1947 have become bases of political action. For instance, in the villages of northern India, the grouping seldom took (or takes) the form of Hindu and Muslim, but that of Jat, Ahir, Rajput, Brahmin, Chamar, Bania, Muslim, etc.; in Malabar, Muslim, Nair, Ezhava, etc.; in

[18]It was especially so when the appeal had to be made to the peasantry. As P.C. Joshi has pointed out: "The spontaneous political articulation of the peasant often proceeds through rise of religious heresies, through the reorientation of the religious world-view rather than its outright rejection. The peasantry may for long respond to the modern problems in the language of the past." "Myths: Old and New."

[19]K.B. Krishna, *The Problem of Minorities,* pp. 277, 292. Moreover, he states that "this expression again depends on the classes and individuals who generalize their experience and needs." *Ibid,*, p. 292.

Maharashtra, Muslim, Maratha, Mahar, Brahmin, etc. In other words, Muslims were treated just as another social group of the caste-type and not seen in contrast to 'Hindus' but to other village castes.[20]

Thus, the religious identity or the consciousness of being different from one's neighbours because of one's religion as also the intrusion of religion into other areas of life, including the political, was inherent in the given, inherited social situation. What was, however, not inevitable was the manner of religion's entry into modern politics—politics of popular participation—and its transformation into communalism. The use of religious grouping or identity for forming political communities or as the basis for political formation and action was a new feature of Indian political and social development. To understand this, one has to go, as suggested in Chapters 2, 3 and 4, into the socio-economic roots of communalism: religion was brought in (as also caste, etc., later) primarily because it could be utilized to 'mask' the politics of classes and social groups arising in the secular, non-religious spheres.

It has often been noted that the purely religious or theological content of communalism has tended to be rather meagre.[21] The communalist seldom relied on theology and, in fact, actively avoided theological issues. K.B. Krishna gives the example of Muslim money-lenders who went against their religion to practise usury and then used religion to fight against Hindu money-lenders.

That religion played, in communalism, an entirely extraneous or vicarious role—the role of a mask—is clearly brought out if we take a look at the religious side of the communal leaders or personalities. The average Muslim League leader, for example, was not an orthodox or even a practising Muslim. "In most cases even his knowledge of the Quran and *Sunnah* was only marginal.... To him the Islamic appeal

[20]See Chapter 1, Section III.

[21]Louis Dumont, for example, writes: "The religious element that enters into its (communalism's) composition seems to be but the shadow of religion, i.e., religion taken not as the essence and guide of life in all spheres, but only as a sign of the distinction of one human, at least virtually political, group against others." "Religion/Politics and History in India," pp. 90-91. Similarly, casteism today has hardly any ritual aspect; quite often even caste taboos are ignored.

was simply an instrument of rabble rousing."[22] This statement would have been true of most Aligarhian communalists, and was, above all, true of M.A. Jinnah.[23] Most of the Muslim communalists used Islam in a general sense, as a banner and not in its religious functioning. On the other side, the very heterogeneous character of Hinduism made the Hindu communalist keep all religious aspects out of communal politics. Many staunch Arya Samajists, opposed to idolatory in any form, virtually became cow worshippers in their communal practice. V.D. Savarkar, the high priest and theoretician of communalism, was a rationalist and a practising atheist.[24] Because of the diversity of Hindu religious beliefs, he tried to define Hindu dharma, *Hindutva* and Hindu nation in purely cultural terms. He explicitly denied the role of religion in the determining of *Hindutva* or the Hindu political identity. Rather, he used *Hindutva* to explain Hinduism.[25] Hindus were not the followers of Hinduism but Hinduism was the religion of Hindus! While Savarkar tried to explicitly exclude religion from his definition of Hindus as a community or nation, even those who did

[22]Iqtidar Alam Khan, "The Origin and Rise of Muslim Obscurantism." Also see Humayun Kabir, *Muslim Politics 1906-47 and Other Essays*, p. 41.

[23]Keith Callard has remarked: "The background of the men who organized the campaign (for Pakistan) was not theology and Islamic law but politics and the common law, not Deoband but Cambridge and the Inns of Court. Mr Jinnah and his lieutenants such as Liaquat Ali won Pakistan largely in spite of the men of religion. They led a secular campaign to create a state based on a religion." *Pakistan, A Political Study*, p. 200. Also see K.B. Sayeed, *op. cit.*, pp. 198-99. Maulana Maudoodi, the leader of the anti-Congress Jamat-i-Islami, wrote at the time: "From the League's Quaid-i-Azam down to the humblest leader, there was not one who could be credited with an Islamic point of view." Quoted in K.B. Sayeed, *op. cit.*, p. 198.

[24]D. Keer, *Veer Savarkar*, pp. 201-07.

[25]See his *Hindutva*. He defined a Hindu not by his religion but by his belief in India as his motherland and *poonyabhuomi*. This was done deliberately.... "We have deliberately refrained ourselves from referring (to) any religious beliefs that we as a race may hold in common. Nor had we referred to any institution or event or custom in its religious aspect or significance. Because we wanted to deal with the essentials of *Hindutva* not in the light of any 'ism' (like Hinduism) but from a racial point of view." *Ibid.*, p. 80. He was also fully aware of the fact that reliance on Hinduism as a religion for definition of *Hindutva* or nationhood would divide Hindus. *Ibid.*, pp. 3-4, 64-65. Also his presidential address to the Hindu Mahasabha in 1937 in *Hindu Rashtra Darshan*, p. 8.

not do so, kept religion more as an abstraction than as a *concrete* religion with specific religious content. Thus Golwalkar, whose political thought was otherwise a virtual echo of Savarkar's, and who included religion as a basic determinant of nationhood in India, defined Hindu dharma, *sanskriti* and Hinduness themselves either by circular reasoning or equated them with "following varnas and Ashramas."[26] Similarly, Bhai Parmanand defined nationalism as love of language, territory and religion, but then immediately back-tracked on the religious aspect. Firstly, he said, "religion *per se* is altogether different from nationalism." Secondly, "religion lays down a few dogmas.... Religion presupposes the truth of a few postulates, and thus lays the foundations of narrow-mindedness and bigotry." Hindu religion was not like that; but then the Hindu shastras only infer the existence of a supreme power that controlled the universe and declared everything else to be "unknownable (sic)." Moreover, it was difficult to define a Hindu. Tilak, he said, had declared in 1901 that "A Hindu is he who believes that the vedas contained self-evident and axiomatic truths." But, Bhai Parmanand pointed out, this definition would leave out Jains and Sikhs. Some others said that a Hindu was one who venerated the cow and the Brahmin; but many Hindus did not do so. In the end, he opted for Savarkar's definition of a Hindu and concluded: "He who calls and considers himself a Hindu is a Hindu"![27]

On the other hand, most of the orthodox Ulama and theologians, who were deeply religious and whose politics were more firmly based on religion, were opposed to communalism till the early 1940s or were at least less communal.[28] Similarly, Gandhi's or Maulana Azad's deep religious commitment did not come in the way of their commitment to secularism.[29] Apart from the fact that religion might

[26]M.S. Golwalkar, *op. cit.*, pp. 63-64. Also see pp. 26-31.

[27]Bhai Parmanand, *Hindu Sangathan*, pp. 5-11.

[28]S. Ansari, *Pakistan—The Problem of India*, pp. 63-64.

[29]Gandhi, for example, said in 1942: "Religion is a personal matter which should have no place in politics." And in 1947: "Religion is the personal affair of each individual. It must rot be mixed up with politics or national affairs." Quoted in M.K. Gandhi, *The Way to Communal Harmony*, pp. 39, 398. Of course, his use of the Hindu religious idiom, which

have satisfied certain personal urges which were not a part of the personal or group interests of the believers, there was also a basic difference between religion as a source of nationalist inspiration and communalism. For example, the early twentieth-century revolutionary terrorists took to religion and mysticism for inspiration and ideology, but they were not communalists. To them, religion was a source of inner strength and not the *basis* of their politics. It inspired them to become fighters for the national liberation of all Indian people and not organizers of communal politics, spouting hate against other sections of the Indian people. While the religious and mystical beliefs of the revolutionary terrorists led them to fight against imperialism, the communalists were often pro-imperialism subjectively and invariably served imperialism objectively by dividing the Indian people and turning the edge of their politics against other Indians and not against imperialism.

In contrast, most of the middle class Hindus and Muslims, who formed the social base of communalism, were hardly religious. What W.C. Smith has said of communal Muslims is equally true of communal Hindus:

> ... for many middle-class Muslims, communalism is the most important part of their religion.... Without communalism many of these (Indian) Muslims too would be Muslim in little more than name. For it is exceedingly difficult to discover what, if anything, they mean when they say "Islam," except the Muslim community and loyalty to it; or, more usually, the Indian Muslim community and loyalty to it; or even, the Muslim League and loyalty to it. Usually they do not govern their lives by their religion in any other sense, their decisions are not influenced by it, their ideas and objectives do not derive from it. Often they do not know very much about their religion in any other sense. There is little concern with God; with personal salvation; with morality; with worship.[30]

he used less and less with the passage of time, could and was to some extent misunderstood by the masses, both Hindu and Muslim, though not to the extent that many writers believe.

[30]W.C. Smith, *op. cit.*, pp. 203-04.

Thus, communalism was in this sense also a sleight of hand. Though relying on religion for communal demarcation, it had hardly any religion in it. (For example, Savarkar went to the extent of saying that a person could be a Hindu even if an atheist.) The communalists used religion to appeal to an existing consciousness of religious demarcation to create quite another type of fresh consciousness of political demarcation. They used religion merely as a grouping and a separating principle for political purposes. They used religion to create a false consciousness. They hardly had any other use for religion.

While religion as such was not responsible for the origins and growth of communalism, religiosity was a major contributory factor and, at the popular plane, imparted communalism the passion and intensity which made it politically effective. Religiosity may be defined as deep and intense emotional commitment to matters of religion and as the tendency to let religion and religious emotions intrude into non-religious or non-spiritual areas of life and beyond the individual's private life, to refuse to separate religion from politics, economics and social life—that is, to be over-religious or to have too much religion in one's life. As Jawaharlal Nehru repeatedly pointed out, there was "too much religiosity" in India.[31] While the peasantry usually took their religion seriously but with a pinch of salt, the lower middle classes and their women, especially those untouched by modern education and culture, had a tendency to fall prey to religiosity and religious passions.

Too much religiosity enabled the religious factor to come into play in Indian politics. It made the people susceptible to emotional appeals by the communalists in the name of religion. Moreover, religiosity tended to get out of hand for it had no defined boundaries. Without religiosity, religious fervour could not be aroused; and without religious fervour, communalism could not acquire the character of a mass movement as in 1946-47. Religiosity also made it difficult to oppose communalism ideologically. And, of course, the communalists

[31]Jawaharlal Nehru, *SW*, Vol. 3, p. 1.

made every effort to promote religiosity and to strengthen the hold of religion over the popular mind. They strenuously opposed the notion that religion was "an individual question" or that it should be kept out of politics. Indians, they argued, were a religious and spiritual people in whose case religion had to pervade all areas of life.[32]

One reason for the greater success of communalism among Muslims, Sikhs and the Arya Samajists lay in religiosity being stronger among them. Nehru noted this as early as 1935:

> I avoided discussing this subject of religion with him (Mohammed Ali), because I knew we would only irritate each other, and I might hurt him. It is always a difficult subject to discuss with convinced believers of any creed. With most Moslems it is probably an even harder matter for discussion, since no latitude of thought is officially permitted to them. Ideologically, theirs is a straight and narrow path, and the believer must not swerve to the right or the left. Hindus are somewhat different, though not always so. In practice they may be very orthodox; they may, and do, indulge in the most out-of-date, reactionary 'and even pernicious customs, and yet they will usually be prepared to discuss the most radical ideas about religion. I imagine the modern Arya Samajists have not, as a rule, this wide intellectual approach. Like the Moslems, they follow their own straight and narrow path.[33]

One reason for this could be the character of Muslims, Sikhs and Arya Samajists as religious minorities—and Arya Samajists and Hindus were a religious minority in Panjab, the only province where the Arya Samaj could become popular. Possibly, the greater religious cohesion promoted by Islam and Sikhism, the existence of a single book to which appeal could be made to keep down heresies and heterodox sects, the existence of common religious symbols and

[32]See, for example, M.S. Golwalkar, *We*, p. 28; F.K. Khan Durrani, *The Meaning of Pakistan*, pp. 34-35, 37.

[33]Jawaharlal Nehru, *An Autobiography*, p. 118.

beliefs, and the fact that the two religions were born in recent recorded history and their founders were real historical characters may partially account for this stronger religiosity. All Muslims were supposed to belong to one society—the *Millat-e-Islamia,* just as all Sikhs were supposed to belong to one *Panth.* The *maulvis,* mullahs and Ulama and *granthis*—the religious priests or elite—had a very strong hold over the minds of Muslims and Sikhs, especially as they imparted religious instruction to young children. Among Muslims whatever education was imparted to children was mostly religious. The Khilafat and the Akali Movements, otherwise historically progressive and anti-imperialist, strengthened the hold of orthodoxy and priesthood over the minds of men and encouraged religiosity and the habit of looking at political questions from the religious point of view. At the Aligarh college and university, religiosity was consciously encouraged. The Arya Samaj and its schools and colleges too had this effect in Panjab. For example, while claiming to revive the Vedic learning, not a single Hindi or Urdu translation of the Vedas was published by the Arya Samajists. But the question of cow protection was taken up on a large scale. Other denominational educational institutions, such as Sikh, Islamia, and Sanatan Dharama schools and colleges, too encouraged and inculcated religiosity.

This greater religiosity opened Muslims and Sikhs to greater communal penetration and to the emotional cry of "*Islam* (or *Panth)* in danger" and made them readily believe in communal propaganda. It also generated intolerance, fanaticism and prejudice. These were then consciously utilized by the communalists.

A major reason for the weakness of the Hindu communal effort to grow and consolidate has been the much weaker religiosity among Hindus. Hindus were divided by the caste system. Orthodoxy was weak because of heterodox religious sects. Different castes had different concepts of *dharma* (many lower castes were denied access to Vedic religion; many others were beef-eaters). Among Hindus, therefore, there was less religious cohesion and a more diluted sense of religious identity and, consequently, a very weak response to the religious emotion and the cry of Hinduism in danger. Moreover, the priestly class was virtually absent. The task of the Hindu communalist was therefore doubly difficult. While the Muslim communalist had only to transform the Muslim religious identity into communalism, the Hindu communalist had also to *create* the Hindu religious identity. Because of sectarian diversity and inner divisions, the multiplicity of religious beliefs, dogmas and doctrines, the Hindu communalist could not appeal to religious orthodoxy and found that it was difficult to have any religion-based unity. He therefore found it expedient to adopt a definition of who was a Hindu that was not religious at all.[34] While the Muslim divines or Ulama could issue *fatwas* to propagate political causes, among Hindus the very authority to issue such religious edicts would have had to be first created. Efforts to copy the Ulama and make appeals through the so-called Shankaracharyas proved to be complete flops. Even the *Shuddhi* (conversion) campaign divided Hindus, for the questions immediately arose: Was it permitted by the shastras? And *Shudhhi* to which sect or caste? Similarly, the Hindu Mahasabha's efforts to better integrate the Scheduled Castes ran into heavy weather with the Sanatanist pundits.

Consequently, Hindus would respond more readily to the slogan of caste or sect in danger, or to a specific religious issue which made them active participants in a communal riot rather than in communal politics. The one major exception to this generalization were the followers of the Arya Samaj which consciously promoted religiosity and orthodoxy as part of a conscious policy of copying Islam.[35]

It may, therefore, be pointed out, in conclusion, that those who tried to perpetuate the medieval position of keeping religion a very

[34]See, for example, V.D. Savarkar, *Hindutva,* pp. 85, 88-89,102-06; M.S. Golwalkar, *We,* pp. 29-30, 48-49; Bhai Parmanand, *op. cit.,* pp. 5-11.

[35]The contribution of weak religiosity to the weakness of Hindu communalism has been recognized by the Hindu communalists who have made a conscious and vigorous effort since the 1960s to spread religiosity, especially among urban lower middle classes, even if this meant sacrificing their personal religious scruples; for example, the promotion of Bhagwati Jagran by the Arya Samajists among the RSS leaders. A similar effort to spread regular congregational prayers was made by the Hindu Mahasabha during the Second World War. The RSS also consciously set out to expand the role of religion to cover politics and other areas of life. See Golwalkar, *We,* pp. 27 ff.

large part of life under modern conditions, that is, those who spread religiosity, contributed, however indirectly, unconsciously or unwillingly, to the spread of communalism. They did so, in fact, even when they consciously opposed it.

Here, the role of the Ulama and Pan-Islamism was particularly negative. By asserting that Muslims constituted one single society, the *Millat-e-Islamia,* founded on the religious idea alone, by proving all their positions through the authority of the Quran and other religious texts, by demanding that Muslims should live under the *Sharia,* to be interpreted by the Ulama and not courts of law, so that there should be two separate systems of laws, that Hindu and Muslim children should go to separate schools, and that, in general, Muslims should be kept away from all modern culture and thought, by constant stirring up of religious sentiments, by constantly stressing that religion should encompass all other areas of personal, social and national life and by asserting the value of traditional religious forms of education, even the nationalist Ulama helped spread communalism by contributing massively to religiosity and the sense of religious and even communal identity among Muslims.[36] And, of course, when a section of the Ulama joined the Muslim League, this religiosity was turned massively against nationalism; any opposition to Pakistan being declared unislamic and even against the *Sharia.* The pro-Pakistan Ulama had a definite edge over the nationalist Ulama: while they could declare that Pakistan would be ruled according to *Sharia,* the nationalist Ulama could give no such assurance regarding a united India or Muslims in it. Nor could the nationalist Ulama issue a *fatwa* declaring Pakistan *haram* or *dar-ul-harab.* Similarly, Swami Dayananda, Swami Vivekananda, Aurobindo Ghose and Bipin Chandra Pal and

[36]One aspect of Pan-Islamism was, however, opposed to communalism. If Muslims were a world community, obviously Muslims in India did not need to be a separate community or state in India; they could as members of a world community be citizens of different states—including India. Moreover, this world community then could not be a community for secular purposes but only for religious purposes. Pan-Islamism would then strengthen a religious approach towards life but weaken the communal approach in India.

others encouraged religiosity and thus indirectly a sense of communal identity among Hindus.

Vast new areas of life were opened up in modern times. Either religion would intrude here or it would accept a steadily narrowing sphere of life for itself. In other words, secularism was partially the result of the expansion of life. Religion was not the cause of communalism but its elements served as an ideological vehicle for communalism. Secularization did not therefore mean removing religion or religious consciousness but it did mean reducing religiosity or increasingly narrowing down the sphere of religion to the private life of the individual. It may be noted in this respect that modern secular nations have shed religiosity and not religion.

The role of religious and social reform movements of the nineteenth and twentieth centuries, especially their revivalist wings, also deserves elucidation. These movements, known collectively as the Indian Renaissance, represented not just modernization but also a return to religious fundamentals and the 'great traditions' of Hinduism and Islam. That is, modernization was often accompanied by what sociologists describe as 'Sanskritization' and 'Arabization' or 'Islamization.'

The medieval period had witnessed a certain cultural rapprochement and the synthesis and the gradual development of a common culture among the upper and middle class Hindus and Muslims in different parts of the country. At the popular plane, popular religions with their mutual influences and therefore 'corrupted,' that is, unorthodox, forms had been bringing the common people together socially and culturally. There was adaptation by the high religions to a variety of tribal and local cultures and beliefs and to different caste traditions. Moreover, most Muslims were converts who carried with them into the new religion old religious and social beliefs and practices. The popular religions were highly eclectic in their beliefs and practices. The common popular culture and ways of life tended to prevail. Marriage and other social customs and practices tended to be uniform, or at least mutually influenced, in both their good and bad features. Hindus and Muslims shared common saints and *pirs, mazaars, dargas* and other holy places, and even popular gods and goddesses. Various syncretic cults had developed in different parts of the country. Some elements of the caste system, for example, food taboos, pollution and marriage restrictions, had become common to both. Holi, Dussehra, Durga Puja, Diwali, Rakhi and Id were often celebrated together by the common people as well as the ruling classes in the eighteenth century in Avadh, Bengal and many other areas. Even when these or other festivals, etc., were not celebrated or observed together, they were shared to a certain extent with the neighbours. The Muharram *Tazia* was an occasion for all, particularly for the Hindu women who, it was believed, could get a child if they walked under the *Tazia*. Astrology, palmistry and almanacs were used in common. Common literary tradition had developed based on secular heroes and heroines or common religious characters, symbols and myths. In this respect, a rather long extract from Dezil Ibbetson's late nineteenth century study of Panjab castes in the Census of 1881 is rather difficult to resist:

> As a fact in the east of the Panjab conversion has absolutely *no* effect upon the caste of the convert. The Musalman Rajput, Gujar, or Jat is for all social, tribal, political, and administrative purposes exactly as much a Rajput, Gujar or Jat as his Hindu brother. His social customs are unaltered, his tribal restrictions are unrelaxed, his rules of marriage and inheritance unchanged; and almost the only difference is that he shaves his scalplock and the upper edge of his moustache, repeats the Mahomedan creed in a mosque, and adds the Musalman to the Hindu wedding ceremony ... he even worships the same idols as before, or has only lately ceased to do so.

The fact is that the people are bound by social and tribal custom far more than by any rules of religion. Where the whole tone and feeling of the country-side is Indian, as it is in the Eastern Panjab, the Musalman is simply the Hindu with a difference. Where that tone and feeling is that of the country beyond the Indus, as it is on the Panjab frontier, the Hindu even is almost as the Musalman. The difference is national rather than religious.

Ibbetson further states:

> The laxity allowed by Mahomet in the matter of intermarriage has no effect upon the Musalman Jat of the Delhi division, for he has already refused to avail himself even of the smaller license allowed by the Hindu priests and scriptures, and bound himself by tribal rules far stricter than those of either religion. But the example of the Pathan and the Biloch has had a very great effect upon the Jat of the Multan division; and he recognizes, not indeed the prohibitions of Mahomet,—or rather not only them, for they represent the irreducible minimum,—but the tribal rules of his frontier neighbours, more strict than those of his religion but less strict than those of his nation. I believe that the laxity of the rules and restrictions imposed by the customs of castes and tribes which is observable in the Western Panjab, and among the Hindus no less than among the Musalmans, is due far more to the example of the neighbouring frontier tribes than to the mere change of faith. The social and tribal customs of the eastern peasant, whether Hindu or Musalman, are those of India; while in the west the people, whether Hindu or Musalman, have adopted in great measure, though by no means altogether, the social and tribal customs of Afghanistan and Bilochistan. In both cases those rules and customs are tribal or national, rather than religious.[37]

The social and religious reform movements, especially their revivalist wings, tended to reverse this trend. They attacked popular religious beliefs and practices as irrational and corrupted and debased forms of the original faith. Their emphasis was on the purity of faith

[37]Denzil Ibbetson, *Panjab Castes,* pp. 13-14. (Reproduces pp. 178-79 of the Census of Panjab, 1881.)

and the purging of popular religions of the so-called 'alien accretions.' Purity meant making religion more fundamentalist and less universal and returning to the distant and divergent traditions—traditions of periods when Hindus and Muslims had not known each other and which therefore separated them and widened the religious, cultural and social gulf between them. Thus, returning to the pristine purity of Hinduism and Islam and the purification of religious rites, rituals, beliefs and practices and social customs, traditions and values meant condemnation of religious syncretism, gradual elimination of common elements, checking the process of the evolution of a composite culture initiated during the medieval period and the creation of a greater distance between religions and people, producing a sense of cultural and social exclusiveness. In fact, quite often the revivalist reformers emphasized and proclaimed precisely those features of their religion in which it differed from other religions. The reformers also made an attempt to stop participation in each other's festivals, etc., or the offering of reverence to each other's *pirs,* saints, holy places, etc., or participation in common religious cults. This divisive aspect of the reform movements was noted in 1939 by Gandhi: "That we [Hindus and Muslims] appear to be farthest apart from one another today is a natural outcome of the awakening that has taken place. It has emphasized the points of difference and accentuated prejudices, mutual suspicions and jealousies."[38] The entire question has been clearly brought out by Beni Prasad, a fine representative of the medieval tradition of cultural synthesis and of the Allahabad school of secular social sciences. A rather long extract from his work on the communal question will not, therefore, be out of place:

> Revivalism weaned away the half-converts from the lingering Hindu beliefs and practices. On the other hand, the Hindu sub-castes which had adopted Muslim ways of living gravitated towards Hindu revivalism or modernism. Hindus and Musalmans alike began to give up many practices which they had imbibed from one

[38]M.K Gandhi, *Collected Works,* Vol. 69, p. 280.

another and which had formed bridges between the two communities. Many areas of common life and thought have thus been restricted and many meeting places obliterated. Revivalism leads to the withdrawal of one community from the other's festivals which the natural forces of sympathy and imitation tend to make common to both. It fosters a conscious retention and accentuation of existing divergences and the invention of new ones in regard to diet and dress, manners and etiquette and magnifies them all into profound 'cultural' diversities. It tends to diminish the common elements in the literary productions of the Hindus and the Musalmans and fosters itself by claiming control over the education of the young and founding separate schools, academies, colleges and universities. It imparts its tone to literature, favouring the elimination of Sanskrit terms from Urdu and that of Arabic terms from Hindi, Bengali and other languages. Revivalism prompts organization on communal lines and often assumes an aggressive tone which brings the different communities into acrimonious debate over theological and other matters.[39]

Reformist and revivalist movements also spread religious orthodoxy where heterodoxy had prevailed earlier. Even if they did not spread greater commitment to religion they spread religiosity and religious self-consciousness, that is, consciousness of being Hindu, Muslim or Sikh. Though often not communal by themselves, they made the

[39]Beni Prasad, *The Hindu-Muslim Questions,* pp. 25-26. Denzil Ibbetson also took note of this aspect in his study cited earlier. Continuing his analysis, he wrote: "At the same time there can be no doubt that both the artificial rules of Hindu caste, and the tribal customs which bind both Hindu and Musalman, have lately begun to relax, and with far greater rapidity among the Musalmans than among the Hindus. And this difference is no doubt really due to the difference in religion. There has been within the last 30 years a great Musalman revival in the Panjab; education has spread, and with it a more accurate knowledge of the rules of the faith and there is now a tendency which is day by day growing stronger, to substitute the law of Islam for tribal custom in all matters, whether of intermarriage, inheritance, or social intercourse. The movement has as yet materially affected only the higher and more educated classes; but there can be little doubt that it is slowly working down through the lower grades of society." *Op. cit.,* p. 14.

people, both the middle classes and the masses, more susceptible to communal propaganda.

Moreover, the revivalist movements in particular often affected and represented in the religious and social fields, the same social classes and groups as were evolving communal politics to serve their material and class needs, namely, the ruined zamindars, the emerging rural landlords and other intermediaries, the rising but insecure middle classes and the merchants and money-lenders. Also, these same social classes and groups monopolized the literary professions and were therefore in charge of ideology formation in the schools and colleges and through the Press, publications and political parties. They were in a position to use the growing modern means of communication to disseminate their ideas and ideologies among other sections of society.[40]

II. SOCIAL AND CULTURAL LAG

Due to numerous social and historical reasons, modern education and trade and industry did not make as much headway among Muslim (and Sikh) middle and lower middle classes as among other Indians of the same classes.[41] They lagged behind by decades in industry, trade, professions and higher education.[42] This resulted in the lag of

[40]We may point out in the end that we have dealt here only with the role of reform and revivalist movements in respect of the growth of communalism. Their other roles relating to cultural defence against the assault of colonial culture, promotion of self-respect and self confidence in face of constant imperialist denigration of Indian society and culture and the search and struggle for cultural identity and cultural autonomy were certainly important. Also, all reform movements did not bear the same relationship to religiosity and religious differentiation. Brahmo Samaj was, for example, more syncretic. I owe this point to K.N. Panikkar.

[41]The poor and the lower classes, as also the traditional upper class of zamindars and landlords, were educationally and economically backward both in case of Muslims and non-Muslims. Aparna Basu, *The Growth of Education and Political Development in India 1889-1920,* p. 152.

[42]Contrary to popular belief, except in Bengal, there was not much of a lag in employment in the government services in the last decades of the nineteenth century. Peter Hardy, *op. cit*,, pp. 123-24; Francis Robinson, *Separatism among Indian Muslims,* p. 46.

about half a century in the development of a modern intelligentsia, modern middle classes and a modern bourgeoisie—in short of modern civilization—among Muslims (and Sikhs).[43] This lag and not the lag in government jobs was to play the more important role in the growth of Muslim communalism.

What were the historical reasons for the aforementioned lag and the delay in the emergence of a modern intelligentsia and a modern bourgeoisie among Muslims? One important reason lay in the structure, character, mode of life and traditions of the upper classes of Muslims m northern India in the pre-British period. Almost all of them were 'feudal,' that is, based on land (as zamindars and jagirdars), the military and higher civil administration. Hindus predominated in positions in the lower rungs of civil administration and in trade and banking even during the medieval age. Thus, among Muslims what K. M. Ashraf describes as the jagirdari elements were the dominant elite. British rule deprived *all* Indians of top posts in the army and administration, while the lower posts proliferated further. The upper classes, which were more Muslim or among whom the number of Muslims was more, were hard hit, while the lower middle and middle classes, who were more Hindu or among whom the number of Hindus was more, proliferated. The latter took to modern education to protect positions in the lower and middle rungs of administration, while there was no way in which the upper classes could maintain their previous position in higher government posts in the face of the British policy of Europeanizing all higher services in the army and civil administration. At the same time, the upper classes, whether Hindu or Muslim, were not willing to stoop down to occupy the available inferior clerical posts which the lower middle class Hindus, traditionally used to occupying such posts, were glad to do. The Sikh upper classes also lost out in Panjab for similar reasons.

[43]Among Muslims, independent professionals such as lawyers, doctors, journalists and teachers in modern schools and colleges were fewer and zamindars and government servants and pensioners (serving or having served in British India or the princely states) greater in number.

Similarly, as we have seen earlier in Chapter 3, while the traditional zamindars, both Hindu and Muslim, were increasingly expropriated and deprived of administrative power, money-lenders, bankers and traders, who were mostly Hindus during the pre-British period, grew in numbers and economic strength and even moved into land as zamindars and landlords and into modern banking and industry.

Secondly, British conquest and its impact occurred at different times in different geographical areas of the country. Areas of Muslim upper class dominance—areas where Muslim elites lived—were conquered later and therefore felt the colonial impact later.

Thirdly, the traditional Muslim intelligentsia, the Ulama, were impoverished during the nineteenth century. Under the Mughals, they had been dependent on official grants and employment as judges *(qazis* and *muftis)* which now came to an end. This also initially led to the decline of the old educational system among Muslims.

Fourthly, the strata from which the modern middle classes and the intelligentsia could have initially arisen were also impoverished. Landed classes could have served as a major recruiting ground of the new intelligentsia and professionals. But they were undergoing rapid expropriation by the colonial state, urban merchants, money-lenders, officials, etc. Even so, they remained, among Muslims, the chief source for the supply of the modern intelligentsia, explaining both the short supply and its largely conservative character.

The British followed a policy of disfavouring the employment of Muslims in the higher branches of administration in northern India immediately after 1857, that is, just when the modern intelligentsia was being born in the country.

Lower middle class Muslims were thrown out of jobs on a large scale from the administration and the courts. They had been earlier dependent on service in the army and police, and, the educated ones, as munshis and clerks in the civil administration. Replacement of Persian by English as the official language struck them a major blow. Changes in the army and police had a similar effect. Still, in UP, the number of Muslims in the police bureaucracy was very large. This once again gave a conservative character to the Muslim intelligentsia which emerged from these bureaucratic strata.

Fifthly, Muslim revivalism and reaction kept modernization and 'renaissance' weak and thus hampered the emergence of a modern intelligentsia. It is interesting that Muslim revivalism was fully half a century ahead of Hindu revivalism and was much more backward looking, hide-bound and orthodox.

One form this reaction took was the effort to boycott modern, secular education. The mullahs and maulvis, aided and encouraged by sections of the old 'feudal' or jagirdari classes, incited Muslims against modern education and culture in the name of religion. They urged Muslims not to join modern schools and colleges because they were secular, imparted 'foreign' knowledge and were therefore 'unIslamic.'[44] Three other aspects were also significant. First, the relative weakness of the business and professional elite and of the lower middle classes meant that in some parts of the country there were not enough Muslim students who could pay the high fees in schools and colleges or could promote private educational institutions under the grants-in-aid system. Secondly, even when a Muslim student reached the new school or college, he was handicapped, in comparison with a Hindu or Parsi student, by the fact that religious orthodoxy had forced him to spend his earlier years in a traditional religious school. He was further handicapped by having to learn Arabic and/or Persian and in the case of Bengalis and Indians from the south or west also Urdu. Lastly, women's education was successfully opposed by the orthodox virtually till the 1920s. This weakened not only the emergence of a modern intelligentsia among Muslims but diluted its commitment to modernity when it did emerge. The neglect of modern education not

[44]Their success in delaying the spread of modern education among Muslims is brought out by the fact that as late as 1890 nearly half (47 per cent) of Muslims going to school in UP went to private, mostly religious, schools. The corresponding figure for Hindus was 18 per cent. Even in 1910 the two figures were 26.6 and 7.4 per cent, respectively. Moreover, new institutions imparting higher traditional religious education were established and gained in strength among Muslims. Francis Robinson, *op. cit.*, pp. 39, 274.

only strengthened the elements of cultural backwardness, but also further weakened the position of Muslims in the professions.

To sum up: the reasons for the smaller size of the middle classes among Muslims and for the backwardness of Muslim middle classes in modern education and modern culture and thought lay in specific historical circumstances and not in any effort by 'Hindus' to keep them backward.

All this meant that the modern intelligentsia, middle classes and bourgeoisie remained weak among Muslims, especially in northern and eastern India. Consequently, and this is the important part, the weight of landlords, zamindars and aristocracy in general—the jagirdari element—and the higher bureaucrats in the emerging political, social, cultural and economic elite among Muslims remained preponderant.[45] Or, in more recent terminology, not the modern intelligentsia but the jagirdari and bureaucratic elements remained the dominant elite among Muslims, exercising social, cultural, intellectual and political leadership and hegemony. Thus, for example, while in Calcutta, Bombay and Madras movements of social, economic, educational and political reform were led by modern intellectuals, the Aligarh movement was primarily led by nawabs, zamindars and bureaucrats—the main audience of Syed Ahmed Khan—and backed by the colonial administration.

By the time the Muslim intelligentsia was born in North India, the social context had changed. The process of a differential social development had left its mark. No doubt the educated Muslims were an educated 'class' or stratum, but they were a modern intelligentsia to a much lesser extent. Moreover, even the middle classes and the intelligentsia that did emerge had a 'feudal class affiliation' and colonial bureaucratic connections to a large extent. While the Hindu and Parsi educated had produced a major section imbued with radical ideas of rationalism, social reform, nationalism

[45]In fact, recent research shows that this is the only correct part of the theory of Muslim backwardness. In UP where Muslim communalism was the strongest Muslims were not backward in jobs, including higher jobs. See Francis Robinson, *op. cit.*, pp. 22-23, 38-39, 45-46.

and democracy, the late-comer Muslim educated stratum often grew under the patronage of imperialist authorities, big zamindars and big bureaucrats, and under the shadow of the orthodox Ulama. Since the role of the intellectuals was crucial in understanding the processes of social change under colonialism and in popularizing modern ideas, this development created a crucial lacuna among Muslims; it encouraged a conservative outlook among middle and lower middle class Muslims and made them an easy prey to communalism.[46] Moreover, when later the intellectuals and middle class politicians did acquire political leadership, they were compelled to form a political bloc with the jagirdari elements and ex-bureaucrats.

An interesting example of this jagirdari linkage of the emerging Muslim intelligentsia is provided by the melancholy and pessimism—the sense of 'heart-breaking grief' — that pervaded much of the poetry of Hali, Iqbal and other Muslim writers at the end of the nineteenth century and which is often explained as the expression of the Muslims' sense of plight and socio-economic deprivation because of the loss of power. After all, it was only the jagirdari elements which were 'losing power.' The mass of Muslims, as also the mass of Hindus, never had it. Moreover, only the jagirdari elements faced a future that was 'dark and bleak without any ray of hope'; the common people, the

[46]See K.M. Ashraf, *op. cit.,* pp. 61-62: "When fully half a century after Raja Rammohan Roy, Sir Syed laid the foundation of modern education, the social environment of Muslims had undergone a change. Instead of helping the struggle to get rid of British capitalism and imperialism, the Muslim middle class became a tool in the service of British interests; and in the new period Muslims were deprived of the leadership of a new healthy element. In short, a middle class did in the end emerge among Muslims half a century later; but this was a child born in old age which, instead of fighting the jagirdari camp-followers of British imperialism, began to grow up under their patronage under a system of job reservations. It also tended to acquire bureaucratic ambitions and a bureaucratic ethos. If one compares the Aligarh movement with the educational and social movements at Bombay, Calcutta, or Madras, at every step one will find Nawabs and jagirdars, who are spokesmen and tools of British rulers and British imperialist interests and who have come to monopolize both Aligarh educational movement and the 'national' politics of Muslims." One result was that "in the new era of the awakening of India and Asia, such camp-followers of imperialism as the Nawab of Dacca and Aga Khan came to be known as the leaders of Muslims." Translated from Urdu.

bourgeoisie and the new intelligentsia were beginning to fight for a bright future. Through Hali's *mussadas,* Iqbal's *Shikwa,* etc., the jagirdari ethos came to be identified with the ethos of all Muslims. In other words, most of the modern Muslim intellectuals—and much of the intellectual expression—of the late nineteenth century served as the organic intellectuals of the jagirdari elements of society, who were, for their own reasons, also pro-imperialism.

All this was of course true mainly of northern India, In southern and western India, the middle and upper classes of Muslims had a different historical background and pattern of social development under colonialism since there developed both a modern business class and a modern intelligentsia among them. Also there were no large jagirdari elements dominating their social, cultural, educational and political development. The result was that nationalist politics, social reform and modern education made headway among middle class Muslims in these areas. Moreover, Muslims constituted a very small part of the population in these areas. Also, in Bombay, Muslims were divided into a large number of heterodox sects, which lent a certain liberalism to their social outlook.

It should be kept in view, at this stage, that landlords and zamindars or jagirdari elements tended to be obscurantists, backward-looking, communal and pro-imperialist because of their social outlook and class position, irrespective of the fact whether they were Hindu or Muslim. They had fully accepted, especially after 1857, the policy of total subordination to the British rulers and increasingly based their politics on this position. But while among Hindus and Parsis the modern intelligentsia and the rising capitalist class had, by and large, pushed out the jagirdari elements from leadership and were exercising political and ideological hegemony with the ideology of nationalism, democracy, secularism and independent capitalist economic development, leadership over the Muslim masses and lower middle classes was exercised by the reactionary and loyalist jagirdari elements and by the backward-looking and communal intelligentsia. For example, Syed Ahmed Khan and Raja Shiva Prasad shared a common social background; and in the 1880s the two joined hands to launch an attack on the National Congress from the point of view of the landed, upper caste, pro-colonial elite. But while Syed Ahmed Khan occupied, till his death, a powerful social and political position among Muslims of North India, Shiva Prasad's influence among Hindus was soon overshadowed by the Congress leaders. On the other hand, where, as in Panjab, ex-bureaucrats, money-lenders and landlords and loyalist, castiest and communal intellectuals exercised hegemony over the Hindu masses and middle classes, the Congress failed to make much headway or retreated after the first advance.

A similar allied factor was the predominance of the bureaucratic element among the educated Muslims. Among the educated Indians in general, on the other hand, partially because of the very large size of the educated, the bureaucrats and ex-bureaucrats did not constitute the dominant element.

Once again, and this is often forgotten by those who treat all educated Indians as a single homogeneous social stratum or group, the bureaucrats and the ex-bureaucrats among Hindus, Parsis and Christians were also loyalist, reactionary and often communal. Nor were their interests compatible with nationalism. But the weight of the bureaucrats in the Hindu and Parsi middle classes was small. The pace-setters, the leaders and the makers of public opinion in the country as a whole were the modern intellectuals who were anti-colonial and on the whole secular and who tended towards radicalism in the contemporary sense; for example, Dadabhai Naoroji, Surendranath Banerjea, B.G. Tilak, G.K. Gokhale, early Badruddin Tyabji, M.K. Gandhi, Abul Kalam Azad, Jawaharlal Nehru and Subhash Chandra Bose. Consequently, while communalists and loyalists did emerge among Hindus and Parsis, they did not become a significant political and ideological force.

Among Muslims, at the end of the nineteenth century and the beginning of the twentieth century, the educated were few and these few could be absorbed and accommodated readily, to a larger extent than Hindus and Parsis, into government service in British India or the princely states. For example, a few well-placed job offers virtually eliminated the first generation of the Muslim nationalist intellectuals from the nationalist scene.[47] Moreover, the social aspirations of the few, newly educated Muslims tended towards government service, especially as professional openings were also getting reduced during the early years of the twentieth century and the economic basis for openings in trade and industry was very narrow among Muslims. Consequently, the bureaucrats and pensioners enjoyed a prominent social and political position within the Muslim middle classes, leading once again to politics of loyalism and communalism. One other result was that the Muslim masses and lower middle classes were, to some extent, deprived of modern ideas and ideologies. The modern secular and democratic intelligentsia did, of course, develop among Muslims in the 1930s and, as pointed out earlier, it took a turn towards left nationalism. But this development came rather late, for by then communalism was thriving. Moreover, the process of the leftward turn of the Muslim intelligentsia was reversed in the 1940s partially because of political errors by the National Congress and the Communist Party. The new intelligentsia was swept aside by or swept into the communal maelstrom of the 1940s

Among the zamindars and government servants, the very style and habit of taking a stand on demands against the government or of opposing the government were missing. They could only generate politics of loyalty or communalism and often both at the same time. And since the emerging intelligentsia among Muslims was also largely recruited from the jagirdari and bureaucratic strata, it tended to imbibe some of their conservatism and communalism.

Thus, except for the short period from 1916 to 1923 when the Muslim League joined the nationalist ranks and younger intellectuals took over, its leadership was studded with names such as Aga Khan, Nawab of Dacca, Nawab Mohsin-ul-Mulq, Nawab Waqar-ul-Mulk,

[47]Towards Hindus and Parsis too, the government followed the policy of coopting the emerging nationalist leaders. But in view of their large numbers, this policy could not absorb or eliminate the leadership group.

Raja of Mahmudabad, Nawab of Chhattari, Sir Sikandar Hayat Khan, Sir Feroz Khan Noon, Sir Zulfiqar Khan, Nawab Liaquat Ali Khan. In general, officials and ex-officials, big landlords and knights and Khan Bahadurs predominated in the League leadership up to 1947. The same was the case with the Hindu Mahasabha which was dominated by rich businessmen and landlords and successful bureaucrats such as Raja Rampal Singh, Raja Narendra Nath, Sir Gokul Chand Narang, Rai Bahadur Ram Saran Dass, Kurakoti Shankaracharya or their hangers-on such as Ganesh Dutt and B.S. Moonje. The big difference lay in the fact that while the weight of the Hindu Mahasabha in the country's politics was small, the weight of the Muslim League was significant.

This entire aspect can be summed up in the words of W. C. Smith:

> Rather than saying that the Muslim middle class was economically more backward, and more pro-British than the Hindu middle class, it would be more accurate to say that the economically backward, pro-British middle class was more Muslim than was the older, stronger, now fault-finding middle class.... He (Syed Ahmed Khan) was not, of course, able to persuade those few Muslims, who were members of the economically advanced sections, not to join the nationalist movement. But he was able to persuade the many Muslim members of the less advanced sections, who did not want to join it anyway, that they should not join it 'as Muslims.'[48]

We may only add that they, the less advanced, would not have joined it 'as Hindus' or 'as Parsis' either. Only, the Shiva Prasads the Bhingas, the Peary Mohan Mukerjis and the D.N. Petits failed to carry the middle class Hindus and Parsis with them.

The roots of the renaissance, the social and religious reform movements and modern ideas were no doubt quite shallow among the Hindu and Parsi middle classes, especially when compared with the

[48]W.C. Smith, *op. cit.*, p. 187.

penetration of the renaissance and the rationalist movement in thought among the European middle classes. But, none the less, these ideas and movements were present. The Muslim middle classes were much less open to renaissance and modern ideas. There was a much lesser spread of enlightenment. They remained much more traditional and backward,[49] and therefore easier prey to pre-modern forms of self-perception. This was so for several reasons: the lateness of and the delay in the reform effort; the stronger hold of orthodoxy, the very revivalism having occurred during the first half of the nineteenth century;[50] the large social influence of landlords and bureaucrats and the strong affiliation of the new intelligentsia with these two social strata; and the virtual absence of an organized movement for social and religious reform.

Thus, for example, Syed Ahmed Khan had planned and initiated a comprehensive religious, intellectual, cultural and educational reform movement during the 1860s and 1870s. In some of his efforts, he had taken the support of enlightened Hindus. But he soon came under pressure from the orthodox Ulama and big zamindars. In order to save his educational efforts and to promote the Aligarh College, he found it necessary to placate the jagirdari elements and colonial authorities, who could hamper or even thwart these efforts both directly by withholding financial grants and because of their influence over the jagirdari and bureaucratic elements, and gave up all reform efforts in other directions and also abandoned all politics. As S. Abid Husain points out, he had to "sacrifice some of his most cherished objectives. He had to close the organ of his mission of reform. *Tahzib-ul-Akhlaq,* and promise that religious education in the Aligarh College would be given in the strictly traditional way without the slightest

[49]As S. Abid Husain remarks: "This darkness of their (Muslims') ignorance was so profound that the light of the various reform movements was lost in it. The movements with which Sir Syed, the nationalist Ulama and Badruddin Tyabji were associated, tried, each in its own way, to bring about reforms, and achieved some measure of success. Yet having reached a certain point they found their way blocked...." *Op. cit.,* p. 53.

[50]The Mughal period itself witnessed two major reactionary revivalist movements based on and preaching rigid orthodoxy—those of Shaikh Ahmad Sirhandi in the seventeenth century and Shah Walliullah in the eighteenth.

tinge of his own particular ideas."[51] Moreover, as brought out in Chapter 4, he openly denounced ideas of democracy and social equality which his contemporary nationalist intellectuals were adopting and vigorously propagating. We should note that Lala Hansraj also abandoned nationalist politics to be able to promote and preserve the Dayananda Anglo-Vedic schools and colleges. But then, he never became a major political figure even in Panjab, not to speak of northern India.

Similarly, the Aligarh College and the Aligarh University, which were from the 1870s to the 1940s the cradle of the modern Muslim intelligentsia, included from the beginning a large component of religion.[52] Religious conservatism and orthodoxy and the religious content of the syllabi were further strengthened in the first decades of the twentieth century as a result of a conscious effort to come closer to the Ulama. Even otherwise, the character of education at Aligarh had a conscious bureaucratic and jagirdari orientation. Consequently, the Aligarh student was intellectually much less liberated than his contemporaries. Moreover, the education imparted at Aligarh College, as also in many of the government colleges in the North, where other Muslim students went for higher education, was much more colonial.[53] There was a preponderance of colonial culture and intellectual milieu, and the student was carefully guarded against nationalist ideas and agitation. Similarly, the resurgence of higher religious educational institutions from the end of the nineteenth century weakened the spread of modern ideas among Muslims and increased priestly authority in the realm of ideas and ideologies.

[51]S. Abid Husain, *op. cit.,* p. 31.

[52]"The first period of each day's work in Aligarh College was devoted to lectures on Islam. Attendance at these lectures was enforced by regulations as stringent as those relating to ordinary class work of the College. All Muslim students were required to pray 5 times a day. Absence from prayers was punished by a fine. Fasting during the month of Ramzan was mandatory, except in exceptional circumstances." H. Malik, *Muslim Nationalism in India and Pakistan,* p. 215.

[53]According to an old Aligarh graduate, S. Bashiruddin, those who controlled the Aligarh College and the Aligarh University "succeeded in producing generations of young men with no political awareness of any description and with deep-rooted obscurantist ideas about Islam." "Pan-Islamism in Indian Politics and the Khilafat Agitation."

All this also made the Muslim middle classes much more prone to religiosity and reactionary socio-political ideas and reduced the social weight of the modern democratic and nationalist intelligentsia among Muslims. And, of course, the effects of middle class conservatism penetrated downwards to the masses. The effects of the Hindu tinge of the national movement were also intensified by this social, religious, intellectual and political conservatism. A more modern and radical intelligentsia could have opposed the Hindu tinge more successfully and without falling into the communal trap.

Also, the very conservatism of Muslim intellectuals and middle classes made them view modern nationalism, especially as it gradually became more and more radical, as inimical to their social and religious institutions and traditions, which they prized because of the lack of renaissance and modernity. Quite often, the 'Hindu' threat was the threat of modernity. Once the nationalist movement came to represent strong modernity and colonialism began to support orthodoxy and the *status quo* in almost every field, the social reactionaries, the orthodox and the vested interests saw in the former a greater threat to their position. This is one reason why both Hindu and Muslim communalists and reactionaries saw in the mass-based secular nationalism of Gandhi and the left nationalism of the irreligious Nehru, socialists and communists a grave threat to their 'communities' while the foreign Western colonial authorities were often seen as guardians of their communal interests and even as 'defenders of the faith.'

Two other aspects of the weak renaissance also need to be kept in view. The fact that it was confined in the main to the middle classes meant that it was weak among Muslims for another reason—they had a much smaller modern middle class. If it had been a more thorough-going cultural phenomenon, it would have touched all sections of society and not let unevenness develop in its impact and permeation, because unevenness in class formation among Hindus and Muslims was confined to the formation of the capitalist and middle classes. Not the Muslim 'community' but the Muslim middle classes and bourgeoisie lagged behind their counterparts among Hindus; the Hindu and Muslim masses were after all equally backward.

It should also be remembered that the shallow social base of the renaissance among the masses and its weak and compromising character among the Hindu middle and lower middle classes kept a potential base for overt communalism and an actual base for covert or hidden communalism among them. Thus, communalism in some form was quite strong among Hindu middle classes till the early 1930s. Similarly, the Hindu denominational colleges and the Benares Hindu University too were hotbeds of obscurantism and communalism. Only, most of the intellectuals among Hindus were not educated and trained there. Not so much the Hindu middle classes as the modern intelligentsia was basically secular and democratic. Herein lies the significance of the nineteenth-century renaissance and the twentieth-century socialist movement. With all their weaknesses, the two guaranteed that from Raja Rammohan Roy to Jawaharlal Nehru the intellectually and politically hegemonic intelligentsia, the intelligentsia whose vision of society, of its social, cultural, economic and political development would prevail and would face no serious challenge, would be among Hindus and Parsis secular, rationalistic and democratic. The opposite was the case among Muslims.

The combined result of the two factors just discussed, namely, that the dominant or hegemonic class bloc among Muslims consisted of the jagirdari and bureaucratic elements and that there was a lesser spread of modern ideas among Muslims, was that the predominant social and political influence among them was not that of the democratic intelligentsia and secular and democratic ideologies but that of landlords, bureaucrats, mullahs, *maulvis* and semi-feudal (jagirdari) and colonial culture and ideas which gradually consolidated around the communal ideology.

III. CULTURAL BACKWARDNESS, ETHICAL VACUUM AND SOCIAL BARRIERS

The cultural and intellectual backwardness of the Indian people contributed to the growth of communalism because it enabled the communal leaders to misrepresent their socio-political situation and to misdirect their struggles to improve their existing social condition into communal channels.[54] It was this backwardness which made it possible to give, as we have seen earlier, the class struggles of the workers and peasants a communal or caste colour or to turn petty bourgeois frustrations into communal channels. It also enabled the vested interests, both Indian and foreign, to use communal issues and identities to serve their own interests.

Also important here was the fact that the cultural and intellectual level of the mass of educated Indians was also quite low. Because of the colonial character of the Indian educational system, which discouraged the development of critical faculties and independent thought, the literate and the educated were equally ill-equipped to resist communal ideology.[55] In fact, in the absence of adequate cultural, intellectual and political content, literacy and modern means of communication such as the Press, pamphlets and posters made possible the easier and more rapid penetration of communal propaganda. On their part, the nationalist and anti-communal forces failed to seriously take up the question of raising the cultural level of the people.

Crisis in and the disintegration of the old world and the gradual erosion and breakdown of traditional moral values under conditions of colonialism tended to create an ethical vacuum and moral root-lessness which, in their turn, produced an ideal ground for the propagation and flourishing of modes of thought and action based on

[54]For example, the class struggle of the Mappila tenants against Hindu land-lords and their anti-imperialist sentiments could be readily turned into communal channels because of the tenants' cultural backwardness, illiteracy and intense religiosity.

[55]The widespread belief that pre-1947 education was superior to today's is nothing but a myth. It might have enabled its recipients to write better English; but its intellectual content was rather shallow. The positive cultural and intellectual impulses in the colonial period came almost entirely from the nationalist movement and the non-academic nationalist intelligentsia. Today, the communal forces are trying their best to prevent the development of higher standards in education. Using populism, they have been attempting to reduce the school and college curricula to pre-1947 levels.

communal and fascist immorality,[56] irrationality, hatred, fear, conflict and violence.

Similarly, colonialism (and underdeveloped capitalism) introduced acquisitiveness, competitiveness and 'naked self-interest' on a large scale without full-fledged growth of capitalism and economic development which could satisfy them. Colonial capitalism created desires which colonial underdevelopment frustrated. This was a basic feature of colonialism and one of its most negative aspects. Entire groups and strata were engendered which wanted wealth and power and which had few traditions or values which could deter them from following any and every means of acquiring them. Yet, the social existence, desires and ambitions of most of them were destined to be frustrated. Moreover, traditional social ties and loyalties to family, kin and locality were gradually getting dissolved, especially in the cities, but no new, strong ties were getting formed. This social milieu without values and full of material, social and psychological frustrations was ideally conducive to irrational philosophies and ideologies, movements of hate and fear, crass individual strivings and the setting of one group against another.[57] The extreme barbarism, brutality and cruelty witnessed during the communal riots were also due in part to the cultural backwardness of the people, in part to the fact that the main participants in these riots were the urban poor who had lost all moral inhibitions in the course of their struggle for bare subsistence and in part to the middle strata's bitter fight to preserve their existing social position. There was a need to fill this moral vacuum; there was a need for new, positive values and morality to combat the irrational

[56]"There can be nothing more immoral and cowardly than the killing of innocent people in individual stabbings in the dark or virtual lynching by hysterical crowds which far outnumber their victims. Communal killings seldom take place in the form of pitched battles between well-matched crowds or "volunteers."

[57]Or, as K.B. Krishna has put it: "This conflict between traditional moral precepts and actual needs has produced a class, a decaying class, whose social instincts are dead, whose private interests are everything, who have become the hirelings of political padres. These weak classes who realize their private instincts in stealth, who disregard moral precepts in the dark.... To observe religion in the open to back up their interests, crawling on their bellies, and to disregard it in the dark to back up some other needs are the characteristics of these weak decaying classes." *Op. cit*,, p. 284.

and immoral doctrines. Gandhian 'villageism' and emphasis on traditional moral values and, to a certain extent, even revivalism were partly a reaction to the moral disintegration of colonial society. Once again, the national movement and the left-wing forces failed to move into the breach and take up in earnest the struggle for the inculcation of new values and the preservation of the best of the old values. This was in a way surprising because the leaders and cadres of these movements had themselves joined them basically out of a sense of moral commitment and should have therefore seen the need for the moral renovation of society.

The Hindus' tendency towards social exclusiveness made its own contribution towards the growth of communalism. The caste system is based on social narrowmindedness and exclusiveness and on a system of social taboos. Social intercourse among Hindus was guided by this rigid system of caste hierarchy. They also extended it to their relations with Muslims who were treated socially as outsiders and therefore outside the caste system and caste hierarchy. As between different Hindu castes, there was also no intermarriage between Hindus and Muslims. What was much worse, traditionally there was also no interdining. Moreover, the average Hindu would not take food or water from the hands of a Muslim or even if touched by a Muslim. A constant reminder of this 'touch-me-notism' was the cry of 'Hindu *pani* and 'Muslim *pani* at the railway platforms and bus stands. In big cities, Hindus and Muslims had a tendency to live apart in different *mohallas* or areas. Because of the relative absence of interdining and intermarriage, social contact between the urban lower middle class Hindus and Muslims tended to be minimal.

However, though such social taboos and exclusiveness created a certain social distance and perhaps even psychological separation or a sense of separate identity among Hindus and Muslims and, to a certain extent, acted as a psychological irritant, they were not a causative factor in the rise of communalism. They arose out of certain ritualistic and caste considerations. Since Muslims (and Christians) were by definition outside the caste system, all caste taboos automatically applied to them. While this led to social taboos in certain fields, Muslims (and Christians) were not untouchables; they were just outside the caste society. Hence, basically there was no racial or superiority or inferiority complex involved in them from either side, except to the extent that one considered one's own religion to be superior.[58] They had prevailed even when the rulers and many high officials had been Muslims. And even in modern times they prevailed between socially and economically superior Muslims' and their inferiors among Hindus, that is, between Muslim masters and Hindu servants, Muslim landlords and Hindu tenants They often prevailed between the English Sahibs and their humblest chaprasis or clerks. For centuries, Muslims had not seen these social taboos and exclusiveness, as well as the social practices in which they were manifested, as derogatory or as signifying discrimination and degradation. Instead, they were seen as peculiar features of the religion and caste-based social order of Hindus.[59]

Consequently, they did not produce a sense of resentment or degradation and oppression as was produced among the untouchables. They also did not produce, nor were they seen as grounds for, social tensions between Hindus and Muslims. Nor should the social distance between Hindus and Muslims be exaggerated. The gap was never unbridgeable or nasty. There certainly was social heterogeneity but too much should not be made of it—it was not true that Hindus and Muslims were 'in all social matters total aliens.' There existed a great deal of common social and cultural life. As a pro-Pakistan writer acknowledged at the height of the movement for Pakistan: "Among ordinary folk not connected with the court, the same old relations of

[58]In particular, to an orthodox Hindu a Muslim was a *mlechchha* and to an orthodox Muslim a Hindu was a *kafir.*

[59]Even upper caste Hindus practised all types of social taboos against each other. A Brahmin cook would observe food taboos against his Rajput or Baniya or Khatri employer. The Muslim upper classes were no less split by 'racial' and social differences, only the social taboos took less naked and less extreme forms. Moreover, often even caste taboos were not, except in the case of untouchables, symbols of discrimination, degradation and social oppression. See, B.C. Pal, *Memories of My Life and Times,* Vol. I, pp. 106-08.

courtesy, regard and good neighbourliness continued and did so to our times.... (There was) an atmosphere of social harmony and peace. Hindus and Muslims participated in one another's festivals, marriages and other domestic events and shared their joys and sorrows."[60] Similarly, B.C. Pal, after discussing the wide participation of Hindus in Muharram in a Sylhet village in the 1860s and 1870s, pointed out in his autobiography that ritualistic considerations in no way affected social life in the village among Hindus and Muslims:

> The community in our village was ... a very mixed one. We had not only almost every important Hindu caste but a fairly large Mohammedan population also. And the intercourse between the Hindus and the Mohammedans was almost as free and friendly as that among the different Hindu castes themselves. In my father's house we used to invite our Mohammedan neighbour, the zemindar, to all our domestic functions, except the Pujas, which they could not attend, though there was regular exchange of presents between us during the Mohammedan festival of Id as well as on occasions of marriage or death.

Pal continues:

> This Mohammedan neighbour, I still remember, used to send a piece of cloth and a couple of rupees whenever there was any *shradh*

[60]F.K. Khan Durrani, *op. cit.*, p. 43. Similarly, what Beni Prasad says about the medieval period was in general equally true of nineteenth and twentieth century India: "Caste and creed forbade inter-marriage but there were classes to which Hindus and Musalmans alike belonged—classes of peasants, landlords, traders, artisans and labourers, soldiers, government servants, etc. Within a class, Hindus and Musalmans were often indistinguishable from each other in dress, housing, etiquette and manners, whether in villages or in towns. The position of women, the age of marriage and even some wedding rituals were uniform within a class and common to its Hindu and its Muslim members. It was only natural that Hindus and Muslims should join one another's festivals. There was a broad identity of economic interests which held a class together and cut across the religious cleavage. Behind it all was the similarity in the standards set up by Hindu and Muslim ethical codes." Also: "Painting, another of the great modes of the expression of a people's soul, develops from the sixteenth century onwards in common schools at the hands of Hindu and Muslim masters and becomes truly Indian. Styles of music and dance became and have remained absolutely common." *Op. cit.*, pp. 12-13 and 11, respectively.

> or after-death ceremony in our house; and we used to return these to them on similar occasions. We were permitted to catch fish from their tanks on every festive occasion in our house as they were permitted to freely use our fish preserve for their own use on festive occasions in their own house. In these matters no manner of distinction was made between our Hindu and our Mohammedan neighbours. And the general Moslem population of the village were (*sic*) treated similarly and practically on the same footing of social equality, within the limitations that caste and religion imposed, as the Hindu peasantry used to be treated. Our differences in religious faiths and practices made not the slightest difference in these social amenities and relations. There was perfect toleration of one another among members of both the communities.[61]

A survey of a Panjab village carried out by the Panjab Board of Economic Inquiry in the early 1930s noted:

> There are two mosques built of burnt bricks and in very good condition. Separate rooms in the compound are provided for travellers and marriage parties of all faiths and creeds. The investigator saw a Hindu marriage party staying in these rooms and singing songs, but, of course, stopping at the times of Muslim prayers. The inhabitants of the village have been accustomed to these conditions from time immemorial.[62]

Regarding life in his twin-villages, Zeradei and Jamapur, Rajendra Prasad noted in his *Autobiography:*

> As one could see, religion permeated the village life, and there was perfect harmony between Hindus and Muslims. Muslims would join Hindus in the boisterous festival of Holi. On the occasion of Dasahra, Diwali and Holi, the Maulavi would compose special verses.... Hindus participated in Mohurrum by taking out Tazias.

[61]B.C. Pal, *op. cit.,* Vol. I, pp. 109-110. Comments regarding Muharram are on pp. 88-92.

[62]*An Economic Survey of Naggal,* p. 2.

> The Tazias of the well-to-do Hindus in Zeradei and Jamapur were bigger and brighter than those of the poor Muslims.... [In the Tazia procession] the atmosphere would be surcharged with enthusiasm and all distinctions between Hindus and Muslims would disappear.[63]

Moreover, the social gap and social taboos differed from province to province, from city to town to village and from class to class. The upper classes and the professionals always had a large number of avenues for social intercourse, irrespective of religion. The social gap was also much less in villages and small towns than in big cities. At the village level, Hindus and Muslims lived within a common socio- economic framework, based on a network of common ties and a large number of common social customs and conventions and cultural forms. In general, except for interdining and intermarriage, there was a great deal of free social mixing within the same social class or group, irrespective of religion. It was among the urban lower middle classes, especially among the women, that the social gap tended to become a gulf. And this had an exaggerated effect later, when lower middle classes became the most active element in Indian politics.

Nor should too much be made of food taboos. They were often overcome by Muslims entertaining their Hindu friends by getting food or sweets from a Hindu shop or the house of another Hindu friend or neighbour. No sense of inferiority was felt. For example, after Shahu, the grandson of Shivaji, and his mother fell into Aurangzeb's hands, the latter saw to it for years that the strictest of Hindu social and food taboos were observed in housing and feeding them.[64] Rajendra Prasad also notes in his *Autobiography* that when after festivals, etc., "sweets were distributed, everyone would put out his hand, but the Hindus would not take water from a Muslim. The Muslims, however, understood Hindu sentiments and did not mind it."[65]

[63]See pp. 13-14. Also see Shibli Nomani, quoted in K. B. Sayeed, *op. cit.*, pp. 36-37; M.L. Darling, *Rusticus Loquitor*, pp. 22, 42, 62-63, 75, 137, 288-89.

[64]H.N. Sinha, *Rise of the Peshwas*, pp. 12-13.

[65]See p. 14.

A bit of autobiography may not be out of turn here, for Indians of today, brought up in the communal atmosphere of the 1940s and after, may not be able to capture the social spirit of the pre-communal times when communalism was yet weak or even absent.[66] In my home town, in the then Panjab, it was usual for the Hindu middle class families to send Diwali sweets to their middle class Muslim friends. The latter in their turn sent Id sweets—only they would be brought directly from the Hindu sweet shop to the Hindu homes. I still remember a dramatic incident of my childhood which to me is a constant reminder of the true state of affairs as late as 1937. I was eating *chat* during the school break when my Muslim friend ran into me and touched my chat-holding hand. When he found that I was not throwing the *chat* away, he urged me to do so since otherwise I would become *bhrasht* (polluted). Being enlightened, the result of nationalist propaganda, and perhaps greedy, I refused to do so. He threatened to report my behaviour to my parents. When this produced no effect, he, being bigger and tougher, forcibly snatched the *chat* plate and threw it away saying that he could not permit a friend of his to go to hell. Similarly, according to Prof. Moonis Raza, in his hometown in UP, social distance was maintained horizontally according to social class differentiation and not religion. Food taboos were observed but accommodated *within* the social differentiation. Thus, when a Muslim hosted a dinner, all upper class and upper caste Hindus and Muslims ate at the same time, though in separate dining areas, and all lower classes and lower castes ate later, again at the same time, though again in separate dining areas. Social distance was therefore symbolized not by separate areas of dining but separate, hierarchical timing of the dinner service. Thus, a Hindu upper class Rajput or Brahmin ate simultaneously with the Muslim host while a Muslim *julaha* (weaver) or a Hindu lower caste servant of the same caste rank ate afterwards but simultaneously with each other. Of course, during the 1930s, many educated Hindus and Muslims,

[66]Similarly, most foreign scholars working on the communal problem tend to quite wrongly view the social problem against the background of white racism or anti-Semitism of their own societies.

especially lawyers, doctors and government servants, also dined together. According to Raza, many pious old Muslim ladies, etc, would not eat food cooked or served by Hindus as a part of their practice of piety, without being conscious of any sense of social superiority except that of class, caste or racial origin, i.e., foreign descent such as Irani, Turki and Arab, or native 'Hindustani' descent.

However, the social exclusiveness and the taboos always contained certain potentialities for mischief and misunderstanding. In a new socio-political situation, and once communalism started burgeoning, though for other reasons, these taboos began to be seen by the educated Muslims in a different light. To modern persons brought up on ideas of social equality, they appeared to be derogatory and discriminatory. They became constant irritants and reminders of the social distance between Hindus and Muslims. Above all, they could be used by the communalists to spread anti-Hindu feelings and a sense of social bitterness among the Muslim lower middle classes and thus to stoke the fires of communal hatred. These social taboos were now seen or portrayed as proofs of the fact that Hindus despised and disliked Muslims and held them in total contempt. This was in particular true of Bengal where, unlike in Panjab, Kerala or UP, social taboos against Muslims were an aspect of the Hindu zamindars' class contempt for the poor Muslim tenant-cultivators.[67]

Thus, in 1918, the *Al-Eslam* from Bengal wrote that one of the four reasons for Hindu-Muslim friction was that: "Ordinary Muslims complain that Hindu zamindars behave unfairly towards them, and even ordinary Hindus make insinuations and behave in a hostile contemptuous manner towards them on the streets, in trains and steamers and in the market place."[68] Similarly, *Banga Nur* wrote in 1920 that among the sources of Hindu-Muslim tension were "fear of

[67]Interestingly, the Muslim zamindars and the other Muslim upper strata in Bengal were nearly as contemptuous and socially distant from the Muslim peasantry. Unlike the Hindu zamindars, they did not share even a common language with them. They took pride in using Urdu in place of Bengali. Kamruddin Ahmad, *A Social History of Bengal*, pp. 12-13.

[68]M.N. Islam, *Bengal Muslim Public Opinion as Reflected in the Bengal Press 1901-1930*, p. 111.

Muslim pollution (and) use of abusive terms such as *Yavana* and *Mlechchha*."[69] A correspondent of *Saugat*, again from Bengal, wrote in 1928 that though historically *Yavana* meant foreigners "those who now use it to mean 'Muslim' feel in their hearts a very definite abhorrence."[70] M.A. Jinnah was to assert in 1940 that one of the reasons why Hindus and Muslims could never form one Indian nation was because "they neither intermarry nor interdine together."[71] By the 1930s, the social exclusiveness of Hindus was being seen even by nationalist writers as a factor that contributed to the spread of communalism. Thus Shaukatullah Ansari wrote in 1945: "The crux of the problem is that the Hindus are small-minded in the social field, and that has touched the Muslims to the quick. Hindus have treated Muslims as untouchables.... Whatever reasons the Hindus may have, the Muslims cannot help being aggrieved by this attitude.... The Muslim heart-burning remains acute and engenders hate in the hearts of those who are humiliated by the Hindus."[72] Similarly, Humayun Kabir wrote in 1942: "The attitude of the Hindu in social matters towards all non-Hindus in general and the Moslem in particular has been one of the most potent causes of Hindu-Muslim misunderstanding and ill-feeling. Social disabilities obtrude themselves upon the consciousness in a way in which economic or even political ones do not...." He however added: "Social disabilities are in the end only symptoms which express a deeper malaise and this will be found to

[69] *Ibid., p.* 115.

[70] *Ibid., p.* 121.

[71] M.A. Jinnah, *op. cit.*, Vol. I, p. 160. Also see *ibid.*, pp. 217, 230; C. Manshardt, *The Hindu-Muslim Problem in India*, pp. 37-38.

[72] S. Ansari, *op. cit., p.* 27. Similarly, an Ahrar leader, Ch. Afzal Haq wrote: "Musalmans of the Aryan race, Musalmans of the Sufi cult, Musalmans of the High Houses, Musalmans of good education were treated alike as untouchables of the Hindu society. You may be a pucca nationalist and a four-square Gandhite, yet you will be treated as an untouchable as soon as you announce to a Hindu that you are a Musalman. However justified the Hindus feel and however innocent they plead in their treatment of the Musalmans, in justice they cannot blame the latter if they cultivate an ill-feeling towards them." A. Mehta and A. Patwardhan, *The Communal Triangle in India*, p. 182.

lie in economic and political inequities."[73] Gandhi too acknowledged the force of this argument. Answering a question on untouchability, he wrote in the *Harijan* of 25 May 1940: "I regard untouchability as the root cause of our downfall and of Hindu-Muslim discord."[74]

The relative social gap or lack of social contact among urban Hindus and Muslims contributed to the spread of communalism in another, more serious manner. It tended to breed on its own, as well as made it easier to breed, stereotypes. This tendency was fully utilized by communal propagandists to spread contempt as well as fear and hatred of persons following other religions. Though not a causative factor in the rise or growth of communalism, it was a major weapon in the communal armoury.

The Hindu communalists portrayed the Muslim as lacking in culture and as a *goonda,* a bully and a bloodthirsty brute whose natural instinct was to loot, kill, burn and rape. In the communal image, a Muslim was a man of low morals and uncontrolled sexual lust who was ever ready to seduce, abduct and assault Hindu women. It was therefore not safe for Hindu women to go into Muslim localities. Nor were they safe even in their own localities unless the Hindu youth were organized to defend their honour. This stereotype of Muslims was then used to create fear and a defensive mentality among Hindus even though they were a majority in the country. The Hindu communalists also created the stereotype of the 'mild,' 'docile' and 'emasculated' Hindu in order to goad Hindus to transform themselves

[73]H. Kabir, *op. cit.,* p. 30. Earlier still, Rabindranath Tagore had written in 1907: "Wc know, that in many places in Bengal Hindus and Muslims do not sit side by side on the same mattress. If a Muslim comes to a (Hindu) home, the carpet is removed and the water inside the *Hookah* is thrown away, thus wc suffer from a sinful attitude regarding Hindu-Muslim relations. We cannot escape now, without paying the price for our sin." Quoted in G. Chattopadhyay, *Role of Bengal Legislature in the Freedom Struggle,* Chapter 3.

[74]M.K. Gandhi, *Collected Works,* Vol. 72, p. 77. The situation has a parallel in Panjab today. For decades Sikhs did not mind jokes made at their cost. But once Hindu and Sikh communaiisms hostile to each other have developed, they are seen as anti-Sikh and today certainly their narration leads to growth of communalism. Surprisingly, as was the case with food and drink taboos earlier, secular forces are doing little to oppose the propagation of such jokes, etc.

into a 'militant people' by organizing along communal and fascist lines. In fact, they said, once Hindus became 'strong,' it would bring about Hindu-Muslim unity for Muslims would no longer dare attack them![75]

The Muslim communalists created the stereotype of the Hindu as a calculating, crafty, dubious Baniya who could not be trusted and whose every word must be watched for a twist. Consequently, all assurances given by 'Hindu' politicians were useless. Moreover, all Hindus were money-mad exploiters in deep contrast to Muslims who cared little for money and had "no idea of exploitation."[76] Hindus were a nation of capitalists and pen-pushing babus. Indian nationalism was consequently branded as 'Baniya imperialism.' Above all, Hindus were cringing cowards whose cowardice was symbolized by the *dhoti.* The stereotypes of the cowardly Hindu and the strong Muslim were also used by the Muslim communalists to create bellicosity and prove the viability first of minority fascist communalism and then of Pakistan, which would be much smaller than the remaining India.

[75]See, for example, Shraddhananda quoted in G.R. Thursby, *Hindu-Muslim Relations in British India,* p. 164; M.M. Malaviya in *ibid.,* p. 162; Lajpat Rai, quoted by Bhai Parmananda in Indra Prakash, *op. cit.,* pp. xiii-xxi; V.D. Savarkar, *Hindu Rashtra Darshan,* pp. 134-35; Shyama Prasad Mookerjee, *Awake Hindusthan,* pp. 83-84. In other contexts, Muslim communalists repeated this argument. See, for example, Jinnah quoted in Z.H. Zaidi, *op. cit.,* p. 250.

[76]See, for example, F.K. Khan Durrani: "The Hindu lives to earn and hoard, while the Muslim earns to live and spend. The Hindu's inordinate love of money is a most amazing phenomenon. It governs his whole life and thought and occupies his whole mind till he dies. The food he eats is wretched. He seems to live upon nothing in fact. The Muslim, on the other hand, is a notorious good eater. When he marries, he looks for a self-contained suite of rooms, where he will enjoy decent privacy and an independent home life. Hindus of equal and even better incomes live promiscuously. A tenement building of fifty rooms might be housing as many as fifty families, and the rooms in Hindu houses are usually small. One might say, they do not live at all; they just earn, save and die. So much love of money is a curse; to individuals and nations it is all round a curse. It creates economic inequalities which lie at the bottom of many a social evil." He further states: "To the Hindu it has given a peculiar character, a peculiar cast of mind, a habit of thought which we Muslims of northern India just do not understand, and the same is more or less true of the Muslims of other parts of India. Europeans and Americans, too, cannot understand it, for there is nothing like it in their countries, except among the Jews. But, then, Jews are but small minorities in Western lands, whereas our Jews are the overwhelming majority." *Op. cit.,* p. 198. Also see pp. 196-97.

Similar stereotypes have been actively propagated about each other by Sikh and Hindu communalists ever since the rise of anti-Sikh and anti-Hindu communalism in post-1947 India. Interestingly, not much innovation has taken place. Often, the Muslim stereotype has been transferred to Sikhs while the Sikh communalists have adopted the Muslim communalist's stereotype of Hindus.

The rise of communalism and communal stereotypes in post-1947 Panjab (as also casteism all over India) also shows that social exclusiveness or gap plays a very minor role in the rise and growth of communalism for there is hardly any such gap between Sikhs and Hindus who interdine and intermarry, have free social contact and social relations and live in common *mohallas* in cities. Among them exists *'roti beti ki sanjh.' Nor* are there any grounds for antagonism between the two on account of religious practices, festivals, conversions, etc. Lakhs of Hindus worship the Granth Sahib as a holy scripture while lakhs of Sikhs revere the Hindu scriptures. Furthermore, only a few years earlier, the Hindu communalists used to hail Sikhs as the defenders of Hinduism.

Similarly, the modern, Westernized intellectuals to be found in colleges, courts and newspapers seldom practised or came across food or other social taboos in the 1930s and 1940s or today. The social gap among them was otherwise also quite narrow. Yet quite often they were (and are) the chief carriers, leaders or ideologues of communalism.

Finally, it may be pointed out that it was essential at this stage and as a part of the struggle against communalism and colonialism, to fight and overcome these social taboos, exclusiveness and narrow-mindedness, particularly their discriminatory aspects. The failure to wage such a struggle was particularly surprising because very similar struggles were being waged in the case of similar taboos and discriminations against the Harijans and against women. In part at least, it may be suggested, this failure was due to the wide prevalence of socially reactionary ideologies in the nationalist ranks. That the promotion of the process of the nation-in-the-making required active social radicalism was recognized by many thinking Indians. Rabindranath Tagore, for example, had written in the early 1920s:

> When our nationalists talk about (nationalist) ideals they forget that the basis of nationalism is wanting. The very people who are upholding these ideals are themselves the most conservative in their social practice. Nationalists say, for example, look at Switzerland where, in spite of race differences, the peoples have solidified into a nation. Yet, remember that in Switzerland the races can intermarry, because they are of the same blood. The India there is no common birthright.[77]

IV. ONE COMMUNALISM AS A REACTION TO THE OTHER COMMUNALISM

Often in the past, but even today, it is common for a communalist—and sometimes for a non-communalist too—to ascribe the origins of one communalism to the existence of the other communalism. It was and is seen as a reaction to, or the consequence of, the other communalism, which arose autonomously or on its own. Thus, by assigning the blame or the original sin to the opposite communalism, a sort of back-door justification was provided for one's own communalism or the communalism one was studying and supporting. At the same time, a holier-than- thou status was smugly claimed for one's own 'community.' A recent example of this approach is provided by Prabha Dixit who says that while Muslim communalism developed as a struggle for power and "did not arise as a reaction to Hindu communalism," "Hindu communalism, on the other hand, grew as a reaction to Muslim communalism."[78] Elaborating further on "Hindu Communalism: Its Genesis and Growth," she writes: "In their own interest as well as in the interest of the country, therefore, all Hindu leaders devoted themselves to the cause of national freedom and democracy."[79] But the foundation of the Muslim League in 1906 "delivered a rude shock to the Hindu leaders. The Muslim leadership

[77]Quoted in Sasadhar Sihna, *Indian Independence in Perspective,* p. 72.
[78]Prabha Dixit, *op. cit.*, pp. vii, 9.
[79]*Ibid.*, pp. 138-39.

was obviously determined to keep their community aloof from the mainstream of national politics." Consequently:

> It would not be an exaggeration to state that the Act of 1909 which granted separate electorate and weightage to the Muslims was directly responsible for the birth of organized communalism amongst the Hindus. The Congress which had stood for ideals of secularism and common nationhood got discredited in the eyes of one section of the Hindus. The wisdom of the Congress policy of putting the entire burden of national unity on the Hindus was questioned.... It was felt that the Hindus should establish a separate organization to defend their "just rights...." The success of the Muslim League in obtaining special status and privileges for the Muslims without any agitation or struggle made communal politics an honourable and profitable profession. The advantage(s) of the Muslim model of communalism over the Congress model of nationalism were too obvious to be ignored. Instead of agreeing to what they considered to be a surrender of their rights, one section of the Hindu elite chose to walk in the foot-steps of the Muslim communalists.[80]

A similar viewpoint is adopted, though from the opposite angle, by Mushirul Hasan. After discussing B.S. Moonje's communal utterances

[80] Dixit has a similar explanation for the growth of Hindu communalism after 1947. The latter is the result of the Muslim minority's claim for special rights, etc. To quote her in full: "If the special concessions enjoyed by the Muslim minority under an imperial and alien government in the '30s did not meet their expectations, guarantees spelled out in the constitution of an independent India have even lesser chance to make it feel secure and contented. Mr. Jinnah had not asked for anything more than 'an honourable settlement.' But unfortunately, a settlement which may prove 'honourable' to the minority is not always acceptable to the majority. In a democracy the grant of special rights and privileges to a minority on grounds of its religious identity is bound to arouse religious susceptibilities of the majority also. All such measures disturb the confidence which the majority group possesses on account of its greater numbers. Once the confidence is shaken, it starts campaigning against the minority with religious and cultural slogans similar to those adopted by the minority for self-preservation. In the extreme, it tries to eliminate the minority from all positions of political power." *Ibid.*, pp. 216-17.

and activities, Hasan writes: "They revealed the ineffectiveness of the dominant Congress leadership in curbing the growing influence of the Hindu Mahasabhaites, *stimulated an increased awareness among Muslims to protect their interests* and confirmed the suspicion of some Muslim groups that Swaraj in Congress terms meant Hindu domination." (Emphasis added.) Discussing the growth of anti-Congress politics and the Muslim League from the 1880s to the first decade of the twentieth century, which he does not see as the growth of Muslim communalism, he writes:

> Its narrow political interests apart, the Muslim League provided organizational expression to the sentiments of those who were either affected or concerned with the activities of the firebrand cow-protectors and militant linguistic reformers. The League provided the platform where such concerns could be voiced, while the continued alliance with the British ensured that *Muslim interests,* howsoever differently perceived, would be adequately protected. The cornerstone of Muslim politics from 1906 to 1919 was the consolidation of the League as an *effective spokesman of Muslim interests;* it was a vehicle to articulate both political and religio-cultural demands.[81] (Emphasis added.)

Undoubtedly, once the two communalisms developed, they 'fed and fattened on each other.' Instead of cancelling each other out, they promoted each other even in geometrical progression. As Mehta and Patwardhan observe: "Each has provided the raison d'etre and the stimulus needed for the other."[82] Their exploitation of each other led to a snowball effect. This is the true part of the theory of 'one

[81] Mushirul Hasan, "Communal and Revivalist Trends in Congress," pp. 210-12. Both Prabha Dixit and Mushirul Hasan are perhaps subjectively secular and their notion of the original communalism being other than the one they are studying originates in their inability to rigorously analyse or understand communalism. Consequently, they constantly fall into the communal trap that the contemporary sources set for them. The frankly communal writers put forward this view in a far more blatant manner.

[82] A. Mehta and A. Patwardhan, *op. cit.,* p. 181.

communalism as a reaction to the other communalism.' For example, Muslims reacted to the strengthening of Hindu communalism; it seemed to justify the fears sought to be aroused by the Muslim communalists. The more the Hindu commual or commual nationalist newspapers and other media smugly and patronizingly pointed to the Hindus' devotion to nationalism and asked Muslims to give up their 'selfishness' and 'narrowmindedness' and to join the mainstream of nationalism—a holier-than-thou approach that is exemplified by the extract from Prabha Dixit given earlier—the more strongly did Muslims feel that Hindus sneered and looked down upon them, and there was, therefore, truth in the Muslim communal approach. Similarly, Hindus reacted to the constant propaganda that Muslim interests were separate and that Hindus were constantly planning to dominate and destroy Muslims.

A special case of this mutual communal reaction was the two-nation theory. Both Savarkar and Jinnah asserted, after 1936, that Hindus and Muslims were two separate nations.[83] The two assertions reinforced each other and created conditions for the emergence of separatism.

But while it is wrong to say that either communalism arose as a reaction to the other, the existence of Hindu communalism and its aggressive propaganda, along with the Hindu tinge in much of the national movement, were contributory factors in the failure of the national movement and later of the class movements to overcome Muslim communalism.

The answer to the trap of mutual communal reaction, of their fattening on each other, lay in the realm of practice. Both were equally invalid and neither could legitimize or validate the other. Both should have been subjected to a simultaneous critique and exposure. Operationally, one should have criticized Hindu communalism more if one was addressing a Hindu audience or if one was a Hindu and

[83]V.D. Savarkar, *Hindu Rashtra Darshan,* pp. 21,26, 64, 101; M.A. Jinnah *op. cit.,* Vol. I, pp. 116-17. Also see M.S. Golwalkar, *We,pp.* 52, 62 (footnote). There was another Hindu communal version of the two-nation theory—that Hindus were the only nation in India, Muslims and others being foreigners.

Muslim communalism more if one was addressing a Muslim audience or if one was a Muslim, Otherwise, sometimes, even criticism of the other communalism before a communal audience, for example, of Muslim communalism before a Hindu communal audience or vice versa, led only to the stoking of the communal fire.

V

However, in conclusion it should be kept in view that, above all, communalism grew and acquired greater popular support from stage to stage mainly because of social conditions. It became cumulative or self-perpetuating because it was constantly being fed by social forces which found in it an available, ready-made and serviceable ideology.

CHAPTER 7

The Use of History

A communal and distorted unscientific view of Indian history, especially of its ancient and medieval periods, was both a major instrument for the spread of communal consciousness and a basic constituent of the communal ideology as also its product. In fact, it would be no exaggeration to suggest that the communal interpretation of history has been the main ideology of communalism in India; without it little would be left of communal ideology. This was particularly true of Hindu communalism.[1] While using 'history,' Muslim communalism depended more on religious and minority feelings for creating a feeling or psychosis of fear. The Hindu communalists could hardly do so successfully in view of the Hindu majority in the present; they, therefore, relied upon the past for the purpose. Similarly, the Muslim communalists demanded a separate and special status for Muslims as a distinct political community on the basis of their role in Indian history. Both communalisms used the communal interpretation of Indian history to create an atmosphere of fear, passion, prejudice and hatred.

Stereotypes of various religious groups, especially Hindus and Muslims, and myths, symbols and legends were major parts of the communal ideology; history-teaching at various levels was used to create and propagate them, often on parallel communal lines, thus separating Hindus from Muslims and strengthening the rival communalisms. The past, interpreted to suit a particular communalism, was also used as its major intellectual justification or legitimation.

[1]This is clearly brought out in the three basic texts of Hindu communalism before 1947: V.D. Savarkar's *Hindutva,* his presidential speeches to the Hindu Mahasabha collected in the *Hindu Rashtra Darshan* and M.S. Golwalkar's *We.*

In particular, the basic conceptions of Hindu communalism, of Hindus constituting a distinct nation and of possessing a common culture, depended on their particular interpretation of history.[2]

The teaching of Indian history in schools and colleges contributed in a major way to the growth of communal feeling. For generations, almost from the beginning of the modern school system, communal interpretations of history of varying degrees of virulence at different levels were propagated, first by imperialist writers and then by others. So deep and widespread was the penetration of the communal view of history that even sturdy nationalists accepted, however unconsciously, some of its basic digits which came to be seen as basic 'truths' of Indian history. They also formed constituent parts of the Hindu tinge in the nationalist ideology to which Muslims and other minorities took serious objection. So much so that it would require a veritable revolution in history-teaching, and perhaps a cultural revolution in society, to undo the consequences. The role of history-teaching and interpretation in the spread of communalism was seen clearly by contemporary observers; and a few examples may be cited. Gandhi wrote: "Communal harmony could not be permanently established in our country so long as highly distorted versions of history were being taught in her schools and colleges, through the history textbooks."[3]

Lajpat Rai writing about his childhood said in his autobiography: "At that time a book on Indian history called *Waqiat-i-Hind* used to be taught at Government schools. That book created in me the feeling that Mussalmans had subjected the Hindus to great tyranny. Gradually the respect for Islam that I had acquired from early training began to change into hatred because of study of *Waqiat-i-Hindi.*"[4]

Mohammed Ali wrote in the *Comrade* in February 1912:

> The race antagonism owes its virulence mainly to a false reading of history. The past has flung out its dead hand to paralyse the present.

[2]See, for example, V.D. Savarkar, *Hindutva,* pp. 75-77.

[3]Quoted in A.N. Vidyalankar, *National Integration and Teaching of History,* p. 3.

[4]Lajpat Rai, *Autobiographical Writings,* p. 77.

> Practical issues of politics are swayed by the foolish but eminently real resentment of the Hindu "patriot" at the political domination of the Muslims in a bygone period of Indian history and by the equally foolish yet powerful sentiment of the Muslim about his vanished power and prestige and empire.[5]

The "Foreword" to the *Report of the Kanpur Riots Enquiry Committee,* appointed by the National Congress, pointed out in 1932 that the communal view of medieval history found in school and other history books "is playing a considerable part in estranging the two communities" and went on to add:

> We feel that unless the people begin to see the past in a truer perspective it will be very difficult or well-nigh impossible to restore mutual confidence and to arrive at a real and permanent solution of the present differences. We consider, therefore, that an attempt to remove historical misconceptions is the first and the most indispensable step in the real solution of the Hindu-Muslim problem.[6]

Even more than through the textbooks, the communal view of history was spread widely through poetry, drama, historical novels and short stories, newspapers and popular magazines, pamphlets and books and, above all, orally through the public platform, class-room-teaching and private discussion and conversation. Moreover, at this level—the level of popular history—the communal content was even more rabid as well as more fictitious. Its effect was also more vicious for it was more difficult to refute. Yet, in the popular mind it passed as history, possessing the solidity of 'well-known' facts. These virulent versions of communal history, propagated virtually as myths, were seldom written down despite their wide prevalence and are therefore difficult to document. However, some idea of their content may be

[5]Mohammed Ali, *Selected Writings and Speeches,* p. 78.
[6]See p. 43.

derived from the speeches and writings of V.D. Savarkar, M.S. Golwalkar, Z.A. Suleri, F.K. Khan Durrani and other similar communal political writers and leaders, including some of the later speeches of M.A. Jinnah.

A few other aspects of the use of history as communalism may be noted. An integrated and often communal view of history at the level of research or full-fledged scholarship was found very rarely before 1947 mainly because of the hegemony of nationalism among the intelligentsia. Communal forces gained significant and open intellectual adherents in India and Pakistan only after 1947.[7] Consequently, history-teaching and research at the higher, i.e., post-graduate and doctorate levels, were seldom openly communal. But this did not fully promote a secular, scientific understanding of history even at these levels, for the postgraduate student went to his studies with his mind already prejudiced.

One result of classroom history being communal ideology was that the spread of education meant the further spread of communalism, especially in the denominational institutions such as the Dayanand Anglo-Vedic and Sanatan Dharam, the Islamic and the Sikh schools and colleges.

Because of being subjected to the communal view of history from childhood, elements of this view came to prevail widely even among the nationalists. A large number of Congress leaders and members imbibed some of these elements and propagated them freely, however unconsciously and unaware of the consequences. For example, they glibly talked of India having suffered under foreign rule for a thousand years and of the sharp decline of Indian society and culture under 'Muslim rule.' In fact, any secular Indian will recognize on serious introspection how much his or her view of history has incorporated the communal view and assumptions in the form of 'settled' or 'proven' facts or as historical truths.

[7]The post-1947 communal historians adopted in their research the conceptions and framework evolved by the communalists before 1947 which they had imbibed consciously or unconsciously. They developed no new concepts or hypotheses; often, they merely filled in the blanks with better researched data.

Though often adopting diametrically opposite and hostile positions, the two communal interpretations of history—the Hindu and the Muslim—adopted basically the same historiographic framework, premises and assumptions. Often the only difference was that the other 'community' was the villain.

Moreover, quite often, the two communal interpretations and generalizations were based on those earlier put forward by British historians, administrators and publicists.[8] Nor were the latter in all cases simple innocents. Many of them were often guided by broad considerations other than those of historical enquiry. First, to show that the Indian people had always been ruled by cruel tyrants and uncontrolled despots. Consequently, there was nothing wrong if the British rule too was autocratic or despotic; only it was benevolent and just and operated under the Rule of Law. Moreover, Muslims were also foreigners just like the British; therefore, the British had not introduced foreign rule, but only replaced a barbaric and inhuman foreign rule with a humane and civilized foreign rule. Secondly, to show that Muslims had oppressed, subjugated and maltreated Hindus in a most cruel and frightful manner; the British had virtually 'liberated' them. Hindus, being much better off under British rule, should feel indebted to the British and extend them full support. Thirdly, to assert that Hindus and Muslims were always divided and at each other's throats and they could, therefore, never live peacefully with each other in the absence of a third party—the British. Thus, the leading British historian of medieval India, H.M. Elliot, in his "Original Preface" to his *The History of India As Told By Its Own Historians,* wrote in 1849, of "the few glimpses we have, even among the short Extracts in this single volume, of Hindus slain for disputing with Muhammadans, of general prohibitions against processions, worship, and ablutions, and of other intolerant measures, of idols mutilated, of temples razed, of forcible conversions and marriages, of proscriptions and confiscations, of murders and massacres, and of the

[8]Most of the communal generalizations can be easily so traced. For example, the periodization of Indian history into Hindu and Muslim periods was first made by James Mill in *The History of British India.*

sensuality and drunkenness of the tyrants who enjoined them." He also frankly confessed his motive in publishing his history. It was to make "our native subjects more sensible of the immense advantages accruing to them under the mildness and equity of our rule" and to make the emerging nationalist intellectuals—"the bombastic Babus" as he called them—see the reality of pre-British India and thus stop their incipient critique of British imperialism.[9]

Quite often, in the hands of the communalist, the entire treatment of the past was allegorical. It was assumed or implied that whatever happened then was bound to happen now. And, therefore, contemporary communal politics were projected into the past and the happenings of the past were so described and historical myths created as to serve the communal politics of the present, to justify present-day communalism. Thus, both communalisms adopted an interpretation of the past, through which feelings of fear, insecurity and separateness could be aroused among their followers in the present. In this sense, while communal history produced and propagated communalism, in its turn communal politics gave a fillip to communal historical writing, teaching and myth-making. It may be noted in this respect that, as pointed out earlier in Chapter 1, it was not medieval history as lived by the medieval people or the medieval historical processes that generated communalism; it was the communal interpretation of medieval history, that is, of what happened, that produced communalism as well as got produced by communalism—this interpretation was itself communal ideology.[10]

Quite often, elements and themes of the communal view of history were found in the nationalist historiographic tradition, often as a

[9]Quoted in Tara Chand, *History of Freedom Movement in India,* Vol. II, pp. 484-85.

[10]This aspect is clearly and dramatically brought out in the novels of Bhai Vir Singh. Writing at the end of the nineteenth century when Sikh communalism was being born, Bhai Vir Singh created a 'double' or two-faced communal version of history to promote Sikh communalism which would be antagonistic to both Muslims and Hindus. His heroes and heroines were persecuted by villainous Muslims and were left undefended by the cowardly Hindus. Either brave Sikhs saved them from Muslim tyranny and Hindu cowardice, or they became Sikhs to acquire the characteristics of brave and heroic men and women. See Harjot Oberoi, "Literature and Society: An Approach to the Novels of Bhai Vir Singh."

Hindu or a Muslim tinge. But communalism exaggerated and distorted them, changed their social, historical and ideological content and put them to a totally different use. A part of the reason for the easy success of the communalists in doing so, of course, lay in the failure of the nationalist historical tradition to measure up fully to the high standards of a scientific approach.

I. THE BASIC CONSTITUENTS OF THE COMMUNAL VIEW OF INDIAN HISTORY

The communalist primarily saw medieval Indian history as one long story of Hindu-Muslim conflict. Hindus and Muslims were permanently divided into separate camps whose mutual relations were bitter, distrustful and hostile. There existed throughout the medieval period distinct and separate Hindu and Muslim cultures. Muslims formed a distinct cultural and political community because of Islam; and for that very reason Muslims found it impossible to get culturally assimilated. A few quotations may not be out of order. In his presidential address at the Lahore session of the Muslim League in March 1940, Jinnah said: "The history of the last 12 hundred years has failed to achieve unity and has witnessed, during the ages, India always divided into Hindu India and Muslim India."[11] V.D. Savarkar was much more virulent. In *Hindutva,* written in 1923, he asserted that "the day when Mohamad Gazani crossed the Indus ... that day the conflict of life and death began" which "ended shall we say with Abdali?" He went on to add: "Day after day, decade after decade, centuries after centuries, the ghastly conflict continued...." In this conflict, all Hindus, belonging to different sects, regions and castes, "all suffered as Hindus and triumphed as Hindus." All Muslims were enemies, and "the enemies hated us as Hindus." And *Hindutva* and the cultural unity of Hindus was the one issue which was "being fought out on the hundred fields of battle."[12]

[11] M.A, Jinnah, *Speeches and Writings,* Vol. I, p. 161.

[12] V.D. Savarkar, *Hindutva,* pp. 34-36. Also see his presidential address to the Hindu Mahasabha in 1939 in *Hindu Rashtra Darshan,* p. 133. This view came to be articulated on

This struggle or hostility between Hindus and Muslims was then, according to the communal view, 'naturally' carried over to the nineteenth and twentieth centuries and served as the cause or basis, as well as the justification, for the current communal antagonism between the two. This was the basis on which the RSS declared Muslims to be the 'old enemies' of Hindus. Thus, for example, in 1939, M.S. Golwalkar condemned the nationalists for spreading the view by which Hindus "began to class ourselves with our old invaders and foes under the outlandish name—Indian." He went on to add:

> The result of this poison is too well-known. We have allowed ourselves to be duped into believing our foes to be our friends and with our own hands are undermining true Nationality. *That is the real danger of the day, our self-forgetfulness, our believing our old and bitter enemies to be our friends.*[13] (Emphasis added.)

V.D. Savarkar said in 1937: "But the solid fact is that the so-called communal questions are but a legacy handed down to us by centuries of a cultural, religious and national antagonism between the Hindus and the Moslems."[14] The Muslim communalists readily accepted and

the academic plane after 1947. In India, R.C. Mazumdar wrote in his *The Delhi Sultanat,* published by the Bharatiya Vidya Bhawan in 1957, as Volumes V and VI of *The History and Culture of the Indian People,* that medieval India remained "permanently divided into two powerful units, each with marked individuality of its own, which did not prove amenable to a fusion or even any close permanent coordination." Vol. VI, p. xxviii. In Pakistan, Ishtiaq Ahmad Quraishi wrote in *The Muslim Community of the Indo-Pakistan Sub-Continent,* published in New York, "at all times the Muslims of the sub-continent were resolute in refusing to be assimilated to the local population and made conscious efforts to maintain their distinctive character."

[13]M. S, Golwalkar, *We,* p.19. He had written a few pages earlier "that though, for the last thousand years or less, the land has been infested with murderous bands of despoilers in various parts, the Nation has not been conquered, far less subjugated; that through all these years it has engaged in a terrible struggle to free the land of this pest and the great struggle is still relentlessly raging with varying success to both sides. In short, our History is the story of our flourishing Hindu National life for thousands of years and then of a long unflinching war continuing for the last ten centuries, which has not yet come to a decisive close." *Ibid.,* pp. 17-18.

[14]V.D. Savarkar, *Hindu Rashtra Darshan,* p. 26.

propagated this view and traced the two-nation theory to the medieval period. So widespread was this theory of past antagonism between Hindus and Muslims that many well-meaning and secular persons accepted it even while working for Hindu-Muslim unity in the present.

Basing themselves on the theory of 'historical antagonism' between Hindus and Muslims, the remedies or social solutions of the communal problem put forth by the two communalists were very similar. While the Muslim communalists raised the demand for the separation of Muslims from Hindus through the creation of the separate state of Pakistan, the rabid Hindu communalists demanded the expulsion or the subordination of Muslims who had refused to be 'absorbed' and had, therefore, remained foreigners.[15]

As a corollary, the communalist denied or underplayed other social tensions and conflicts in medieval society. Not only were class and caste tensions ignored but also overt political conflicts such as between Rajputs and Marathas, northern and southern kingdoms, Rajputs and Sikhs, and Afghans and Turks were papered over.

The Hindu communalists described the rule by medieval Muslim rulers as foreign rule; and, consequently, Muslims as an alien element in Indian society and as permanent foreigners in the land. This was basically because of their religion. A Muslim was a foreigner because he was a Muslim. Hindu Indians, for example Panjabi and Bengali Hindus, became foreigners as soon as they changed their religion to Islam. Because Islam had come from outside, that is, had been founded outside India, it was a 'foreign' religion and this made all its followers foreigners. Thus 'Indianness' or 'indigenousness' or nationhood were linked to religion. In fact, both V.D. Savarkar and M.S. Golwalkar defined nationhood in such a manner as to exclude Muslims, Christians, Jews and Parsis from its ambit.[16] A Hindu or native Indian was one who followed a religion that was founded in

[15]M.S. Golwalkar, *We*, pp. 26-27, 53-56.

[16]See V.D. Savarkar, *Hindutva* and M.S. Golwalkar, *We*. Golwalkar and Savarkar also used the concept of race or common blood to define a nation. But the former was aware of the fact that Muslims had the same 'blood' as Hindus. He therefore used the concept of 'Race Spirit' which was lost with the change of religion. *We*, Chapters II and III.

India; it is this that enabled him or her to see India as a *poonyabhoomi*. For the same reason, a non-Hindu had to remain a foreigner. The very fact that Muslims had remained Muslims showed that they were not willing to be absorbed into Indian society, were perhaps not capable of being absorbed and, therefore, remained foreigners. And, of course, the communal moral for the present was obvious.

The communalists constantly bracketed 'Muslim rule' and British rule as foreign rule. The talk of 'a thousand years of slavery' or 'foreign rule' was common rhetoric, sometimes even used by nationalists, before 1947 as also after that, and was dinned into young and illiterate heads day in and day out on every conceivable occasion from the public platform, through the Press, and in the classroom. As pointed out earlier, it is not easy to document the more rabid and vicious examples of communal propaganda since it was carried on orally. But we may give an example from the rare written word. Drawing the appropriate conclusion from his historical interpretation, Golwalkar wrote in 1939 in *We:*

> The non-Hindu peoples in Hindusthan must either adopt the Hindu culture and language, must learn to respect and hold in reverence Hindu religion, must entertain no idea but those of glorification of the Hindu race and culture, i.e., they must not only give up their attitude of intolerance and ungratefulness towards this land and its agelong traditions but must also cultivate the positive attitude of love and devotion instead—in one word, they must cease to be foreigners, or may stay in the country, wholly subordinated to the Hindu nation, claiming nothing, deserving no privileges, far less any preferential treatment—not even citizen's rights.[17]

And he warned the non-Hindus: "There are only two courses open to the foreign elements, either to merge themselves in the national race and adopt its culture, or to live at the sweet will of the national

[17]Pp. 55-56.

race."[18] Golwalkar repeatedly referred to Muslims as foreigners and invaders who were treating India not as a home but as a *sarai.*[19] Savarkar also suggested that to Muslims India was "only a land of sojourn" while to Hindus it was a home.[20] The view that Muslims were foreigners in India was found quite acceptable by Muslim communalists in a different incarnation. If the idea was to exclude Muslims from India, it was of course totally unacceptable. But if it was to show their complete separateness, to show that Muslims could not be Indians in the same way as Hindus, it was fully in line with their approach. Thus, Jinnah asserted in 1941:

> ... a Muslim, when he was converted, granted that he was converted more than a thousand years ago, bulk of them, then according to your Hindu religion and philosophy, he becomes an outcaste and he becomes a *malecha* (untouchable) and the Hindus cease to have anything to do with him socially, religiously and culturally or in any other way? He, therefore, belongs to a different order, not only religious but social, and he has lived in that distinctly separate and antagonistic social order, religiously, socially and culturally. *It is now more than a thousand years that the bulk of the Muslims have lived in a different world, in a different society, in a different philosophy and a different faith.*[21] (Emphasis added).

[18] *Ibid.*, p. 55. Also see pp. 26-27.

[19] Such references can be found almost on every page of *We.*

[20] V.D. Savarkar, *Hindu Rashtra Darshan,* p. 50. Also see *ibid,* pp. 63-64; Prabha Dixit, *Communalism—A Struggle for Power,* pp. 168-71. Some others went further. It could not be accepted, they said, that the country was 'jointly owned by those who either came running away from their countries end sought protection here or those descendants of ex-Hindus, who for the greed of power and money or out of fear renounced their glorious faith and became converts, or those who are the descendants of those barbarous invaders who spoiled our very sacred land, demolished our sacred temples ... the country cannot belong to them; if they are to live here, they must live here taking it for granted that Hindusthan is the land of the Hindus, of no one else." Indra Prakash, *Where We Differ,* p. *66,* quoted in Prabha Dixit, *op, cit.*, p. 171.

[21] M.A. Jinnah, *op. cit.*, Vol. I, p. 230. Similarly, the Nawab of Mamdot said in 1941 that: "Pakistan had existed in India for nearly twelve centuries." Quoted in Moin Shakir, *Khilafat to Partition,* p. 200.

Thus, the communal view of Indian history directly led, during the phase of extreme communalism, to the clearly articulated notion that Hindus and Muslims formed two separate nations. Only, while the Muslim communalists proclaimed the existence of two nations in India, many of the Hindu communalists held that only one nation, the Hindu nation, existed in India, the Muslims being 'foreigners.'

One of the basic constituents of communal ideology was the view that in medieval India Muslims constituted the ruling class or the dominant group while Hindus were the ruled, the dominated, the subjects or the 'subject race.' It is to be noted that *all* Muslims, including the vast mass of the rural and urban poor, were portrayed as rulers and all Hindus, including the rajas, chiefs, nobles, officials and zamindars, as the ruled. The Muslim communalists put forward this view of medieval society from the early years of the twentieth century in order to claim a large share in the legislatures.[22] It was later propagated as a major component of Muslim communal ideology. Addressing Lahore students in 1941, M.A. Jinnah said: "Our demand is not from Hindus because the Hindus never took the whole of India. It was the Muslims who took India and ruled for 700 years. It was the British who took India from the Musalmans."[23] In 1942, he asserted that if the British handed over the government of India to the Muslim League, they "will be making full amends to the Muslims by restoring the government of India to them from whom they had taken it."[24] Other communal publicists were more crude. Thus, Z.A. Suleri argued that India could not belong to Hindus because they had been suppressed for a thousand years,[25] and Shaukat Ali declared in 1929: "Hindus have been habituated to slavery and they would remain slaves."[26] As we have seen earlier, the Hindu communalist readily

[22]Address presented by the deputation to Viceroy Minto, cited in Ram Gopal, *Indian Muslims: A Political History (1858-1947),* p. 330. Curzon even suggested that Muslims in UP were losing the "reins of power" only at the end of the nineteenth century. S. Gopal, *British Policy in India, 1858-1905, p.* 259. Also see *ibid.*, p. 193.

[23]M.A. Jinnah, *op. cit.,* Vol. I, p. 229.

[24]*Ibid., p.* 404.

[25]Z A. Suleri, *My Leader, p.* 162.

[26]Quoted in Ram Gopal, *op. cit.,* pp. 206-07.

accepted that Hindus were "slaves" under "Muslim rule." For example, in 1937, V.D. Savarkar described the rule of Muslim rulers as "a veritable death-warrant to the Hindu Nation."[27]

The communal theory of Muslims being the rulers and Hindus being the ruled in medieval India prevailed on a large scale in another form also. It was widely suggested that the nineteenth and twentieth century Muslims had an ever-present happy or 'glorious' memory or remembrance of having been the ruling class, and this fact powerfully affected, for better or worse, their current politics. Similar was the case with Hindus—only theirs was said to be a sad memory, the humiliating memory of having been the ruled or 'subject race.' The wide prevalence of this view, which was very clearly a creation of contemporary communal ideology and not a historical or folk memory or revival of a past, forgotten feeling, is testified to by its adoption even by a shrewd observer like C. Manshardt who wrote in 1936:

> This early hostility of the Hindu towards the Muslim has carried over to the present day. Though the Hindu out-numbers the Muslim in practically every province of India, he still seems to fear him. Recalling the days of Muslim domination, he is unwilling to run any risks of present-day Muslim political supremacy. The Muslim, on the other hand, remembers his glorious past and looks to the future.[28]

[27]V.D. Savarkar, *Hindu Rashtra Darshan, p.* 15. Also see *ibid.,* p. 61; M.S. Golwalkar, *Bunch of Thoughts,* pp. 294-95; N.C. Kelkar's presidential address to Hindu Mahasabha, 1925, *Indian Annual Register,* 1925, Vol. II, p. 351. The wide prevalence of the views that "Muslims were the ruling class" and Muslims lost political power is attested to by the fact that even sturdy secularists often accepted it, though unconsciously and without grasping the full implications. See A. Mehta and A. Patwardhan, *The Communal Triangle in India,* p. 182.

[28]C. Manshardt, *Tlie Hindu-Muslim Problem in India,* p. 33. One of the first to put forward this view was Lord Dufferin. Quoted in *Report on Indian Constitutional Reforms,* 1918, p. 91. Also see John Strachey, *India,* p. 239; V.D. Savarkar. *Hindu Rashtra Darshan,* p. 61; M.S. Golwalkar, *We,* p. 19. For recent statements of the historical memory notion, see H.V. Hodson, *The Great Divide,* p. 11; K..B. Sayeed, *Pakistan—The Formative Phase 1857-1948,* p. 179. For the late nineteenth-century communal view, see Sudhir Chandra, "Communal Consciousness in the Late 19th-century Hindi Literature," pp. 173, 177-78.

Several corollaries followed from this view. First was the notion that politics, political power and the distribution of political power in India have always been based on religion and religious differences and that too of, and among, the rulers. The Indian state was a religious state, being Islamic in medieval India; this fact being determined by the personal religion of the rulers. Even more, the basic objective of the medieval state was the propagation and glorification of Islam by every possible means, and this was so because of the inherent character of a state whose rulers were Muslim. As the *Report of the Kanpur Riots Enquiry Committee* pointed out, the communalists regarded the Muslim rulers

> as zealous crusaders whose dominant motive was the spread of Islam and whose method for achieving this object was the destruction of temples and forcible conversions.... The Muslim writers deplore the want of true religious feeling in Muslim kings in permitting idolatory to persist in their dominion and the unbelievers to prosper, while the Hindu writers bewail the weakness of the religious sentiment in Hindu rulers and their want of patriotism in not combining effectively against a foreigner in defence of their religion and their country.[29]

For the same reason, the autonomous or semi-autonomous states ruled by Hindu rajas and chiefs, such as the Maratha empire and the states ruled by Maratha chieftains, Rajput rajas and Jat zamindars, were declared to be Hindu states whose rulers were the defenders of the Hindu religion. Once this basic hypothesis regarding the determination of the basic character of the medieval states according to the religion of their rulers was accepted, all other historical data were fitted in. Inconvenient facts or incidents were usually explained away as aberrations. In fact, the communalists not only explained away the behaviour of the vast majority of chieftains and rulers, who did not conform to the communal scheme in their politics,

[29]P. 105.

but used it to spread communalism by branding them 'bad' Hindus or 'bad' Muslims who were some sort of 'traitors' to their communities.

Secondly, the communalists adopted a purely religion-based definition of culture, and that too based on the religions of their upper classes. Since the two religions were by definition separate, there could be no common cultural ground or even mutual interaction between Hindus and Muslims.

The communalist constantly praised rulers belonging to his 'community' and condemned those belonging to the other 'community.' Real or fictitious incidents were constantly narrated and reiterated to prove this point.[30] And then, by transfer, the character of the rulers was said to reflect the inherent character of the 'communities' to which they belonged. This is how, to a large extent, the communal stereotypes were created and propagated. This was in particular true of literature, especially in Bengali, Hindi and Urdu. Regarding Bengali literature, a Muslim communal publicist, while himself attacking Shivaji in a typically communal manner, complained in 1903 that most of the Bengali Hindu novelists, poets and dramatists

> take immense pleasure in exhuming from their peaceful marble tombs the Muslim emperors of Delhi and depicting them in the pages of their novels and poems as wicked, tyrannical, dissolute devils and hateful lecherous dogs, and these distortions are, when staged in Calcutta and various places in the provinces, earning praise of countless Hindus....
>
> They have dragged out from their solitary rooms in the harem even the daughters of the Badshas, who had been kept in strict purdah, and by the help of their hemp-addicted imaginations they have depicted some of them as desirous of the love of Shivaji, that devil in human form, that mountain-rat and slayer of women, and

[30]As pointed out earlier, such real or fictitious events could be often readily dug up from the writings of the medieval chroniclers, court poets, etc., who earned their livelihood by justifying, on religious grounds, the deeds or misdeeds of their patrons.

> some of them as languishing for the love of pig-eating Rajputs and some as the hand-maids of the Hindu slaves; and they get great pleasure from staging the stories in the theatre.[31]

The Hindu communalist readily adopted and propagated the imperialist view that the medieval period of Indian history represented 'Muslim tyranny.' He depicted the history of medieval Indian society as one long tale of murder, rapine and oppression, hostility to Hinduism and Hindus and the forcible spread of Islam through temple destruction and forcible conversion by the Muslim rulers and their officials. The worst examples of this presentation of medieval history were to be found in oral propaganda. But sometimes this view was articulated in a virulent form in the written word also, as, for example, in Golwalkar's *We,* published in 1939. Golwalkar usually referred to Muslims as "murdering hordes," "murderous bands," "despoilers," "free-booters," "the enemy," "forces of destruction," "old invaders and foes," "our old and bitter enemies," etc.[32] And V.D. Savarkar wrote in *Hindutva:*

> But here India alone had to face Arabs, Persians, Pathans, Baluchis, Tartars, Turks, Moguls—a veritable human Sahara whirling and columning up bodily in a furious world storm! Religion is a mighty motive force. So is Rapine. But where Religion is goaded on by Rapine and Rapine serves as a handmaid to Religion, the propelling force that is generated by these together is only equalled by the profundity of human misery and devastation they leave behind them in their march. Heaven and Hell making a common

[31]Quoted in M.N. Islam, *Bengal Muslim Public Opinion as Reflected in the Bengal Press 1901-1930,* pp. 142-43.

[32]M.S. Golwalkar, *We,* pp. 17-19. Later, in his *Bunch of Thoughts,* he wrote: "Their history of the past one thousand two hundred years, full of incidents of destruction, depredation and all sorts of barbaric atrocities, is there before our eyes. The present-day large Muslim population in our country is one of the results of the fatal devastation that they wrought all over the land. Not only the broken monuments but these pieces of a broken society also are equally an evidence of their vandalism. What has our good behaviour towards the Muslim faith and the Muslim people brought us? Nothing but desecration of our holy places and enslavement of our people." pp. 294-95.

> cause—such were the forces, overwhelmingly furious, that took India by surprise the day that Mohmad crossed the Indus and invaded her. Day after day, decade after decade, centuries after centuries, the ghastly conflict continued and India single-handed kept the fight morally and militarily.[33]

Similarly, referring to the medieval period, Indra Prakash wrote in 1938: "During these days of alien rule, the history of Hindusthan, is a tragic account of Hindus slain, of the intolerant measures, of the temples razed, and mutilated, of forcible conversions and marriages, of proscriptions and confiscations, of murders, massacres and of the sensuality and drunkenness of the tyrants, who enjoyed them."[34]

This 'Muslim tyranny' was moreover portrayed as being a result not of the character of the rulers or the ruling classes but of the basic character of Islamic religion itself. Indra Prakash, for example, wrote in *Where We Differ* in 1942:

> The Muslim religion exalts and heroworships an assassin. This religion encourages its followers to kill men of other religions. According to the tenets of Islam the killing of a Kafir or a man belonging to the fold of any other religion raises the murderer or assassin in the estimation of his fellow-men or community; nay, it makes him a *shahid* and facilitates his transport to heaven.[35]

One proof offered for this generalization was the historical record of the spread of Islam all over the world which was declared to be equally bloody and destructive. In fact, the notion that Islam has spread by the sword was treated as an axiom. Golwalkar, for example, wrote in *We:*

[33]See p. 35.

[34]Indra Prakash, *A Review...*, p. 4. Later, he again referred to "the sleeping consciousness of the great Hindu Nation—dulled, deadened and suppressed within two centuries by the disappearance of that constant terror and direct social and religious humiliation combined with political servitude which was the characteristic of the previous rule." p. 22.

[35]See p. 81.

The same old tale of Islamic invasion, with its attendant Massacres, devastation, destruction, loot and arson, violating all sacred places, desecration of religion and culture, and forced conversion to the faith of the ready executioner, and everything else that ever went in hand with the spread of Islam, was then repeated in all its hideousness in Iran.[36]

The *Report of the Kanpur Riots Enquiry Committee* also noted:

Of the many wrong impressions prevailing at present one which is the most fruitful source of bitterness and ill-will is the impression that Islam is inherently bigoted and intolerant.... The theory that Islam has spread by the sword has been canvassed so widely and so persistently that for the average Indian mind this proposition has become almost an axiom.... (It) gives its edge to the Hindu-Muslim problem....[37]

This political and oral tradition regarding 'Muslim tyranny' was to find academic expression mainly after 1947, as for example in the Bharatiya Vidya Bhawan's *The History and Culture of the Indian People.*[38] But it was quite current in the classroom in the colonial period. For example, a note regarding conditions in the Panjab University said:

Those who have examined university papers in history will know how Muslim rulers and administrators are depicted as blood-sucking vampires and fiends of cruelty. The general impression which they give is that the Muslim rulers came to India simply to destroy the Hindus and their culture and to convert the people to Islam at the point of the sword.[39]

[36]See p. 25. Also see V.D. Savarkar, *Hindutva,* pp. 34-35. The 'inherent' character of Islam was also used to argue that a Muslim could not ever be loyal to a nation-state which was not Muslim. See V.D. Savarkar, *Hindu Rasthra Darshan,* pp. 60 and 135.

[37]pp. 68-69.

[38]See, for example, Vol. VI, pp. 627-36.

[39]Quoted in F.K. Khan Durrani, *The Meaning of Pakistan,* p. 69.

Similarly, the *Report of the Kanpur Riots Enquiry Committee* noted:

> These stories of idol-breaking and forcible conversions give colour to the view generally canvassed in our histories which represents the whole movement as if it was a continued religious war between Hinduism and Islam extending over eight centuries. Even those writers who seem to understand its political nature by their general treatment of the subject, invariably leave upon the mind the same impression.[40]

The myth of Muslim tyranny had also a few corollaries. It aroused communal passions among Hindus and, in reverse, angered Muslims who objected to being always put in the dock. Many of them, in turn, felt it necessary, in self-defence, to defend the record of the medieval Muslim rulers and chieftains, including the record of a ruler like Aurangzeb. This myth in time helped structure the communal stereotype of Muslims being inherently cruel, sexually debauched and aggressive. It was used by the Hindu communalists to create a feeling and even a psychosis of fear which normally a majority would not have felt. It was also used to demand the denial of equal citizenship rights to Muslims on the ground of their ancestors' tyrannical behaviour and to deny the possibility of Hindu-Muslim unity in the present because of the historical memories of tyranny. The more rabid communal elements even promoted the theory that Hindus should seek revenge, or at least compensation, for the wrongs done to them during the medieval period.[41] Since the Muslim communalists could not so use history, they used the big lie regarding the record of the Congress ministries from 1937 to 1939.[42]

[40] *Op. cit.*, p. 105.

[41] As late as 1974, three senior professors of the University of Rajasthan, including the historian G. C. Pandey, publicly damanded that Muslims should raise, through voluntary contributions, funds for at least partial reconstruction of the Somnath temple as historical restitution for the religious vandalism indulged in by their ancestors.

[42] See *Pirpur Committee Report* and *It Shall Never Happen Again.*

The myth of Muslim rapine and destruction was also utilized to deny the positive aspects of medieval economy, polity and culture and their contribution to the development of Indian society.

Above all, the Hindu communal view of history relied on the myth that Indian society and culture—Indian civilization—had reached great, ideal heights in the ancient period from which it fell into permanent and continuous decay during the medieval period because of 'Muslim' rule and domination.

The communal myth of ancient greatness had several constituents. First, there was the totally uncritical approach to the depiction of ancient Indian society.[43] Since a major objective was to depict the depth of the later fall under Muslims, there had to be a great height from which the fall occurred. Consequently, the ancient period was held to be sacrosanct, above critical study. No criticism of the ancient period was to be tolerated, lest it dilute the communal critique of the medieval period. Consequently, even the most negative features of ancient Indian society were defended or glossed over. In his *Hindutva,* Savarkar, for example, defended the caste system and even explained sympathetically the prohibition on overseas travel.[44] Golwalkar too defended the caste system in his *We.*[45]

Second, Indian culture was identified with ancient Indian culture, which was, in turn, identified with Hinduism in its Sanskritic form. Thus, above all, it was the Gupta Age which was glorified as the Golden Age because of the belief that it emphasized Hinduism and the Sanskritic culture. Similarly, 'greatness' was defined by military conquests, strong monarchs and the size of empires. Here too, the Gupta Age seemed to fill the bill.[46]

Third, while the medieval period was shown to be full of conflicts, persecution, etc., the ancient Indian society was declared to be free of

[43]See, for example, M.S. Golwalkar, *We,* pp. 8,10, 13.

[44]See pp. 22-23, 69.

[45]See pp. 62-64,71.

[46]See, for example, V.D. Savarkar, *Hindutva,* pp. 18-21, 33-34; and *Hindu Rashtra Darshan,* p. 39.

social and religious tensions and conflicts. Even the caste system was said to promote social cohesion and not division.

Fourth, antiquity or ancientness was seen as a crucial element of ancient Indian greatness. This antiquity or rather this unique quality of Indian civilization as compared to other world civilizations was proclaimed and defended with great vigour.

Hindus were, declared Indra Prakash, "the earliest people who developed a high type of civilization and disseminated it to the various parts of this earth."[47] Antiquity was also utilized to support the idea that the Hindu nation had already been formed in the ancient period.[48] It was essential to the claim that India was solely the Hindus' 'hereditary territory' or possession[49] and to thus emphasize the 'foreignness' of Muslims and to deny that long residence in India could give them the right to become Indians. It was this need to prove the Hindus' 'ancient title' to the land and to deny it to Muslims that increasingly pushed the communalists to adopt the position that India was the original home of the Aryans and that the latter had not migrated into India from outside. Whatever the scientific aspect of the Aryan migration theory, to the communalist its denial became an ideological and emotional necessity which sometimes produced ludicrous situations. We may take Golwalkar's treatment of the subject as an example. While Savarkar had, in the early 1920s, been willing to entertain the theory that the Aryans entered India from outside,[50] in 1939 Golwalkar refuted it vehemently and said that its real objective was to show "that the Hindus are mere upstarts and squatters on the land." But there was a major hitch in this refutation. Lokamanya Tilak had written a book about the Arctic home and origin of the Aryans; and he could not be declared to be anti-national and

[47] *Indra Prakash, A Review...*, p. 4. Also see V.D. Savarkar, *Hindutva,* pp. 4-5, 111; and M.S. Golwalkar, We, pp. 8-10. Interestingly, as was done quite often by the communal writers, Indra Prakash sets out to prove his point by producing certificates from Western writers; in this case, Lord Curzon and Max Muller! *Op. cit.,* p. 3.

[48] V.D. Savarkar, *Hindutva,* pp. 5, 10-12,20, 23-24, 26, 33-34 and *Hindu Rashtra Darshan,* pp. 41-42; M.S. Golwalkar, *We,* p. 72.

[49] M.S. Golwalkar, *We,* p. 48.

[50] V.D. Savarkar, *Hindutva,* pp. 7, 10, 24.

anti-Hindu. Golwalkar therefore came to the conclusion that the North Pole was earlier where Bihar and Orissa are at present and, consequently, while Aryans remained in India the Arctic zone travelled north on a zigzag course. To quote him: "...the Arctic Home in the Vedas was verily in Hindusthan itself and that it was not the Hindus who migrated to that land but the Arctic zone which emigrated and left the Hindus in Hindusthan." The moral was clear: "We Hindus come into this land from nowhere, but are indigenous children of the soil always from times immemorial and are natural masters of the country."[51]

The second step in the communal scenario of the stages of Indian history consisted of the 'terrible' fall of the Indian people and their culture and civilization during the medieval period.[52] "From such heights," declared Indra Prakash, "they fell into the depths of slavery and foreign subjection. The fall was really a terrible fall."[53] This negative view of the Muslim impact on Indian society and culture was dinned into the minds of middle class Hindus day in and day out through every possible means of communication. Most of the social and cultural ills of Indian society, all its backwardness, were ascribed to 'Muslim rule' and 'Islam.' The entire medieval period was represented as the dark age "during which the national life of India was deflected from the normal course of its evolution and plunged into a social and religious chaos from which it is difficult for it to extricate itself."[54] As we have seen earlier, the entire medieval period was characterized as a period of "evil,"[55] of "denationalization" of Hindus,[56] and of "conflict of life and death" between Hindus and Muslims.[57] Usually, two additional points were made. First, the "tide of Hindu cultural degeneration" continued during the modern

[51]M.S. Golwalkar, *We,* pp. 11-13.

[52]Though the fall is also postulated as beginning earlier in order to explain the defeat of the Hindu rulers by the Muslim invaders. See *ibid.,* p. 14.

[53]*Indra Prakash, A Review...,* p. 4.

[54]*Report of the Kanpur Riots Enquiry Committee,* p. 130.

[55]M.S. Golwalkar, *We,* p. 17.

[56]*Ibid.,* p. 66.

[57]V.D. Savarkar, *Hindutva,* p. 34.

period.[58] Second, not everything was lost forever; the Hindu 'race' had evolved "a culture, which despite the degenerating contact with the debased 'civilizations' of the Musalmans and the Europeans, for the last ten centuries, is still the noblest in the world.... And even those, spoiled by contamination with foreign influences do not but compare favourably with the best in the rest of the world."[59]

The third communal theme was that of the 'Hindu revival' in the eighteenth century after centuries of decadence, tyranny and foreign domination, though even during 600 years of "defeats" and "humiliations" and of "Muslim ascendancy," Hindus had "carried on a life and death struggle to regain their national honour and glory."[60] But complete Hindu recovery and revival, it was said, started taking place under Shivaji's leadership. By the middle of the eighteenth century, Hindu supremacy had been re-established. The communalists described the rebellions, revolts and struggle for territory and political power by petty zamindars, Rajput rajas and Maratha chieftains as Hindu struggles and their states as Hindu kingdoms and empires. Moreover, it was said, all these struggles strengthened the dormant Hindu national feeling.[61]

Savarkar repeatedly hammered at this theme in his presidential addresses to the Hindu Mahasabha during the late 1930s. A long quotation may therefore not be out of place:

> Thousands upon thousands, princes and peasants alike, revolted and rose as Hindus under Hindu flags and fought and fell in fighting against their non-Hindu foes. Till at last Shivajee was born, the hour of Hindu triumph was struck, the day of Moslem supremacy set. Under one common name 'The Hindus,' under one common banner, the Hindu banner, under one common Hindu leadership, with one common ideal of the establishment of 'Hindu-

[58] M.S .Golwalkar, *We,* pp. 68-70.

[59] *Ibid.,* p. 49.

[60] *Indra Prakash , A Review...,* p. 6.

[61] V.D. Savarkar, *Hindutva,* pp. 36-56, 63-64 and *Hindu Rashtra Darshan,* pp. 15-16, 30, 39-40, 293-94; M.S Golwalkar. We, pp. 14-15, 69.

> Pada-Padashahi' (the Hindu Empire), with one common aim, the political liberation of 'Hindusthan,' the emancipation of their common Motherland and Holyland, the Hindus rose from province to province till at last the Maratha confederacy succeeded in beating to a chip the Moslem Nababs and Nizams, Badashahas and Padashas in a hundred battlefields.[62]

Similarly, he had, in 1923, in the *Hindutva* described the eighteenth century Maratha struggle as "the Great Movement of National liberation"[63] and had written:

> In this prolonged furious conflict our people became intensely conscious of ourselves as Hindus and were welded into a nation to an extent unknown in our history.... Sanatanists, Satnamis, Sikhs, Aryas, Anaryas, Marathas and Madrasis, Brahmins and Panchmas—all suffered as Hindus and triumphed as Hindus.... The enemies hated us as Hindus and the whole family of peoples and races, of sects and creeds that flourished from Atak to Cuttack was suddenly individualized into a single Being.[64]

The Hindu communalists chose nearly all their symbols and heroes, whose tales of bravery were used to inspire their followers, from the medieval period, ignoring those who had fought or were fighting determinedly against British conquest or British rule. There were two reasons for this: only 'anti-Muslim' heroes could be made to serve communal emotional needs; this was also the safer course, for while the British authorities ignored the glorification of such heroes, they came down heavily on any praise or propagation of anti-British heroes. It may also be noted that in treating those who fought against

[62]V.D. Savarkar, *Hindu Rashtra Darshan,* p. 40. He had written earlier in the *Hindutva:* "The rise of Hindu power under Shivaji had electrified the Hindu mind all over India. The oppressed looked upon him as an Avatar and a Saviour." P. 47.

[63]See p. 53.

[64]See p. 36. In fact, Savarkar devoted in this work over 20 pages out of 116 to this theme of Hindu rivival. See pp. 36-56, 63-64.

Mughal rulers as national heroes a basic aspect of communal history was being evoked as well as propagated: they were not just local or regional patriots but 'national' heroes because they fought against 'foreigners'; and the Muslim rulers were foreigners by no other definition than that they were Muslims.[65]

The task of Hindu revival and liberation was, however, said the communalists, interrupted by British conquest.[66] But even that conquest was made possible by the help that the British got from Muslims.[67] Nor did the Muslim perfidy end at that point of time. When Hindus had started a struggle against the British, Muslims were not cooperating. So, Hindus had to carry out the task on their own. In fact, enjoined the communalists, they had to link the two struggles, the struggle against Muslims and the struggle against the British.[68] It was the task of the present generation of Hindus, said Savarkar in 1938, to "resume the thread of our national life where ... our grandfathers left it at the fall of our Maratha and Sikh Hindu Empires."[69]

Before we conclude this aspect of the Hindu communal view of history, we would like to throw some light on a related aspect. Many nationalists also maintained a panegyric view of ancient Indian society, polity, economy and culture as a basic element of nationalist ideology; and the Hindu communalists borrowed this view from the nationalists. But the two differed in a few basic aspects in its use as well as in its form. The nationalists, starting with Dadabhai Naoroji and R.C. Dutt and ending with Gandhi and Nehru, had presented a positive picture of both the ancient and the medieval periods. The nationalist glorification of the past was part of the effort to bolster

[65]For a detailed discussion of this aspect, see Romila Thapar *et al.*, *Communalism and the Writing of Indian History*, pp. 54-61.

[66]V.D. Savarkar, *Hindu Rashtra Darshan*, pp. 30, 43; M.S. Golwalkar, *We*, pp. 15, 67.

[67]M.S. Golwalkar, *We*, p. 15; V.D. Savarkar, *Hindu Rashtra Darshan*, p. 43.

[68]Or, as M.S. Golwalkar put it: "We, Hindus, are at war at once with the Moslems on the one hand and British on the other." *We*, p. 19. Also see *ibid.*, pp. 16-18; V.D. Savarkar, *Hindu Rashtra Darshan*, pp. 17, 21, 51, 71-73.

[69]V.D. Savarkar, *Hindu Rashtra Darshan*, p. 63.

national self-confidence and pride, especially in the face of the colonial ideological effort to undermine them and create a psychology of inferiority and dependence. The Hindu communalists praised or idealized the ancient period in order to contrast it with the fall and decline during the medieval period and thus create anti-Muslim feelings. The nationalists went to the past looking for positive features in order to prove India's fitness for modern parliamentary democracy, modern civic and political rights, popular representation through elections and self-government. Nationalist historians like K.P. Jayaswal, P.N. Banerjee, B.K. Sarkar, U.N. Ghosal, D.R. Bhandarkar and even the early R.C. Mazumdar emphasized the democratic, constitutional, non-despotic and even republican, non-religious and secular, and rational elements of the ancient Indian polity and social life.[70] Thus, in nationalist hands, the glorification of ancient Indian society was a weapon in the anti-imperialist struggle. Despite its unscientific features and the potential for mischief in a multi-lingual, multi-cultural, multi-religious and multi-caste country, it had a certain historically progressive content. Moreover, the nationalists readily adopted and accepted scientific criteria for the evaluation and the further development of their views. The communalists, on the other hand, used the ancient past to create communal feelings and consolidation. They also held up for praise some of the most negative features of ancient Indian society and polity. They would also not tolerate the scientific treatment or criticism of any of its aspects.

The educated Muslims, and later the Muslim communalists, reacted to all this by harking back to the Golden Age of 'Islamic' or Arabic and Turkish achievement. The heroes, myths and cultural traditions they appealed to belonged not to the ancient or medieval periods of Indian history but to medieval West Asian history. Many turned their faces towards Turkey; symbolic was the popularization of the Turkish fez (cap) by Syed Ahmed Khan. Nor could they possibly

[70]R.S. Sharma, *Aspects of Political Ideas and Institutions in Ancient India,* pp. 3-13, 44; Romila Thapar, *Ancient Indian Social History,* p. 13. Similarly, Dadabhai Naoroji, the founding father of India's anti-imperialist struggle, contrasted the low level of British civilization in the ancient period with the heights reached by its contemporary Indian civilization.

accept that their religious, social and cultural impact had been the causative factor in the 'decay' of Indian civilization. Many of them, therefore, began to defend all, or at least most, aspects of medieval Indian society, culture and polity. The more rabid communalists defended even Aurangzeb's policies of religious bigotry, imposition of *Jaziya* and destruction of temples. He was hailed as the builder of *Dar-al-Islam* in India and pronounced to be a great and pious ruler. Akbar, on the other hand, was condemned for weakening Islam. To counter the theory of 'Islamic destruction' in India, they stressed the beneficial impact of 'egalitarian' Islam on the Hindu society ridden with superstition, caste, untouchability and inequality.

One aspect of this reaching back for the task of glorification to 'historical Islam,' that is, the past of the kingdoms whose rulers were Muslim in other parts of the world, was Pan-Islamism, which provided the notion of a worldwide 'Muslim people' and their great achievements both in terms of empires and religious unity in the past. The objective of Pan-Islamism was not only to defend 'Muslim' interests threatened by Western powers on a world scale but also to restore the past glory of Islam or the 'Muslim people.' Two aspects of Pan-Islamism should, however, be noted. Though it contributed in a major way to the growth of Muslim communalism, it was not, in the main, directed against Hindus. It was, on the other hand, till the early 1920s, on the whole, anti-imperialist, since on a world scale it was imperialism that was colonizing or threatening to colonize countries with predominantly Muslim populations. At the same time, even when anti-British on a world scale, Pan-Islamism was not in general anti-imperialist in the Indian context, except during the Khilafat phase.

In any case, in their search for Golden Ages and periods of glory, many educated Muslims and almost all Muslim communalists popularized the achievements of the medieval Muslim rulers and empires in West Asia and North Africa.[71] The history, the traditions,

[71]This effort sometimes produced hilarious results in the hands of the ignorant. In 1945-46, for example, Feroz Khan Noon glorified Chengiz Khan's massacres under the impression that because of the word 'Khan' in his name, he was a great Muslim conqueror! As is well known, Chengiz Khan, a believer in a nomadic Mongol religion whose God was Tengiri, killed Muslims in 'enormous numbers.' See M. Habib, "Chengiz Khan and the Mongols."

the mythology and the heroes of that period and those regions were used to create a feeling of community among Indian Muslims coming from different regions, belonging to different cultures and speaking different languages. As the Report of the *Kanpur Riots Enquiry Committee* noted:

> Pan-Islamism seemed to open up before them a new vista of hopes and aspirations more congenial and attractive than Indian nationalism, as in this new vista their imagination could find security against the harrowing horror of Hindu Raj and at propitious times, even revel in dreams of a possible Muslim world domination. This new outlook and sentiment were exclusively the possession of the educated sections of the Musalmans.[72]

The Muslim communalists also propagated their own version of the 'fall.' In their view, while Hindus were 'going up,' Muslims 'fell' or declined as a 'community'—and not as a part of the Indian people when the Mughal empire fell. Muslims, it was said, declined throughout the nineteenth century after 'they' lost political power. Their social condition was becoming pitiable. Their culture, religion and economic interests were threatened with ruin. They were increasingly becoming weak and helpless.[73] Many writers, such as Altaf Husain Hali, now took up the theme of 'Muslim melancholy' which was seen to be the result of Muslim decline.[74] Inevitably, this theme generated the fear of ultimate 'extinction' of Muslims in India and their domination by 'other communities' unless they took to communal consolidation.

As an illustration, we may take up the treatment of this theme by Z.A. Suleri, a major Muslim League ideologue during the 1940s.[75]

[72]pp. 207-08.

[73]The widespread nature of this belief is brought out in Syed Tufail Ahmed Mangalori's *Musalmanon Ka Roshan Mustaqbil,* "Foreword" by M. Bashiruddin and "Introduction" and Chapter 1 by Mangalori. One of Mangalori's major aims in writing the book was to refute this belief.

[74]For the class nature of this 'melancholy,' see Chapter 6 of this volume.

[75]*Z.K.* Suleri, *op. cit.,* pp. 11-23, 61-65.

According to Suleri, Indian Muslims were passing through a critical period and were facing disaster till Jinnah re-emerged on the scene in the 1930s. They were facing the danger of being "drowned" or "blotted out." The entire history of "Muslims from 1757" was a tale of British support to Hindus and suppression of Muslims. While Hindus were "pushing forward," Muslims were "sinking down." Especially after 1857, Muslims were "pushed into the vast sea of degeneration." Moreover, Hindus were getting united while Muslims were divided. By the end of the nineteenth century, "the century-long prosperity and patronage of the new power had made the Hindus solid, strong, educated and what is more important conscious of their political rights, on the other hand while the century-long suppression had thrown the Muslims into the very mire of misery...." It was Syed Ahmed Khan who arrested "the degeneration of a whole people." In any case, by the end of the nineteenth century, "one community had at its back a century-long prosperity and education, while the other had a century-long suppression and ignorance. How could the interests of the two be the same?" This degeneration of the "defeated" Muslims expanded further in the 1920s and 1930s till Jinnah came on the scene: "By the year 1934, the Hindu occupation of the Muslim mind was almost complete. Triumphant Hindu hordes were busy shepherding the disunited, confused and demoralized bands of the Mussalmans into the fold of Hindudom."

The Sikh communalists could not, of course, accept the medieval period as a period of their fall. But they too argued that it was a period of Muslim tyranny and of the decline and degeneration of Hindus. Sikhism arose, according to this view, to save Hindus from their cowardice and from Muslim tyranny. This could not be done by regenerating the decadent, caste-ridden Hinduism, as Hindu communalists argued, but by founding a new casteless, free-of-superstition and egalitarian religion, society and polity.

II

This is perhaps not the place to examine the scientific validity of the communal view of Indian history. Numerous historians have in recent years provided a convincing refutation of its basic premises and constituents. We refer the reader to their writings.[76] Here we would only like to reiterate that this view was to play an important role in the formation and the propagation of communal ideology and the growth of communal politics in pre-1947 India. It continues to play this role since 1947. It has, in fact, gained strength in some ways. It has now found support in academic writing at the research level and the university level text books while continuing to enjoy heavy representation in the school textbooks and popular 'made-easies.' It also finds literary and graphic representation at the level of novels, poems, stories, popular magazines and children's magazines, story-books and comics.

[76]See, for example, Irfan Habib, "The Contribution of Historians to the Process of National Integration in India—Medieval Period" and "Economic History of the Delhi Sultanate—An Essay in Interpretation"; Romila Thapar *et al*,, *op. cit.;* R.S. Sharma, *op, cit.;* Romila Thapar, *Past and Prejudice* and " Interpretations of Ancient Indian History"; Harbans Mukhia, "Commimalism: A Study in its Socio-Historical Perspective"; Satish Chandra, *Communal Interpretation of Indian History,* "History Writing in Pakistan and the Two-Nation Theory" and "Jizyah and the State in India during the 17th Century"; *Kanpur Riots Enquiry Committee Report;* Iqtidar Alam Khan, "Mughal Nobility and Akbar's Religious Policy"; M.Athar Ali, *The Mughal Nobility under Aurangzeb,* "Causes of the Rathor Rebellion of 1679" and "The Religious Issue in the War of Succession"; Tara Chand, *Society and State in the Mughal Period.*

CHAPTER 8

The Role of British Policy

British rule and British policy hold a special responsibility for the growth of communalism in modern India. The British took advantage of it, encouraged it and helped it reach the monstrous proportions that it ultimately did in 1946-47.

It has been quite fashionable, first among colonial administrators and now among certain scholars, to sneer at this view. This view, it has been said, arose to meet or serve the needs of the national movement[1] and is now nothing more than an aspect of the nationalist hangover, bias or emotion. A recent expression of this critique is by Gopal Krishna, who writes in a historiograhic, survey article:

> In the pre-independence period the theory of communalism (especially of Muslim communalism) most popular with nationalist writers was that communalism was *essentially a product of British policy....* This was a nationalist argument, developed, it appears in retrospect, from the point of view of the contemporary needs of the national movement rather than justified by historical evidence.[2] (Emphasis added.)

[1]But is not new understanding, or theory and thought, usually evolved to meet the fresh needs of society or of some of its sections at a particular moment; for example, the thought of Adam Smith, Ricardo, Keynes, Marx, Lenin, Mao, or Gandhi? This is also true of the view that denies the validity of the critique of colonial policy in this respect.

[2]Gopal Krishna, "Religion in politics," pp. 363-64. We may taks note of a strange bias in this author (and many others, e.g., Robinson cited in footnote 3). Nationalist writers and arguments are described as 'nationalist,' but the ideologies of other writers and of other arguments are left unmentioned. For example, the obviously imperialist writers, etc., arc not so described. It seems that nationalism made writers and argumerts ideological, but imperialism did not!

Similarly, Francis Robinson writes: "A second proposition is that the British deliberately *created division in Indian society* for their own imperial purpose.... Indian nationalist historians found the argument particularly attractive and accuse their imperial rulers of having broken an evolving synthesis of Hindu-Muslim culture."[3] (Emphasis added.)

Thus, one way of demolishing the critique of British policy regarding communalism and of, 'covering up' the British role has been to present the critique in such an *extreme or* simplistic form that it appears or becomes ridiculous or absurd. The critique is supposed to suggest that communalism was "essentially a product of British policy"; or that the British created the entire involvement of religion in politics or communal antagonism out of whole cloth, from nowhere; or that British policy was solely responsible for the rise and growth of communalism; or that the entire communal antagonism or politics can be attributed to British policy. This is to create a paper tiger which can then be easily blown away with one puff.

It is obvious that the British policy of 'divide and rule' could succeed only because something in the internal social, economic, cultural and political conditions of society favoured its success. We have already shown that these conditions were remarkably favourable for the rise and growth of communalism and for the policy of divide and rule; and communalism could grow not only because it served the political needs of colonialism but also because it met the social needs of some sections of Indian society.

Whatever might have been said at the level of popular agitation by lower-level political workers,[4] no responsible leader or writer has ever maintained that British rule was solely responsible for communalism or that communalism was basically created or produced by British policy or that the removal of colonialism would automatically solve the

[3]Francis Robinson, *Separatism among Indian Muslims,* p. 2. Also see G R. Thursby, *Hindu-Muslim Relations in British India,* p. 173.

[4]And a certain vulgarization of analysis is inevitable at that level. Imagine the results if an analysis of Marxism or of the liberal writings on the Second World War, etc., was made through citations from the popular agitational level.

problem. What the anti-imperialist writers have maintained is that the colonial authorities followed a policy of divide and rule, encouraged and promoted communalism, accentuated communal conflicts and used communalism to perpetuate their rule; and that, consequently, the removal of colonialism was one of the necessary conditions, though not a sufficient condition, for the 'solution' of the communal problem. So dense is the fog of misrepresentation created around this question that to bring out British responsibility in this respect is to be accused of being a nationalist bigot. So, before bringing out this responsibility, I would like to quote at length representative nationalist writers to show that they did not put forward the absurd version of the critique ascribed to them by the apologists of imperialism.

Thus, among the nationalist leaders, Motilal Nehru said in his presidential address to the National Congress in 1928: "Nor is the Government solely accountable for all the communal differences which have contributed a dark chapter to the recent history of our own times." And: "It is difficult to stand against the foreigner without offering him a united front. It is not easy to offer a united front while the foreigner is in our midst domineering over us."[5] One of the most authoritative nationalist documents on the communal problem, the *Report of the Kanpur Riots Enquiry Committee,* 1931, ascribed communalism to "the social, religious and political factors which have been *in the main responsible for the birth of the communal problem."* At the same time, it set out to discuss "the part which British policy has played in *working it up* and in *bringing* matters to the present crisis." Similarly, it correctly posed the problem of studying the role of British policy as follows: "To discover the real social and political causes which have given birth to this problem we shall have to study *along with other factors* the undercurrents of British policy during the whole period of British administration."[6]

[5]Motilal Nehru, *The Voice of Freedom: Selected Speeches of Pandit Motilal Nehru,* pp. 52-53.

[6]See pp. 45 and 161. (Emphasis added.) Similarly, discussing the politics of the British and that of Syed Ahmed Khan, the *Report* says that, despite different motives, the two were "converging towards the same centre," p. 183. The following were members of the Committee: Purshottam Das Tandon, Pandit Sunder Lal, Bhagavan Das, Manzar Ali Sokhta, Abdul Latif Bijnori and Maulana Zafrul Mulk.

In his address to the Lucknow session of the National Congress in 1936, Jawaharlal Nehru pointed out that the Congress had always "argued that the communal problem had arisen from a certain set of circumstances which *enabled the* third party to exploit the other two."[7] (Emphasis added.) And, again, in 1936 in his letter to Lord Lothian, he gave voice to the real nationalist critique of colonial policy in this regard:

> Obviously, no one can say that there was not an inherent tendency towards division in India, and with the prospect of the approach of political power, this was likely to grow. It was possible to adopt a policy to tone down this tendency; it was also possible to accentuate it. The Government adopted the latter policy and encouraged in every way every fissiparous tendency in the country.[8]

Earlier, in January 1934, in a major essay on communalism, he had written: "Communalism thus becomes another name for political and social reaction and the British Government, being the citadel of this reaction in India, naturally throws its sheltering wings over a useful ally."[9] In 1943, in his prison diary, he commented:

> What a lot Jinnah and his Muslim League have to answer for! ... But is it any good cursing others? They have misbehaved and betrayed the cause of our country and freedom! Agreed—What then?... Why did we permit them to do so? True the British Government helped them and created the conditions under which they flourish. That too is not enough! There must have been, must be, something wrong with our thinking. To blame others is never good enough.[10]

[7]Nehru, *SW,* Vol. 7, p. 190.

[8]*Ibid.,* pp. 69-70.

[9]*Ibid.,* Vol. 6, p. 182

[10]*Ibid.,* Vol. 13, p. 244, entry on 21 September. Similarly, in the chapter on communalism in his *An Autobiography,* nowhere does Nehru assign the British a causative role in the rise of .communalism. In a letter to J.T. Gwynne in 1933, he accused the British Government of having "deliberately aggravated this disease by their policy." *Ibid.,* p. 56. For Gandhi's views see his collection, *The Way to Communal Harmony,* pp. 6-7, 194-99.

Rabindranath Tagore repeatedly expressed similar views. He warned the political leaders in 1907 that: "That Muslims could be used against Hindus is the really worrying fact, who used them is not as important. Satan cannot enter till he finds a flaw...."[11]

What has perhaps led to a certain misunderstanding of the nationalist leaders' viewpoint was their belief that divide and rule or a policy of counterpoise was a basic aspect of colonial policy and that there could be no long-term solution of the communal problem till the 'third' party, i.e., the colonial administration, left the scene.

The much-criticized nationalist or anti-imperialist writers have also not been guilty of the charge preferred against them. The most important Indian analyst of the communal problem, K.B. Krishna, who has been accused by both Gopal Krishna and Francis Robinson of creating and propagating the myth of British responsibility for the origin of communalism, analysed at length the social roots of communalism and then wrote:

> These struggles, (within Indian social classes and groups), arising from the social economy of the country, are *accelerated* in an epoch of the development of Indian capitalism under feudal conditions, by British imperialism, by its policy of counterpoise.... Even if imperialism were overthrown, the problem of overcoming the social forces which give rise to careerism or communalism has to be faced. It is here that socialism presents itself as the solution of the problem.[12] (Emphasis added.)

A.R. Desai fully accepts this view.[13] Similarly, R. Palme Dutt, after analysing the socio-economic rivalry among the rising middle classes,

[11]Quoted in Sumit Sarkar, *The Swadeshi Movement in Bengal 1903-1908,* p.83. Tagore said that the root of the evil lay in the social traditions of Hindus which led them to treat Muslims as inferior. He also pointed to the 'great ocean' that separated the educated few, who were mainly Hindus, from the masses. To build a powerful national movement, he said, it was necessary to bridge this 'ocean.'

[12]K.B. Krishna, *The Problem of Minorities,* pp. 296 and 346. Also see p. 277 where British policy is accused of "accentuating" the tension arising out of "the general economy of the country." Also see p. 263.

[13]A.R. Desai, *Social Background of Indian Nationalism,* pp. 360-98. See in particular pp. 362-63.

wrote: "This was the soil which made it easy for official policy to play on the latent antagonisms and build upon them a whole political system."[14] C.G. Shah, another major analyst of communal politics, was even more explicit: "British imperialism, though it did not create (it is a misconception that it *created* it) political Muslim communalism, however, accentuated and utilized it in pursuance of its *divide et impera* strategy with a view to perpetuating its domination over India."[15] Beni Prasad also expressed a similar opinion. While the British did not originate communalism, "in the course of piecemeal adjustment to various factors and exigencies of the Indian situation during the last 80 years, the British Government did strike on policies and actions calculated to sustain and accentuate the differences between the two communities."[16] Even the much-maligned Asoka Mehta and Achyut Patwardhan did not take an extreme or stupid position on the question and placed their critique of colonial policy in the context of "the favourable soil" provided by the "fissiparous tendencies in our social structure" and "the social forces acting on our body-politic for the last hundred and fifty years."[17]

In fact, it is to avoid this type of cheap accusation that I have placed this chapter entitled "The Role of British Policy" at the tail-end of the work, after discussing at length the social, economic and cultural roots of communalism in modern India.

II

To come back to the main point, the British rulers did play an important role in the promotion, spread, growth and the ultimate partial success of communalism in modern India. Their role became crucial precisely because they held state power, a crucial determinant in the political fortunes of any political ideology or movement. And to deny this role directly or indirectly by misrepresenting those who bring it out is to become an apologist for imperialism. In fact, this is one of

[14]R. Palme Dutt, *India Today*, p. 425. Also see pp. 428ff.

[15]C.G. Shah, *Marxism Gandhism Stalinism*, p. 191.

[16]Beni Prasad, *The Hindu-Muslim Questions*, p. 163.

[17]A. Mehta and A. Patwardhan, *The Communal Triangle in India*, p. 79. Also see the "Introduction," pp. 7-9.

the major fields of colonial policy taken up for defence and apologetics by the neo-imperialist school of historians, often in the name of sophistication.

In fact, apart from the socio-economic situation, British policy was the determining element of the communal question. After all, the social classes and groups involved—from landlords to the petty bourgeoisie—lacked the political power to push their interests through communal politics and could hardly have gone far, or even dared to try to do so, in the absence of support from the colonial state. Here, the contrast with the present is instructive. Today, in India, even the existence of a weak and compromising secular state has made it possible to keep communalism under check and to prevent it from becoming a mass phenomenon.

The policy of dividing Indians on communal lines and giving support to the communalists became, from the end of the nineteenth century onwards, an important instrument of colonial policy in the effort to thwart the rising national movement. Virtually since the founding of the National Congress, parallel with its growth through different stages, and as an accompaniment to the process of constitutional reforms, the official policy of active promotion of communalism was developed. This policy was also developed to meet the exigencies of politics back home in Britain where the growing democracy and labour movement were increasingly questioning imperialism in general and the policy of suppression of the popular national movement in particular, Communalism was presented by the colonial administrators as the problem of the defence of minorities. And the defence of minorities became a major part of the theory of imperialist legitimation, as its other components—welfare of the colonized, civilizing mission, white man's burden, etc.—got increasingly discredited. The imperialist statesmen, officials and ideologues at that stage said that Britain had to continue to rule India because it alone could protect the minorities from domination, exploitation and suppression by the majority.[18]

[18]The Indian, particularly the Muslim, communalist agreed and lent active support to this view. As we have seen earlier, it was this that made him an instrument of imperialism and reaction, even when he might have subjectively been a nationalist.

It should be remembered in this respect that the communal division was not the only constituent of the policy of divide and rule, just as divide and rule was not the only weapon in the armoury of colonialism for its preservation and continuance. An effort was made to set as many groups and interests against one another as possible and to find and widen as many social gaps as possible; and different permutations and combinations were tried at different times to split up the Indian people and prevent their emerging unity. Regionalism (such as Bengali versus Bihari, Panjabi versus Bengali, the rest versus Panjabis), linguism, province-against-province, caste-against-caste or the balancing of castes (Brahmins versus non-Brahmins in West and South India), martial versus non-martial 'races,' agriculturists versus non-agriculturists, landlords and peasants versus the educated middle classes, moderate versus extreme nationalists at every stage of the national movement,' young India' versus 'older India,' leftists versus rightists, communists versus conservatives, reformers versus the orthodox—no possible division was considered too paltry as grist for the imperialist mill, no grouping was too humble to be exploited as a counterpoise to the national movement. In addition, every effort was made to mobilize the vested interests—the *talukdars,* zamindars, landlords, princes, big merchants and capitalists—against the nationalists. Nor were class divisions completely ignored. Despite obvious constraints, efforts were made to utilize the class contradictions between peasants and landlords, workers and capitalists, and debtors and creditors. Divide and rule was thus a 'many-splendoured' policy which became a basic and all-pervading element of colonial policy. It is, of course, a matter of history that it was the communal division which survived to the end and proved the most serviceable.

It is usual to quote from leading British policy-makers to show that the British followed the policy of divide and rule or of using Muslim communalism as a counterpoise to the anti-imperialist movement. Quotations from Malcolm (1813) and Ellenborough (1843) through Dufferin, Colvin, Curzon and Minto to Oliver, Birkenhead and Churchill are, and can be, easily given. This is a valid and important historical method. But we will not follow it here, for, apart from other reasons, it would take up too much space,[19] Instead, we will examine the nature and character of this policy, for much of the criticism of the critique of British policy towards communalism or the defence and

[19]The temptation to give a few examples from the long string of quotations is, however, irresistible. Thus, Lord Elphinstone in 1858: "'*Divide et impera*' was the old Roman motto, and it should be ours." A.R. Desai, *op. cit.,* p. 363. Charles Wood, Secretary of State for India, wrote to the Viceroy in 1862 that the antagonism of Indian 'races' was an element of strength to the British in India. Therefore, "a dissociating spirit" should be kept up, for "if all India was to unite against us how long could we maintain ourselves." S. Gopal, *British Policy in India 1858-1905,* p. 36. Cross, Secretary of State, wrote to the Viceroy in 1887: "This division of religious feeling is greatly to our advantage." *Dufferin Papers,* Reel 518. Birkenhead, Secretary of State, wrote to the Viceroy in March 1925: "I have placed my highest and most permanent hopes in the eternity of the communal situation." G.R. Thursby, *op. cit.,* p. 173. Oliver, ex-Secretary of State, wrote in a letter to the London *Times* that British officialdom in India followed the policy of using the Muslim community "as a make-weight against Hindu nationalism." W.C. Smith, *Modem Islam in India,* p. 201. Churchill's views as expressed in the Cabinet meeting of 2 February 1940 are recorded as follows in the Cabinet Papers: "...he did not share the anxiety to encourage and promote unity between the Hindu and Muslim communities. Such unity was, in fact, almost out of the realm of practical politics, while, if it were to be brought about, the immediate result would be that the united communities would join in showing us the door He regarded the Hindu-Muslim feud as the bulwark of British rule in India." Quoted in R.J. Moore, *Churchill, Cripps and India, 1939-1945,* p. 28. Churchill had earlier, i.e., on 3 November 1937, written to Linlithgow: "I think the main difference between us is that you consider a united All-India an end desirable in itself; whereas I regard it as an abstraction which in so far as it becomes real will be fundamentally injurious to British interests. I look upon India as one on the same scale as Europe with all its divisions and counterpoises, and upon the British function being to preserve the balance between these great masses, and thus maintain our own control for our advantage and their salvation." He further added: "Following this line of thought I should rather like to see the Muslims of the North joining together as a counter-check upon the anti-British tendencies of the Congress. I hope the 'princes' India will preserve a separate entity and outlook from the rather dismal and bleak outlook manifestation of British India. I should have thought that it was in the preservation of these forms of culture and thought that one of the essentials of British strength rested.... I'm not at all attracted by the prospect of one united India which will show us the door. We might not be able to prevent it, but that we should devote our best efforts to producing it, is to my mind distressing and repugnant in the last degree.... Of course, my ideal is narrow and limited. I want to see the British Empire preserved for a few more generations in all its strength and splendour. Only the most prodigious exertions of British genius will achieve this aim." *Linlithgow Papers,* Roll No. 150.

apologia of this policy arises out of the failure to understand its mainsprings and its nature and character.

III

The British Indian administration did not support a particular 'community' or communalism for the love of that 'community' or communalism. The aim of the British policy of divide and rule was to check the politicization of the Indian people, to curb their consolidation and unification and to *disrupt* the process of the Indian nation-in-the making. Once the anti-imperialist nationalist movement arose, the policy was also directed towards checking its growth, dividing its actual or potential supporters and preventing Muslims (as also landlords, capitalists, Panjabis, etc.) from joining it. To meet the nationalist onslaught and to perpetuate their own rule, the British needed to find support among some sections of the Indian people, to create some political support base. The long-term policy adopted was that of stimulating communal antagonism and communal politics and organization through appropriate short-term administrative policies which could have a certain diversity to suit the given moment as well as the personalities and the outlook of the given administrators. This would divide the Indians, make them fight each other as enemies and secure the active or passive support of communal forces for colonial rule because they would treat the other community as the main and immediate enemy. It should be remembered in this context that official support to Muslim communalism was a part not of an anti-Hindu policy but of an anti-nationalist policy. It was for this purpose that the National Congress was dubbed a Hindu body. Also, the British policy-makers were frightened not only of the rising anti-imperialist movement but also of its attempts to weld the Indian people into a nation.

The official British commitment was not to communalism in itself but to its use for their own particular ends. The policy of divide and rule was not *a perverse* one. The aim was not to divide Indian society for its own sake or out of perversity or malice. It was not followed for itself or as a matter of principle but as a political instrument and as a part of a broader political strategy of maintaining colonialism in the face of the nationalist challenge. For that reason, among others, it was used only to the extent needed. Similarly, its edges and contours were not the same throughout. It evolved gradually and changed to meet the changing times and the changing needs of colonial politics. It also differed from region to region. For example, it was not followed as one-sidedly in Panjab as in Bengal or UP; nor as actively between 1911 and 1923 as before 1911 and after 1930. The commitment to Muslim communalism became total only after 1939.

Moreover, this policy was not necessarily a well-worked out strategy which was developed as a blueprint at any particular date by a particular administration or policy-maker. A policy of this order does not get evolved through a single act of decision-making or planning or conspiracy. It evolves gradually even without the full knowledge or concurrence of all the policy-making officials. Its evolution is like that of the market-place decisions which are the result of capitalist interest or profit motive but not necessarily willed by any single capitalist. In the case of divide and rule, the perpetuation of colonial rule took the place of the profit motive.

Nor did this policy evolve out of nowhere as a sort of outside imposition on Indian society. As we have shown earlier, divisive tendencies existed and were being formed in Indian society. The forces of integration were also active. The state, with all its massive power, could either promote national integration or keep up and promote all kinds of divisions. The colonial state, because it was colonial, chose the latter course.

One reason that enabled the colonial state to support communalism and to make this policy a success was the common social base of both in the jagirdari elements in general and the landlords and bureaucrats in particular, who felt threatened along with the colonial state by the radical changes in the political and economic structure projected by the anti-imperialist forces. Furthermore, the communal demands did not in any way lessen colonial control or weaken colonialism.

The policy of divide and rule was complex and subtle. Both its critics and those who criticize them have tended to a rather simplistic or crude understanding of it. It seldom, except perhaps near the end, took the form of a conspiracy by the officials. As we shall see, communalists were seldom given open and all-out support by the colonial state. They were encouraged through the ready acceptance of their demands, welcoming of their initiatives, 'non-frowning' upon their agitations, non-action against their ideological misdemeanours, extension of official patronage and so on. The degree of support also varied in time as well as space.

Nor were all divisions favored and promoted indiscriminately. Some divisions were curbed. For example, in Panjab, the semi-communal leaders such as Fazli Husain, Sikandar Hayat Khan, Chhotu Ram and Sunder Singh Majithia were prompted into mutual co-operation in the name of unity of the agriculturists against non-agriculturists. Similarly, in 1916, when the Muslim League was threatened by a double-edged split between Bombay and UP leaders and Khojas and Sunnis, the Governor of Bombay intervened and chaired the meeting where the differences were resolved.[20]

The colonial state did not extend to communalism, except near the end, its open and all-out support for several reasons. Uncontrolled, extreme communal tension and hostility and extremist communal politics carried several dangers to the colonial state and contradicted its interests in some respects. They had therefore to be controlled, promoted and permitted only in muted or 'bottled-up' versions. In particular, violent communal outbreaks were to be avoided. This meant that, within the overall framework of supporting communalism, the colonial administrators also tried to check communal tensions, to avoid 'heating up communal relations' and to minimize communal violence, especially when it led to and reflected 'lower class turbulence.'

Militant communalism and communal violence posed administrative problems and were a threat to law and order and to socio-political stability which were seen as necessary for the maintenance of colonial

[20]Francis Robinson, *op. cil.,* p. 244.

rule. Nor could local administrators be expected to welcome serious communal trouble. The colonial authorities, therefore, tried in general to minimize communal violence and to bring down communal passions when they rose too high. But they preferred to face administrative problems created by communalism rather than let the process of the unification of the Indian people in an anti-imperialist movement proceed unhindered. As Hamilton, the Secretary of State, wrote to Elgin, the Viceroy, in 1897: "One hardly knows what to wish for. Unity of ideas and action (among Indians) would be very dangerous politically, divergence of ideas and collision are administratively troublesome. Of the two the latter is the least risky, though it throws anxiety and responsibility upon those on the spot where the friction exists."[21]

Extreme communal feelings or involvement of religion in politics could also lead to mass politics and to popular outbreaks which could turn against the colonial authorities and, simultaneously with communalism or religious feelings, promote anti-imperalism. At the level of religion, the experiences of the Wahabi movement, the Revolt of 1857 and the Akali Movement were obvious. At the level of communalism, the Calcutta riot of 1897, the Kanpur mosque affair of 1913 and the Mappila rebellion of 1922 served as examples.

Communalism was clearly undesirable if its edge turned against the government. This should not happen. Communalism should not get out of hand. We may, for example, notice the fate of the militant Khaksar Movement in Panjab in the 1930s. This movement was based on artisans and other lower class Muslims and was not merely communal but was also developing as a mass movement and posing a threat to law and order. It was anti-Congress but it was also becoming anti-government. Consequently, it was suppressed vigorously. The more middle class-based, elitist and politically passive Rashtriya Swayamsevak Sangh was carefully watched for any anti-government potentialities, but was left alone for the time being when it was found that it had no immediate intention of opposing the government.

[21]Quoted in S. Gopal, *British Policy in India, 1858-1905,* p. 201.

This fear of communalism becoming a popular force which might turn against the government also explains certain other aspects of government policy. Hindu communalism was not given as much support as Muslim communalism because it could, because of Hindus being in a majority, become a popular force and prove as dangerous to colonialism as Catholic-based nationalism in Ireland or Islam-based nationalism in Indonesia or the Arab countries.[22] This is brought out by the general alarm expressed by officials at the end of the nineteenth century as the cow protection agitation spread. Moreover, Hindus were seen as splintered by caste and sect and, consequently, not as dangerous as a 'community' as the more cohesive Muslims. Encouragement to Hindu communalism would integrate them into a 'community' and would therefore serve a purpose opposite to that of divide and rule. Consequently, the British used the Muslim League and not the Hindu Mahasabha (which was quite anxious to be used by them) as their chief instrument against the National Congress. Similarly, because of the legacy of the Akali Movement, sections of Sikh communalism tended to be anti-imperialist and were therefore given little support. Equal support to Hindu communalism was also incompatible with active support to Muslim communalism and the full play of the divide and rule policy. Even among Muslims, as was the case with the Khaksars in the 1930s or the Kanpur mosque affair agitators, such communalists, the edge of whose politics turned against the authorities, were firmly put down. Similarly during the second decade of the twentieth century, the government intervened against the younger Muslim leaders because, even though they tended to be communal, their political ideals were becoming no different from those of the Congress. In other words, communalism was to be supported only when it was quite compliant. The government also refused to extend franchise to all adults even though that would have met one of the major Muslim communal demands by automatically ensuring that the majority of the voters would be

[22]Thus, the British officials were highly critical of the Arya Samaj because, though it tended to foster communalism, it was suspected of also being anti-British.

Muslims in Bengal and Punjab; but that would have also compelled the communal leaders to acquire support of the masses as well as strengthened the mass base of the Congress in all, especially the Hindu majority, provinces. And throughout the late nineteenth century and in the twentieth century, the colonial officials and statesmen followed a schizophrenic policy towards Pan-Islamism. On the one hand, they wanted to utilize it as a part of their divide and rule policy within India and of their shifting policy of winning over West Asian and North African regimes by claiming to be the friends of 'Islam'; on the other hand, they were mortally afraid of its potential mass base and its tendency towards anti-imperialism.

Another reason for being careful and cautious in the matter was that a very open, active and all-out support to Muslim communalism could have been very dangerous to British rule for it would have earned the hostility of Hindu communalism, pushed it and its supporters into the Congress camp and tended to spur 70 per cent of India's population against imperialism. In other words, Hindus could not be antagonized overmuch as Hindus. Many of the colonial administrators saw this quite clearly. Viceroy Irwin, for example, wrote to John Simon in February 1928: "I do not wish, if I can help it, to see the lines of opposition between Government and the Hindu political intelligentsia irrevocably set."[23] Earlier, in 1927, while explaining to the Secretary of State why Hailey, the Panjab Governor, had appointed the Hindu Mahasabhite Manohar Lal as minister in place of the Unionist Chhotu Ram, Irwin had written: "Hailey's difficulty was that if he carried on with the old ministry, the Hindu Party as such would have been permanently excluded.... They would probably have been driven back on opposition ... and possibly to swaraj."[24] In the elections of 1926, the forces of Hindu communalism had split from the Swarajist nationalists, administered them a drubbing, and then followed a policy of giving responsive cooperation to the government in order to 'safeguard Hindu interests' by 'weaning'

[23]Quoted in G.R. Thursby, *op. cit.*, p. 173.

[24]Quoted in Prem Choudhry, "Role of Sir Chhotu Ram in Punjab Politics," p. 228,

it from a 'pro-Muslim' policy. Hailey felt that if the government ignored these men and relied only on Muslims and Unionists, they would be driven back into the arms of the nationalist "extremists."[25] Earlier still, Morley had warned Minto in January 1909 that "we have to take care that in picking up the Mussulman, we don't drop our Hindu parcels"; it was, however, clear, he said, that the administration had to go in "the Moslem direction" though it was "impossible to blurt out the full length to which we are, or may be, ready" to do so.[26] Similarly, in 1913, Meston, the UP Governor, had reversed his predecessor's recommendation of giving a large weightage to Muslims in municipal committees because it would "arouse a storm of indignation among the Hindus which will do us more harm with them, than good it will do us with the Muhammadans."[27] This hesitation to antagonize Hindu communal feelings also explains why the government adopted a policy of giving all-out support to Muslim communalism only after 1939, by which time the support of the Hindu masses and middle classes was already lost as the elections of 1937 and the popular movements against the imperialist authorities from 1930 to 1942 revealed.

In certain regions, communalism was also kept under control because of the particular political position they occupied in the Indian empire and the nature of alternative political strategy followed to control them. Panjab was one such area, where a different version of divide and rule was followed. It was a strategic border province. It was moreover the sword-arm of the empire. Its Muslim, Sikh and Hindu Jat and Rajput population provided nearly half the men for the Indian army. Uncontrolled communal passions and disorder would have divided the countryside, affected the contentment of the army and otherwise endangered the security of the border province. In Panjab, therefore, open and vicious forms of communalism were kept under check virtually till 1945, and not the Muslim League but the Unionist

[25]For a detailed discussion of this aspect, sec *ibid.*, pp. 227ff.

[26]Quoted in M.N. Das, *India under Morley and Minto*, p. 237.

[27]Quoted in Francis Robinson, *op. cit*,, p. 245.

Party was extended official patronage. The Panjabis were sought to be divided not along lines of religion but along the recently created divide of agriculturists and non-agriculturists, which pitted the landlord-led peasant castes against the 'urban' Hindu merchants and money-lenders. The attraction of this divide was that it did not affect the soldiers negatively; rather, it tended to keep them as well as the bulk of the other Panjabis out of any kind of nationalist politics. Any encouragement to the communal division would also have threatened the Unionist politics of agriculturist versus non-agriculturist by promoting intercaste Hindu solidarity. The British administrators therefore opposed the merger of the Muslim League with the Unionist Party or the growth of direct Muslim League influence in Panjab even after the Muslim members of the Unionist Party had joined the All-India Muslim League. Support from the Unionist Party was withdrawn in favour of naked communalism only near the end when the transfer of power was on the agenda and the alternative strategy of using an independent Pakistan against an independent India was being worked out. Perhaps a minor factor in the change in the British stance was the frustrated anger of the British officials against 'Hindus' for having 'deprived' them of the empire.

However, while not utilizing communal division as a major political instrument in Panjab, the British did encourage it as a subsidiary theme so long as it could be accommodated within the framework of the agriculturist versus non-agriculturist strategy. The Unionist Party and its ruling coalition were based on the semi-communal politics of Fazl-i-Husain and Sikandar Hayat Khan in West Panjab, Sunder Singh Majithia in Central Panjab, Raja Narendra Nath and Gokul Chand Narang among middle class Hindus, and Jat casteism in South-East Panjab (Haryana).

A similar non-communal strategy was tried off and on in UP where the *talukdars* and zamindars were seen as the strongest social force opposing nationalism and underpinning British rule. Communalism would have weakened it by separating Hindu zamindars from Muslim zamindars. Thus, the first open opposition to the National Congress was sought to be built in the late 1880s on this non-communal zamindari base; Syed Ahmed Khan and Raja Shiva Prasad were the joint leaders of the anti-Congress United India Patriotic Association. Only when this opposition failed to get off the ground did the officials and Syed Ahmed Khan decide to mobilize Muslim zamindars as Muslim opponents of the Congress.

Once again, in the 1920s and 1930s, in meeting the challenge of the non-cooperation movements and electoral politics, the UP officials set out to build an intercommunal political alliance of all zamindars as a counterpoise to the Congress, which was acquiring an increasing influence over the tenants, and, consequently, to keep the Hindu Mahasabha and the Muslim League out of state politics. Thus, in the 1937 elections, the chief opponent of the Congress was the National Agriculturist Party (NAP), and the officials used their influence to turn the Muslim *talukdars* and zamindars away from the Muslim League into the fold of the NAP.[28] This effort failed. The NAP was riven with communal disputes and infighting and it failed miserably at the polls in 1937. Both the zamindars and the British then shifted to communal politics.

There was another reason for the British unwillingness to countenance open communal violence. The responsibility, as rulers of the country, to maintain law and order and social stability was a part of the worldview and the colonial ethic in which the administrators were trained and which provided the inner moral justification for their activity in the colonies. No civilized rulers could openly encourage communal riots or even countenance them and remain totally passive in their face without breaking their own morale or fracturing and splintering their worldview. The British officials could follow such a passive policy in the face of barbarism only during 1945-46 when they no longer felt responsible for what happened in India and could even justify their passivity as a *quid pro quo* for Indians having driven

[28]The Raja of Mahmudabad narrates how in an interview in 1936 the UP Governor ordered him to withdraw support to the Muslim League and to join the NAP, hinting that the British had the authority to withdraw the grant of his lands. "Some Memories," p. 384.

them out. Also, the breakdown of law and order would remove, from the public mind, one of the most important justifications for the acceptance and toleration of British rule, namely, its ability to maintain law and order.

IV

Because of some of the considerations discussed above, till 1937, the British encouraged controlled communalism with some effort to hold the balance between different communalisms and to check its untrammelled growth. Thus Fuller, the Lieutenant-Governor of Bengal, was made to resign in 1906 when he created the impression of being anti-Hindu and of being a vigorous supporter of Muslim communalism. And as late as 1940, Zetland, the ex-Secretary of State, could write to the Viceroy regarding the Pakistan demand: "Taking a long view, I should myself doubt very much if a cleavage between the Muslims and the Hindus as fundamental as that contemplated by the present leaders of the All-India Muslim League would prove to be to our advantage."[29]

It is important to note in this respect that, in the beginning, the Muslim communalists were encouraged by the officials not with a view to stimulating communal politics, organization or agitation but to *prevent the emergence of modern politics and political agitation of any kind among Muslims.* Colonial policy at that stage was to prevent the politicization of the Indian people, a process which any form of political organization, including communal, would have encouraged. The objective therefore was not only to prevent the Muslims from joining the national movement but also to keep them aloof from politics and to discourage any move in the direction of even communal political agitation and organization. Thus, one reason why Syed Ahmed Khan could get massive official support throughout his career was his policy of keeping upper class Muslims away from any kind of modern politics and political agitation and of relying upon

[29]Zetland, *Essayez: Memoirs of Lawrence, Second Marquess of Zetland,* p. 292.

official patronage instead.[30] The early local societies founded by him in the 1860s discussed many topics from education and philosophy to science and literature but avoided politics. The Muhammadan Anglo-Oriental Defence Association, founded by him and others under official inspiration in 1893, decided to oppose the National Congress and defend 'Muslim' interests; but it also laid down that it would "discourage popular political agitation among Mohammedans." It would hold no political meetings nor affiliate other Muslim associations. One of its aims was to curb the tendency towards politicization among younger Muslim intellectuals.[31]

This policy was rigorously enforced at the turn of the century when the UP Government's Nagri resolution angered UP Muslims and produced a vigorous agitation in defence of Urdu, which, conservatives like Mohsin-ul-Mulk, the Secretary of the Aligarh College, joined. The Lieutenant-Governor of UP went down to Aligarh, threatened Mohsin-ul-Mulk with withdrawal of the grant to the College and thus forced him and others to give up all anti-government agitations, drop the Urdu Defence Association and stop the formation of a Muslim political association.[32]

This colonial political strategy had to be changed after 1905 when the Indian national movement entered the new stage of active political struggle. New ways and means had to be found to check the process of the nation-in-the-making and to obstruct the emerging united struggle against imperialism. The existing divisions within Indian society had to be actively fostered. Above all, the political Indians had to be split into rival communal camps. But non-political communalism had outlived its usefulness. Only organized political communalism could perform this task. The British at that stage promoted the political communalism of the Muslim League against the Congress.

[30]This is also one reason why the official approach to him differed so completely from that towards the moderate nationalists who also professed loyalty to the Raj. But the latter were, apart from being critics of colonialism, also propagators of modern politics and political agitation.

[31]Francis Robinson, *op. cit,,* pp. 86, 121-26.

[32]*Ibid.,* pp. 136-41.

Moreover, the younger generation of Muslim intellectuals were restive and were beginning to veer towards nationalism, Hindu-Muslim unity and political agitation and were threatening to join the Congress. (As pointed out in an earlier chapter, the younger Muslim intellectuals were powerfully attracted by left-wing nationalism till about 1942.) Even the loyalist, upper class Muslims were being pushed by the younger men into taking to some form of agitation. Though the tendency was suppressed, it could not be kept bottled up for too long. This was brought out with great clarity by Mohsin-ul-Mulk in two letters written in August 1906 to Archibold, the Aligarh College principal. In the first, he warned that Morley's announcement of constitutional reforms "will produce a greater tendency in them (the young educated Muslims) to join the 'Congress.'" In the second letter, he said that he had received letters from all over India telling him that "Mohammedan feeling is very much changed ... people generally say that the policy of Sir Syed and that of mine has done no good to Mohammedans ... that Government has proved by its actions that without agitation there is no hope for any community, and that if we can do nothing for them we must not hope to get any help for the college...." He warned that "if we remain silent ... people will leave us to go their own way...."[33]

Thus, some political organization and modern politics, apart from further political concessions by the government to the traditional loyalist communal elements, were inevitable if sections of Muslims were not to be lost to the Congress. These had to take non-agitational and communal forms. The loyalist elements had now to be encouraged to take to politics, but only to constitutional, parliamentary and dependent politics. Accordingly, the ready acceptance by the British authorities in 1906 of Muslim communal demands and of the claim of the upper class communal leaders of being the representatives of all Muslims had, in part, the objective of preventing Muslims from taking to political agitation and joining the Congress. Clearly, it is

[33]M.N. Das, *op. cit.*, pp. 164-65, 167-68; and B.L. Grover, *A Documentary Study of British Policy towards Indian Nationalism 1885 1909*, pp. 255, 259-60.

wrong to describe this policy as 'pro-Muslim.' Rather, its aim was to keep upper and middle class Muslims pro-British.

The policy of supporting parliamentary and dependent communal politics was followed from 1906. Whenever communalism tended to become militant or to come closer to the nationalist forces, it was cold-shouldered or even opposed. Thus, the younger, semi-communal intellectuals were frowned upon from 1906 onwards. Jinnah was never the official favourite and was treated virtually on par with the Congress leaders from 1930 to 1934. Vestiges of official antipathy to him were to be found even in 1936-37. Nor was communalism given all-out support till 1939, even though it was made a major issue and sedulously nurtured through sympathy, consideration and concessions during the constitutional discussions of 1930-34. It was also already seen as the most important political weapon against the burgeoning national movement.

After 1937, the British shifted from balanced to uncontrolled communalism, encouraged total communal division, gave virtually open support to the Muslim League especially in its anti-Congress role and tolerated its efforts to acquire a mass character. In the period after 1937, communalism increasingly became the only recourse of colonial authorities and their policy of divide and rule.

This was because nearly all other divisions, antagonisms and divisive devices promoted and fostered earlier by the colonial authorities had lost political force and had become politically non-viable from their point of view. The balances of 'classes and interests' carefully fostered since the days of Minto and Morley were failing. The nationalist movement had gradually succeeded in either overcoming them or reducing their political weight. The Non-Brahmin challenge in Maharashtra and South India had fizzled out. The Scheduled Castes and other backward castes could no longer be mobilized against the Congress except in stray pockets. Workers and peasants were increasingly mobilized behind radical anti-imperialism. The capitalists were already pro-Congress. The effort to pit the zamindars and landlords against the Congress in the 1937 elections had failed as had also the policy of strengthening constitutionalist forces outside the Congress. The right and left wings of the Congress could also not be split. The Lucknow session of 1936 and the decision to fight elections and form governments in the provinces in 1937 buried all fond hopes of the officials in this respect. The right wing would not split from the left and the latter was following at the time a 'united front' policy. The Liberal Federation was no longer an important political force. The constitutional and non-constitutional wings of the Congress also remained united. The moderate card had been played out. Moderate nationalist elements could be separated from the radicals only by giving up political power as was done in 1947. Princes were still in the field as props of the Raj, but they were being hard-pressed by popular states' peoples' movements. Reliance on the princes, on which the three-legged race of the Federation was planned, was likely to prove futile from the start. Interprovincial and interlingual rivalries had exhausted themselves much earlier.

Thus, just when the elections of 1937, in which the Congress came out victorious in large parts of the country, and the clear emergence of the Congress as a hegemonic force in Indian politics had created an alarming situation for the colonial rulers, many of their major props lay shattered. The communal card alone was available for playing against the national movement and the rulers decided to use it to the limit. They were also pushed to do so by the fact that the Muslim intellectuals and masses were being increasingly attracted to the national movement, especially its left wing.

The force of several considerations which had earlier dictated a policy of cautious and limited support to communalism was now very much weakened. Rampant communalism and communal violence could still create law and order problems. But the latter paled into insignificance when the very existence of colonial rule was at stake. Similarly, the loss of the support of Hindus was not much of a deterrent, for it was already more or less lost. On the other hand, the Hindu Mahasabha was already a spent force.

There was also not enough time or political space for the organization of a fresh political strategy to meet the nationalist challenge which had become more immediate and dangerous, especially in the context of a world war looming on the horizon and the growing left-wing strength in the national movement. The rulers were, on the other hand, familiar with communalism and had acquired a certain dexterity in manipulating it. Moreover, Muslim communalism was, as has been brought out earlier, for its own reasons, a strong political phenomenon at the time.

Thus, increasingly after 1937, communalism or the division among Hindus and Muslims became the chief political or 'civil' prop of imperial authority and presence in India. The British decided to stake all on it.[34] The Secretary of State in 1938, Zetland, wrote later that at that time he "could not resist a steadily growing conviction that the dominating factor in determining the future form of Government in India would prove to be the All-India Muslim League."[35]

The outbreak of the Second World War on 1 September 1939 further strengthened the reliance on the communal card. All policy was now geared to the successful waging of the war and to the maximum mobilization of Indian resources for the war effort. Several attempts were made to get the Congress cooperation for the war, but they failed. The Congress withdrew its ministries and demanded that the British make a declaration that India would get complete freedom after the war. They threatened to organize a powerful mass struggle to achieve their aim. Thus, the British faced a life-and-death struggle both for the maintenance of colonial rule in India and for the use of Indian resources in the world-wide conflict. They were willing to subserve all else to a victory on this dual front. Both for countering the Congress demand and dividing Indian opinion and response and for

[34]Political prop, because administratively one other was available and was freely used, that is, naked suppression or 'leonine violence' including bombing of the unarmed civilian population from the air. But the nature of British society at home and British rule in India and the huge size of the Indian population made it impossible to rely entirely on this prop over a long period. It is also to be noted that the nationalist agitation from the 1870s had already gradually destroyed the elements of civil hegemony of colonialism, such as faith in British benevolence, over the minds of the Indian people.

[35]Zetland, *op. cit.,* p. 247.

maintaining normal administration in as many provinces as possible, reliance was placed on the Muslim League whose politics and demands were counterpoised to the nationalist politics and demands. The League was, as will be shown, recognized as the sole spokesman for Muslims and given the power to veto any political settlement and its demand for Pakistan was virtually conceded in principle. India could not be given freedom, it was said, so long as Hindus and Muslims did not unite. But such unity was made impossible by the wholesale official backing to Muslim communalism. Thus, with lip-service to unity, division was promoted and ensured.

However, while giving all-out support to communalism, some efforts to maintain communal peace were made in the interests of the war effort. This check disappeared after 1945 and the people had a full taste of the bitter fruits of the poisonous tree during 1946-47.

V

The political settlement of 1947 revealed that British commitment was neither to the principle of the protection of minorities nor to Muslims nor even to Muslim communalism. Their policy towards communalism was geared to serving their own political ends. All promises and pledges to protect the rights of the minorities were at that stage forgotten. No safeguards were provided for the millions of Hindus in Pakistan and Muslims in India. If Muslims in post-independence India were able to live as equal citizens it was because the nearly century-old communal and British propaganda that the Congress was a Hindu body whose aim was to dominate and 'destroy' Muslims was false. What is even more interesting is that once the British could no longer maintain their rule in the subcontinent and had therefore no overriding interest left in using or supporting Muslim communalism against the nationalist movement, they unhesitatingly ditched it. In this respect, the partition of India has hidden an important part of the reality. Because the nationalists failed in keeping India united, it is assumed that the Muslim League got what it wanted. But the Pakistan that finally came into being in

1947 was very different from its 1940 conception; it was after all a 'truncated' or 'moth-eaten' Pakistan. The failure to carry through the original concept of Pakistan undoubtedly represented a betrayal of the Muslim League by the colonial rulers, While the partition represented a partial defeat for Indian nationalism and both Hindus and Muslims lost by it, history is likely to record that as between the Congress and the League, or as between nationalism and Muslim communalism, the latter was the bigger loser in terms of the achievement of their objectives, the materialization of their concepts and the long-term viability of their gains. Thus, once the British found that they were not capable of fighting for the continuation of their rule, they had no desire—or reason—left to fight for the League's demands or for the protection of the rights of the minorities.[36]

VI

With what instruments was the policy of divide and rule through communalism implemented? What were the different ways in which the British encouraged and supported communalism? This was done, first of all, by treating Muslims as a separate community or political entity in India and, in general, by acting upon the assumptions that India consisted above all of structured religious communities, that

[36]When, in 1944, C. Rajagopalachari had, with the backing of Gandhi, presented a scheme for Pakistan similar to the one accepted in 1947, that is, self-determination on the basis of the contiguous Muslim majority districts of the Muslim majority provinces, Jinnah had rejected it on the ground that "it was a shadow and a husk, a maimed, mutilated and moth-eaten Pakistan." In 1947, the radical Muslim League leader, Abul Hashim, asked Jinnah not to accept a truncated Pakistan. Claiming that the Mountbatten Plan was inferior to that of Rajagopalachari, he said that such acceptance would betray "the Lahore Resolution and the whole Pakistan movement." The Pakistan it created would be "a monster with two far-flung wings on the two extremities of a hostile India." He would rather give a ten-year trial to the Cabinet Mission Plan. Jinnah's reply was to make a sentimental appeal to the League Council: "'Do you want to have Pakistan in my lifetime?" and almost the whole House shouted in the affirmative. After a pause he said: 'Then, my friends, you have to accept this truncated and moth-eaten Pakistan." Kamruddin Ahmad, *A Social History of Bengal,* pp. 63-64, 79. It may, of course, be said that earlier Jinnah and the League had not expected even what they got.

religion took the place of nationality in India and that religion was the most meaningful division among Indians.

Most British policy-makers, administrators and writers emphasized the essential disunity of India, especially because of religious plurality or diversity. The notion that India was a nation or was becoming a nation or a *people* was rejected out of hand. Moreover, unlike the West, India was not held as consisting of individuals either. It consisted, it was said, of interests and communities,[37] and the most important interests were those of religious communities which were mutually exclusive and antagonistic.[38]

In the political field, not parties and individuals but religious communities were seen as acting, organizing, etc. The role assigned to parties and factional groupings or interest groups in contemporary political writing was, in India, assigned to communities. Even when parties existed, it was said that they merely represented the wills of religious communities, though often the Congress was denied the right to speak not only for most Indians but also for most Hindus. Consequently, the government insisted on approaching all questions of politics, administration, education, etc., on a communal basis and encouraged others to do the same.

This communal view of Indian society and politics was maintained and propagated from the beginning of modern politics in India to the end of the British rule. Dufferin was one of the first Viceroys to encourage Muslims to regard themselves as a distinct political entity in India.[39] Colonial administrators increasingly saw India as "a country of unintegrated communities."[40] Similarly, in his reply to the 'Muslim' delegation in 1906, Minto referred to "the beliefs and traditions of the communities composing the population of this

[37] *The Economist* of 27 February 1909 wrote: "Whatever may be the political atom in India, it is certainly not the individual of Western democratic theory, but the community of some sort." Quoted in K.K. Aziz, *op. cit.*, pp. 171-72.

[38] Nor was it a case of misapplication of Western political theory. A new principle of political organization not provided for in contemporary Western political theory was being applied here.

[39] S. Gopal, *op. cit., p.* 158.

[40] D.A. Low, *Soundings in Modern South Asian History*, p. 19.

continent." He also expressed approval of the views that in bodies such as legislative councils "the Mohammedan community be represented as a community," and that a Muslim elected with Hindu votes would sacrifice his views "to those of *a majority* opposed to his community."[41] Here, one gets full endorsement of the entire gamut of communal ideology as it was developing in India.

In 1926, Irwin referred to Hindus and Muslims as "two ancient and highly organized societies."[42] In 1930, the report of the Simon Commission referred to the relationship between Hindus and Muslims as that of "a basic opposition manifesting itself at every turn in social custom and economic competition, as well as in mutual religious antipathy." One result was that "representation of rival communities and different interests is the only principle upon which it has been found possible to constitute, by the method of direct election, the legislative bodies of India...."[43] The Joint Select Committee on Indian Constitutional Reforms went further: Hindus and Muslims "may be said indeed to represent two and distinct separate civilizations."[44] On 18 October 1939, Linlithgow spoke of the British Government's willingness "to enter into consultation with representatives of the several communities, parties and interests in India...."[45]

Apart from such official pronouncements, a large number of officials put forward, over the years, the two-nation theory as also the

[41]Reproduced in Ram Gopal, *Indian Muslims: A Political History (1858-1947),* p. 338; and B.L. Grover, *op. cit.,* p. 272. Minto also wrote to Morely on 23 January 1907 that the "only representation for which India is at present fitted is a representation of communities...." Quoted in B.N. Pandey, *The Break-up of British India,* pp. 75-76. Similarly, Morley, the Secretary of State, told the House of Lords on 23 February, 1909: "The difference between Mohamedanism and Hinduism is not a mere difference of articles of religious faith. It is a difference in life, in tradition, in history, in all the social things as well as articles of belief that constitute a community." *Parliamentary Debates,* House of Lords, 1909, Vol. I, Column 126.

[42]Lord Irwin, *Indian Problems,* p. 238.

[43]*Report of Indian Statutory Commission,* Vol. I, Paras 36 and 152. For similar views in the earlier *Report on Indian Constitutional Reform,* 1918, see pp. 84-85, 91, 99.

[44]*Report* of the 1933-34 session, Vol. I, Para 1.

[45]*Indian Annual Register,* 1939, Vol. II, p. 387; and M. Gwyer and A. Appadorai, *Speeches and Documents on the Indian Constitution 1921-47,* Vol. II, p. 491. For similar language in the Wavell Plan in 1945, see *ibid.,* p. 559.

theory of the incompatibility of the two 'community-nations.' They also constantly egged on the Muslim communalists to stick to the track and run the full course. They virtually assumed the role of the builders of communal ideology in India; a role they performed with great energy and acumen, till the Indian communalists were able to produce their own competent ideologues in the 1930s and 1940s.[46]

A recent scholar who has made an in-depth study of Muslim communalism in UP has summed up this aspect as follows: "There can be no doubt that British policy played the main part in establishing a separate Muslim identity in Indian politics."[47] Of course, once established, both Hindu and Muslim communalisms were to play an active part in sustaining the communal identities. And, later, the British were to portray these identities and differences based on them as the major impediment to constitutional concessions or to the transfer of power. Linlithgow, for example, was to tell the Indian political leaders in November 1939 that the British failure to evolve greater devolution of power to Indians was "because of the lack of prior agreement between the major communities such as would contribute to harmonious working at the centre."[48]

The British also gave direct encouragement and support to communal individuals, groups and parties in general and to the Muslim League in particular to oppose the national movement. From the beginning, Muslim participation in the National Congress was seen as deplorable by the dominant group of British officials and policy-makers, who made every effort to check this tendency and to disrupt the emerging national movement. Bureaucrats, jagirdari elements, job-seekers and petty bourgeois elements in general among Muslims were pitted against the Congress by encouraging them to

[46]K.K. Aziz has given extracts from the writings of many of these men whose ranks included V. Chirol, J.D. Rees, W.S. Lilly, J. Morrison, S. Low, Meston, E.A. Home, C.H.V. Tyne, H.G. Rawlinson, M.F. O'Dwyer, Verney Lovett, T. Morison, R. Craddock, J. Coatman, William Barton and editorial writers of journals like *The Economist* and *The Observer.* See *op. cit.*, pp. 50ff. and 167ff.

[47]Francis Robinson, *op. cit.*, p. 349.

[48]*Indian Annual Register,* 1939, Vol. II, p. 411.

think of Muslims as a separate political entity and then to fight for special rights *vis-a-vis* Hindus, while viewing the British as protectors of Muslims. While the opposition of upper class Hindus to the Congress was seen in class terms and not as 'Hindu' opposition, and Hindu communal opposition was rightly seen as communal opposition, opposition by upper class Muslims or by Muslim communalists was invariably portrayed as 'Muslim' opposition to the Congress.

For example, Syed Ahmed Khan was shown a marked favour at the personal and family plane and given conspicuous support in his educational and other activities. It was official patronage that made the Aligarh College and Syed Ahmed and other collegians a major political force, so much so that Francis Robinson has rightly concluded that "through government policy, Sayyid Ahmad ... was raised up as the advocate of his community," and the government gave the Aligarh College conspicuous financial and political support because it "played an important part in Government's scheme of political control."[49]

Similarly, in Bengal, the hereditary title of Nawab Bahadur was conferred on Sir Salimullah in order to enable him to acquire the glamour of being a traditional ruler so that he could emerge as a leader of the Muslims of Bengal. Titles were also conferred upon his cousins later. In addition, the Government gave him a loan of several lakhs of rupees to save him from his creditors.

During 1899-1900, A.P. Macdonnell, the Lieutenant-Governor of UP, tried to counterbalance this support to Muslim communalism by supporting Hindu communalism in the province. He tried to increase the number of Hindus in government employment and supported the advocates of Hindi against Urdu, thus pushing many nationalist Hindus and Muslims into respective communal camps.

Another form of official encouragement to communalism was that of support to denominational universities such as the Benares Hindu University and the Aligarh Muslim University. As Harcourt Butler, Lieutenant-Governor of UP, told the Viceroy in 1911, the

[49]Francis Robinson, *op. cit.*, pp. 131 and 348, respectively. Also see pp. 128ff.

denominational universities would give religious instruction and thus keep alive the Hindu and Muslim feelings.[50]

Also, whatever the other motives for effecting the partition of Bengal might have been, in order to strengthen Muslim communalism, Curzon declared in February 1904 that one of its purposes was to be able to "invest the Mohammedans in Eastern Bengal with a unity which they have not enjoyed since the days of the old Mussulman Viceroys and Kings."[51]

The divide and rule policy was implemented primarily by readily accepting communal demands and thus politically strengthening communalism and communal organizations and their hold over the people. This is clearly illustrated by the reception given by Viceroy Minto to the Muslim communal deputation and its demands in 1906. On 1 October that year, a deputation of leading conservative, upper class Muslims, headed by the Agha Khan, met the Viceroy at Simla with a charter of demands based on a communal understanding of Indian society and politics. The Viceroy then and there accepted most of the demands and endorsed the underlying communal approach.[52]

The deputationists had claimed to represent "a large body of the Mohammedan subjects of His Majesty the King Emperor." At the very outset of his reply, the Viceroy acknowledged "the representative character of your deputation as expressing the views and aspirations of the enlightened Muslim community of India." He went on to add that "all you have said emanates from a representative body...." He went further when he referred to "the position of the Mohammedan community for whom you speak." The deputationists had based their entire claim on the recognition of Muslims as "a distinct community." The Viceroy accepted this claim too.

The deputationists demanded for Muslims privileged representation beyond their numerical strength in the reformed councils on

[50]Cited in Aparna Basu, *The Growth of Education and Political Development in India, 1898-1920,* p. 163.

[51]Quoted in S. Gopal, *op. cit.,* p. 271.

[52]For the address by the deputation and for the Viceroy's reply, see Ram Gopal, *op. cit.,* Appendices B and C, or B.L. Grover, *op. cit.,* pp. 263-73.

grounds of their "political importance" and "the position which they occupied in India a little more than hundred years ago...." Accepting the demand, the Viceroy said: "You justly claim that your position should be estimated not merely on your numerical strength but in respect to the political importance of your community and the service it has rendered to the Empire. I am entirely in accord with you...." He also referred to the deputationists as "the descendants of a conquering and ruling race."

The deputationists had claimed that the existing system of joint electorates did not lead to the election of Muslims who represented their own 'community.' They had therefore demanded separate electorates. The Viceroy agreed that the Muslims "should be represented as a community." While refusing to make a commitment on the question of a separate electorate, he affirmed that "any representation in India would be doomed to mischievous failure which aimed at granting a personal enfranchisement regardless of the beliefs and traditions of the communities composing the population of this continent."

The deputationists demanded an assurance that in the future constitutional rearrangements care and caution would be exercised to see that the interests of the Muslim community did not suffer. The Viceroy promised: "The Mohammedan community may rest assured that their political rights and interests as a community will be safeguarded in any administrative reorganization...." Future concessions to Muslim communalism were to be justified by this promise.[53]

In historical literature, the significance of the Simla deputation has been clouded over by a controversy around the questions: Who took the initiative in organizing the deputation—the officials or the deputationists themselves? Was it a genuine deputation? Was the deputation really organized by the officials with the Viceroy's prior

[53]For example, when finalizing the Constitution Bill of 1909, Morley telegraphed to Minto: "No scheme will be sanctioned here which does not either fulfil the pledges, or, without fulfilment of pledges, commend itself to Muhammedan leaders here." Quoted in Francis Robinson, *op. cit.*, p. 171.

connivance? Did the Viceroy and the officials enter into a conspiracy with a handful of Muslim leaders? Was it therefore a 'command' performance? In fact, these questions are not important or are rather of minor significance.

The real question is how could the deputation be so promptly received, its demands and the logic behind them so easily accepted and basic undertakings so readily given? No political agitation or struggle had to be waged. After all, the Viceroys were not so accessible, nor used to receiving deputations, nor to so readily granting their requests or demands. As a recent scholar has put it: "If the deputation was not a command performance it was guaranteed box-office success in advance."[54]

On the other hand, the National Congress, quite loud in its proclamations of loyalty and ideologically closer to the British as it stood for Western liberal democratic values and a capitalist economic and political order, had been agitating for years, and yet even its mildest demands were not accepted. Why were the nationalists reviled, abused and ignored? Why was official patronage not extended till 1905 even to the Moderates who were loud in proclaiming their faith in the Raj? Similarly, the Simla deputationists were immediately acknowledged as representing Muslims without their having given any political proof of it, while the claim of the far more popular and politically representative body, the Indian National Congress, to speak for the Indians was rejected outright. The latter was, on the other hand, branded as a spokesman for a microscopic minority.

Despite the use in common of certain expressions of loyalty, a crucial difference demarcated the nationalists from the communalists. This difference then explains the totally dissimilar attitude of the colonial authorities towards the two. The nationalists, including the Moderates, generated nationalist politics and an anti-imperialist ideology and undermined colonialism and its hegemony, while the communalists practised and propagated the politics of loyalty and were therefore rightly seen by the rulers as the pillars of colonial rule.

[54]Peter Hardy, *The Muslims of British India*, p. 157.

The fact is that the Simla deputationists' pleasant fate and their 'remarkable achievement' in getting concessions can only be explained as part of the deliberate British policy of favouring and encouraging Muslim communalism with a view to disrupting the rising anti-imperialist struggle. Minto was helping to establish a separate communal identity for Muslims, and then trying to control the emerging younger Muslim intellectuals, who were beginning to veer towards the Congress, through the older, upper class leaders who were helped with concessions so that they could rally the young men round in the name of defending Muslim communal interests. Lady Minto was to record in her diary immediately after the Simla deputation:

> This evening I have received the following letter from an official: "I must send Your Excellency a line to say that a very, very big thing has happened today. A work of statesmanship that will affect India and Indian history for many a long year. It is nothing less than the pulling back of sixty-two millions of people from joining the ranks of the seditious opposition."[55]

The policy of ready acceptance of Muslim communal demands continued to be followed during the preparation of the Constitutional Act of 1909. The recently founded Muslim League agitated for (1) privileged representation for Muslims through the reservation of a certain number of seats in the new legislative councils in excess of Muslim proportion in the population on grounds of 'political importance', and (2) separate electorates, that is, only Muslims should vote for these seats. The Government of India immediately supported these demands. Morley, the Secretary of State, resisted for some time. He wanted reservation of seats for Muslims in multi-seat constituencies for which all voters in a constituency would vote. But,

[55]Mary, Countess of Minto, *India, Minto and Morley 1905-1910,* pp. 47-48. Similarly, Minto's Private Secretary, Dunlop Smith, told Butler a few hours after the deputation had met the Viceroy: "It meant that the M's declared to the H's that they would not join the Congress, (and) that they preferred appealing to their Ma-Bap to stumping the country...." Quoted in Francis Robinson, *op. cit.,* p. 167.

ultimately, under the joint pressure of Muslim communalists, British Conservatives, right-wing politicians and a large part of Indian officialdom, he fell in line and agreed to meet the communal demands 'in full.' Thus, while the Congress demand for representative government put forward for over 25 years was to be denied,[56] the Muslim League demands for separate electorates and reservation of seats for Muslims in excess of their proportion in population were to be accepted in full.

The danger of alienating the Moderates, the growth of discontent and nationalist feeling among young Muslim intellectuals, the rise of Pan-Islamist feelings, and the Khilafat-Non-Cooperation Movement led, during the second decade of the twentieth century and the early 1920s, to a certain passivity in the official policy towards Muslim communalism, though the conservative communalists continued to be favoured and encouraged. The failure of Hindu-Muslim unity efforts at the top level and the resurgence of the anti-imperialist movement in the late 1920s gave the British a fresh opportunity to resume this policy.

In choosing the delegates to the Round Table Conferences during the early 1930s, the government showed a marked favour to the communal leaders and ignored the nationalist leaders and individuals. This was one of the reasons why no agreement on the communal problem could be arrived at these Conferences. Moreover, the entire discussion was organized within the ambit of communal digits, thus making any solution of the basic political problem of political advance impossible.

In 1932, the government announced its decision on communal demands known as the Communal Award. The Award accepted all the major Muslim communal demands of the time. It guaranteed through reservations Muslim majority in Bengal and Panjab; it assured Muslims thirty-three and one-third per cent of the seats in the central

[56]Morley told the House of Lords in 1909 when speaking on the reforms of 1909: "If it could be said that this chapter of reforms led directly or necessarily to the establishment of a parliamentary system in India, I for one would have nothing at all to do with it." *Op. cit.*

legislature; it separated Sind from Bombay and introduced reforms in the North-West Frontier Province; and it decided to continue separate electorates. It was thus less an award than a pronounced favour shown to Muslim communalism. And it was based on an approach that fully accepted communal digits and the perpetual division of Indian political life on communal lines.

Thus, by 1935, when a new Constitution Act was passed, all the communal demands had been accepted. This had two further consequences. First, the ready acceptance of Muslim communal demands made it nearly impossible for negotiations at the top between the nationalist and communal leaders to succeed. Whatever concessions or compromises were offered by the nationalists, the colonial government could overbid them and thus remove any incentive to the communal leaders to compromise. Moreover, those Muslim leaders who agreed to settle with the nationalists could at that stage be made to appear 'pro-Hindu' as also unrepresentative of 'Muslim opinion.' Thus, the colonial authorities could by giving timely concessions authenticate the intransigent communal leaders as better if not the sole 'Muslim' leaders and help them dig political roots.

Secondly, once the communal demands regarding reservation of jobs and seats in the legislatures had been fully satisfied, as finally by the Communal Award incorporated in the Act of 1935, the communalist was left without any negotiable communal demands which could be rationally put forward and argued. Consequently, liberal communalism would either wither away or move 'forward' to a fascist, irrational position and programme. It was the absence of any visible demands which could be put forward that forced Jinnah to refuse to negotiate with the Congress after 1937 unless it first accepted the impossible condition that the Congress was a Hindu body and the League represented all Muslims. This posture could also not be carried on too long. The move towards Pakistan was then inevitable, for separatism was the only part of the communal ideological programme left unfulfilled, though here too Jinnah refused to explain as to what Pakistan would be like and how it would solve the problems of millions of Muslims allegedly resulting from Hindu predominance.

The policy of ready acceptance of communal demands was to continue till 1945. It is interesting, for example, as brought out in the next section, that the Muslim League demand for a veto on constitutional development was readily accepted during World War II and the demand for Pakistan was accepted even before the demand for dominion status had been conceded.

The British also followed the policy of supporting communalism by accepting communal organizations and leaders as the authentic or real spokesmen for 'the communities' and by strengthening their political position. Once the Muslim League was founded, it was given immediate political recognition. During the 1930s, it was continuously played up and increasingly recognized as the sole representative party of Muslims, even though it had organized no mass agitation or movement, had fared quite badly in the 1937 elections and, in fact, represented till the 1940s a very small section of Muslims.[57] The government also began to encourage the traditional loyalist politicians to join the Muslim League. Nationalist Muslims were, on the other hand, deliberately ignored and discouraged. This was done not only in the 1940s, when their influence among Muslims had been reduced drastically, but also in the 1930s when they were politically quite a force. For example, as pointed out earlier, they were completely ignored and only communalists were nominated as Muslim delegates to the Round Table Conferences. This official recognition was one of the important factors which helped the Muslim League to grow in the late 1930s and the early 1940s.

The height of this aspect of British policy was reached in 1939 and after when, in order to keep tight control over India during the war

[57]The government both recognized the League as a representative body and actively worked to make it so. For example, in 1939, in a letter to Zetland, dated 5 September, Linlithgow expressed his anxiety "to shepherd all the Muslims into the same fold." *Linlithgow Papers,* Vol. 8. In the same year, in November, Zetland, at that time Secretary of State for India, said that the Congress represented Hindus and the Muslim League Muslims. *Indian Annual Register,* 1939, Vol. II, p. 409. The Viceroy wrote to Amery, the new Secretary of State, on 18 January 1941: "I do not dispute Jinnah's claim to have 90 percent Muslim support." *Linlithgow Papers,* Vol. 10.

and to face the nationalist demand for the effective transfer of power, the British insisted that before any constitutional or administrative arrangements towards independence were discussed, the two 'communities,' Hindus and Muslims, must arrive at an agreement. Combined with the official acceptance of the Muslim League as the sole representative party of Muslims, this gave the League an absolute veto over any constitutional advance. Jinnah, in turn, persisted with his impossible demand that before any negotiations between the League and the Congress could take place Congress must renounce its secular character and declare itself or transform itself into a Hindu communal body. Till then the League would, and did, go on saying 'no' to every Congress proposal. This meant that negotiations between the two could never begin in earnest. The British could then assume a self-righteous pose and declare that responsibility for India's failure to make political advance lay with the failure of the 'communities' to unite and with the Congress's inability to win over the minorities. They, on their part, could not abdicate their responsibility towards the minorities.[58] This stratagem was at this stage such an important part, in fact the kingpin, of the British policy of bolstering up Muslim communalism, the Muslim League, and Jinnah and of pitting them against the Congress and the national movement that it may be traced here at slightly greater length, though it is not possible to discuss all aspects of the wartime British policy towards the League.[59]

The Muslim League Working Committee put forward its claim for a veto on all further political progress in the country on 18 September 1939 when it demanded that "no declaration regarding the question of constitutional advance for India should be made without the consent and approval of the All India Muslim League." It further demanded the ending of the federal scheme. It also claimed to be "the only organization that can speak on behalf of Muslim India."[60]

[58]For example, Amery, Secretary of State, declared in August 1940: "The constitutional deadlock in India is not so much between His Majesty's Government and a constituent Indian opposition as between the main elements in India's own national life." *Indian Annual Register,* 1940, Vol. II, p. 374.

[59]For a detailed discussion of this policy, see R.J. Moore, *op. cit.,* Chapters 2 and 3; and S. Gopal, *Jawaharlal Nehru—A Biography,* Vol. One, Chapters 16-19.

[60]*Indian Annual Register,* 1939, Vol. II. p. 352.

The British were willing to oblige the League for the British Cabinet "saw the growing rift between the Congress and the Muslim League as their trump card.... Most members of the Cabinet also looked to the communal divide as the most effective trap for the forces of nationalism."[61] On 11 September, the Viceroy announced the suspension of all moves towards federation.[62] On 5 November, he went a long way towards accepting the League demand for a veto when he told Gandhi and Jinnah that introduction of further Indian element in the Viceroy's Executive Council and restoration of popular ministries in the provinces were contingent on an agreement between the Congress and the League.[63] Zetland, the Secretary of State, responded on 2 November by asking the Congress as the representative of Hindus to reach a settlement with the Muslim League, the representative of Muslims.[64]

Jinnah and the League repeatedly reiterated the demand for a veto in the succeeding months, including at the famous Lahore session in March 1940 where the demand for Pakistan was first put forward.[65] The positive official response continued. On 18 April 1940, Zetland said in the House of Lords that Britain would not force a constitution on unwilling Muslims.[66] On 19 April, Linlithgow told Jinnah that no constitution would be enforced without the prior approval of Muslims.[67] And finally came the famous authoritative August (8) statement of the Viceroy which gave the League the desired veto. The Viceroy pledged that the British could not contemplate transfer of their present responsibilities for the peace and welfare of India to any system of government whose authority is directly denied by large and powerful elements in India's national life. Nor could they be parties

[61]B.R. Tomlinson cites Cabinet Papers for this view. See his *The Indian National Congress and the Raj, 1929-1942,* p. 144.

[62]Linlithgow, *Speeches,* Vol. II, pp. 140-41.

[63]*Indian Annual Register,* 1939, Vol. II, p. 411.

[64]*Ibid., p.* 409. Also see Uma Kaura, *Muslims and Indian Nationalism,* pp. 139-40.

[65]M.A. Jinnah, *Speeches and Writings,* Vol. I, pp. 89, 154.

[66]V.P. Menon, *The Transfer of Power in India, p.* 85.

[67]*Ibid.*

to the coercion of such elements into submission to such a Government.[68]

The British had thus by a series of prouncements, capped by the August declaration, given the Muslim League a veto over all further political progress in India. This veto bolstered the League, increased its bargaining power *vis-a-vis* the Congress and enhanced its prestige among Muslims. Jinnah and the League would not need to make any compromises with the Congress. They could afford to 'sit it out.' The Congress, on the other hand, had now either to concede Pakistan or to wage a two-front battle against the British and the Leauge.

The logic of the 'pledge' of 8 August was taken to its conclusion when, in March 1942, the Cripps proposals implicitly conceded the Pakistan demand. They suggested that any province or provinces which did not want to join the projected Indian union with dominion status to be created after the war could opt out of it, frame their own constitution and establish a similar, separate dominion relationship with Britain. Once again, this easy acceptance of the demand for Pakistan gave a boost to the League, increased its self-confidence, and demoralized the nationalist forces among Muslims. The League could now grow rapidly even in Muslim majority provinces where it had earlier faced many obstacles.

The policy of rallying the Muslim communalists was followed even more rigorously during and after the Quit India Movement of 1942. Apart from suppressing the Congress and removing its leaders from the political scene, the government helped the League by removing non-League ministries and installing League-dominated ministries in Assam, Sind, Bengal and the North-West Frontier Province, that is, in all but one of the provinces constituting the prospective Pakistan. The League in return fully supported the government's repressive policy towards the nationalists. This acquisition of the limited levers of power was to play a crucial role in the political growth of the League, its increasing political ascendancy over Muslims and the political

[68]C.H. Philips (ed.), *The Evolution of India and Pakistan 1858 to 1947,* p. 371; and Gwyer and Appadorai, *Speeches and Documents on the Indian Constitution 1921-47,* Vol. II, p. 505.

demoralization of the nationalist and other non-League Muslim leaders. By 1945-46, the League and its main demand had acquired a popular base, as was revealed in the elections of 1946.

Apart from the immediate objective of keeping India politically passive during the war, the policy of supporting the League including its demand for Pakistan formed an important part of the Conservative strategy of maintaining British dominance over the subcontinent after the war. Churchill's objective was that "we might sit on top of a tripod—Pakistan, Princely India and the Hindus."[69] Linlithgow hoped that Britain would "carry on with some scheme of Government imposed by ourselves with, of course, the inevitable corollary that we shall remain there to hold the balance."[70]

Jinnah and the League continued to exercise a veto over the post-war constitutional discussions for some time, for example, at the Simla Conference, so long as the British still hoped to maintain some sort of presence in the subcontinent. Once it became clear that was not possible, the British on the one hand openly conceded the demand for Pakistan and on the other withdrew the veto. The partition of India was now a part of the policy of ordered withdrawal from India rather than the policy of divide and rule. Hence, Prime Minister Attlee's declaration on 15 March 1946:

> We are very mindful of the rights of minorities and minorities should be able to live free from fear. On the other hand, we cannot allow a minority to place a veto on the advance of the majority.[71]

[69]Quoted in R. J. Moore, *op. cit.*, p. 138.

[70]*Ibid.*

[71]*Parliamentary Debates,* House of Commons, Vol. 420, Column 1422. The crutch of differences among Indians was also now abandoned: "I should like today, therefore, not to stress too much the differences between Indians. Let us all realise that whatever the difficulties, whatever the divisions may be, there is this underlying demand among all the Indian peoples." *Ibid.,* Column 1420. Similarly, the other prop, the princes, was also kicked aside: "There is the problem of the Indian states. Of course, the feelings in India in regard to nationalism and the unity of India cannot be confined by the boundaries that separate these states from the Provinces. I hope that the statesmen of British India and princely India will be able to work out a solution of the problem of bringing together, in one great polity, these disparate constituent parts. There again, we must see that the Indian

Also, the usefulness of the League as an alibi for remaining in India having come to an end, it was conceded a 'truncated' or 'moth- eaten' Pakistan. And the principle of the protection of all the minorities which had been offered as an excuse for delaying constitutional advance umpteen times was suddenly forgotten.

The system of separate communal electorates, developed almost parallel to the growth of the national movement and the process of constitutional reforms, was an important instrument for the development of communal politics. Along with elected legislatures and municipal bodies, communal representation, weightage, reservation and, above all, communal electorates were introduced. The system was extended through successive stages of constitutional reforms till 1935.

Under this system, Muslim voters and later others were put into separate constituencies from which only Muslims or other members of specific 'communities' or castes could stand as candidates. According to the 1909 Act, only Muslims could vote in Muslim constituencies, while they could vote along with Hindus in the general seats. After the Act of 1919, Muslims could vote for Muslim candidates only and Hindus for Hindu candidates only. Three basic assumptions underlay the system. First, that the political, economic, social and cultural interests of Hindus and Muslims were separate so that they could not be represented by candidates belonging to the other religion. Secondly, in a system of general electorate, since people would only vote for their co-religionists, either Hindus would swamp all elections because of their majority and thus few Muslims would be elected or mostly those Muslims would be elected who would be under Hindu influence because of their obligation to the majority for having elected them.[72] Thirdly, the legislators would work only for their own 'community' and use their 'power' to dominate the other 'communities.'

states find their due place; there can be no positive veto on advance, and I do not believe for a moment that the Indian princes would desire to be a bar to the forward march of India. But, as in the case of any other problems, this is a matter that Indians will settle themselves." *Ibid.*, Columns 1422-23.

[72]Minto had another apprehension that joint electorates would bring into the legislatures younger Muslims of 'advanced' political views and not the conservative, upper class Muslims. See M.N. Das, *op. cit.*, p. 233. Also see p. 228 for a similar opinion by the Lieutenant-Governor of Bengal.

Separate electorates turned elections and the legislative councils into an arena for communal conflict. Since the voters were exclusively the followers of one religion, the candidates did not have to get votes from persons of other religions. They could therefore make blatantly communal appeals. During elections, the voters listened to communal speeches and appeals; many of them tended therefore to think and vote communally and in general to think in terms of communal power, progress, and to express their socio-economic grievances in communal terms.[73]

The effect of separate electorates was heightened by the restricted nature of the franchise which was limited by property and educational qualifications. This meant that elections were mostly confined to the middle classes which were, as brought out in Chapter 2, otherwise involved in communal politics because of their hunt for jobs and other economic opportunities. Separate electorates thus meant institutionalization of middle and upper class needs, rivalries and politics along communal lines. It also meant partial transforming of the emerging anti-imperialist sentiments among the middle classes into communal rivalry among Hindus and Muslims for seats in legislatures and for government jobs.

Consequently, separate electorates strengthened communalism not only among Muslims but also Hindus. The general constituencies often returned nationalists but also communalists. Even the nationalists had to respect many communal prejudices of their middle class voters and thus became susceptible to communal ideological influences. In

[73]The political effect has been graphically described by Beni Prasad: "The Muslim constituencies ... rang with cries of danger to religion, language and culture and need of protection in all possible ways. The Hindu reaction conjured up a danger to Hindu rights, stigmatised the Congress as pro-Muslim and often looked upon compromise as surrender." *Op. cit., p.* 46. Similarly, D. Petrie, in his secret C.I.D. Memorandum, wrote in 1911: "More especially is this true of the Reform Scheme which has driven home the lesson that representation and consequently power are in direct proportion to numerical strength. There has been a great awakening of intercommunal jealousy and there is no community that is not fired with the idea of consolidating and improving itself to the utmost of its power." *The Punjab Past and Present,* October 1970, Vol. IV, Part, II, No. 8, p. 320.

any case their capacity to wholeheartedly fight Hindu communalism was undermined. As the *Kanpur Riots Enquiry Committee Report* noted, among other factors "the exigencies of the electoral campaigns ... made it almost impossible for the Congress openly and directly to come to grips with communalism."[74]

The system of reservations of seats and weightage in representation to minorities also generated communalism. To the minorities it appeared that communalism, as also the government, was protecting their interests, while the majority tended to feel deprived of its 'natural' right to be in a majority. The Hindu communalists could therefore turn the anger of the majority against the minorities. This was particularly so as the system of reservation of seats for other 'interests' tended to reduce the majority's representation to a minority. For example, in the projected federal assembly under the 1935 Act, Muslims were allocated 82 out of 250 seats (thirty-three and one-third per cent), while the general seats (intended for Hindus) were 105 (forty-two percent).

Separate electorates did not in reality serve the objective they were supposed to serve. They did not protect the interests of Muslims or other minorities in any meaningful or long-term sense. By freeing the majority of representatives from canvassing the support of the minorities, they created a situation where the minorities had no capacity to influence them.[75] If the majority of representatives also behaved in a communal manner, the minorities would be either faced with 'the position of a perpetual ineffective minority' and perhaps permanent communal oppression or forced to move towards territorial and political separatism.

[74]See p. 256.

[75]In post-independence India, under the system of joint electorates, Muslim voters, constituting barely 10 per cent of the total electorate, compel the different parties to tone down and even mute their communalism, at least in public. They also play a crucial role in defeating the communal parties. Similarly, even though there is reservation of seats for the Scheduled Castes, the system of joint electorates means that the Scheduled Caste candidates must canvass for non-Scheduled Caste voters and the non-Scheduled Caste candidates have to get Scheduled Caste votes. This has prevented the emergence of aggressive anti-Scheduled Caste or anti-non-Scheduled Caste ideologies, politics and propaganda.

The system of separate electorates had a disastrous effect on the process of national integration and nation-in-the-making. It created a regular political mechanism for the spread of communalism. It helped create a political milieu in which communal elements could flourish. It encouraged and reinforced the habit of looking upon Hindus and Muslims as separate political entities. Communal views could now spread through election propaganda into a widening circle of social groups which were otherwise free of the communal struggle for loaves and fishes of jobs and office. It made it difficult for the secular nationalist elements to carry out an ideological, political struggle against communalism. In general, it exasperated and perpetuated communal feeling and heightened communal consciousness.

The system was moreover self-perpetuating. It created vested interests which would not let it be abandoned once it had come into being. In India, it took independence and partition of the country to discard it.

The British also extended the system of communal patronage and reservation to employment in government and to education leading to such employment and professions such as medicine and engineering. This policy was to play a crucial role in transforming the economic competition among individuals of the middle and upper classes into communal politics. Once in operation, this policy continuously escalated communalism. The Muslim communalists asked for more and more reservations and patronage, while the Hindu communalists continuously bemoaned and attacked the loss of opportunities. Moreover, not the British or colonialism but the individuals of the other 'community' appeared to be the obstacles standing in the way of one's success in landing a job or enhancing one's capacity to do so. The edge of middle class politics could be turned against the other 'community' or caste instead of against the foreign rulers, and Indian society and politics could be continuously fragmented.

Immediately after the Revolt of 1857, the British distrusted Muslims and tried to suppress the Muslim upper and middle classes. A deliberate policy of favouring Hindus in government appointments and reducing the number of Muslims, especially in the army and among civil officials, was followed. The education of Muslims, which faced certain obstacles because of the hold of religious orthodoxy, was also neglected—no attention being paid to its specific problems. The result was that Muslims were not only losing out in government employment but also lagging behind in the modern professions.

Gradually, from the 1880s, this policy was reversed partially because of the rise of a vocal nationalist intelligentsia among the newly educated and partially because of the rise of a group of Muslim intellectuals and leaders of the upper classes who argued that Muslims should follow a policy of loyalty to the rulers and of dissociation from the rising national movement in order to remove official distrust and thus get back official favour and patronage in education and employment. The latter were encouraged in their endeavours by officials from the Viceroy downwards who were increasingly getting worried by the national movement and were looking for counter-weights to it. Muslim middle and upper classes under communal leadership along with the landlord and bureaucratic elements in general appeared as likely to fill the role.

The new policy was initiated in the 1880s, when the government promised special assistance to Muslims for spread of education among them and in matters of employment in public services, though in practice the favours were granted only to the upper class Muslims. The policy was however followed rather feebly till the end of the century except for vigorous support given to Syed Ahmed Khan's educational efforts at Aligarh. Moreover, perhaps because of the weakness of the national movement and the early emergence of Hindu communalism in UP, where it was the Hindu middle classes which felt deprived of a share in government appointments, A.P. Macdonnell, the Lieutenant-Governor, supported Hindu communalism in the late 1890s and actively sought to increase the number of Hindus in administration.

But from the first decade of the twentieth century the principle of reserving posts and promotions in public services through fixed quotas for Hindus and Muslims was vigorously pursued in Bengal and Panjab. The principle was extended to all the provincial and all-India services in 1934. It was also increasingly applied to admissions to professional and other government colleges.

The government also carefully managed educational development through municipal committees and district boards, colleges and universities, and denominational schools, colleges and universities so as to promote communal rivalry.

Even apart from jobs and education, the government had numerous other avenues of patronage, such as grant of contracts and conferment of titles, appointment of honorary magistrates, nominations to municipal and legislative bodies, which were used to strengthen communal leaders and their political base.

The British also encouraged communalism through non-action against it. Certain positive measures which the state alone could undertake were needed to check the growth of communalism. The British failure to undertake them served as an indirect encouragement to communal forces.

First of all the Government of India refused to take action against propagation of virulent communal ideas and communal hatred. The communalists used almost every form of vicious and inflammatory propaganda: speeches, rumours, popular Press, leaflets, pamphlets, poems, dramas, novels, satire, caricature, parody. Rarely did the government take any action to curb it or punish its perpetrators. The rare action was taken only in the worst cases of religious attacks when religious susceptibilities were hurt so as to avoid extreme excitement which might threaten law and order.

It is to be noted that the colonial regime had by the 1920s evolved an extensive system of police-reporting, intelligence-gathering, and Press censorship and other laws to control the Press. But this machinery of suppression was directed and used almost wholly against the nationalist movement. In this the government was active, rigid, vigilant and effective. Even the slightest effort to produce 'disaffection' and 'sedition' was taken note of and often acted against.[76] But the

[76]For example, in 1934, when almost all the Congress leaders had been released, Jawaharlal Nehru was tried and sentenced to a fresh two-year term in jail for making two speeches in Calcutta in January in which he had criticized revolutionary individual terrorism but argued for an organized peaceful revolutionary movement against imperialism.

same legislative, police and administrative machinery suffered from fits of absent-mindedness and relative inactivity where even the most vicious forms of communal propaganda and other activities giving direct incitement to communal murder and rioting and in general perpetuation of communalism were concerned. Here, the principles of, and love of, civil liberty and rule of law were often invoked. Numerous instances of this double-standard can be given. For example, while discussing the communal riots of Bengal in 1907, Sumit Sarkar has pointed out: "Ibrahim Khan, the author of the communal *Red Pamphlet,* was let off with a warning, while Liakat Husain and Abdul Gafur (supporters of the Swadeshi Movement) were being hounded down for sedition."[77] Earlier, in 1890-91, when communal rumours were widely disseminated in the northern Indian Press, some officials proposed the amendment of Section 505 of the Indian Penal Code to make it easier to take legal action against false reports, but the Viceroy, Lansdowne, rejected the proposal on the ground that it would stir up "a storm of protest." But in the same years, stringent Press laws were passed to control 'seditious' writings which promoted hatred, contempt or disaffection towards the government.[78] This differential policy towards nationalism and communalism became glaring in the 1920s when communalism first emerged in a violent and disruptive form. The communal and British-owned newspapers were given free reign to publish and highlight sensational reports of alleged communal occurrences, including rape, abduction and killing, in terms which were blatantly designed to incite extreme communal emotion among the readers. The following account of Mappila activities was, for example, published in the *Times of India* of 7 September 1921 and later widely reproduced:

> The rebels ... captured beautiful Hindu women, forcibly converted them ... and utilised them as their temporary partners of life. Hindu women were threatened, molested and compelled to run

[77]Sumit Sarkar, *op. cit.*, p. 80.

[78]G.R. Thursby, *op. cit.*, p. 20. Also see p. 23.

> half-naked for shelter to forests abounding in wild animals. Respectable Hindu gentlemen were forcibly converted and the circumcision ceremony performed with the help of certain Musiiars and Thangals.[79]

At a time when the emerging film medium was rigidly controlled by the government, films of the Mappila atrocities on Hindus, with their immense emotional, visual impact, were permitted to be freely screened.[80] The discrepancy between government action against nationalist propaganda and its utter inaction against communal incitement in the case of the Mappila uprising was noted by contemporaries. The Urdu paper *Zamindar* of Lahore noted in its issue of 21 October 1921:

> The correspondents of Anglo-Indian and moderate papers are publishing long stories of Moplah atrocities.... Misstatements are being circulated to create Hindu-Muslim dissensions. Any one publishing a report that might be harmful to the government is at once arrested, but section 153A has become paralysed against those who publish baseless and wild statements intended to sow feelings of enmity between the Hindus and the Muhammadans.[81]

The period from 1923 to 1926 marked the worst years of communal violence before the holocaust of 1946. Several Hindu and Muslim members of the Central Legislative Assembly proposed legislation to curb activities which promoted discord and breach of peace among followers of different religions. The Home Department successfully opposed such legislation on the ground that it would restrict religious and civil liberty![82]

[79]Quoted in *ibid.*, p. 140. Such exaggerated accounts were not permitted to be published when the rapists were the British soliders, tea-planters, etc.

[80]*Ibid., p.* 152.

[81]Quotcd in *ibid.*, p. 139.

[82]*Ibid.*, p. 119. And this when the most draconian ordinances had been passed to suppress the Non-Cooperation Movement barely four years earlier.

The same differential policy was followed in the sensitive area of the writing and teaching of history. Communal or semi-communal or communal-tinged historians faced no bar to their appointment or promotion. The pro-nationalist historians suffered in every way. The nationalist K.P. Jayswal was made to resign his post in the Calcutta University in 1912-13, while the Calcutta Vice-Chancellor was frustrated in his endeavours in 1929-30 to appoint S. Sanyal, Ph.D. from London University, to the post of lecturer because he was suspected by the Governor of harbouring nationalist leanings. Private schools and colleges faced loss of government aid and even of recognition if their teachers or students took active part in the nationalist movement or wrote against imperialism. On the other hand, teachers and students were often allowed to be active in communal politics and dissemination of communal ideology.

Non-communal nationalist writers and other intellectuals fared no better. Prem Chand was first compelled to destroy a collection of his nationalist short stories and later dismissed from the Education Department for persistence in writing stories and novels in the same vein. For writing a poem praising Rani of Jhansi, Subhadra Kumari Chauhan had to go to jail. Similarly, biographies of Tipu Sultan, Bahadur Shah, Rani of Jhansi, Tantia Tope, Kunwar Singh, Khudiram Bose, Bhagat Singh, etc., were promptly banned. On the other hand, writers, who aroused and inflamed communal feelings by writing plays, poems, stories and literature glorifying medieval zamindars, chiefs and rulers for their mythical struggles against their opposite members of the other religion, faced little difficulty in getting official patronage or at least retaining their jobs and promotions.

This fact partly explains why not a single history textbook or monograph or thesis which subjected colonial rule to a basic critique was published by an academic historian before independence. The early example of Bankim Chandra Chatterjee in a way set the trend. In the first version of *Anand Math,* as published in the literary journal, *Bangadarshana,* the struggle of the Sanyasis had many sentences, place names, etc., which indicated that the struggle was also directed against the British. Bankim was at the time a Deputy Collector. Official hints were given to him as to the impact of such a literary construction on his official career. Bankim promptly made changes in the text so that the hostile references to the English were removed and the Muslim officials of the Nawab appeared as the only villains against whom patriotic struggle was directed. For example, in the *Bangadarshana* as well as the first edition, Bankim referred to the opponents of Jivananda as the English, but in the second edition they were referred to as *Yavana* and in one place as *Nede,* that is, low class Muslims. Later, in the fifth edition, he also felt it necessary and safer to introduce many sentences in praise of British rule.[83]

While frowning upon and sometimes directly or indirectly punishing any anti-imperialist writing or other activity, the government freely rewarded communal political leaders, intellectuals and government servants with titles, positions of profit and high salaries, appointments as honorary magistrates, and other rewards. Retired government servants were a fertile recruiting base for communal parties and groups—a large number of Muslim League and Hindu Mahasabha leaders came from within the ranks of the bureaucracy. On the other hand, nationalist activity often led to the loss of pension. Even in case of serving officials, nationalist activities were strictly put down while communal activities were often overlooked unless they took a virulent form.

The British administration also practised a policy of relative inactivity and irresponsibility in dealing with communal riots. When the riots occurred, they were not crushed energetically. The well-known steel-frame strangely became utterly inefficient and the trigger-happy police developed qualms of conscience in using counter-violence. The official Kanpur Riots Enquiry Committee noted in 1931:

> Every class of witness ... agreed in this one respect that the police showed indifference and inactivity in dealing with various

[83]For a lengthy treatment, see B.B. Majumdar, "The Anand Math and Phadke."

> incidents in the riot. These witnesses include European businessmen, Moslems and Hindus of all shades of opinion, military officers, the Secretary of the Upper India Chamber of Commerce, representatives of the Indian Christian Community and even Indian officials.... There is no doubt in our mind that during the first three days of the riot the police did not show that activity in the discharge of their duties which was expected of them.... A number of witnesses have cited instances of serious crimes being committed within view of the police without their active interest being aroused.[84]

The *Report* also noted that during the three days of fierce rioting from 24 to 26 March there was not a single case of police firing and only eight persons were arrested except for 25 arrested in Colonelgunj on 25 March.[85] Once again this 'masterly inactivity' and administrative apathy were in deep contrast to the police handling of the nationalist movement, the peasant and trade union struggles, or even such movements of social reform as the Akali Movement and the movement for temple entry. Here, we would witness mass persecutions and arrests, police firings galore on unarmed men, women and children, and preventive 'strikes' by the police. Moreover, whenever action was taken during the riots it was the lower class participants who were punished; the middle and upper class instigators were permitted to go scot-free. In the case of the national movement, the leaders were arrested first. The administration also seldom made proper preparations or adopted preventive measures to meet situations of communal tension. This dereliction of elementary administrative duty was particularly glaring because most of these situations, such as coincidence of Holi and Muharram, municipal by-laws, cow-slaughter or protest against public sale of beef, could be foreseen months ahead of time. Even otherwise a communal riot seldom occurred without

[84]Quoted in K.B. Krishna, *op. cit.*, p. 273.

[85]G. Pandey, *The Ascendancy of the Congress in Uttar Pradesh*, pp. 138-39. Also see K.B. Krishna, *op. cit.*, pp. 272-73; Sumit Sarkar, *op. cit.*, pp. 448, 451-52; Tanika Sarkar, "The First Phase of Civil Disobedience in Bengal, 1930-1," pp. 91-92 and "Communal Riots in Bengal," pp. 285-90.

warning signals days and weeks ahead. For a riot to occur, tension had to build up to the requisite pitch. This took some time. The C.I.D. and the intelligence system functioned fairly well. Provocations such as music before mosque, organization of sacrificial cow processions and the efforts to stop them were normally known to the police and magistracy. The administration invariably got enough time to take precautionary measures. That administrative inactivity in the face of communal tension was not the result of an inherent difficulty in dealing with it is shown by the fact that whenever the administration decided to prevent a riot or to suppress it, the task was performed efficiently and successfully.[86] In fact, a firm maintenance of law and order and the public knowledge that such firmness would be forthcoming would in most cases prevent the riots, check their spread and in any case mitigate their ferocity.

A large number of contemporary public persons and the Press expressed the opinion that the British authorities deliberately instigated and engineered or at least connived at communal riots, especially when faced with nationalist or class upsurge, through agent provocateurs, aid to the instigators and organizers of the riots and such other methods. Recent historical research at the micro level tends to confirm this view.[87] Of course, till the secret police records are opened, we cannot know the extent of government's involvement in this respect. At the same time, in terms of our analysis, it is not necessary to take a definitive or strong position on this aspect. We can accept that the British had their own 'civilized' logic regarding riots. They encouraged communal politics and division, but would not perhaps go very far at the level of policy in deliberately organizing the more barbaric riots. But under the impact of the divide and rule policy and

[86]See, for example, Thursby, *op. cit.,* pp. 83, 88; G. Pandey, *op. cit.,* p. 139; Tanika Sarkar, "Communal Riots in Bengal," p. 290; C.E. Buckland, *Bengal under the Lieutenant-Governors,* Vol. II, pp. 1004-05.

[87]See, for example, Sumit Sarkar, *op. cit.,* pp. 451-52; Tanika Sarkar, "The First Phase of Civil Disobedience in Bengal, 1930-1," p. 91 and "Communal Riots in Bengal," pp. 286-90; G. Pandey, *op. cit.,* p. 142; K.B. Krishna, *op. cit.,* pp., 272-73; Kirpal Singh (ed.), "Sardar Bahadur Mehtab Singh's Report on Rawalpindi Riots—1926".

colonial ideology, they certainly did little to suppress them. Certainly, they gave such suppression a very low administrative priority. For example, an official who was sympathetic to the national movement or lax in dealing with it could suffer a setback if not disaster in his official career, while empathy with communalism and communal leaders or a failure to deal effectively with communal tension was easily overlooked.

This policy of inactivity was to cost thousands of lives during the communal killings of 1946-47. Both in Bengal and Panjab, officials from the highest to the lowest remained passive, inactive, indifferent, irresolute and supine in the face of massive killings, butchery and one-sided pogroms, when elementary administrative integrity and activity would have saved thousands of lives. Many of the officials were of course deeply embittered with the Indians for succeeding in throwing them out along with colonialism.

The administration's inactivity during communal riots had one other drastic consequence. Once people could not get police protection during communal riots, they were forced to organize self-defence along Hindu or Muslim lines and to rely upon their respective communal organizations. This inevitably strengthened communalism and aggravated communal suspicion and estrangement.

VII

The role of colonial policy in the growth of communalism should not be underestimated for one important reason. What were involved in this policy were state power and state apparatuses and not a mere political party. The state always has immense power for good or for evil. This is even more true of the colonial state which covered wider areas of life, had greater untrammelled administrative constitutional power and disposed of many more instruments of intervention in society than did other democratic states. Moreover in certain spheres of life it alone could act. It alone could take action against malicious and provocative communal propaganda, vicious lies and rumour-mongering, biased teaching of history in schools and colleges, and the communal Press; it alone could take preventive police measures in case of communal tension—and quite often firm law and order steps would check communal riots; it alone had the legal sanction and the requisite apparatus for using force against rioters; it alone could punish the instigators and organizers of riots and reward those who tried to prevent them. The state alone possessed a battery of instruments such as the educational system, radio, official propaganda machinery, and a structure of patronage including appointments to various services, which could be used to oppose and eradicate communalism. Certainly a national government committed to national unity and integration would have done so.

The colonial state disposed of large patronage which acquired even greater significance in view of the underdevelopment of the economy in general and industry in particular. Combined with the large relative size of the middle classes, this power to dole out jobs and other patronage gave the colonial state immense capacity to influence the politics of the petty bourgeoisie. This power was used to set sections of the petty bourgeoisie against one another, to crystallize their search for jobs, ensure security and identity around communal ideology and politics and to increase in their eyes the attraction of communal leaders, through whom part of the colonial patronage was exercised. The colonial state also had a very large capacity to manipulate the constitutional, administrative and educational structure to favour communal political forces. Its political, administrative and economic strength could therefore be successfully used to counteract the efforts of the nationalist leaders to integrate Indians into a united people in their struggle against imperialism and to spread for the purpose secular outlook and ideology. In the absence of this weight of the state being thrown behind communalism, the nationalist leaders would perhaps have found it possible to keep communalism under check even if they had not been able to eliminate it. Above all, the colonial state and its policies and the ideology generated and propagated through official pronouncements, colonial writers, official or British controlled media, and the educational system created a wide space and favourable terrain for the growth of communalism.

A political corollary follows from the analysis presented in this chapter. Once the colonial state and its apparatuses supported communalism, a solution of the communal problem was not easily possible so long as colonial rule remained. Only a national state, a state that was interested in national integration and nation-building, could undertake the necessary administrative measures to minimize sectional inequalities and reduce and 'manage' communal tensions and lessen their impact on politics, promote through its numerous channels a secular outlook, and, above all, by promoting rapid transformation and development of the economy remove the economic imbalances which were the tap-root of communalism. Of course, overthrow of colonialism and the colonial state was a necessary but not a sufficient condition for a successful struggle against communalism.

The importance of the role of the colonial state in the growth of communalism can also be seen if we compare the communal situation of the colonial period with that of the post-1947 period in India and Pakistan. Despite favourable conditions, including the partition of India and the accompanying mass communal killings, Hindu communalism has not been able to become a predominant social or political force in India, or a mass phenomenon, even though a large segment of the middle classes and the bureaucracy has been responsive to communal ideology and politics. Nor has this been because the state has taken active steps to fight communalism in the ideological and other fields. It has not. But it has not supported communalism either. And secularism has been enshrined in the Constitution and the official ideology of the ruling party and most other parties. In other words, even a weak secular state has enabled Indian people to keep communalism under check; and the absence of state support has been a major obstacle to the growth of communal forces. The reverse has been the case in Pakistan where communalism became enshrined in the state structure and official ideology.

The very large role of colonial policy in the growth of communalism should not, of course, lead us to underrate or ignore the basic causative role or primary responsibility of colonialism and the colonial structure that evolved under its impact. Colonialism was not merely or rather mainly a policy or a 'factor' in the situation. It was the foundation of India's social system during the colonial era. It was within colonialism and the colonial structure that various factors, including colonial policy, operated and by which they were shaped. It is the logic of the colonial structure that provided the parameters within which communalism grew and functioned. It is the colonial structure, and the resulting economic underdevelopment and the paucity of economic opportunities, which created conditions conducive to communal antagonism on the one hand and the successful working of the colonial policy of divide and rule on the other. In the absence of these conditions this policy would not have been so easy a success.

In the end, we may also note that our analysis of the role of colonial policy reinforces what was suggested earlier in Chapter 4. In the colonial context communalism did not serve only the indigenous social classes and strata, namely, the middle classes, money-lenders and landlords and other jagirdari elements; it was also the channel through which petty bourgeois politics were placed at the command of colonialism. In other words, communalism served above all as a social prop—and in the end the chief social prop—of colonial rule. It was the function of colonial policy to bring about this result. On the other hand, in the absence of state power the indigenous social classes and strata favourable to communalism lacked the capacity to push their interests through communalism and therefore relied upon the colonial state to be able to do so. Communalism was therefore in a sense one of the major political and ideological media through which mutual dependence and interaction between colonialism and these classes and strata were established.

CHAPTER 9
Retrospect

What was the way out for the forces of secular nationalism? And what are the lessons of the historical experience of communalism for us today?

The way out of the communal morass lay in a long-term political and ideological strategy and not in a one-shot solution at any particular political conjuncture. Certainly no such solution existed at the moment of the partition of India during 1945-47. There is never an instant solution to a social problem like communalism. To look for such instant solutions while ignoring the past and the present interconnections is to indulge in false comfort, vain hope and futile romanticism. And the failure to find such solutions often leads to a search for scapegoats. Conditions and forces for a solution have to be prepared over a number of years and even decades. Moreover, nations and societies are sometimes placed in situations which brook no piecemeal solutions however genuine and well-meaning the desire and effort of those who seek them.

I

A major school of thought has held that the nationalist failure in this regard lay in the inability to conciliate and appease minority communalisms in general and to secure a rapprochement between the Congress and the Muslim League in particular. In reality, a compromise with communal forces was neither feasible nor desirable. And the terms on which it was available would have destroyed the secular integrity and identity of the nationalist forces themselves, leading to the creation of a Hindu communal, possibly fascist, India. On the other hand, even the efforts that the Congress and the Communist

Party made to conciliate Muslim communalism did great harm: these efforts bolstered Muslim communalism, indirectly encouraged Hindu communalism through a backlash and hampered and weakened the struggle against both. The effort to compromise with forces which were incapable of being accommodated in a secular and nationalist framework–the effort 'to repair the damage by decreasing forces, by dispersal, by a peace treaty with real needs'–could only end in failure and even disaster.

The secular nationalists also attempted or propagated a few other liberal solutions.[1]

(i) Individuals of different religious persuasions were constantly urged to be friendly and fair-minded towards each other and to look upon each other as brothers or '*bhai-bhai*'. This solution was especially vigorously promoted whenever a communal riot occurred, and was accompanied by peace committees, public demonstrations of Hindu-Muslim fraternization, etc.

(ii) Religious bigotry, intolerance and narrow-mindedness should be opposed and religious broad-mindedness and tolerance encouraged. Religion should be increasingly personalized and kept out of public questions. Religion should be deritualized, emphasis being placed more and more on its spiritual aspects. The unity of all religions and not their differences should be emphasized.

(iii) A bigted outlook was often the result of ignorance and illiteracy. Education should be rapidly expanded so that knowledge and rational thinking might spread.

(iv) Communalism fed on half-truths, rumours, distortions, false stereotypes, and biased and unscientific interpretations of history. Every effort should be made to disseminate correct information and scientific knowledge so that people learn to discriminate between truth and lies.

(v) Minorities should be given protection against discrimination and domination by the majority. Every effort should be made to allay

[1]A good summary of the liberal solutions is given in C. Manshardt, *The Hindu-Muslim Problem in India*, pp. 121-23

their fears and anxieties, real or imaginary. Their genuine grievances must be removed and their interests safeguarded or assurances given to this effect.

The liberal remedies were tried, and were failures. Yet they were not 'false'; they were certainly part of a wider solution of the communal problem and the political-ideological struggle against communalism. Only the liberal nationalists did not effectively deal with the questions: Why was communalism growing? Why were the liberal solutions failing? What were the deeper social and ideological roots of communalism? They could have asked at least one question: Why did the liberal communalists remain firm communalists in spite of their expressed belief in all the liberal solutions including emphasis on Indian unity and Hindu-Muslim brotherhood, spread of education, opposition to religious bigotry and communal riots, and a negotiated settlement of the 'communal differences'?

II

As we have seen earlier, communalism and its growth were products of the Indian social, economic and political developments and conditions during the nineteenth and twentieth centuries. Economic backwardness, interests of the semi-fedual, jagirdari classes and strata, the precarious economic condition of the middle classes, social cleavages within Indian society, its heterogeneous and multifaceted cultural character and the ideological-political weaknesses of the nationalist forces–all combined to promote communalism or to weaken the struggle against it. Consequently, a multi-sided, multi-causal understanding of the complex Indian reality and the struggle to change it were needed.

But, above all, the social framework for the growth of communalism was provided by the colonial economy and polity. Colonialism was the foundation of the social structure which generated and then propelled forward communal ideology and politics. While many other aspects of the Indian social condition helped the growth of communalism, it was the logic of the economic, political, cultural and idelogical system structured by colonialism that created the space for the growth of communalism. This logic was, of course, supplemented by colonial policy, which in its turn fully exploited the conditions produced by colonialism itself as also other weaknesses of Indian society.

Colonial underdevelopment and the crisis of the colonial economy in the 1920s and 1930s created a fertile field for the rapid growth of communalism. Above all, they resulted in widespread unemployment, which led to the desperate struggle for jobs among the middle classes, and thus helped communalism acquire its real mass base. The colonial agrarian structure also led to the peasants' struggles against landlords and money-lenders being given a communal form in several parts of the country. The colonial political structure and policies provided the ground on which communal politics could flourish.

Consequently, to uproot communalism it was necessary to change the social reality which gave birth to it and provided scope for its growth; there was no lasting solution to the communal problem within the existing colonial social framework. It was impossible to put an end to communalism or communal-type ideologies, politics and movements without the overthrow of colonialism and the colonial state. Similarly, the jagirdari classes and strata had to be expropriated. But even if that was not done and the agrarian relations were not completely restructured, the struggle for peasant demands, especially in areas such as Punjab, Bengal and Malabar, had to be organized in such a manner that Muslim peasants' hostility to Hindu landlords and money-lenders was not transformed into communal hatred. Such a struggle against landlords and money-lenders would have helped to arouse the national and secular consciousness of Muslim peasants and made them conscious of the communal game being played by the jagirdari elements and the colonial authorities.

Even if by a supreme effort a compromise with communal political leaders had been successfully concluded during the 1920s or 1930s, the solution would most probably have been temporary, as was the case with the Lucknow Pact and to some extent the Nehru Report. Communalism or some other communal-type movement would have grown again so long as the original social condition continued; for example, if opportunities for employment remained scarce. Thus, no real and long-term success in the struggle against communalism or similar forces was possible without economic, political, social and cultural transformation and development. The fact is that some social problems have no other but basic social solutions. This does not of course mean that communalism was not to be opposed till society as a whole was transformed. It was necessary to do so, but with the full awareness that till society itself was transformed the soil for the growth of communalism would remain fertile.

We may at this stage remind the reader of an important aspect of our analysis in Chapter 1 of this work. Communalism was based on a false consciousness, on a wrong understanding of the reality. It completely misunderstood not only the Indian people's social condition but even the problem of Muslims as a religious minority. It consequently posed this problem wrongly and offered a false solution to this problem as also to the social condition of Muslims. But it was not only the communalist's understanding of the reality of colonial India that was wrong. There was a reality—a real social situation—of which communalism was a distorted reflection, a reality which provided a favourable soil for the growth of communalism. In a sense, communalism interpreted the social reality wrongly because the reality itself was upside down. Therefore, not only did the reality have to be rightly interpreted, not only had there to be a critique of the communalists for interpreting the social condition wrongly, but the reality itself had to be criticized and transformed. It was not merely that the distorted reality had to be *understood* rightly, it had also to be *made* right. For example, it was necessary to show not only that Hindu middle classes were not responsible for the unemployment among Muslim middle classes and that both suffered in common from unemployment generated by colonial underdevelopment, but also to 'break' the economic underdevelopment and stagnation which created unemployment and to open the way for the creation of more jobs. For so long as the scramble for posts continued communalism in some form would be used by the middle classes to improve their individual chances of getting a job. There could, therefore, be no division of work between those who analysed communalism and opposed its interpretation of reality and those who changed the social reality which spawned it. Changing the reality was an essential part of the struggle against all forms of false consciousness-including communalism. There had to be a constant dialectic between interpretation and change.

This is not to underplay the role of a scientific interpretation of communalism, for there could be no effective struggle against communalism, or for that matter against any negative social phenomenon, without its correct interpretation, but to emphasize that it was only the beginning of the task. Suppression of communalism demanded the transformation of the social condition. No amount of conciliation or compromise would have solved the problem. The road ahead lay in a new direction, in the direction of a direct struggle against communalism and for social change.

A basic feature of colonial India was that the anti-communal nationalist forces had no control over the objective economic and social conditions which were conducive to the growth of communalism. It was the colonial rulers who wielded the state power and therefore only they could take economic and administrative measures to promote national unity and to undermine communal forces; for example, by developing the economy and thus creating job opportunities leading to the toning down if not disappearance of petty bourgeois rivalries, by introducing land reforms, by suppressing communal riots with a heavy hand, by introducing adult franchise and thus reducing the influence of zamindars and bureaucrats in politics, by improving school syllabi, by checking propagation of communal hatred and false rumours. However, instead of undertaking any such measures, the colonial state played a crucial role, by its acts of omission and commission, in aiding and abetting the communal forces. Consequently, the secular and nationalist forces could not weaken communalism by directly affecting the social condition and thus drying up its social roots except by working for the overthrow of colonialism and for the transformation of the internal social structure, especially the agrarian structure, and by waging a political and ideological struggle against communalism so that the social conditions promoting communalism were ultimately transformed while being made inoperative or 'subverted' in the short run so far as their negative effects were concerned. Unfortunately, the nationalist movement, including its left-wing composed of the socialists and communists, revealed major weaknesses in these respects. In a sense, the burgeoning of communalism after 1937 may be seen as a punishment for these weaknesses.

III

If communalism could not be ended without changing social reality, i.e., by overthrowing colonialism, the reverse was also true: a scientific understanding of communalism, its exposure as the false consciousness of the reality and an intense political-ideological struggle against it were an essential part of the broader struggle against imperialism and for changing the reality. There was thus a dialectical relationship between the two struggles. One could not merely wait for structural change, that is, for colonialism to go and social change to occur, and to thus solve the communal and other similar problems as a consequence; one had to wage the ideological struggle while simultaneously being fully aware that structural change was basic for a long-term solution. As Karl Marx put it in the third of his Theses on Fuerbach:

> The materialist doctrine that men are products of circumstances and upbringing, and that, therefore, changed men are products of other circumstances and changed up-bringing, forgets that it is men who change circumstances and that the educator must himself be educated.... The coincidence of the changing of circumstances and of human activity can be conceived and rationally understood only as revolutionary practice.[2]

The role of the political and ideological struggle was even greater in the short run, for that was where immediate effectivity of social action

[2]Marx and Engels, *Collected Works*, Vol. 5, p. 7.

lay. Moreover, if effectively waged, this struggle could contain communalism for a period of time and by that very effect create conditions for the development of secular forces which would, in the long run, ensure a more favourable outcome of the battle between secularism-nationalism and communalism as well as of the struggle against colonialism.

This is in fact a major lesson of the pre-1947 historical experience. The freedom struggle suffered from major weaknesses in this respect. Firstly, a vigorous political and ideological struggle against communalism, and its feeders—religiosity, caste, social distance, the Hindu tinge in nationalist thought, the communal interpretation of history, obscurantism, etc.—was not carried out. However, this does not mean that the Congress and its leaders were communal or semi-communal. Leaders like Gandhi and Nehru were sturdy secularists. The ideology, organizational structure, programme and policies of the Congress were basically secular. Despite the fact that Hindus formed the overwhelming mass of the Congress members and supporters and Muslim support to and participation in it was limited, the Congress remained a basically secular and national organization. The Congress leaders also made strenuous attempts to promote Hindu-Muslim unity. Their weakness lay in the fact that they were not able to take an effective and vigorous line of action to oppose the rising tide of communal forces or to protect even their own ranks from penetration by elements of communal ideology. While they recognized the importance of struggle against the economic and political elements of imperialist ideology as part of the anti-imperialist struggle, most of them did not sufficiently realize that communal ideology was also, in one of its aspects, an important element of imperialist ideology and had therefore to be fought equally vigorously. There was a tendency to see communalism as just another obstacle to national unity which had to be opposed politically. Gandhi, Nehru and the left did of course recognize the deep connection between the struggle against communalism and the struggle against imperialism, but, as we shall see, their approach suffered from other weaknesses. Moreover, the preoccupation of the Congress leaders with day-to-day politics and political mobilization left them with little time, and weakened their inclination, for ideological work on this front. This was even more so during 1937-39, when many of them were busy running the administration in the provinces, and the war years from 1939-42 when their time was taken up by political negotiations, agitations and movements. After 1942, they were in jail and were therefore cut off from the people. By the time they came out in 1945, it was perhaps too late to change the communal scene. In any case, immediately thereafter the Congress leaders became preoccupied with the INA Prisoners' Release Campaign and political negotiations. This once again led them to ignore ideological and political struggle against communal forces. Instead, they tended to rely on negotiations with communal leaders for finding a solution to the communal problem.

Even at the purely political level, no mass campaigns of the type carried out against colonialism were organized. At no stage did the Congress come directly to grips with the communal problem or the communalists. It did not explain to the people in a patient manner the real dimensions of the problem or the connection between communalism and colonial backwardness or the linkage between communalism on one side and the colonial authorities, the jagirdari strata, and the narrow petty bourgeois interests on the other.[3] At the most, the Congress propaganda blamed colonial policy or administration in a general and sweeping manner and in deep emotional tones but without much analytical content, which would bring out the complex relationship of communalism with colonialism. Nor was there a vigorous and sustained educative propaganda campaign against communalism. Instead there were spasmodic exhortations to people not to fall a prey to communalism, to give up communalism and to feel, think and act as Indians. While the spirit of Hindus and Muslims as '*bhai-bhai*' was stressed, there was little explanation of the nature of economic, social and political relations between the followers of different religions or of the true nature of

[3]The left wing too did not take serious note of the petty bourgeois social base of communalism. Consequently, its ideological critique of communalism too remained shallow and half-hearted.

exploitation in colonial society, which did not occur on a communal basis. For example, that Hindus or the Hindu 'community' did not exploit Muslims or the Muslim 'community' but capitalists and landlords, whether Hindu or Muslim, exploited workers, peasants, and lower middle classes, whether Hindu or Muslim, or that all Indians were jointly exploited by imperialism; and that, therefore, just as the interests of all exploited classes were common *vis-a-vis* the landlords and capitalists, the interests of all Indians were the same *vis-a-vis* colonialism; or that unemployment was not caused by the other 'community' but by colonial underdevelopment. The Congress failed to bring to surface the real problems and anxieties of the minorities, whether in the country as a whole or in a region, to deal with their causes, or to combat the communalists' efforts to misdirect the anxieties and fears of the minorities. The need was to direct the debate with the communalists into hard, rational, analytical channels so that the latter were forced to fight on the terrain of reason and science and not of emotion and bias.

Instead, the basic strategy followed by the Congress to tackle the communal problem and to bring about Hindu-Muslim unity was either, as in the 1920s, 1930s and 1940s, to arrive at a compromise through top-level negotiations with Muslim communal leaders through conferences, individual negotiations, etc. By doing so, the Congress tacitly or by implication accepted to a certain extent the claim of the communal leaders that they were the representatives of the communal interests of their respective 'communities', and, of course, that such communal interests and religious communities existed.[4] By negotiating with communal leaders, it legitimized their politics, 'invested the communalists with greater importance and

[4]Cf. "It began to be widely assumed that religious communities, such as Muslim community, Hindu community, and Sikh community, existed in real life.... The only major difference between the nationalists and the communalists was that the former wanted these communities to unite and fight together as communities against imperialism and the latter to shun and fight each other. Both sides accepted the logic of communalism. The nationalists would then fight for the unity of the communities while the communalists would carry the logic further. The early Jinnah could do both. Thus the basic communal

prestige', or at least made them respectable. It also tacitly weakened its right to carry on a hard political-ideological campaign against communal parties and individuals. Constant negotiations with communal leaders also weakened the position of the anti-imperialist Muslims who were increasingly forced to think and act as Nationalist Muslims. Men like Abul Kalam Azad and Asaf Ali, that is, simple nationalists, increasingly became a rarity. Moreover, the repeated failures of negotiations at the top tended to create communal distrust and bitterness and a feeling of despair and helplessness regarding the solution of the communal problem. This unity-from-the-top strategy contained another built-in mechanism to promote community-wise thinking among the political leaders involved in the Hindu-Muslim unity talks. The political position of many of these leaders was due to their being 'Muslim' or 'Hindu' or 'Sikh' leaders. Consequently, most of them found it difficult to give up communalism altogether for that would suddenly reduce their political stature.[5]

The only serious effort to understand the broader social, economic and political dimensions, character and causation of communalism and to organize an ideological and political campaign based on this understanding was made by Jawaharlal Nehru and the left during 1933-37. Nehru's writings on the subject had a certain freshness of approach and contained deep insights. He was able to see clearly that national unity should be a unity between the masses and not an artificially arranged marriage of convenience between the leaders. His was also one of the first efforts to apply a Marxist approach to the problem. To the efforts at patchwork unity at the top, he counterpoised the alternative political line of militant anti-imperialism, refusal to

way of looking at politics, that is, of seeing the basic task of Indian politics not as that of uniting and integrating the diverse Indian people but of uniting the distinctly formed communities and their leaders, was permitted to enter the heart of the Indian political process." "Indian National Movement and the Communal Problem", in Bipan Chandra, *Nationalism and Colonialism in Modern India,* pp. 257-58.

[5]For a detailed critique of the nationalist approach to the communal problem, see *ibid.* and *Report of the Kanpur Riots Enquiry Committee*, pp. 225-28.

confine the national movement to middle class politics, basing politics on the masses, and the direct winning over of the Muslim peasants and workers through political work among them on the basis of their class demands and an anti-imperialist programme. Thus not only bypassing the middle and upper class communal leaders but also exposing their pro-colonial, pro-feudal and pro-capitalist bias as also their narrow job-oriented petty bourgeois approach. The highlight of Nehru's campaign of 1933-37 was the Muslim Mass Contact Programme. This hastily conceived and ill-planned and ill-organized programme was never implemented in right earnest and was soon abandoned under the pressure of the Congress right wing. Such a programme could not be seriously undertaken in several areas such as Bengal, Punjab and Bihar. To do so, the Congress had to commit itself there more fully to a radical agrarian programme and pro-labour and pro-artisan policies in the towns and cities. Moreover, it was not possible to heighten the class understanding and social consciousness of the Muslim masses without doing so also in case of the Hindu masses.

Thus, Nehru and the left did have glimpses of the reality; unfortunately, they failed to grapple with the total situation. In any case, after 1937 Nehru and the left too began to neglect the fight against communalism, especially at the ideological plane. He one unfortunate exception was the ill-fated Communist Party support to the Pakistan demand in the name of the doctrine of the right of self-determination of nationalities. The treatment of the Muslim League as a nationalist and not a communal party followed suit. One important consequence was to provide respectability to the League in the eyes of the Muslim intellectuals who could now join or support it without any feeling of guilt.

Secondly, the Congress leaders in general and Nehru and the left in particular suffered from a certain mechanical and simplistic approach and an economistic and deterministic bias in their treatment of the problem. This led to the underplaying of conscious ideological struggle against communalism; sometimes the communal issue itself was belittled and underplayed as secondary.[6] It was often assumed that development of the 'real' struggles, that is, the economic struggles of workers and peasants and the anti-imperialist political struggle, and economic development would automatically dissolve communalism.[7] The people would then automatically be able to see it as a reactionary and outdated ideology. What was not fully realized was that these movements would not grow and develop fully unless communalism was ideologically and politically opposed; that ideological struggle was as 'real' as the economic and national struggles;

[6]See, for example, the following extracts from Nehru. "I am afraid I cannot get excited over this communal issue, important as it is temporarily. It is after all a side issue, and it can have no real importance in the larger scheme of things." (Presidential address to the ucknow Congress session, *SW*, Vol. 7, p. 190.) "Europe has to face basic and fundamental problems which is not the case with our communal question. Our question is a ghostly thing, and of no substance.... I submit that if the question is placed before the masses, the solution will be found readily enough." (Speech at Aligarh Muslim University, 15 December 1933, *SW*, Vol. 6, pp. 132-33.) "social and economic forces will inevitably bring other problems to the front. They will create cleavages along different lines, but the communal cleavage will go." ("Hindu and Muslim Communalism", 27 November 1933, *SW*, Vol. 6, p. 170.) "But this idea of a Muslim nation is the figment of a few imaginations only, and, but for the publicity given to it by the Press, few people would have heard of it. And even if many people believed in it, it would stll vanish at the touch of reality." (*An Autobiography*, p. 469.) Gandhi did not make this type of error and fully recognized the strategic importance of eliminating communalism. He did not, however, know how to go about the task except through moral exhortations to the people or conciliation of the communal leaders through negotiations.

[7]For example, Nehru wrote in January 1936 that though communalism was not to be ignored because it was a "tremendous obstacle in our way and is likely to interfere with our future progress", yet "it is overrated and over-emphasised.... With the coming of social issues to the forefront it is bound to recede into the background." *SW*, Vol. 7, p. 69. Similarly, C.G. Shah, a very perceptive Marxist writer on communalism, wrote: "The material interests of the exploited classes are identical. Joint struggles based on this identity of material interests and resultant common demands can alone build up their unity. In proportion that such united movements grow, they will cease to feel as Hindus or Muslims and begin increasingly to feel as workers, peasants, etc. Communal consciousness will increasingly be replaced by class consciousness. Thus the only effective method to combat and liquidate communalism is to mobilize the masses, Hindu and Muslim, round a programme of demands reflecting their own common interests, to strengthen their class organizations.... Their communal consciousness will disintegrate in proportion that their class consciousness grows as a result of the experience of united class effort." And again, "communalism among masses will steadily decline and finally disappear only in proportion that their united movements for improving their conditions grow." *Marxism Gandhism Stalinism*, pp. 186-87 and 195.

that 'class struggles', seen in terms of economic struggles, did not automatically obliterate the influence of communalism, caste, region, etc., that even the classes in Indian society would be constituted through the constitution of the nation or 'Indian people' or the process of the nation-in-the-making; that class consciousness and class struggles themselves would be hindered and blocked by communalism; and that along with class outlook and organization confronting communalism, nationalist ideology must confront and overpower communal ideology. Nehru and others were, of course, right in not seeing communalism as real or as based on real conflict and seeing it, instead, as a 'replacement' and distorted reflection of real conflicts. But then it was necessary to bring to the surface the real conflicts and show the falsity of communalism not only by taking up the real national and class conflicts but also by patient ideological educational work leading to changes in the thinking and culture of the people.

Thirdly, the nationalists often made emotional appeals in the name of nationalism and national interest of persons under communal influence to give up communal outlook or not to fall prey to it. Assuming that national consciousness had already permeated society, they appealed to the people to give up communalism because it was anti-national. This made little impact on those who were not already nationalist in their consciousness. This ignored the fact that India was not yet a fully structured nation but a nation-in-the-making, that, consequently, the process could not yet be seen to be a complete one, and that the Indian nation had yet to be fully built. Nor would the development of national consciousness be an automatic process simply because India was objectively becoming a nation. The emergence of a national or Indian identity or the feeling of nationhood could, therefore, not be taken as a prior fact. This feeling itself had to be inculcated. Prolonged and patient political-ideological work on this central question had to be a necessary part of the conscious process of making India into a nation. Indian people would acquire the new, national identity through conscious political and ideological activity and not simply because it was an objective fact. Only as the people became conscious of nationhood and acquired the new identity would it be possible to make an appeal to it against communalism. While for various reasons the upper caste Hindu intelligentsia and middle classes and some sections of the peasantry and the working class had gradually imbibed the feeling of belonging to the nation, this feeling was weak among Muslim intellectuals and middle classes as also among many sections of both Hindu and Muslim peasants, workers and lower castes.

In this respect, there was even a certain throwback from the early nationalist period when the national leadership was acutely aware that India was just beginning to become a nation, that this process had to be consciously promoted and could not be taken for granted, that the Indian people had to be made aware of unity as also the need for this unity had to be argued and struggled for, and that, consequently, differences based on religion, caste and region had to be patiently eliminated from the political and social arena.

Then there was the problem of defining the social character of national independence in more socially radical terms. The Karachi (1931) and Faizpur (1936) resolutions of the National Congress had marked important steps in this direction. During the 1930s, the burgeoning left wing of the Congress was popularizing the slogans of socialism, land reform and *Mazdoor-Kisan* Raj. The intelligentsia was increasingly becoming socialist-minded. There was serious competition among several social visions of a free India. Several ideologies and social perspectives were contending furiously inside the national movement. At the same time, by the very nature of things, there was no single social vision to which all Congressmen could appeal. In many cases, the nationalist propaganda and agitation were broadly confined to the notions of the expulsion of the colonial rulers and the ending of colonial exploitation and to vague promises of removal of poverty and the development of industry and agriculture. This enabled the communalists to mislead the middle classes and the masses and to appeal to their fears and anxieties. There were some other serious weaknesses, which cannot however be discussed here, in the character of the anti-imperialist movement led by the National Congress. By the 1930s, colonial economy and polity had entered a period of prolonged crisis and thus created a situation where its social, economic and political problems cried out for a simultaneous and radical change. Unfortunately, the Congress leadership failed to tackle adequately the political and ideological problems resulting from colonial rule and underdevelopment.

Fourthly, to fight communalism successfully it was necessary to have a deep comprehension of communalism in all its complexity and opacity—its ideology, its sources and roots, its social base, reasons for its growth and stubbornness in face of the nationalist attack. Even though the *Kanpur Riots Enquiry Committee Report* and the writings of Jawaharlal Nehru, K.B. Krishna, K.M. Ashraf, Tufail Ahmed Mangalori, C. Manshardt and Beni Prasad contained deep insights, on the whole they as well as other nationalist leaders failed to meet adequately the intellectual challenge in this respect. Even Gandhi's usually inspired political understanding was shallow where communalism was concerned; and he was constantly baffled by it so much so that in the end he could counterpoise to it only his personal moral and physical courage.

Also important here was the general ideological weakness of the national movement. As pointed out earlier, socially reactionary and obscurantist ideas as also the Hindu tinge permeating much of nationalist propaganda were never frontally opposed or rooted out by the Congress leaders and were widely prevalent in the nationalist ranks. The communal elements were able to use their existence both directly by appealing to them and indirectly by utilizing them to cast doubts on the genuineness of the national movement's secular credentials.

We have indicated in the main body of this work the lines along which ideological and political attack on communalism had to be made. We may also stress once again that mere propaganda or ideological campaign would not have sufficed, it was also necessary to organize the people into a common struggle against colonialism, for social transformation of society and around the objective material reality of common interests. The unity of the Indian people would be the result of the effect of two simultaneous phenomena: common struggle of the people for their common real interests and aims based in part on a common outlook, and the evolution of a common understanding of their social condition, based in part on common struggle.

IV

One of the major reasons for the weakness of the nationalist political and ideological struggle against communalism lay in the common middle class social base and orientation of both the national movement and communalism. As we have seen earlier in Chapter 2, colonial underdevelopment created a serious social situation for the petty bourgeoisie which, on the one hand, took an active part in the national movement in its search for a long-term solution of its problems and, on the other hand, took to communal politics in its scramble for government posts and educational facilities and thus to serve its immediate, short-term interests. While communalism served colonialism and the jagirdari classes and merchants and money-lenders and also in certain areas represented class struggles in a distorted form, its main social base, its mass base, was constituted by the middle classes—it was a petty bourgeois phenomenon *par excellence*. Consequently, so long as the middle classes occupied a strong position in Indian politics, especially in the politics of municipal committees and legislatures, the solution of the communal problem would remain elusive.

The petty bourgeois domination of politics created several problems so far as the struggle against communalism was concerned. Even when the national movement adopted a broad-based national programme, it could not go far in opposing middle class urges and interests which the communal parties projected. In the short run, and put in a tight economic corner, the middle class individuals did get a certain differential advantage out of communalism. These two features placed a severe constraint on the secularism of petty bourgeois politics in general and on the politics of struggle against communalism in particular. This factor was responsible for the general tendency in nationalist ranks to turn a blind eye towards communal ideology and politics, to adopt a soft political and social attitude towards communal ideologues and leaders, to try to compromise with them, and even when opposing communalism to wage no intense struggle against it.[8] This also made it difficult for the nationalist movement to oppose the social, cultural and psychological narrow-mindedness of the petty bourgeoisie. In fact, it could not itself avoid imbibing this narrow-mindedness.

After all, in the existing situation, it was a fact that any real ideological and political struggle against communalism and communal ideology would tend to alienate, however temporarily, sections of the middle classes. This alienation could prove quite disastrous in electoral terms since the middle classes constituted the largest section of the urban voters under the system of restricted franchise in colonial India. In fact, even the left wing, which frontally opposed communalism, failed, with some exceptions such as Nehru, to comprehend communalism as a petty bourgeois phenomenon, or at least seriously underestimated the role of the middle classes in it and tended to emphasize in the main its semi-feudal and colonial base. This was perhaps due to its own strong roots in the petty bourgeoisie.

The middle class weight in Indian politics was one of the reasons for the failure of the nationalist strategy of solving the communal problem through negotiations with the communal leaders. This strategy to be a success required appeasement of the middle class-based minority communalism through generous concessions on the questions of jobs and seats in the legislatures. Even when the Congress leadership accepted this logic,[9] it was not able to act on it because of

[8]Today a similar weakness prevails to a greater or lesser extent among all the major political parties and groups *vis-a-vis* casteism.

[9]According to Nehru, one of the major aspects of the Congress policy towards communalism was that "the majority community must show generosity in the matter to allay the fear and suspicion that minorities, even though unreasonably, might have". *SW*, Vol. 7, p. 190.

the pressure of the communal-minded Hindu middle classes on its flanks. The latter opposed any such concessions; and the Congress leadership, though secular, did not have the political will to defy them. Instead, it tried to satisfy all sections of the middle classes and to appease middle class Muslim communalism without annoying overmuch middle class Hindu communalism. However, this is not to suggest that appeasement of communalism or accepting the demands of the Muslim middle classes was a viable or desirable policy. The criticism is that the Congress leaders failed to explore to the full the possibilities of their own strategy. As pointed out earlier, the real answer lay in an all-out opposition to communalism in all arenas—ideological, cultural, social and political—and in a greater shift of the national movement's social and ideological base from the petty bourgeoisie to the mass of peasants and workers.

Because the Congress had wider mass roots and because the Hindu middle classes did not, because of political-ideological influences, wholly go over to communalism and retained strong nationalist loyalties, the Congress could on the whole follow secular politics. But its weakness among the masses in several regions and dependence on the middle classes, especially for electoral purposes, opened it to communal pressures to a certain extent. At the same time, its failure to acquire a base among the Muslim peasantry and artisans, except in small pockets, and the strong tilt of the Muslim middle classes towards communalism disarmed it when faced with Muslim communalism. Consequently, it was forced to negotiate with Muslim communal leaders and in the end to bow before them. In other words, in order to solve the communal problem and to fight communalism successfully, it was necessary to reduce the weight of the middle classes in Indian politics and end their predominance over the social ethos. This aspect acquired added importance because the national movement was not in a position to wean away the middle classes from communalism by drastically changing their social condition for the better.

The ending of petty bourgeois predominance over socio-political development should not, of course, be understood in a simplistic or mechanical manner. In a loosely structured colonial society, where classes were in the process of formation and were far from being ideologically or socially structured, even workers in the factories, railways, etc., as well as the newly emerging strata of the middle and rich peasants thought and functioned within a petty bourgeois ethos; and unless intense and conscious ideological remoulding occurred, movements and politics based on them could also suffer from petty bourgeois deformations. Furthermore, because of agricultural and industrial stagnation, the educated youth of peasant and working class origin, as also of landlord origin, rapidly acquired petty bourgeois aspirations and outlook. For these reasons, even individuals, groups and parties who claimed to speak for, or to be based on, workers and peasants could acquire communal overtones or at least fail to struggle against communalism politically and ideologically.

To recognize the negative features of the dependence of the national movement on the middle classes and of the middle class orientation of nationalist politics was not to project a political programme or tactic of anti-middle classism. Throughout my analysis I have been emphasizing the social base that the middle classes or the petty bourgeoisie provided to communalism. But this has been done to point to the key factor in the struggle against communalism. The purpose has not been to condemn this stratum or to sneer at it.

For complex historical reasons, the petty bourgeoisie was, and had to be, an important component of the national movement. This was especially so because constitutional or electoral politics and political agitations through the Press and the platform were a necessary and inevitable part of nationalist political strategy. Given the way the electorate was defined or public opinion was historically constituted in India, the petty bourgeoisie could by no means be eliminated as an important element of the social base of the anti-imperialist movement. It was true that to successfully oppose communalism the movement had to get out of the groove of middle class-oriented politics. But it was not possible to ignore or banish the petty bourgeoisie from politics simply because communalism was above all its ideology. It was therefore necessary, even while reducing its weight in the social processes, to struggle to change and remould its ideological make-up. The secular nationalist forces had to take a positive approach towards its economic as also social, cultural, ideological and psychological needs. And this was the conglomeration of strata among whom the focal point of ideological struggle had to be located. Struggle against communalism was basically a struggle to prevent the petty bourgeoisie from becoming communal. Not to see this was to suggest that this struggle was to be equated with the struggle against colonialism.

The middle classes under communal influence had to be patiently weaned away from communal politics and prejudices and *to be encouraged to understand their social condition and its causation and to transcend through ideological and political practice the effects of their social condition.* It was necessary for them to understand that their grievances, while being real, were due to the colonial character of Indian society, polity and economy and not to the machinations or domination of the other 'communities', and that not only could there be no middle class solution of the national or the communal problem but that there could be no communal solution of the genuine social problems of the middle classes either. For example, while benefiting some individuals of the middle classes, reservation of jobs would not solve the wider problem of unemployment among the middle classes; this problem would be solved only when the economy was set on the path of development leading to the creation of jobs for the middle classes in industry, trade, professions, education, social services, the Press, radio, arts and literature, films, drama, etc.

There was another important reason why ideological remoulding of the middle classes was important. By the 1920s, the middle classes were the main recruiting base of the intelligentsia, nationalist and other political workers, socialists and communists, and trade union and peasant cadres who carried politics to the other sections of society. A significant change in the orientation of the ideology and politics of the middle classes would therefore have had an immediate and compounded impact on politics as a whole.

CHAPTER 10

Communalism Today: The Way Out

What of the future? Communalism and communal-type movements and ideologies are very much with us today and have even grown to an extent that they were in power from 1999 to 2004 and rule several states even to-day. Indian society continues to provide objective social, economic and political bases as also ideological and cultural soil for the rise and growth of such movements. Since the late 1950s, the country has been repeatedly racked by a spate of communal, regional linguistic and caste riots. Communal and caste appeals are used on a large scale for electoral as well as non-electoral political mobilization of the people. Today, communalism is the most serious challenge facing Indian society and polity. It marks, on the one hand, the growth of forces of national disintegration which constantly threaten the unity of the Indian people, and, on the other hand, the growth of forces of barbarism. Moreover, it is a problem facing the entire Indian society. Conjecturally, it breaks out in a virulent form sometimes here, sometimes there; but, in varying degrees of intensity, it has been pervading the entire country. It has had a strong pressence since the 1950 in Assam, U.P., and Madhya Pradesh. But who could have imagined that it would assume such major proportions in Punjab, Gujarat, Kashmir, Madhya Pradesh, Rajasthan and Kerala?

While not giving way to and opposing the feeling of helplessness and hopelessness, in facing the communal challenge, the starting point has to be the realization that the way out is going to be a long haul. Historical problems generated over decades and generations do not have short-term or instant solutions. Such solutions—pacts, compromises and accords and electoral alliances by secular parties—often tend to worsen the problem. Communalization of Indian society has been a prolonged process which has been going on for over 100 years; de-communalization has also got to be a process.[1] The real answer to the communal challenge lies in initiating and pushing forward the process of the long haul.

Whatever our failures on the communal question in the past—and the price of the failure to tackle the communal problem as its roots was paid by the partition of the land in 1947—it is necessary to use the insights we gain by the study of our historical experience to understand and deal with communal and communal-type movements and ideologies in a more rigorous and scientific fashion.

The study of communalism during the colonial period cannot, of course, be utilized mechanically by directly transferring its analysis or remedies to post-colonial India, for the socio-political context of communalism underwent basic structural changes after 1947.

The most important of these changes has been in the role of the state. While the colonial state was a major prop of communal forces, the independent Indian state has so far been largely secular as well as opposed to communalism except during the short period 1999 to 2004. Similarly, the ruling political party, the Congress, as well as most of the major all-India opposition parties—the Communists, Socialists, Swatantra, dissident Congress, Janata, Lok Dal and Janata Dal, that is, all except the RSS and BJP (Jan Sangh) and the Muslim League—have been secular. But the quality of the secularism of the Indian state and most of the political parties has had varying degrees of weakness. In fact, their secularism has seldom been very sturdy.

Moreover, communalism has made serious inroads into the state apparatuses. Many of the officials of the government and middle-level leaders have openly or secretly compromised with or even supported communal forces and sometimes themselves practised communalism. Neither the Central and State Governments nor the political parties, especially the ruling Congress Party, have fought communalism scientifically or with enthusiasm and commitment. They have often

[1]Interestingly, nobody expects or tries to find an 'instant' solution to the caste problem or the problem of poverty or class oppression—here we turn to political, economic, social or ideological processes.

permitted and sometimes encouraged the intrusion of religion into politics. They have opportunistically compromised and even allied with communal parties and individuals; for example, with the Muslim League in Kerala and the Akalis in Punjab. Similarly, several secular groups and parties did not hesitate to join hands with the RSS-Jan Sangh in 1967-69 and in 1977-80 and in 1999-2004 with the BJP. They are continuing to do so with the BJP in Bihar and Orissa.[2] But it is still very important that they have themselves not been communal. This fact has been a major obstacle in the path of Hindu communalism, preventing its burgeoning, and is responsible for keeping India basically secular. But it has not prevented the growth of communalism, especially in its ugly, barbaric form of communal riots.

The social, class character and base of communalism have also undergone a major change after 1947. In the colonial period, communalism represented in the main the interests of the jagirdari classes and strata, moneylenders and merchants, sections of the petty bourgeoisie, and colonial rulers. The colonial factor as a prop of communalism has by now virtually disappeared. The jagirdari classes and strata have been disintegrating and merging with the capitalist farmers and rich peasants, who constitute a strong base of Sikh communalism in Punjab, and who tend to support communalism and casteism in other parts of the country too as a means of keeping their hegemony over the poor peasants of the same caste or religion. Moneylenders and merchants still constitute a major social base of communalism all over India. With the creation of Pakistan and the gradual abolition of the zamindari system and landlordism during the last 30 years, communalism seldom now represents, except in Punjab, a distorted form of class struggle. There is however a tendency for the rural class struggle between agricultural labourers and rich peasants-capitalist farmers and landlords to take on the forms of caste and communal struggles. This is particularly so in Punjab today. Similarly,

[2]Their record of compromise with the casteist parties and groups is perhaps even worse.

though the struggle among the capitalist strata and groups is once again beginning to take on a communal form in a few areas, its main form still is that of regionalism. The struggle of the rural bourgeoisie against the urban bourgeoisie sometimes takes casteist forms, though its main form is the ideology of peasantism. The Indian intelligentsia continues to be on the whole anti-communal or at least not pro-communal, though it is not able to stand up to the communal forces once they enter a vigorous phase as the example of Punjab and Gujarat shows.

In other words, apart from the petty bourgeoisie, whose ranks are being rapidly replenished by the children of the peasantry and working classes, communalism has failed after 1947 to get significant support from any major social class or stratum. In particular, it cannot be said that it has been getting or is likely to get in the immediate future from the Indian bourgeoisie the type of strong social support it derived from the jagirdari or semi-feudal classes and strata and from colonialism. The Indian bourgeoisie continues to feel, as it did before 1947, that it needs national unity and integration and that communalism (and casteism) operates against the economic, social and political development of India along capitalist lines. Its role in the spread of both communalism and casteism is minimal, being confined to certain socially reactionary sections and individuals. Its dominant sections and class leaders do not yet feel that the class can survive only with the help of communalism (or casteism). Therefore, any analysis or strategy of political and ideological struggle against communalism (or casteism) which is based upon treating it as the ideological instrument of the capitalist class would be incorrect and is therefore likely to be politically infructuous. At the same time, it cannot be said that this attitude of the capitalist class towards communalism would remain for ever. World historical experience from Japan to Germany indicates that communal type fascist ideologies tend to serve as the second or last line of defence of a capitalist class faced with political and economic crises and the threat of expropriation or overthrow. Any long-term strategy against communalism must therefore take account of such a possibility. In other words, it cannot be dogmatically asserted either that the Indian bourgeoisie at present backs communalism or that it would never do so in the future.

II

While the state policy of independent India has not been basically procommunal, the logic of the socio-economic system continues to provide favourable ground for the spread of communalism. To reiterate what has been brought out in Chapter 1, communalism is the product of a particular situation of a particular society, economy and polity, which creates problems for its people—problems whose cause the people are not able to easily understand. Communalism often represents the effort of the people to come to grips with the situation of their personal and social crisis without correctly grasping what the situation is and why it is so. Communalists quite often are people who cannot understand the world around them and are frustrated. Communalism is, of course, neither a correct diagnosis of the social situation, nor its correct solution. At the same time, there is a social situation lying at its back, which is funnelling it, without which communalism could not have survived for long; and unless that social situation is righted or efforts are made to set it right to solve it in a right way, ideologies like communalism and casteism will go on arising and growing. Therefore, the way out of communalism in a permanent direction lies in making right the social situation.

But, having said that, two other points have to be made. Firstly, one cannot rest with this formulation, for while communalism is the product of a particular social situation, to right that situation communalism itself has to be opposed and eradicated, otherwise the situation cannot be transformed. Secondly, social analysis of communalism should not be used, as many people do, as an alibi for not actively fighting against communalism. Fighting for the ultimate solution does not take away from the task of fighting against communalism here and now.

III

The capitalist path of development in post-independent India created the soil for the growth of communalism in, broadly speaking, two ways. Firstly, the capitalist economy has failed to solve the basic problems of poverty, unemployment and inequality which breed frustration and generate unhealthy competition for the inadequate economic and social opportunities. It became obvious by the late 1950s that though the overthrow of colonial political power was a necessary condition for opening the path to economic development, it was not a sufficient condition.

In particular, after the initial spurt in job opportunities following independence, unemployment among the lower middle classes tended to become endemic after the mid-1960s. The coming of freedom and the Five Year Plans did open up a wide range of opportunities to the middle classes because of the immense expansion of the administrative apparatuses, Indianization and expansion of the officer cadre of the armed forces, Indianization of the higher cadre of foreign firms, development of banking, trading and industrial companies, rapid growth of school and college education and phenomenal expansion in the training and recruitment of engineers, doctors and scientists. For nearly 20 years after 1947 the middle classes not only had a respite but were in a state of euphoria. In politics there prevailed not only the social stability of the Nehru era but also the relative weakness and stagnation of the communal and other similar socially disruptive forces as well as of the forces of social transformation. But fresh opportunities for the middle classes soon began to dry up. The pattern of capitalist economic development was such that while it led to a certain economic growth over time, it failed to generate large-scale employment in the industrial and commercial sectors. It also placed limits on the expansion of social services. At the same time, the spread of education and the population explosion led to the accertion of hundreds of thousands of new youths from the peasantry and working class into the ranks of the job-seeking petty bourgeoisie. Thus, gradually, from the 1960s, conditions similar to those of the 1930s began to emerge, leading to intense discontent and rivalry among the middle classes. Moreover, changes in agrarian relations threw up new strata of rich and middle peasants and capitalist farmers, that is, rural bourgeoisie and petty bourgeoisie, who provided a fertile ground for the germination and spread of communal and casteist ideologies, movements, and parties. Expectations of these youth, especially the educated among them, were aroused without the society developing the requisite capacity to fulfil them to the needed extent. The countryside has been full of disoriented educated youth who cannot be absorbed in the agricultural sector and who do not know what else to do with their lives.

Secondly, capitalist development in agriculture and industry did generate higher incomes and even prosperity for certain strata and in certain regions and brought new social groups to the fore. These developments brought in their wake new social strains and new social anxieties. The accompanying competitiveness, rising expectations, skewed distribution of income and sharp and visible inequality have been straining the social and political system creating fresh ground on which both communalism and populism can flourish. Moreover, as new groups gain in social strength, others decline in power and prestige and become open to the appeals of revivalism and communalism. Political, economic and social development and various poverty-removal programmes, such as the Intensive Rural Development, food for work, employment guarantee scheme, old age pensions for the poor, and reservation of jobs for the socially deprived, produce resentment among those who have been, or at least have had the feeling of being, dominant in the rural areas. Both groups of social strata tend to fall prey to casteism and communalism.

The problem, however, does not lie merely in the economic realm, with people turning to communalism to redress their existential economic grievances. It also involves the breakdown of traditional social institutions such as caste, the joint family, and village and mohalla communities, which had the positive aspect of providing a sense of identity and a support system, accompanied by the failure of class, political (party) and national solidarities to take their place.

Many turn to communalism as a kind of refuge, as an alternative focus of unity and solidarity. There is also the attraction for individuals and groups of taking the quick and easy route to political power in a situation of popular sovereignty—whether through the use of ballot-box or through a populist authoritarian manner—by arousing communal sentiments and passions. The possibility emerges strongly in a situation of crisis in the political system.

Consequently, once again, since the late 1950s, the disruptive forces of communalism, casteism and regionalism have been on the move in Indian society, bringing within their net newer and newer sections of Indian society.

IV

Communalism has been aided by the undermining and even breakdown of values and ideals consequent upon the unbridled sway of the profit motive. A kind of moral vacuum has been coming into being. For decades, the struggle for freedom and social reform provided the framework and inspiration for this sway of idealism. After 1947, the people needed a new unifying, anti-divisive goal or vision which could generate hope for the future, rekindle healthy national feeling, and inspire and unite them in a common nation-wide endeavour, pushing forward the process of nation-in-the-making. That endeavour can only be the building of democratic, civil libertarian, egalitarian, socially just, nationally united and economically developing society, that is, a socialist society.

The minorities in particular can live and prosper with full dignity and security and without fear only in a social system in which they would not be permanent potential scapegoats for its failures. As Abid Husain, no fire-brand revolutionary, has put it, when Muslims come out of "the 'valley of doubt' and are able to think clearly, they will become warm supporters of the general idea of a socialist society and prove to be an effective force in giving the movement the right orientation and leading it to success."[3]

[3]Abid Husain, The Destiny of Indian Muslims, p.6.

A caveat may however be entered at this stage. Great care has to be exercised in making a social analysis of communalism. It has to be based on hard research and analysis; it has to be a serious and complex empirical, analytical and theoretical effort. The roles of economy and polity, culture, social classes and strata, different social and political forces, the state, and different religions in India as a whole as also in its different parts have to be examined in all their complexity. We must not give way to easy generalizations or to 'simple attempts at solving complex problems'. The price of not making such a deep and complex study in the 1920s and 1930s and of relying on easy formulas was the partition of India in 1947.

V

As we have observed several times, communalism is a long-term problem which requires intense and complex struggle on the political front and in the field of ideas. This is because communalism is basically and above all an ideology, and politics based on that ideology, and not, in the main, communal rioting or communal violence, including its latest version, terrorism. The two are linked but basically the latter are episodic or conjectural consequences of the former, they are the concrete manifestations and products of the spread of communal ideology. Communal ideology can prevail without violence but communal violence cannot exist without communal ideology. A person can be a believer in, and even a propagator of, communalism even while opposing and condemning communal violence, rioting and terrorism.

Consequently, it is possible for communal ideology to exist and grow for years and even decades without any communal violence at all taking place. For example, more communal riots took place during 1923-28 than during 1937-46 when communal ideology had a far greater reach and spread and was in fact burgeoning forth. There was no communal violence in Punjab during 1948-1981. But, in fact, the communal violence unleashed there after 1981 has its roots in the communalization of Punjab in the pre-1981 years. We may also note that Muslims in India after 1947 have seldom initiated communal violence—they have invariably been its victims. Yet, Muslim communalism has remained quite strong and has, in fact, grown in the last several decades. Similarly, the horrendous communal violence in Delhi and northern India in early November 1984 was the result precisely of the spread of communal ideology during 1981-84, as was the wave of brutal killings in Punjab after 1982. The same is true of Gujarat riots of 2002. They were the result of the communalization of the Gujarat society since the late 1970s.

As an aside, we may take note of an interesting phenomenon which throws light on the role of communalism as an ideology. In Punjab, both Hindu and Sikh communalisms had developed as political allies before 1947. Sikh communalism, from the days of Bhai Vir Singh's novels at the end of the 19th century, postulated that Sikhs were the defenders of Hindus and Hinduism against Muslim tyranny, that the later Gurus were the defenders of Brahmins and cows. Hindu communalists fully accepted the theory that Sikhs were the sword arm of Hinduism. That is why the main Hindu communal organization since the late 1930s, the RSS, made Guru Govind Singh one of its three main hero-figures, 'who fought against Muslim domination', the other two being Shivaji and Rana Pratap.

Consequently, till recent years, Hindu and Sikh communalists tried to avoid preaching of hatred against each other or against Sikhs and Hindus respectively even while developing anti-Sikh and anti-Hindu communalism. The Akalis did not preach hatred of Hindus because that would go against the entire grain of their communal ideology as developed during the 20th century and against their particular mythology regarding the history and role of Sikhs in the past. Even more recently, when the Akali ideologues such as G.S. Tohra and Sant Longowal, in their virulent phase, propagated the notions that Sikhs were being crushed and eliminated and the Sikh religion was in danger of being wiped out, it was to the 'Centre' (i.e., the Central Government) that they pointed as the villain and not Hindus as such, though the disguise was very thin indeed. Similarly, the RSS and the BJP (in its various reincarnations) found it extremely difficult, and even unpleasant, to arouse hatred against Sikhs, because a part of their communal mythology was the belief that Sikhs were a part of Hindus and that, in fact, Sikhs were the doughtiest defenders of Hindus and Hinduism from Muslim onslaught. Hence they could not easily breed and preach hatred against Sikhs as they have been doing against Muslims and Christians.

But the important point is that despite the Hindu and Sikh communal parties and groups making every effort not to preach or spread hatred against Sikhs and Hindus respectively and to confine their communal politics in Punjab within the bounds of liberal communalism, hatred and extreme communalism did finally come, because communal ideology—the ideology of separate communities—had its own logic. Once one holds and propagates communal ideology, the consequences are not in one's hands. Nor is Punjab's a lone instance. We have already seen how Jinnah, the youthful 'ambassador of Hindu-Muslim unity' and the cultured and civilized communalist of his middle years, found this out in the late 1930s and decided to follow the logic through, as did the erstwhile nationalist V.D. Savarkar and the liberal Shyama Prasad Mookerji in early 1950s. Sant Longowal went all the way during 1981-85; and when he tried to retreat, he had to pay with his life. As we have pointed out, it was the logic of communal ideology and communalization that resulted in normal people prepetrating, the horrors of early November, 1984. Similarly, it was under the liberal communalist Atal Behari Vajpayee's prime ministership that the communal carnage occurred in Gujarat in 2002. In Punjab the two groups of communalists have not been able to prevent their own development to the 'hatred stage'. In other words, while the final unfolding of the logic of communalism in the form of communal violence is dependent on a variety of conjectural factors, the ground for this denouncement is prepared by the continuing and long-term process of the structuring of communal ideology and politics.

Unfortunately, however, we have tended to ignore communal ideology, the prologue to communal violence. We become aware of communalism only when a riot occurs. But, once it is recognized that communalism is above all an ideology, it is at the level of struggle against that ideology that the way out of communalism has to be found. The way out of communalism means de-communalizing the people at all levels. Communalism cannot be opposed successfully without liquidating the heritage of communal ideology inculcated among our people for over 100 years. At different levels and with different degrees of virulence, communalism and other similar ideologies have penetrated our people, though often subconsciously, so much so that many of its elements have acquired a certain legitimacy even among secular-minded people, many of whom carry large communal elements in their thinking. No class or social stratum or group is free from the reach of communal and communal-type ideologies. Nor would a mere struggle for social transformation automatically lead to and guarantee the disappearance of communal ideology as is shown by the survival of its elements among those who have participated in the nationalist, peasant, working class and other popular movements. For this it is necessary to fight communal ideology and politics in a conscious and all-sided manner.

Before 1947, the anti-imperialist struggle was a powerful force for national unity. Despite its many weaknesses, it kept in check most of the disruptive and divisive forces including Hindu and Sikh communalisms. This led to the foundation of a secular state in India after 1947 and the acceptance by the Indian people of the secular ideal as a basic feature of our society. Similarly, even though obscurantist ideas were not rooted out, they were kept in check, for the thrust of the national movement had been towards modern, scientific, humanitarian and rational ideas.

Unfortunately, the impetus given to secular ideas by the national movement was gradually and inevitably exhausted after 1947 and found no replacement. Moreover, in the euphoria of the 1950s, there was a general tendency to ignore communalism. It was felt that as a result of Gandhiji's martyrdom and with Nehru at the helm communalism was on the way to withering away. Moreover, the official expectation was that economic development, spread of education, science and technology, and construction of the new 'temples' of science and technology such as hydro-electric dams, steel plants, and science laboratories would automatically weaken and extinguish communal (and casteist) thinking. Similarly, the left-wing forces hoped that popular struggles and class organizations of workers and peasants and the spread of leftist political ideas would automatically weaken communal (and casteist) forces. There was thus a general tendency on the part of the secular forces to neglect direct ideological struggle against communalism (and casteism). Nor was any long-term strategy to combat communalism evolved. The secular forces continued to live from hand to mouth in their opposition to communalism. This was also true of Nehru[4] and the Socialists and Communists. There has hardly been a single major all-India movement or mass campaign against caste oppression and communalism in independent India even of the type organized earlier by Gandhiji and the Congress. Consequently, there was little effort to assess the impact of history textbooks, to prevent the use of films, radio and television for spreading religiosity, irrationalism and vicarious 'communal' nationalism, to eliminate the deep-seated Hindu tinge from much of secular thinking, and in general to promote scientific thinking and a

[4]Nehru fully grasped the different dimensions of communalism, the dangers that it posed to Indian people and social development, and the nature of steps to be taken against it. We may illustrate by taking examples from the first two years of tenure as Prime Minister of independent India. The examples are taken from his Letters to Chief Ministers, Vol. I, 1947-1949 (New Delhi 1985). He repeatedly described communalist organizations as fascist which take Hindu, Muslim, and Sikh forms (pp. 11, 33, 243, 428). He warned against exploitation of religion for political purposes (pp. 60, 329). Declaring that "We cannot, therefore, so long as we are the Government, tolerate the encouragement and spread of this wrong ideology," he asked the state government not to "permit the spread of communal doctrines in whatever shape" (p. 179). Communalism preached by the RSS, he again said, "cannot be permitted to poison our national life, and we have to take strong steps against it" (p. 251). It was necessary, he wrote on another occasions, that communal propaganda by Hindu, Muslim and Sikh communalists was "combated in every way, because if this is not done, it may lead the country towards discord and disruption" (p. 513). Yet, it was tragic that Nehru took no steps to mobilize the people and secular forces in a political and ideological struggle against the communal menace. Such steps were not taken even after he saw the surge of communalism in the late 1950's and set up the National Integration Council in 1961. This body remained, and remains to this day, a merely decorative forum.

secular nationalist outlook. Hence, the need to develop a powerful ideological movement against communalism, casteism, linguism, and regionalism remains as urgent as ever. It is also important to remember that it is not enough to denounce them or to demonstrate their wrongness; today most persons would accept them as wrong, at least in the abstract. It is necessary to interpret and expose them for what they are, to bring out the different elements which constitute them as ideologies, to explain their socio-economic and political roots and to show the way to successfully opposing and eradicating them.

Several corollaries follow once we see communalism as an ideology. Communalism cannot be suppressed by force, for no ideology can be suppressed by force or through administrative bans. Ideology has to be overcome at the level of ideas. While communal violence can and must be put down by the state, the weakening and eradication of communalism is the task not only of the state but also, and perhaps even more so, of intellectuals, political parties, media, voluntary groups, trade unions and kisan sabhas, etc. The state can contribute by not encouraging communalism through its acts of omission and commission and by using its media and educational institutions to combat communal ideology.

There can be absolutely no compromise with communalism at the ideological plane. As Nehru put it in December 1948:[5] "No government can be absolutely uncompromising where its own citizens are concerned. It tries, or should try, to win over as many people as possible to its own side. Nevertheless, it is always a dangerous thing to compromise with something that is definitely evil." The example to be followed should be that of Bhagat Singh who did not hesitate to strongly criticise and condemn Lala Lajpat Rai, whom he otherwise respected and whose death he avenged with his life, when Lajpat Rai began to propagate communal ideas after 1922.

This point has to be stressed because our experience since the beginning of the century has been that whenever there is a resurgence of communalism many political parties and leaders and intellectuals

[5]Letters to Chief Ministers, 1947-1964, Vol. 1, 1947-1949, New Delhi, 1985 pp. 251-2.

reel under its pressure and begin to make or advocate compromises with communal ideology in one form or another and tend to accept, or at least refuse to criticize, the underlying idioms, concepts and themes of communal ideology. In recent years, such was the case vis-a-vis Hindu communalism and Jan Sangh in 1967, Sikh communalism and Akalis after 1981 and Lal Krishen Advani and the resurgent. BJP after 1988 and, more recently, Narendra Modi in Gujarat. Similarly, in the last several years, themes and concepts, which were basic to communal ideology since the early 1920s, have been picked up, quite often unconsciously, by many secular persons. Thus there has again been a great deal of talk of Hindu, Muslim or Sikh identity, Hindu, Muslim or Sikh history, sharing of power by communities, and so on.

All this shows how deep are communal ideology or elements of communal ideology in our minds. When we suddenly come out with concepts, symbols and ideas which we thought we had long burried; and when they come up in our minds though we have been struggling against them for years and decades; then it is seen how important it is to go to the marrow, not only to the bone but the very marrow, of communal ideology in order to fight communalism.

Special efforts in this respect have to be made to spread a scientific interpretation of history at research and teaching and popular levels since communal ideology, especially its Hindu variant, is based almost entirely on a perverted view of history which is inculcated among the people from their childhood onwards through various media, including oral communication, and through socialization in the family, school and the mohalla. Another area calling for a major effort is regarding the wrong notion that Hindus, Muslims, Sikhs and Christians constitute structured and homogeneous communities or in fact communities of any sort in India.

Ideological struggle to eradicate communal ideological influences has to be waged among all sections of the people; and not only among the communal-minded but also among those who are secular and who support secular parties. In periods of crisis communalism burgeons forth precisely because secular persons start falling prey to it. This is because there are communal elements in the thinking of even basically secular persons. This point may be elaborated. Communalism as an ideology is constituted of several elements; it manifests in and articulates with one or more such elements. Consequently, it is possible for a person to be secular and yet have some communal elements in his or her thought and personality. Existence of some of these elements in a particular mix may lead to full-blooded communalism; but communal elements may and do exist in an overall secular personality and may not yet amount to communalism. It would be wrong to brand or treat such a person as a communalist and throw him or her into the ranks of communalists. Yet, there is the great danger that if these elements are not opposed and eliminated in normal times, they will grow and develop in a crisis situation and lead to the burgeoning forth of communalism. This is what happened in Punjab during 1982-84 especially after Operation Blue Star, in Delhi and other parts of India during 31 October-3 November 1984, in Bombay in 1991 and 1992, and in Gujarat in 2002. It is on these elements that the Vishwa Hindu Parishad or opponents of the Shah Bano judgement or proponents of Babri Masjid or perpetrators of Gujarat pogroms play. Neither Lokamanya Tilak, nor the Khilafat Agitation, nor the original Akali movement were communal, but they generated certain communal elements among the masses and even among the nationalists which were later used by the communalist ideologues and political leaders to generate and promote communalism.

It is therefore necessary to pinpoint and analyse these communal elements and oppose them much before they develop into full-fledged communal ideologies or become a part of the communal ideological discourse. This, of course, once again requires an in-depth analysis of communal ideology and its manifestations as also a long-term programme of ideological work.

Another corollary follows: We need to distinguish between communal leaders and ideologues and their communal followers. The latter should be neither ridiculed nor scorned and abused. They are to be treated not as villains but as victims, who have been misled by communalism and whose social condition has propelled them in that direction. They have to be helped in a friendly way to overcome their communal thinking and prejudices. This is particularly true of the petty bourgeois social base of communalism which, because of the peculiar social development of India, extends today to large sections of the working class and peasantry. The ideologues and leaders of communalism are, on the other hand, the generators and carriers of the communal germs and are therefore to be seen and branded as the enemies of society and to be given no quarter. We, however, tend to do the very opposite. While the communal leaders and ideologues are treated with kid gloves and more often dealt with as respectable persons, who are even invited to national integration conferences, committees and councils, their followers are condemned and treated as anti-social elements for participating in communal riots, etc. In other words, those who forment communal riots or generate and propagate the ideology that leads to communal riots escape not only legal punishment but often social diapproval and condemnation, while their victims often pay with their lives.

It is necessary to distinguish between liberal communalism and extreme or fascist communalism. But this distinction is not to be made in order to avoid ideological struggle against liberal communalism or to take a softer attitude towards it or to condone it or to give good chits to the liberal communalists or to make them respectable or to legitimize them. This distinction is to be made because the two have to be opposed and attacked in different ways. Liberal communalism has invariably to be opposed via ideology while extreme communalism may in many cases have to be dealt with through the use of state force. Moreover, if liberal communalism is not opposed successfully, it tends to grow into extreme or fascist communalism. Quite often the two forms of communalism go on inter-changing depending upon political circumstances. RSS and BJP (Jan Sangh, etc.) have constantly shifted positions. Muslim communalism became extreme during 1938-47, resumed a liberal form in India after 1947 and is once again assuming extreme forms in recent months. Akali Dal and Sant Longowal were liberal communalists till 1981, became increasingly extreme after 1981 till they could not be distinguished from Bhindranwalites, and then again gradually shifted to liberal communalism after the death of Bhindranwale and Operation Blue Star.

In this context, we may take note of another aspect of the necessity of seeing communalism as an ideology. Since all shades of communalists share a common ideology, liberal communalists cannot be expected or depended upon to fight extreme communalism ideologically. While the political differences among the two may become important, the ideological struggle against extreme communalism can be waged only by secular persons and forces. (In fact even secular persons with communal elements in their thinking are hampered in the task). In the past, for example, liberal communalists like the poet Iqbal, Sikander hayat Khan, H.S. Suhrawardy, and others (including even the leftists who joined the League after 1942) failed to oppose Jinnah and the Muslim League in their extreme phase. It was only the sturdy nationalists like Abul Kalam Azad, Maulana Husain Madani, Rafi Ahmed Kidwai and Asaf Ali who undertook the task facing heavy odds. Similarly, liberal communalists like Shyama Prasad Mookerjee, N.C. Chatterjee, and Madan Mohan Malaviya did not oppose the RSS and Hindu Mahasabha under V.D. Savarkar when they took to extreme communalism after 1937. More recently, even the most moderate elements and leaders of the Bharatiya Janata Party have refused to criticize the RSS ideology or raised their voices against the fascist pronouncements of M.S. Golwalkar or the vicious propaganda carried out in the RSS shakhas (branches) or by Narendra Modi. The same was the case during 1981-84 with Akali liberal communalists like Sant Longowal, Prakash Singh Badal and S.S. Barnala, who not only did not oppose Bhindranwale but increasingly competed with him in rabid communalism. It was only the Communists and sturdy secular Congressmen like Darbara Singh who had the courage to oppose extreme communalism. Similarly, the liberal communalist, Atal Behari Vajpayee failed to criticise or condemn Narendra Modi and Vishwa Hindu Parishad and the hate campaign against Muslims in Gujarat. Thus, the liberal communalists may have political contradictions with extreme communalists and these may be of some tactical use in the fight against communalism, but to expect the former to fight the latter ideologically and consistently is to expect the impossible.

Intellectuals have to play a crucial role in any ideological struggle and we do not agree with the tendency, especially among intellectuals themselves, to decry their own role in society. But in order to effectively play this role, they have themselves to be free of the communal virus. While a large majority of Indian intellectuals are on the whole secular, many others are the main purveyors of communalism. Even otherwise secular intellectuals, as in Punjab since 1983, tend to sometimes suffer from intellectual cowardice in the face of the communal onslaught. Consequently, the struggle against communalism has not only to be conducted with the help of the intellectuals but also first of all among the intellectuals.

We should also distinguish between communalization and secularization of the state and of society. There is a certain difference in the types of efforts needed to secularize the two. This aspect is important because there is a tendency among Indian intelligentsia to be obsessed with the state level and neglect the social level. The state does, of course, play an important role, especially because of its command over the media, educational institutions, and job opportunities. But it is, to say the least, an exaggeration to believe that if the state is secular, it will follow that society will also be or increasingly become secular. In fact, more often it is the other way around. If, for various reasons, society gets communalized the state will tend to follow suit, especially where the system of popular franchise and elected government prevails. Quite often a democratically elected political leadership fails to take drastic action against communal propaganda or violence or yields to communal pressure for reservations, poll adjustment, etc., not because it is inherently communal but because it lacks the courage to stand upto the communalized society and public opinion. Also it may happen that secularization of the state may be accompanied by the desecularization or communalization of society. Also, it is at the level of society that intellectuals, cultural workers and voluntary bodies can be most effective.

There is another advantage in seeing communalism as an ideology. One does not then distinguish one communalism from another; they are seen as varieties of the same ideology: communalism. One does not then fight against Hindu or Sikh or Muslim communalism, but communalism as such and its different manifestations. In other words, it is necessary to wage a simultaneous struggle against all forms of communalism.

While, in my view, as pointed out in Chapter 6 above, religion as such is not responsible for communalism nor does secularism require struggle against religion, the intrusion of religion into secular fields has to be opposed. In particular, religion has to be completely separated or detached from the state and the political and economic realms. There should also be an increasing narrowing down of religion's parameters in the realm of even personal life. Increasingly marriage, divorce, abortion, family planning, and inheritance must be divested of religious control. Moreover, while religion does not lead to communalism, irrational attitudes and cults, religious narrowmindedness and obscurantism in the name of going to fundamentals of a religion—currently fashionable as fundamentalism—and inordinate growth of religiosity (that is, intrusion of religion into areas other than that of personal belief) do create a certain receptivity to or openings for communal ideology and politics. In this respect, different religions have different historically evolved elements in their functioning, structure, ideologies and practices which contribute to or are conducive to communalism. These elements should be brought out, analysed, criticised and eliminated. This process has to be different for different religions. In practice, the opposite is happening and efforts are being made to strengthen precisely such elements in different religions. For example, precisely such universally respected religious-cultural figures as Ram and Krishna (respected equally by Hindus, Muslims, Sikhs, and Christians) have been communalized. Similar is also the case with such religious festivals as Dussehra, Ram Navami, Janam Ashthami, various Puja days of local gods and goddesses, Muharram, Ids, Shaab-e-Barat, and birthdays of Sikh gurus, Ramdas, Valmiki, etc. In this context, the propagation of scientific knowledge and ideas and the inculcation of the scientific temper have to be an essential part of the fight against communalism in the field of ideas and ideologies.

Here the role of education and the press is crucial. The spread of literacy and education was expected to play a major role in weaning people away from communalism and casteism. But the educational system, both at the school and college levels, and the printed word through the press, etc., is being used to inculcate and spread communalism, casteism and chauvinist regionalism. Consequently, the spread of education has resulted in the further reach of communal, obscurantist and irrational ideas and ideologies. Reorientation of education, especially of its social science component, along scientific lines, is therefore an urgent necessity. Similarly, the spread of the reading habit has failed to check communalism in view of the paucity of popular secular literature. On the contrary in the past 30 or 40 years there has been a proliferation of communal magazines, cartoon strips, etc., meant for the consumption of children and neo-literate adults. The communal press also continues to expand its influence as the number of its readers goes up.

The communal forces also increasingly tend to absorb and ally with socially and culturally backward and conservative forces. Consequently, the struggle against caste oppression and the caste system, inequality of women, the cultural, social and economic exploitation of the tribal people, and elitism in society in general becomes part of the anti-communal fight. In general, it is necessary that all radical and liberal national and secular forces, parties, groups and individuals should join in bringing about a veritable cultural revolution in Indian society.

We have also to avoid a few major errors in the ideological and political struggle against communalism. Communalism and casteism should not be confused with the question of the defence of minorities and lower castes. In Indian society, minorities and lower castes suffer from a multiplicity of disabilities, deprivations, discrimination, and oppression and the consequent anxieties and fears. A part of the appeal of minority communalisms and casteism lies in their claim to allay these fears and anxieties. The secular forces have to find out and concretely analyse the genuine sources of these anxieties and fears, put forth and struggle for the real ways of removing them and of protecting the minorities and lower oppressed castes, and to bring out the falsity of communal and casteist premises and promises. In other words, the interests of the minorities are to be defended but not through communalism. That would be a self-defeating defence.

While before 1947 the main damage to national unity was done by Muslim communalism, since 1947 it is Hindu communalism which poses the fascist threat and which has to be made the main target of attack by the secular forces. The existence of minority communalisms should not detract from this fact.

This does not mean that we should ignore minority communalisms or adopt a soft and tolerant attitude towards them. They have to be opposed as strongly as majority communalism. Firstly, a minority communalism is dangerous because it hands over a minority to communal leaders whose politics are invariably harmful to the interests of the members of the minority concerned. Secondly, minority communalism, unless one struggles against it, makes the struggle against majority communalism very difficult.

Take, for example, the case of extreme Sikh communalism in Punjab. The real danger from it lay in this respect. It could not have been and cannot be successful in creating Khalistan—that would not be permitted by the rest of the country. The real danger was and is that of Hindu communalism burgeoning forth—as happened in early November 1984—by making an appeal to the strong sentiment of the Indian people for national unity and declaring, in the face of passivity by the secular forces and the State in opposing extremist violence, that Hindu communalism-fascism alone could keep this country united and strong and protect the Hindus of Punjab from terrorist violence. Therefore, to avoid Hindu communalism-fascism, it is very necessary to oppose minority communalisms. Lastly, it is our experience since the 1920s all over the country, and also in Punjab since 1948, that if we are soft towards minority communalisms, we tend to become passive in the fight against majority communalism also. Thus the different communalisms feed on each other and any strengthening of one inevitably strengthens the other. They have all to be fought simultaneously.

We may also take note of two other aspects. Just as the logic of majority communalism is fascism, the logic of minority communalism is separatism. Once the view is accepted that a minority is prepetually and inevitably threatened by a majority and it must therefore stand on its own legs, no guarantee, political or constitutional, can satisfy its communal proponents. And this for the simple reason that even the most cast iron guarantee has to be implemented by a state in which, by the communal definition, the majority prevails. In the Indian context, once the twin notions of communal identity and politics based on communal identity are accepted, minorities can exist in the long run either through the mediation of an outside power or through a separate state of their own. It is therefore not accidental that Muslim communalism before 1947 first wanted prepetuation of British domination as a safeguard of 'Muslim' interests and later moved on to separation. Similarly, during 1982-84, Sikh communalists repeatedly appealed not to democratic secular opinion for defence of 'Sikh' interests but either to the United Nations or to an autonomous or independent Panthic, i.e., Sikh state.

When warned of the dangers that reiteration of minority communal themes can pose in terms of the growth of Hindu fascism, apologists and exponents of Muslim and Sikh communalism have been putting forward the dangerous theory that Hindus can never be solidified around Hindu 'identity' or Hindu communalism. While it is true that luckily, for various reasons, and above all because of the strong secular leadership from Dadabhai Naoroji to Gandhiji and Nehru and the existence of a strong secular intelligentsia, Hindus have not been solidified into a community, it would be foolhardy to rely on such a theory for a guarantee of future well-being. Hindu communalism, in its various forms and guises, has always had a strong presence in

India—witness for example the defeat of the secular Swarajists in several parts of the country in 1926 or the communal riots of the 1920s and 1946-47 or the Hindu communal fury in Delhi in early November 1984, or in Bombay in 1991 and 1992 or in Gujarat in 2002. Today the opposition to Hindu communalism is beginning to weaken on a large scale. For the first time in modern history, a significant section of the intelligentsia is beginning to talk of a Hindu religious identity or the BJP succeeded in forming a government at the Centre in 1999. Moreover, it should be realized that even if the process of Hindu identity-formation and communalism remains limited, given the size of Hindu population even this limited Hindu communalism would pose a massive social and political danger.

Communalism can also not be eradicated by conciliating and appeasing communal leaders, groups and parties. Concessions only whet the appetite of the communalists; they do not lead them to give up communal politics. In fact, with every concession their demands escalate; and when no further viable demands are left, the last stage of separatism is invariably reached. Moreover, even if one group of communal leaders is appeased, another more 'extreme' group invariably makes its appearance. The growth of communalism assumes an upward spiralling character. This was the nationalist experience with the efforts to appease Muslim communalism from 1907 onwards. By 1937, nearly all conceivable Muslim communal demands had been accepted. Muslim communalism first demanded parity in legislatures and administration with Hindus and then went on to demand Pakistan. Similarly, several times after 1947, compromises with communal forces, both Sikh and Hindu, were made in Punjab. But the problem was not solved and communalism grew from stage to stage. The only result was the communalization of the Congress party in Punjab, making it incapable of opposing communalism, and the paralysis of the secular forces including the Communist parties and groups. Of course, if there is a real crisis—a riot, etc.—some type of compromise may become necessary. But such a compromise makes sense if it is not seen as a solution but as a means of gaining time during which a powerful political-ideological battle against communalism is launched. Concessions to and compromises with the communalists cannot serve as a substitute for political mobilization against them. Not negotiations and compromises but political debate and running argument with the communalists are needed. And part of this argument has to be the clear assertion that communalism shall not succeed, that a price tag is attached to communal politics. Appeasement of communalism, on the other hand, precisely makes the people believe that communalism is the road to political success.

In particular, under no circumstances should one make, under one excuse or garb, communalism and communalist ideology respectable or legitimize them. A positive feature of our society since 1948 is that the word communalist has acquired a bad odour. That odour should remain. The price of making communalism respectable in the 1920s and 30s—and not calling a spade a spade by the national movement as a whole and by the Communist Party during 1942-46 was paid in the form of the partition and the communal killings of 1946-47. If for some reason, it becomes necessary to enter into a compromise with liberal or moderate communalism, say that one has done so with liberal communalism and not with 'liberals' or 'moderates'.

In the post-1947 period, the ideological and political struggle against communalism has been severely vitiated by the tendency of secular parties and individuals to associate and enter into compromises with the different communal parties and groups. Once communalism is thereby made respectable, all talk of ideological campaign against it is seen by the people as hypocritical and makes little impact on them.

In this context, a great deal of political and ideological grit or toughness is needed—as also the recognition of the fact that there are no soft solutions to the communal problem. In no case should one follow the policy of attacking communalism when it is weak and going soft towards it when it acquires mass-support.

Under conditions of poverty and inequality, on the one hand, and rising expectations and democracy, on the other, existing secular parties are increasingly unable to actively promote social and cultural modernization, defeat the communal and other disruptive forces and take the country forward. They find it difficult to discharge this responsibility, as was done, even if inadequately, by the national movement. The secular, national, liberal, democratic and humanitarian elements are not weak in our country; but they have to be brought together and made effective. In this situation, special responsibility devolves on the left political forces who have to play a leading role not only in social transformation but also in national integration.

Unfortunately, while the left has taken correct ideological and political positions on communalism, casteism, regionalism, etc., it has not been able to play the desired role. In fact, it has not even made a serious analysis of these complex phenomena, being satisfied with a few simple formulae. One reason has been its general weakness in Indian society and politics. But more important has been its relative neglect of the problem and its tendency to compromise with caseist and communal forces especially those emerging from among the minorities. One reason for this is perhaps the immense economistic and economic reductionist bias from which the left in India has always suffered. This bias leads it to underestimate and even neglect, at least in practice, serious and complex study and analysis of communalism as well as struggle against it in the realms of ideology and culture. It underestimates the role that a new radical consciousness has to play in the creation of a new society. Consequently, the very cultural, social and ideological backwardness of the masses repeatedly hits back and holds up—and even pushes back—not only the struggle to unify the nation but also the struggle for transformation of society and the efforts to constitute all-India social classes, including the working class.

For example, in the absence of ideological struggle against communalism, economic development has almost every where in India—in Punjab, Gujarat, Bombay, Bhiwandi, Hyderabad, Moradabad, Delhi, Jamshedpur, Kanpur, even Bangalore—led to the growth of communalism, and it is not class struggle which has stymied communalism but communalism which has undermined class solidarity, as in Bombay, Bhiwandi, Baroda, Ahmedabad, Hyderabad, Indore, Kanpur, Jamshedpur and so on.

VI

What about communal violence? Ideological struggle is a long-term phenomenon. But when faced with communal violence, whether in the form of a riot or a knifing in the dark of terrorism, the only answer is the use of immediate and effective counter-violence of the State. When communal ideology manifests itself conjecturally in violent forms then the State alone is capable of saving the situation. When communal violence takes place, whether in Aligarh or Moradabad or Bhiwandi or Gujarat or Punjab, the criticism of the State government should not be, why it sent its police or the army but why did it not use the maximum of State force to crush communal violence in a manner that it would not have lasted one hour or one day instead of continuing for days and months.

Communal violence is bad in itself, but its worst aspect is not the consequent loss of life and property. The real harm is the spread of communal ideology in geometrical proportions. Furthermore, it forces even secular persons to join hands with or even depend upon communal forces to defend their lives and property. If a mob or a terrorist is going to attack one's house or office or shop because of one's religion, whether one is a Congressman, a Janata or Janata Dal, Lok Dal supporter or a Communist, then one is forced to contribute to the organizers of one's defence or even to join them in self-defence, volunteer efforts and organizations. In fact, the major purpose of those who inspire and organize communal violence is not to attack members of the opposite 'community' in order to reduce its numbers this can not be done, but to create situations which communalize secular-minded people.

Consequently, for all these reasons, communal violence must be curbed before it forces a secular person to think communally and join forces with the communalists. This can only be done in three ways: the use of State violence, non-violence resistance by secular persons, and self-defence by the aggressed group. Even Gandhiji and the Congress found it impossible to use the non-violence weapon in case of communal riots, except when Gandhiji himself plunged into the situation. He openly accepted its non-viability during 1937-39 when he asked Congress Ministries to use the full force of the State in case of communal riots. In areas or during times when the colonial State would not act effectively and in time, he advised the group, which felt that it was under the threat of violence, to organize itself and defend itself. This, he said, would check the aggressor group by raising the cost of communal aggression. He was, of course, as was usually the case with him, quite correct in the situation, for whatever the consequences, there was no other way out. Consequently, and in view of the consequences of self-defence, state action is the only viable and correct secular way of meeting the situation created by communal violence. The choice inevitably is between effective intervention by the State and constant aggravation via self-defence a'la Belfast and Lebanon. Not to use state power adequately and at the right moment is to force self-defence and communalization on the people.

In fact, this is also shown by the history of Europe in the 20th century. Organized self-defence failed to check the march of fascism in Italy, Germany and Austria. State action alone could have been effective. But the State played a passive and ineffective role and the result was the victory of fascism. A major form through which the colonial state indirectly encouraged communalism was its refusal, or failure, to take effective action during communal riots and against vicious communal propaganda. It has been noted that communal riots either do not occur or last only a day or two in those areas where effective administrative measures are taken or threatened by secular-minded and strong district officials. The opposite happens when semicommunal or weak officials hold office. State inactivity, for whatever reasons, against communal violence, apart from the absence of political-ideological struggle against communalism, has played a major role in the communalization of Punjab or U.P. and Bihar in recent years. On the other hand, the West Bengal Ministry has several times successfully scotched communal riots and communalization of the State. In fact, the very threat of communal violence would be lessened if it was made clear to all that the Government was both strong and impartial and was determined to put down communal violence or any talk of communal violence at any cost. This points to the need for sturdy secular police and other civil officials who can give confidence to the people and put the fear of God in the hearts and minds of the potential perpetrators and organizers of communal violence.

Our experience in the colonial period, the experience of Pakistan and Bangladesh, and the experience of fascist movements in Italy, Germany, Japan, Spain, France and the USA clearly indicate that communal and communal-type movements cannot win or prevail without state support or at least the neutrality and passivity of state power. That is why the communalists or the fascists try to manoeuvre themselves into state power or to at least neutralize it by postures of innocence and demagogic politics. It is therefore necessary to deny any share in state power to them and to see to it that state power does not remain passive in the face of a communal threat or a communal bid for power. Once again it becomes important for secular parties and forces, whether in the government or in the opposition, not to make unprincipled political alliances with communal groups and parties or to adopt a soft or casual 'negligent' position towards them.

This also means that penetration of state apparatuses by the communalists and communal ideology that has been going on since the 1930s and has been speeded up in the last four decades or so has to be checked and eliminated.

The police and intelligence and administrative machinery has to be rid of communal elements. It has to remain ever vigilant and to extinguish the communal spark before it sets an area or town on fire. Those who instigate and organize riots and incite and spread communal hatred and officials, who betray communalism in their official practice and who, by their acts of omission and commission enable communalism to flourish and communal riots to occur and take a heavy toll of lives and property, have to be dealt with severely and drastically punished. The failure to do so has been a major weakness of the Indian state after 1947.

VII

We may sum up what we have been saying in the form of a warning: unless social reality is changed and intense and wide-ranging political and ideological struggle waged against communal and communal-type parties, movements and ideologies, such divisive and distintegrative movements will break out again and again and continue to impede the processes of national integration and social transformation, even endangering the considerable though limited achievements of the last over 100 years in this direction.

APPENDIX

Forms of Communalism in Modern India

In modern India, communalism has taken three main forms.

I. COMMUNAL NATIONALISM

This form was, properly speaking, not communalism at all. It operated within the broad framework of nationalism, and was more in the nature of a deviation from, or weakness of, nationalism. It was an aspect of unclearly or imprecisely defined nationalism. In this form, nationalism remained primary. The communal nationalist accepted the basic notions of community and special communal interests but believed in the possibility as well as the desirability of their integration into the broader nation and national interests. He believed and propagated that even when the interests of the different religious communities were different, they did not clash and that it was only within the developing nationalism that the different communal interests could be protected. He also believed that his belonging to a particular religious community should not be, at least ideally, a relevant factor in his politics.

Numerous examples of communal nationalist thinking and expression can be given. For example, in his nationalist phase before 1920, when he at the same time worked in the Muslim League, M.A. Jinnah asked Indian people to separate politics from religion and to imbibe secularism. He refuted the Muslim communalist's assumption that self-government in India would lead to Hindu rule. While not actively supporting or opposing separate electorates, he said that the real issue was Home Rule or "transfer of power from bureaucracy to democracy."[1] Similarly, in 1938, Maulana Madani of the Jamat-ul Ulama said: "Now-a-days *qaums* (nations) are determined by their homelands *(watans)*. Race or religion does not make a *qaum*"[2] The Jamat demanded full independence for an Indian state based on a federal structure with full guarantees of religious and cultural liberties.[3] Similarly, presiding over the Muslim League session in December 1915, Mazhar-ul-Haq, an old Congressman, said:

> We are Indian Muslims. These words, 'Indian Muslims', convey the ideas of our nationality and of our religion.... When a question concerning the welfare of India and of justice to Indians arises, I am not only an Indian first, but an Indian next and an Indian to the last, an Indian and an Indian alone, favouring no community and no individual, but on the side of those who desire the advancement of India as a whole....[4]

The early nationalist V.D. Savarkar was also committed to a basically non-communal approach. In the "Introduction" to his book on the Revolt of 1857, he wrote in 1909:

> The nation ought to be the master and not the slave of its own history.... The feeling of hatred against the Mohammedans was just and necessary in the times of Shivaji—but, such a feeling would be unjust and foolish if nursed now, simply because it was the dominant feeling of the Hindus then.[5]

[1]Quoted in Moin Shakir, *Khilafat to Partition*, pp. 181-82.

[2]Syed Mohammed Mian, *Ulama-i-Haq...*, Vol. II, pp. 137-38.

[3]*Ibid., pp.* 164-65.

[4]S.S. Pirzada (ed.), *Foundations of Pakistan...*, Vol. I, pp. 335-36. Similarly, Mohammed Ali during his nationalist phase said at the Round Table Conference: "Where God commands I am a Muslim first, a Muslim second, and a Muslim last, and nothing but a Muslim.... But where India is concerned, where India's freedom is concerned... I am an Indian first, an Indian second, an Indian last, and nothing but an Indian." *Selected Speeches and Writings*, p. 465. For a recent summing up of this view, see Abid Husain, *The Destiny of Indian Muslims*, p. 100.

[5]*The Indian War of Independence 1857.* In discussing the causes of the failure of the Revolt, he wrote: "Though the plan of the destructive part of the Revolution was complete, its creative part was not attractive enough.... If there had been set clearly before the people at large a new ideal attractive enough to captivate their hearts, the growth and completion of the Revolution would have been as successful and as grand as its beginning." *Ibid.*, p. 542.

In their ideological make-up and sometimes in their political practice, many Hindu Congressmen were in reality communal nationalists. They did not see or describe themselves as Nationalist Hindus because, as they belonged to the 'majority community', their communal nationalism was in their minds quite compatible with plain nationalism. On the other hand, communal nationalists following other religions frankly described themselves as Nationalist Muslims, Nationalist Sikhs or Nationalist Christians. Many of the communal nationalists openly joined the Hindu Mahasabha, the Muslim League and the Akali Dal in the 1920s forming a strong nationalist group within these communal bodies.[6] At the same time, they provided the interesting and confusing spectacle of emphasizing Hindu, Muslim or Sikh interests in one meeting and national Indian interests in another. Quite often their entire political position or status depended on their being communal nationalists, i.e., nationalists who were simultaneously 'Hindu', 'Muslim' or 'Sikh' leaders. It was this latter aspect which made others recognize them as leaders. This tended to constantly push them towards communal thinking. In any case, even the best of them found it difficult to rise above the position of a Nationalist Hindu or a Nationalist Muslim to that of a simple nationalist. In fact, many of the nationalist leaders found it difficult to completely ignore the communal factor in their thought or activity. Purely secular nationalist persons like Gandhi, Nehru and Azad were rather uncommon. On the other hand, many communal nationalists bordered on, and easily slipped into, the position of the liberal communalists.[7] In any case the politically unwary persons were often confused about their nationalism and found it difficult to sharply distinguish their position from that of the liberal communalists.

[6]A few examples are: Mohammed Ali and Hakim Ajmal Khan in the Muslim League, Lajpat Rai and Madan Mohan Malaviya in the Hindu Mahasabha, and Manga! Singh, Sardul Singh Caveesher and Kharak Singh in the Central Sikh League.

[7]This was in particular true of the nationalist newspapers whenever they had to deal with the communal demands such as reservation in jobs.

II. LIBERAL COMMUNALISM

The liberal communalist was basically a believer in and a practitioner of communal politics; but he still upheld certain liberal, democratic, humanist and nationalist values. He recognized that ultimately India must be seen and built as a nation. He argued that India consisted of distinct religion-based communities which had their own separate and special interests which they did not share with each other and which often came into mutual conflict. But he also believed that these interests could gradually be accommodated and brought into harmony within the overall, developing national interests, some of which were common even at the outset. He accepted that the ultimate destiny of Indian politics was the merger of the different communities into a single nation, whatever might be the degree of present communal competition and conflict. Thus, the liberal communalist demanded separate communal rights, safeguards, weightage and reservations in jobs and legislatures, separate electorates, etc., within the broad concept of one Indian nation-in-the-making. He accepted national unity as the ultimate goal as also the concept of the ultimate common interests of Hindus, Muslims, Sikhs and Christians. It is to be noted that even though expressing and encouraging communalism, none of the liberal communal demands posed a direct threat to Indian unity. Also, the liberal communalist assumed the possibility of the removal of communal fears and conflicts once conditions were provided for the protection of the 'legitimate interests of the communities', and seldom preached all-out hostility against the other community,[8] and mainly emphasized the fight for special rights for his own community. In time, he also tended to accept the wider principle of democracy, and anti-colonialism, once communal interests were seen as guaranteed.[9]

[8]The resolution founding the All-India Muslim League in 1906 specifically expressed the desire "to prevent the rise, among the Musalmans of India, of any feeling of hostility towards other communities". S.S. Pirzada, *op. cit.,* Vol. I, p. 6. The Hindu Mahasabha and the Muslim League often expressed similar sentiments during the 1920s.

[9]The M.A. Jinnah of the late 1920s was anti-colonial rule at least to the extent of M.M. Malaviya. He wanted Hindus and Muslims to unite against the British once the communal problem was settled.

He also agreed to argue his case rationally; and he was open to discussion and debate unlike the Muslim League after 1937 and the Rashtriya Swayamsevak Sangh (RSS). In actual politics too, it was possible to carry on a political dialogue with him. In fact, during the 1920s, the liberal communalists attended each other's annual sessions. From the historian's point of view, liberal communalism had another important feature. It retained elements of rationality and its content, programme, ideology, etc., could therefore be often analyzed from its self-expression.

Syed Ahmed Khan, Altaf Husain Hali, the Ali Brothers, Mohammed Ali and Shaukat Ali, for most of the time, M.A. Jinnah before 1937, Madan Mohan Malaviya, especially after 1922, Lajpat Rai from 1923 to 1927, N.C. Kelkar of the 1920s and 1930s were on the whole examples of liberal communalists. The Muslim League and the Hindu Mahasabha till the late 1920s in the main practised liberal communalism. Both claimed to be fighting for the 'legitimate' rights of Muslims and Hindus respectively, but otherwise stood for Hindu-Muslim unity and the formation of an Indian nation and an Indian state.

Numerous examples of the liberal communal approach can be cited. For example, the revised constitution of the Muslim League approved by the 1913 Lucknow session laid down as the objectives of the League the protection and advancement of "the political and other rights and interests of the Indian Musalmans", the promotion of "national unity" and "friendship and union between the Musalmans and other communities of India" and the attainment with the cooperation of other "communities" of "a system of self-government suitable to India."[10] Ibrahim Rahmat-Ullah, presiding over the Agra session at the end of 1913, said:

> Every one must recognize that no form of self-government is possible in India unless the two principal communities, the Hindu and the Muslim, are closely and conscientiously united. What can

[10]S.S. Pirzada, *op. cit.,* Vol. I, pp. 258, 279.

be a nobler aim, a loftier goal than to endeavour to secure India united! Once we become sincerely and genuinely united, there is no force in the world which can keep us from our heritage....[11]

The young Mohammed Ali was a good example of a liberal communalist who made an attempt to combine communalism with nationalism. Explaining his motive in starting the *Comrade* in 1911, he wrote that the *Comrade* was to "prepare the Musalmans to make their proper contribution to territorial patriotism without abating a jot of the fervour of their extra territorial sympathies which is the quintessence of Islam".[12] On the one hand, he wrote in February 1912 that "we must clearly recognize that the Hindus and the Muslims dwell apart in thought and sentiment", described the view that the interests of Hindus and Muslims were "identical" as "cant", and supported communal representation, and, on the other hand, he asserted that a common Indian nationality would emerge gradually. Putting together both aspects, he wrote: "Any true patriot of India working for the evolution of Indian nationality will have to accept the communal individuality of the Muslims as the basis of his constructive effort."[13]

[11] *Ibid.*, p. 305. The 1913 (Lucknow) session also passed a resolution expressing "its firm belief that the future development and progress of the people of India depend exclusively on the harmonious working and cooperation of the various communities" as also its hope "that leaders on both sides will periodically meet together to ... find a *modus operandi* for joint and concerted action on questions of public good." It also deprecated "all mischievous attempts to widen the unfortunate breach between the Hindus and Musalmans". *Ibid.*, p. 281.

[12] *Selections from Mohammed Ali's Comrade*, p. 39.

[13] *Selected Writings and Speeches*, pp. 68-69. Similarly, he had written earlier in the *Comrade* of 19 August 1911 that Muslims had "every ambition to live and act as patriotic Indians and work for a nationality of which they would be a component yet conscious part. But they dread the position of the second fiddle which the new-fangled 'Nationalism' of some Indian public men and newspapers assign to them." Muslims were organizing higher education on a communal basis so that they might be enabled "to participate on something like equitable terms in the vast process of political and social change which is going on in this country". Quoted in Francis Robinson, *Separatism among Indian Muslims*, pp. 200-01.

We may take the pre-1937 M.A. Jinnah as the last example. In 1924, he claimed at the Muslim League session that his aim was "to organize the Muslim community, not with a view to quarrel with the Hindu community, but with a view to unite and cooperate with it for their motherland". He was convinced that "once they had organized themselves they would join hands with the Hindu Mahasabha and declare to the world that Hindus and Mohammedans are brothers".[14] As late as 1936, Jinnah took up a liberal communal position and proclaimed his nationalism and desire for national freedom and spoke for Hindu-Muslim cooperation. For example, he said at Lahore in March 1936:

> Whatever I have done, let me assure you there has been no change in me, not the slightest, since the day when 1 joined the Indian National Congress. It may be I have been wrong on some occasions. But it has never been done in a partisan spirit. My sole and only object has been the welfare of my country. I assure you that India's interest is and will be sacred to me and nothing will make me budge an inch from that position.[15]

He still asked Muslims to organize separately so that Hindus might take "Muslims seriously" and consider them "worthy of alliance." "If Muslims would speak with one voice, a settlement between Hindus and Muslims would come quicker." At the same time, he urged Muslims to "stand as firmly by national interest". "In fact", he said, "they should prove that their patriotism is unsullied and that their love of India and her progress is no less than that of any other community in the country."[16]

[14]Quoted in Ram Gopal, *Indian Muslims*, p. 163.

[15]Quoted in S. Gopal, *Jawaharlal Nehru—A Biography*, Vol. One, 1889-1947, p. 223, fn. 5.

[16]Quoted in Z.H. Zaidi, "Aspects of the Development of Muslim League Policy, 1937-47", p. 250. Similarly, addressing the students of Calcutta University in August 1936, he said : "Remember India cannot make any progress and India's salvation lies in the unity of all communities especially the Hindus and Muslims.... It is up to you all, whether as Hindus and Muslims, or Parsees or Christians, it is up to you neither as a Hindu nor as a

During his communal phase during the 1920s, Lala Lajpat Rai also adopted liberal communal positions. For example, in his presidential address to the Hindu Mahasabha in 1925, he simultaneously argued for Hindu unity and solidarity and Hindu-Muslim unity. Only when Hindus were as strong and united as Muslims would the latter agree to join hands with them for political purposes.[17] In September 1926, in a major speech delivered at Lucknow to explain why he had resigned from the Swaraj Party, he laid down his creed of liberal communalism. He said that the policy of non-cooperation could not succeed because Muslims were not supporting it. And, then went on to say:

> The leaders of the Muslim community claim certain rights for their community, the acceptance of which will reduce the Hindu community to a position of subordination, if not immediately, at least in the future.... In the circumstances, the Muslims have allied themselves with the Government.... There are some good men amongst the Hindus who think that the reconversion of the whole Muslim community and the establishment of an all-prevailing, all-absorbing Hindu policy is not only desirable but feasible.... To my mind that policy is impossible. Then there is the Swaraj Party... whose leader maintains that he is constitutionally unfit to think communally, which means that he can only think non-communally. There is a third party to which I have the honour to belong, and who think that nationalism is not inconsistent with justice to Hindu community and that unity cannot be purchased at the cost of Hindu rights.... I do not want the Hindus to return such people to the Councils as are advocates of the idea of Hindu Raj or are in favour of a counter-alliance with the Government. What I desire the Hindu electorates to do is to send genuine nationalists, stern

Muslim but as an Indian to find the solution." *Ibid.*, p. 251, fn. 1. Also see the address of Currimbhoy Ebrahim, Chairman of the Reception Committee of the Bombay Session of the League, 1936, in S.S. Pirzada, *op. cit.*. Vol. II, pp. 236-38.

[17]Indra Prakash, *A Review of the History and Work of the Hindu Mahasabha and the Hindu Sanghatan Movement*, p. xv.

> patriots and firm Hindus who will not compromise in such a way or yield to such an extent as to endanger the position of the Hindu community.

He ended his speech with the basic liberal communal sentiment which contemporary Muslim and Sikh communalists were also expressing: "I want freedom for my country, but I must be sure that I get that freedom without losing my status as a Hindu. I do not want to change masters."[18] From then on till his death he repeatedly proclaimed the slogan: "No Swaraj without safeguarding the interests of the Hindus."[19]

One important aspect of liberal communalism should be noted at this stage. Quite a few Hindu Congressmen, especially at the middle levels of leadership, were deeply communal[20] but they did not have to openly leave the Congress and emerge publicly as liberal communalists. A Muslim liberal communalist had to do so. As a minority communalist, he could not easily conceal himself under a nationalist garb. This is because Hindu communalism was the communalism of a majority 'community'. Communalism of the majority and that of the minority could not assume the same ideological or political shape or form; they were bound to be different in form even though their basic premises and outlook were the same. Because of its very minority character, minority communalism assumed an openly sectional, narrow, undemocratic and divisive approach; and it had to talk of 'minority safeguards' and the like. The majority communalists, on the other hand, knew that the democratic principles of majority rule, open competition, joint electorate, etc., could give them the opportunity to implement their cultural, religious, social and political programmes and the capacity to corner

[18] *Writings and Speeches*, Vol. 2, pp. 318-20.

[19] *The Tribune*, 28 October 1926. Also see the 19 September 1926 issue.

[20] Cf. Jawaharlal Nehru, *An Autobiography*, p. 136 : "Many a Congressman was a communalist under his national cloak." Nehru, of course, rightly added: "But the Congress leadership stood firm and, on the whole, refused to side with either communal party or rather with any communal group."

jobs and other economic opportunities for their middle and upper classes. They could, therefore, safely and readily assume the nationalist garb and talk in terms of the high principles of pure nationalism, putting national interests above sectional interests, democracy, equality of opportunity, competition on the basis of merit, etc. They could employ the authority of nationalism for achieving communal objectives. The minority communalists could not do so. They had perforce to come out in open communal colours. Thus, a Muslim communal leader like Mohammed Ali felt compelled during his communal phase to openly state that he was a Muslim first and an Indian later. Hindu communal leaders like Madan Mohan Malaviya did not have to do so,[21] though when it came to a separate province for Sind, an elected legislature for the North-Western Frontier Province, or democracy in Kashmir, i.e., in situations where Hindus were in a minority, they too acted on that principle.[22] In fact, from this point of view, a Muslim or a Sikh who was a fully secular nationalist was a very special and sturdy nationalist for he could not be a nationalist for any other purpose than nationalism; he could not easily be a hidden communalist.[23]

A student of history or politics, or a practitioner of secular politics, cannot accept such a simple line of demarcation between a nationalist and a liberal communalist as an explicit adherence to national or sectional demands. He must learn to distinguish between genuine nationalism and hidden communalism masquerading as

[21]However, some of the Hindu communalists asserted even this. See, for example, Lal Chand, *Self-Abnegation in Politics,* p. 70: "A Hindu should not only believe but make it a part and parcel of his organism, of his life and of his conduct, that he is a Hindu first and an Indian after."

[22]Similarly, in Panjab and Bengal, many a Congress leader or nationalist newspaper preached nationalism, and simultaneously championed the 'Hindu cause' in respect of jobs, constitutional discussions or communal riots.

[23]We must remind ourselves in this respect that the Nationalist Muslims were very courageous persons and nationalists. We tend to forget their character and contribution because in the end they proved political 'failures'. But as an Urdu poet has put it: "*Zamane ki nazar mein kamyabi asli manzil hat; Zamane ki nazar jahed-e-musalsil per nahin parti.*" (The world sees success as the real goal, the world does not cast its eyes on the constant struggle.)

nationalism. A nationalist must not be so defined as to coincide with or represent a particular section. Not all those who accepted nationalism or the concept of one nation were secular; many harboured to a lesser or greater degree communal thoughts and loyalties and were sometimes as much penetrated by communal ideology as an openly communal Muslim. Moreover, in the extreme, a minority communalist could go over to 'separatism', but a Hindu communalist would not be a 'separatist'; he would think in terms of Hindu 'domination'. In other words, a Hindu communalist would not look like a Muslim communalist. He was more likely to talk of and emphasize national unity and mutual trust; but he might be as viciously communal.[24] A proper analysis had therefore to probe deep into the ideology, psychology and the political approach of the Hindu communalists. The Hindu equivalent of the Muslim League during its liberal communal phase had to be seen not in the Hindu Mahasabha, which often led the nationalist leadership to preen itself on having kept Hindu communalism weak, but inside the ranks of the nationalist leadership and followers where a large number of Hindu communalists of various hues and degrees had taken shelter. Without a struggle against this brand of Hindu communalism, masquerading as nationalism, it was not easy, and perhaps not even possible, to fight against Muslim communalism, which, by the very nature of the case, was in the main outside the ranks of nationalism.

III. EXTREME COMMUNALISM OR FASCIST COMMUNALISM

Extreme communalism, or communalism working broadly within the fascist syndrome, was irrational and based on fear and hatred, and had a tendency to use violence or terror as a weapon against political

[24]This aspect was clearly visible to some of the political leaders of the 1920s and 1930s. For example, Choudhry Khaliquzzaman, who was a Nationalist Muslim at the time, wrote in September 1934 to Dr. Ansari : "If Malaviyaji and Aney can claim to be nationalists, I think every communalist Muslim who honestly fights for the rights of his community without making it a cloak for official favours and personal gain from the Government is a nationalist." Moreover, the liberal communalists were not separatists.

opponents. The social base of communalism was rather narrow till the late 1930s, the masses still looked up to the Congress for redressal of their grievances. Until then, the national movement and national sentiments had continued to spread among both the Hindu and Muslim masses as well as the intelligentsia. It was after 1937 that extreme communalism increasingly acquired a popular base and began to mobilize popular mass opinion. The basic change from liberal communalism occurred during 1937-38 when both Hindu and Muslim communalisms, in the form of the Muslim League and the Hindu Mahasabha and the Rashtriya Swayamsevak Sangh (RSS), started becoming fascist and irrational in their ideology and politics. Communalism was now sought to be organized on a new popular basis and as a mass movement around aggressive, extremist communal politics among the urban lower middle classes which could be done only on an extremist basis or around a fascist outlook. Both the Muslim League and the Hindu Mahasabha had run the election campaign of 1937 on liberal communal lines and both had fared poorly in the elections. The election results made it clear that the Congress had acquired a deep mass base, which it was going to try to strengthen through an agrarian programme, mass contact programmes and its control of provincial ministries, and that the communal parties would gradually wither away if they did not take to militant, mass-based polities. Hitherto, organized mass movements and cadre-based politics had been built by radical, *anti-status quo* nationalists, socialists and communists. The conservatives had shied away from mass movements and proper organization. Now a right-wing model of mass politics, which would not frighten away the vested interests, became available in the form of the fascist movements. Both Hindu and Muslim comnumalists decided to follow this model. Moreover, the Congress had not yet acquired firm roots among all the masses, especially among the Muslim masses; now was the time to take advantage of their political immaturity, before it was too late. The first turn to fascist communalism came in the case of the Muslim League with its Lucknow session in October 1937. In the same year, the

Hindu Mahasabha made a sharp turn in the same direction under V.D. Savarkar's leadership. The RSS had been from the very beginning organized on fascist lines; but it was only from 1937 that it made a serious attempt to spread beyond Maharashtra. It is interesting that during this fascist phase, the League, the Mahasabha and the RSS had also more or less permanent presidents who tended to function on the Fuhrer (leader) principle and cult.[25] The extent and level of communal propaganda, whose nature and methods were deeply influenced by those of Fascism, were now intensified. Skilful, fascist-like propaganda campaigns were launched. The communalists increasingly used the language of war and enemy against their political opponents. In place of stressing the need for protecting and promoting the interests of Hindus and Muslims and demanding effective safeguards, their very existence was seen to be in danger and was to be safeguarded. The cries that Muslims, Muslim culture and Islam, and Hindus, Hindu culture and Hindudom were in danger of being suppressed and exterminated were raised. It was at this stage that both communalists put forward the theory that Hindus and Muslims constituted separate nations whose mutual antagonism was permanent and irresolvable.[26] The extreme Hindu communalists defined Indian or Hindu nation in such a way as to permanently exclude Muslims from its ambit.[27] Muslims were instead seen as a perpetually hostile and alien element within the Indian body politic and social, who as 'foreigners' must either accept total subordination to Hindus or cease being Muslims or should be expelled.[28]

[25]Of course, one reason why Hedgewar, Jinnah and Savarkar could become centres of a leader cult was that all three of them had a certain anti-imperialist past record and they were not integrated with the colonial regime and administration as were most of the liberal communal leaders.

[26]V.D., Savarkar, *Hindu Rashtra Darshan*, pp. 26 and 64; Bhai Parmanand, *The Tribune*, 27 June 1936 and Indra Prakash, *op. cit.*, p. xxxiv; M.S. Golwalkar, *We*, pp. 19-20, 26-27, 52, 62, 73; M.A. Jinnah, *Speeches and Writings*, Vol. I, pp. 116-17, 159-62.

[27]See V.D. Savarkar, *Hindutva*, and M.S. Golwalkar, *We*.

[28]M.S. Golwalkar, *We*, pp. 19, 52-56, 62. We may quote some of the passages: "In Hindusthan exists and must needs exist the ancient Hindu nation and nought else but the Hindu nation.... So long, however, as they (Muslims and other non-Hindus) maintain

The extreme Muslim communalists countered by putting forth the theory that the Indian Muslims constituted not a religious minority but a separate nation. They unilaterally branded the Indian National Congress as a Hindu body and a fascist organization and declared that any democratic rule in India would mean Hindu Raj.[29] The Muslim League now explicitly abandoned the goals of national unity, a united national movement and democracy and a representative form of government.[30]

The extremist communal political positions appealed basically to irrational impulses and fears. They were seldom logically or historically argued. They assumed that to be true which was precisely needed to be so proved. They were proclaimed to be true because they were loudly and repeatedly asserted. The writings and speeches of the communal leaders were intellectually and logically vacuous and often in the nature of catechisms.[31] As was the case with the fascists, their sentences had 'no meaning, only a purpose'. What W. C. Smith has written about Jinnah was equally true of the Hindu communalists:

> As far as reasoning is concerned, the attempt was not so much to convince the audience of certain conclusions, as to infuse in its

their racial, religious and cultural differences, they cannot but be only foreigners.... There are only two courses open to the foreign elements, either to merge themselves in the national race and adopt its culture, or to live at the sweet will of the national race ... they must cease to be foreigners, or may stay in the country, wholly subordinated to the Hindu nation, claiming nothing, deserving no privileges, far less any preferential treatment—not even citizen's rights ... in this country Hindus alone are the Nation and the Moslems and others, if not actually antinational are at least outside the body of the Nation."

[29]See, for example, M.A. Jinnah, *op. cit.*, Vol. I, pp. 69-73, 77, 88, 91-92, 152-53, 185-86, 245-46. Also see Gwyer and Appadorai, *Speeches and Documents. . .*, Vol. II, pp. 620-21. For the more vicious, popular level expression of the same sentiments, see W.C. Smith, *Modern Islam in India,* pp. 296-98.

[30]See Chapter 4 of this volume.

[31]One weakness of communalism and fascism in India after 1947 has been the relative absence of irrationalism in Indian nationalist thought and agitation so that communal propaganda has gone against the grain of the nationalist heritage. This has not been the case with the intellectual and ideological heritage that the new state of Pakistan (and later Bangladesh) inherited from the Muslim League and the *Ulama* of the pre-1947 period. Hence, the easy success of communalism and dictatorship in both these countries.

> minds certain categories of thought, by using them to discuss points on which there could be no disagreement. Objection could hardly then be taken to the statements that he made, but to the way that he made them. That was much more difficult, much less likely to be done. By oft-reiterated implication, he was trying to get his people into the habit of thinking of the Muslim League as equivalent to the Muslims of India; of the Congress as equivalent to the Hindus of India; of the problem that needed solving as being the conflict between the two. The critic could disagree not with the answers proffered by Mr Jinnah, but with the questions that he asked.
>
> The Muslim League never at any time tried to convince anybody that it represented all the Muslims of India. It assumed that it did so; and went on to convince people of something that followed from that. In mass psychology, insinuation is more powerful than argument.[32]

The extremist communal leaders evolved politics without evolving political thought[33] and emphasized the role of political tactics at the expense of a programme.[34] They kept their programme undefined or defined it in a makeshift manner to meet immediate political needs or to cater to the immediate audience. In fact, they lacked any specific

[32] *Op. cit.,* p.291. One example of this approach from Jinnah's address to the League's Lahore session of 1940 may be quoted: "Why should not Mr Gandhi be proud to say, 'I am a Hindu, Congress has solid Hindu backing?' I am not ashamed of saying that I am a Musalman.... Why all these methods to coerce the British to overthrow the Musalmans?... Why not come as a Hindu leader proudly representing your people and let me meet you proudly representing the Musalmans?" *Op. cit,* Vol. I, pp. 152-53. Also see D.R. Goyal, *Rashtriya Swayamsevak Sangh,* p. 50.

[33] The communalists did not produce a single work of political, economic or social thought as was done by anti-colonial nationalism, liberalism and socialism or even by contemporary conservatism.

[34] The Congress leadership opposed a concrete political and economic programme to communal politics but failed to meet or oppose their tactics. It was consequently outmanoeuvred at every step. What was needed was precisely and above all a proper tactical defence against the tactics of the communal leadership. There is a tendency on the part of the secular forces to repeat this error in the post-Independence India and especially in recent years.

social, economic or political programme. This weakness was sought to be concealed through a negative stance on current issues and a savage attack on the Congress and on the other 'communities'. The Hindu communalists so defined Hindu culture and nationhood as to preclude their rational, historical or logical discussion. The RSS programme was confined to three undefined, vaguest possible, almost mystical terms: discipline, character and Bhartiya culture. The RSS and V.D. Savarkar produced hardly any serious writing except the two pamphlets *Hindutva* and *We*. The RSS would not publish even the speeches of its leader till the 1950s.[35]

The Muslim League first refused to put forward any serious demand and when in 1940 it demanded Pakistan it refused to define Pakistan or even its territorial extent, or even whether it would consist of one state or two. Before it would agree to explain or discuss the nature of its demand, it wanted the demand to be accepted. For example, when in April 1941, Rajendra Prasad offered on behalf of the Congress to discuss the Pakistan scheme if its nature and details were made known, Jinnah's reply was that "the Congress should first make up their mind and accept the basic principles laid down in the Lahore resolution" and that "first the principle of partitioning India must be agreed upon, then alone comes the question of what ways and means should be adopted to give effect to that decision."[36] Moreover, from 1937, the League, under Jinnah's leadership, spurned any political discussion or negotiations unless it was accepted at the very outset as the sole authoritative and representative organization of all Indian Muslims, thus unilaterally trying to force the National Congress to transform itself into and declare itself as a Hindu communal organization.[37] It is important to note that this was an impossible

[35]In fact, this (nationalism makes it very difficult to analyse or understand their politics or ideology or organization from their available published materials. For their definition of Hindu culture and nationhood, see V.D. Savarkar's *Hindutva* and M.S. Golwalkar's *We*.

[36]M.A. Jinnah, *op. cit.*, Vol. I, pp. 269-70.

[37]Jinnah to Gandhi, 3 March 1938, *Indian Annual Register*, 1938, Vol. I, p. 361; Jinnah to Nehru, 13 December 1939, in Jawaharlal Nehru, *A Bunch of Old Letters*, p. 404; M.A. Jinnah, *op. cit.*, Vol. I, p. 108; M. Noman, *Muslim India*, p. 361; W.C. Smith, *op. cit.*,

demand for the Congress to meet, for, as Rajendra Prasad put it, for the Congress to accept that it was a Hindu body "would be denying its own past, falsifying its history, and betraying its future";[38] it would amount to the Congress and Indian national movement committing political harakiri.[39]

The two groups of extreme communalists now preached total antagonism and hatred against the opposite 'community'. They attacked the other 'community' with "fervour, fear, contempt and bitter hatred".[40] Unlike the liberal communalists, they declared that no settlement or accommodation or co-existence, not to speak of integration, between Hindus and Muslims was possible. They generated feelings of fear, even of physical destruction, among their own 'communities'.[41] They conducted a virulent campaign of hatred against Hindus or Muslims, as the case might be, and against the Congress and nationalist leaders; in particular, they poured venom on the nationalists belonging to their own 'communities'. They operated largely on the principle of the bigger the lie the better, Thus, Gandhi and other Congress nationalists were denounced as virtual traitors to, and enemies of, the 'Hindu nation' by the Hindu extreme communalists[42] and as enemies of Muslims and Islam, who were out to

p. 286. One reason for this approach was the fact that all the traditional communal demands had been granted by the Communal Award or accepted by the Congress. In the absence of a concrete programme, the League now put forward demands which were clearly petty or such as would be easily accepted by the Congress. Hence all demands were followed by the rider discussed above or often were reduced to this one demand. Choudhry Khaliquzzaman, *Pathway to Pakistan,* pp. 178 and 192; Asoka Mehta and Achyut Patwardhan, *The Communal Triangle in India,* p. 199.

[38]*India Divided,* p. 153.

[39]The long-term political consequences would have been disastrous: independent India would have been a Hindu communal replica of Pakistan and not a secular state.

[40]W.C. Smith, *op. cit.,* p. 295.

[41]See Chapter 5 of this volume.

[42]M.S. Golwalkar, *We,* pp. 20, 52, 68, 70-73, and *Bunch of Thoughts,* pp. 149-52; Savarkar, *Hindu Rashtra Darshan,* pp. 28,125, 260, 280, and *Hindu Sanghatan,* pp. 205, 212; in Indra Prakash, *A Review...,* pp. xviii, xx-xxi, quoted in A. Mehta and A. Patwardhan, *op. cit.,* p. 155; Bhai Parmanand, *The Tribune,* 27 June 1936, in Indra Prakash, *op. cit.,* pp. xxi-xxii, xxx, xxxiv, xxxxv; B.S. Moonje, in Indra Prakash, *op. cit.,* pp. vii, 107, 209, and quoted in Mushirul Hasan, "Communal and Revivalist Trends in Congress", p. 209.

subjugate Muslims and suppress their culture, revive Hinduism and establish Hindu Raj, by the League leaders and publicists.[43] Maulana Azad and other nationalists, who were anti-communal, among Muslims were branded as 'show-boys' of the Congress, traitors to Islam and mercenary agents of Hindus by the Muslim Leaguers and submitted to virtual social terror through appeals to religious fanaticism;[44] they were simultaneously derided by Hindu communalists.[45] On a more popular plane, both communalists aped Hitler. The National Congress was accused by Muslim communalists, in an Indian version of the theory of Jewish capitalism, of founding a "Bania Centre", of practising "Bania Imperialism" and of wanting to turn all Muslims into "a race of workers" at the total mercy of Hindu capitalists.[46] V.D. Savarkar, on his part, warned of the danger of the Hindu peasants, traders, and labourers suffering "at the hands of non-Hindu aggression".[47] During 1938 and after, the Muslim League launched a vicious campaign based on the big lie principle accusing the

[43]M.A. *Jinnah, op.cit.,* Vol.I, pp. 72-73, 77, 88, 91-92, 122-23, 139, 141, 152-53, 185-86, 204-05, passim; Z.A. Suleri, *My Leader,* pp. 12, 38, 42, 52-53, 55-56, 193. Also see S. Gopal, *Jawaharlal Nehru—A Biography,* Vol. One, p. 238; Ram Gopal, *op. cit.,* pp. 257-58; W.C. Smith, *op. cit.,* pp. 282, 285-86. For sheer demagogy of Goebelsian proportions by a leader of Jinnah's stature, the following may be quoted. Addressing Aligarh Muslim University students in March 1940, he said: "It is not that they (the Congress leaders) want the British Government to go but only to cajole and coerce it to give them something which would enable them to dominate the Muslims under British protection." *Op. cit.,* Vol. I, p. 141. Or, "Mr Gandhi's hope is to subjugate and vassalise the Muslims under a Hindu raj"; "He is the one man responsible for turning the Congress into an instrument for the revival of Hinduism. His ideal is to revive Hindu religion and establish Hindu raj in this country." *Ibid.,* pp. 139 and 73, respectively. Other Muslim and Hindu communal leaders were no better and were sometimes even worse. But none of them were of Jinnah's stature. And the fascist character of communalism in this phase is revealed by the fact that he took up politics and agitation at this level.

[44]M.A., Jinnah, *op. cit.,* Vol. I, p. 185; Z.A. Suleri, *op. cit:,* p. 43; W.C. Smith, *op. cit.,* p. 300; Abid Husain, *op. cit.,* pp. 112-13; K.B. Sayeed and others, fn. 15 in Chapter 6.

[45]V.D. Savarkar, *Hindu Rashtra Darshan,* p. 286; M.S. Golwalkar, *Bunch of Thoughts,* p. 149.

[46]F.K. Khan Durrani, *The Meaning of Pakistan,* p. 197; El Hamza, *Pakistan : A Nation,* Chapter XIV. The latter branded the entire people of the "Hindustani Hinterland" as Banias. "There are", he wrote, "over hundred million Banias in India" and their "homeland" was Hindustan (p. 120). Also see W.C. Smith, *op. cit.,* pp. 288-89.

[47]V.D. Savarkar, *Hindu Rashtra Darshan,* p. 142.

Congress of suppressing Muslims and Islam and committing untold atrocities on Muslims.[48] The Hindu extreme communalists used medieval history as the big lie in the same manner and to the same extent.[49]

The relationship between Fascism and extreme communalism was, of course, not of cause and effect, nor were the two the same—there was too much difference in the respective social milieus. Nor can it be said, except in the case of the RSS, the Khaksars, and some of the League publicists, that the latter were consciously and by design adopting the former as a model. Still the influence of the former on the latter was deep-seated, especially at the level of political tactics and propaganda, and the exaltation of the leader and, in the case of the RSS and the Khaksars, of organization, and can be traced in almost all these aspects. It was, however, seldom openly acknowledged or articulated, except in the case of the RSS which did so secretly in its branches to attract young men, because of India being ruled by Britain and because the nationalists and the intelligentsia treated Fascism as a dirty word, especially after 1935. Even so, echoes of Nazi phrases and formulations could sometimes find direct expression in the written word. In his *We,* written in 1939, M.S. Golwalkar said that Italy and Germany were two countries where "the ancient Race spirit" had "re-risen." "Even so with us: our Race spirit has once again roused itself", thus giving Hindus the right of "excommunicating" Muslims. He went on to add:

[48]See, for example, W.C. Smith, *op. cit.,* pp. 295-99; S. Gopal, *Jawaharlal Nehru—A Biography,* Vol. One, p. 239; *Pirpur Committee Report and It Shall Never Happen Again.* Fazlul Huq, holding a responsible position as the Bengal Premier, told the 1938 session of the League: "In Congress provinces, riots had laid the countryside waste. Muslim life, limb and property have been lost and blood has freely flowed.... There the Muslims are leading their lives in constant terror, overawed and oppressed by Hindus.... There mosques are being defiled and the culprit never found nor is the Muslim worshipper unmolested...." Quoted in Ram Gopal, *op. cit.,* p. 258. The very small element of truth in this propaganda lay in the fact that the activities and ideology of many Congressmen had a Hindu tinge. This tinge was blown up out of all proportions by the League propaganda. For the Hindu tinge, see Chapter 5.

[49]See Chapter 8.

> German race pride has now become the topic of the day. To keep up the purity of the Race and its culture, Germany shocked the world by her purging the country of the Semitic Races–the Jews. Race pride at its highest has been manifested here. *Germany has also shown how well-nigh impossible it is for Races and cultures, having differences going to the root, to be assimilated into one united whole, a good lesson for use in Hindusthan to learn and profit by.*[50] (Emphasis added.)

Similarly, an official Muslim League publication declared : "Pandit Jawaharlal's visits to England and other countries in Europe have been cleverly stage-managed by Leftist groups supported by prominent publicity through the Jewish press Reuter."[51] M.H. Gazdar, a League leader of Sind, told a League meeting in Karachi in March 1941: "The Hindus will have to be eradicated like the Jews in Germany if they did not behave properly."[52]

A basic component of Fascism is the role assigned to fascist gangs and storm-troopers, and to an atmosphere of violence as well as concrete violence against its opponents. The extreme communalists tended to absolutize and exalt beyond reasonable political necessity 'virility' and violence and discipline and obedience. They also actively generated an atmosphere of hatred, communal tension and violence both among Hindus and Muslims and against fellow co-religionists who opposed communalism. But they could not take to open acts of violence on a large social scale because of the fact that during the war India was being ruled with a strong hand under the Defence of India Rules, for the British could not permit communal violence to disrupt the war efforts. But the fascist-like communal violence, riots and pogroms—that is, one-sided attacks and killings—broke out with all their virulence during 1946-47, once the colonial regime weakened as well as lost interest in the strict maintenance of law and order. In these

[50]M.S. Golwalkar, *We*, pp. 40-41 and 43.
[51]Quoted in W.C. Smith, *op. cit.*, p. 299.
[52]Quoted in *Ibid.*

riots and pogroms the fascistic youth volunteer corps often played the role of initiators and chief organizers.

It is to be noted that several contemporaries took note of the close resemblance of extreme communalism to contemporary fascism.[53] That communalism was entering a new phase from 1937 was also noted by some.[54] Many liberal communalists showed awareness of the change by dropping out from communal politics.

It was during this extremist phase that communalism deeply penetrated Indian society and many persons whose ideological make-up included communal elements now became full-fledged communalists.

IV

We must, of course, take note not only of the differences between the different forms and phases of communalism but also of their mutual interaction, impact and continuity. There was no rigid barrier between them. Liberal communalism, for example, continued to exist both within and outside the broad framework of extreme communalism during the last phase. Shyama Prasad Mookerjee, N.C. Chatterji, Sikandar Hayat Khan, Choudhry Khaliquzzaman, and Khizr Hayat Tiwana would be good examples of this trend in the post-1937 years. After the Communist Party's support to the Pakistan demand, even certain left-wing persons joined the League; and soon a left tendency, which was weak in Panjab and UP and strong in Bengal, developed inside the League. But the hegemonic tendency in the last phase was the extremist, fascist one, just as earlier liberal communalism had been hegemonic.

[53]Jawaharlal Nehru, quoted in *Nehru, The First Sixty Years,* Vol. II, pp. 344-45; W.C. Smith, *op. cit.,* pp. 280 ff.

[54]S. Wazir Hasan, who was one of the prominent Muslim League leaders during its liberal communal phase and its President in 1936, wrote to Nehru in February 1938 that "propaganda of misrepresentation, lies and religious and communal hatred not only between Mussalmans and Hindus, but also between Mussalmans and Mussalmans was initiated in the presidential address of the Muslim League session at Lucknow in October last. It is being carried on from day to day with ever increasing false statement of facts under the guise of the rights of the minorities and religious hatred." In Jawaharlal Nehru, *A Bunch of Old Letters,* p. 269.

The different phases can also not be always identified rigidly with specific individuals. Leaders and individuals freely floated from one category or form to another. Madan Mohan Malaviya, Lajpat Rai and Mohammed Ali were in different periods of their political lives parts of the communal nationalist and liberal communal tendencies. Even Savarkar went through a liberal phase. Jinnah's political career spanned all the three phases and he actually hoped to revert to the liberal phase in independent Pakistan as his speech of 11 August 1947 showed. Similarly, the Hindu Mahasabha and the Muslim League were before 1937 liberal communal organizations. That is one reason why the Congress leadership did not adopt a very hostile attitude towards them till the mid-1930s. The transition from the liberal to the extremist phase was also imperceptible as well as prolonged, especially in the case of the Muslim League. This was another reason why the nationalists failed to evolve a correct tactical approach towards it.

Communal nationalism fed liberal and extreme communalism and made it difficult to carry on a political struggle against them. It acted as a hostage to them. They, in turn, constantly generated communal nationalism within the nationalist ranks. Similarly, the logic of liberal communalism inexorably led to extreme communalism, for under a democratic system and in the absence of foreign rule there could be no final or absolute guarantee of separate communal 'interests', safeguards, reservations, etc. Once it became clear that colonial administration was on the way out, the liberal communalists wanting to protect the 'special rights' of Hindus or Muslims had either to fade away or had to inexorably turn towards extreme communalism.

Select Bibliography

Addy, Premen and Azad, Ibne, "Politics and Society in Bengal", in Blackburn, Robin (ed.), *Explosion in a Subcontinent,* London, 1975.

Ahmad Imtiaz, "Perspectives on the Communal Problem", *ICSSR, Research Abstracts Quarterly,* Vol. II, No. 1, October 1972, Delhi.

Ahmad, Kamruddin, *A Social History of Bengal,* Dacca, 1970 edition.

Ahmed, Sufia, *Muslim Community in Bengal 1884-1912,* Dacca, 1974.

Ali, M. Athar, *The Mughal Nobility under Aurangzeb,* Bombay, 1966.

________, "Causes of the Rathor Rebellion of 1679", *Proceedings of the Indian History Congress, 1961,* Calcutta, 1963.

________, "The Religious Issue in the War of Succession", *Medieval India Quarterly,* Vol. V, 1963, Aligarh.

Ali, Mohammed, *Selected Writings and Speeches,* edited by Iqbal, Afzal, Lahore, 1944.

________, *Selections from Mohammed Ali's "Comrade",* selected by Jafri, S.R.A., Lahore, 1955.

All India Congress Committee Papers, Nehru Memorial Museum and Library, New Delhi.

Ansari, M.A., *Muslims and the Congress, Select Correspondence, 1912-1935,* edited by Hasan, Mushirul, New Delhi, 1979.

Ansari, Shaukatullah, *Pakistan—The Problem of India,* Lahore, 1945.

Arendt, Hannah, *The Origins of Totalitarianism,* Cleveland, 1962.

Ashraf, Kunwar, Muhammad, *Hindustani Muslim Siyasat Par Ek Nazar,* New Delhi, 1963, in Urdu.

Azad, Maulana Abul Kalam, *India Wins Freedom,* Bombay, 1959 reprint.

Aziz., K.K., *Britain and Muslim India,* London, 1963.

________, *The Making of Pakistan,* London, 1967.

Bashiruddin, S., "Pan-Islamism in Indian Politics and the Khilafat Agitation", mimeographed, presented at the seminar on "The Communal Problem in India 1919-47", organized by the Nehru Memorial Museum and Library, New Delhi, in March 1971.

Basu, Aparna, *The Growth of Education and Political Development in India, 1898-1920,* Delhi, 1974.

________, "Growth of Education and Muslim Separatism, 1919—1939", in Nanda, B.R. (ed.), *Essays in Modern Indian History,* Delhi, 1980.

Board of Economic Inquiry, Panjab, *An Economic Survey of Naggal,* Panjab Village Surveys–5, Lahore, 1933.

Bolitho, Hector, *Jinnah: Creator of Pakistan,* London, 1954,

Broomfield, J.H., *Elite Conflict in a Plural Society: Twentieth-Century Bengal,* Berkeley, 1968.

Buckland, C.E., *Bengal under the Lieutenant-Governors,* Vol. II, Calcutta, 1902, second edition.

Callard, Keith, *Pakistan, A Political Study,* London, 1954.
Chand, Lal, *Self-Abnegation in Politics,* Lahore, 1938 edition.
Chand, Tara, *History of Freedom Movement in India,* Vol. II, Delhi, 1967.
________, *Socieiy and State in the Mughal Period,* Delhi, 1961.
Chandra, Bipan, *Nationalism and Colonialism in Modern India,* New Delhi, 1979.
________, "Gandhiji, Secularism and Communalism," *Social Scientist,* Vol. 32, No. 368-369, Jan. - Feb. 2004.
Chandra, Satish, *Communal Interpretation of Indian History,* New Delhi, no date.
________, "History Writing in Pakistan and the Two-Nation Theory", mimeographed, University of Rajasthan, Jaipur, 1964.
________, "Jizyah and the State in India during the 17th Century", *Journal of the Economic and Social Hisiory of the Orient,* Lieden, Vol. XII, Part II, 1969.
Chandra, Sudhir, "Communal Consciousness in Late 19th-Century Hindi Literature", in Hasan, Mushirul (ed.), *Communal and Pan-Islamic Trends in Colonial India,* New Delhi, 1981.
Chatterjee, N.C., *Hindu Politics, Collection of Speeches and Addresses,* Calcutta, 1944.
Chattopadhyay, Gautam, "Role of Bengal Legislature in the Freedom Struggle", published under the title *Bengal Electoral Politics and Freedom Struggle 1862-1947,* New Delhi, 1984.
Choudhry, Prem, "Role of Sir Chhotu Ram in Panjab Politics", Ph. D. thesis, 1979, Centre for Historical Studies, Jawaharlal Nehru University, published under the title *Punjab Politics—The Role of Sir Chotu Ram,* New Delhi, 1984.
________, "Hindu-Muslim Relations in South-East Panjab: An Analysis of the Operation of Communalism at the District Level, 1920-45", *The Indian Historical Review,* New Delhi.
Colletti, Lucio, *From Rousseau to Lenin,* New York, 1972.
Corrigan, P., Ramsay, H. and Sayer, D., *Socialist Construction and Marxist Theory,* London, 1978.
Coupland, R., *The Constitutional Problem in India,* Oxford, 1944.
Curran, J. A., *Militant Hinduism in Indian Politics,* New Delhi, 1979 reprint.
Darling, M.L., *Rusticus Loquitor or the Old Light and the New in the Punjab Village,* Oxford 1930.
Das, M.N., *India under Morley and Minto,* London, 1964.
Desai, A.R., *Social Background of Indian Nationalism,* Bombay, 1959, third edition.
Dixit, Prabha, *Communalism—A Struggle for Power,* New Delhi, 1974.
Dumont, Louis, "Religion/Politics and History in India", in his *Collected Papers in Indian Sociology,* Paris, 1970.
Durrani, F. K. Khan, *The Meaning of Pakistan,* Lahore, 1944.
Dutt, R. Palme, *India Today,* Bombay, 1949, revised edition.
Dwarkadas, Jamnadas, *Political Memoirs,* Bombay, 1969.
Felice, Renzo De, *Interpretations of Fascism,* Cambridge, Massachusetts, 1977.
Frykenberg, R. E., *Guntur District, 1788-1848,* Oxford, 1965.
Gandhi, M. K., *The Way to Communal Harmony,* Ahmedabad, 1963.
________, *Collected Works,* New Delhi, 1958.

Gangadharan, K. K., *Sociology of Revivalism,* New Delhi, 1970.
Ghose, Aurobindo, *Speeches,* Pondicherry, 1952.
________, *Sri Aurobindo, Collected Works,* Pondicherry, 1972.
Ghosh, Ajoy, *Articles and Speeches,* Moscow, 1962.
Golwalkar, M.S., *We or our Nationhood Defined,* Nagpur, 1947 edition, first published in 1939.
________, *Bunch of Thoughts,* Bangalore, 1966 edition.
Gopal, Ram, *Indian Muslims: A Political History (1858-1947),* Bombay. 1959.
Gopal, S., *British Policy in India 1858-1905,* New Delhi, 1975 reprint.
________, *Jawaharlal Nehru-A Biography,* Vol. One, 1889-1947, London, 1975.
Goyal, D.R., *Rashtriya Swayamsewak Sangh,* New Delhi, 1979.
Grover, B.L., *A Documentary Study of British Policy towards Indian Nationalism, 1885-1909,* Delhi, 1967.
Gwyer, M. and Appadorai, A., *Speeches and Documents on the Indian Constitution 1921-47,* two volumes, Oxford, 1957.
Habib, Irfan, "The Contribution of Historians to the Process of National Integration in India—Medieval Period", *Proceedings of the Indian History Congress,* 1961, Calcutta, 1963.
________, "Economic History of the Delhi Sultanate—An Essay in Interpretation", *The Indian Historical Review,* Delhi, Vol. IV, No. 2, January 1978.
Habib, Mohammed, "Chengiz Khan and the Mongols", *Enquiry,* New Series. Vol. I, No. 1, Spring 1964, Delhi.
Hamza, El., *Pakistan: A Nation,* Lahore, 1942 reprint.
Haq, Mushirul, *Muslim Politics in Modern India, 1857-1947,* Meerut, 1970.
________,"The Background of Muslim Communalism in Indian Politics", mimeographed, presented at the seminar on "The Communal Problem in India 1919-47", organized by the Nehru Memorial Museum and Library, New Delhi, in March 1971.
Hardy, Peter, *The Muslims of British India,* Cambridge, 1972.
Hasan, Mushirul, *Nationalism and Communal Politics in India, 1916-1928,* New Delhi, 1979.
________, (ed.), *Communal and Pan-Islamic Trends in Colonial India,* New Delhi, 1981.
________, "Communal and Revivalist Trends in Congress", in *ibid.*
Hodson, H. V., *The Great Divide, Britain—India—Pakistan,* London, 1969.
Home Department (Political) Proceedings, National Archives of India, New Delhi.
Hunter, W.W., *The Indian Musalmans,* Delhi, 1969 reprint.
Husain, Azim, *Fazl-i-Husain, A Political Biography,* Bombay, 1946.
Husain, S. Abid, *The Destiny of Indian Muslims,* Bombay, 1965.
Ibbetson, Denzil, *Panjab Castes,* a chapter from the Census Report of 1881, Delhi, 1974 reprint.
Indian Annual Register, 1924-46, Calcutta; same as *Indian Quarterly Register* and *Mitra's Indian Annual Register.*
Irwin, Lord, *Indian Problems,* speeches by Lord Irwin, London, 1932.
Islam, Mustafa Nurul, *Bengal Muslim Public Opinion as Reflected in the Bengal Press 1901-1930,* Dacca, 1973.
It Shall Never Happen Again, Foreword by Qazi Mohammed Isa, Delhi, 1946.
Jinnah, M.A., *Speeches and Writings,* two volumes, edited by Ahmed, Jamil-ud-Din, Lahore, Volume I, 1960 edition; Vol. II, 1964 edition.

Joshi, P.C., "Myths: Old and New", mimeographed, presented at the seminar on "Minorities in Nation-Building", organized by the India International Centre, New Delhi, in March-April, 1970.

________, "The Economic Background of Communalism in India—A Model of Analysis", in *Essays in Modern Indian History,* edited by Nanda, B.R., Delhi, 1980.

Kabir, Humayun, *Muslim Politics 1906-47 and Other Essays,* Calcutta, 1969.

Kamat, A.R., "National Integration and Subnational Loyalties", *Mainstream,* New Delhi, Annual 1981, Vol. XX, Nos. 1-5.

Karunakaran, K.P., *Continuity and Change in Indian Politics,* New Delhi, 1964.

________, "Political Philosophy and Practice of the Hindu Mahasabha", mimeographed, presented at the seminar on "The Communal Problem in India 1919-47", organized by the Nehru Memorial Museum and Library, New Delhi, in March 1971.

Kaura, Uma, *Muslims and Indian Nationalism: The Emergence of the Demand for India's Partition 1928-1940,* New Delhi, 1977.

Keer, D., *Veer Savarkar,* Bombay, 1966 edition.

Khaliquzzaman, Choudhry, *Pathway to Pakistan,* Lahore, 1961.

Khan, Iqtidar Alam, "The Origin and Rise of Muslim Obscurantism", mimeographed, presented at the "Conference on Obscurantism", Delhi, December 1967.

________, "Mughal Nobility and Akbar's Religious Policy", *Journal of Royal Asiatic Society,* London, 1968.

Khan, Rasheeduddin, "Self-View of Minorities: The Muslims in India", mimeographed, presented at the seminar on "Minorities in Nation-Building", organized by the India International Centre, New Delhi, March-April 1970.

________, "The Development of Muslim National Consciousness in India: A Political Analysis", mimeographed, presented at the seminar on "The Communal Problem in India 1919-47", organized by the Nehru Memorial Museum and Library, New Delhi, in March 1971.

Khan, Syed Ahmed, *Writings and Speeches,* edited by Mohammad, Shan, Bombay, 1972.

Krishna, Gopal, "Religion in Politics", *The Indian Economic and Social History Review,* Delhi, Vol. VIII, No. 4, December 1971.

Krishna, K.B., *The Problem of Minorities,* London, 1939.

Linlithgow, Marquess of, *Speeches,* two volumes, Simla, 1944.

________, *Linlithgow Papers,* Nehru Memorial Museum and Library, New Delhi.

Low, D.A. (ed.), *Soundings in Modern South Asian History,* Berkeley, 1968.

Mahmud, Syed, *A Nationalist Muslim and Indian Politics: Selected Correspondence,* edited by Datta, V.N. and Cleghorn, B.E., Delhi, 1974.

Mahmudabad, Raja of, "Some Memories", in *The Partition of India,* edited by Philips, C.H. and Wainwright, M.D., London, 1970.

Majumdar, B.B., "The Anand Math and Phadke", *Journal of Indian History,* Trivandrum, Vol. 44, No. 130, April 1966.

Malik, H., *Muslim Nationalism in India and Pakistan,* Washington, 1963.

Mangalori, Syed Tufail Ahmed, *Musalmanon Ka Roshan Mustaqbil,* Delhi, 1945, in Urdu.

Manshardt, Clifford, *The Hindu-Muslim Problem in India,* London, 1936.

Marx, Karl, *Capital,* Vol. III, Moscow, 1971.

________, *The Eighteenth Brumaire of Louis Bonaparte,* in *Surveys from Exile,* Penguin Books, 1973.

Marx, Karl and Engels, Frederick, *Collected Works,* Vol. 5, Moscow, 1976.

Mary, Countess of Minto. *India, Minto and Morley, 1905-1910,* London, 1934.

Mehrotra, S.R., "The Congress and the Partition of India", *in The Partition of India,* edited by Philips, C.H. and Wainwright, M.D., London, 1970.

Mehta, Asoka and Patwardhan, Achyut, *The Communal Triangle in India,* Allahabad, 1942.

Menon, V.P., *The Transfer of Power in India,* Bombay, 1957.

Mian, Syed Mohammed, *Ulama-i-Haq Aur Unke Mujahidana Karname,* two volumes, Delhi, 1946, in Urdu.

Momen, Humaira, *Muslim Politics in Bengal, A Study of Krishak Praja Party and the Elections of 1937,* Dacca, 1972.

Mookerjee, Shyama Prasad, *Awake Hindusthan,* Calcutta, 1944.

Moore, Barrington, Jr., *Social Origins of Dictatorship and Democracy,* Penguin Books, 1977 reprint.

Moore, R. J., *Churchill, Cripps and India, 1939-1945,* Oxford, 1979.

Mujeeb, M., *The Indian Muslims,* London, 1969 impression.

Mukherjea, Ramakrishna, "The Social Background of Bangladesh", in *Imperialism and Revolution in South Asia,* edited by Gougb, K, and Sharma, H., New York. 1973.

Mukhia, Harbans, "Communalism: A Study in its Socio-Historical Perspective", *Social Scientist,* New Delhi, Vol. I, No. 1, August 1972.

Nagarkar, V. V., *Genesis of Pakistan,* New Delhi, 1975.

Namboodripad, E. M. S., *Economics and Politics of India's Socialist Pattern,* New Delhi, 1966.

Nanda, B. R., "Nehru and the Partition of India", in *The Partition of India,* edited by Philips, C. H. and Wainwright, M. D., London, 1970.

Nehru, Jawaharlal, *An Autobiography,* New Delhi, 1962 reprint.

________, *A Bunch of Old Letters,* Bombay, 1958.

________, *Selected Works,* edited by Gopal, S., New Delhi, 1972.

________, *Nehru, The First Sixty Years,* two volumes, edited by Norman, Dorothy, Bombay, 1965.

Nehru, Motilal, *The Voice of Freedom: Selected Speeches of Pandit Motilal Nehru,* edited by Panikkar, K.M. and Pershad, A., Bombay, 1961.

Niemeijer, A. C., *The Khilafat Movement in India 1919-1924,* The Hague, 1972.

Nolte, Ernst, *Three Faces of Fascism,* New York, 1966.

Noman, Mohammad, *Muslim India—Rise and Growth of the All India Muslim League,* Allahabad, 1942.

Oberoi, Harjot, "Literature and Society: An Approach to the Novels of Bhai Vir Singh", unpublished M. Phil. dissertation, Centre for Historical Studies, Jawaharlal Nehru University, New Delhi, 1981.

Pal, Bipin Chandra, *Memories of My Life and Times,* Calcutta, 1932.

Pandey, B. N., *The Break-up of British India,* London, 1969.

Pandey, G., *The Ascendancy of the Congress in Uttar Pradesh,* Delhi, 1978.

Panikkar, K.N., "Peasant Revolts in Malabar in the Nineteenth and Twentieth Centuries", in *Peasant Struggles in India,* edited by Desai, A.R., New Delhi, 1979.

Parmanand, Bhai, *Hindu Sangathan,* Lahore, 1936.

Parliamentary Debates (Hansard), in House of Commons and House of Lords.

Petrie, D., "Secret C.I.D. Memorandum on Recent Developments in Sikh Politics 1911", *The Panjab Past and Present,* Patiala, Vol. IV, Part II, October 1970.

Philips, C.H. (ed.), *The Evolution of India and Pakistan 1858 to 1947, Select Documents,* Oxford, 1965 ELBS edition.

Philips, C.H. and Wainwright, M.D., *The Partition of India,* London, 1970.

Pirpur Committee Report, Report of the Inquiry Committee appointed by the Council of the All-India Muslim Leauge to Inquire into Muslim Grievances in Congress Provinces, 1938.

Pirzada, Syed Sharifuddin (ed.), *Foundations of Pakistan, All-India Muslim League Documents, 1906-1947,* two volumes, Karachi, 1969, 1970.

Poulantzas, Nicos, *Fascism and Dictatorship,* London, 1974.

Pradhan, G.P. and Bhagwat, A.K., *Lokamanya Tilak,* Bombay. 1959.

Prakash, Indra, *A Review of the History and Work of the Hindu Mahasabha and the Hindu Sanghatan Movement,* New Delhi, 1938.

Prasad, Beni, *The Hindu-Muslim Questions,* Allahabad, 1941.

Prasad, Bimal, "British Attitude Towards the Communal Problem in India 1937-1947", mimeographed, presented at the seminar on "The Communal Problem in India 1919-47", organized by the Nehru Memorial Museum and Library, New Delhi, in March 1971.

Prasad, Rajendra, *India Divided,* Bombay, 1947, third revised edition.

________, *Autobiography,* Bombay, 1957.

Przeworski, Adam, "The Process of Class Formation: From Karl Kautsky's *Class Struggle* to Recent Controversies", mimeographed, University of Chicago, 1976.

Rai, Lajpat, *Writings and Speeches,* two volumes, edited by Joshi, V.C., Delhi, 1966.

________, *Autobiographical Writings,* edited by Joshi, V.C., Delhi, 1965.

Rai, Satya, *Partition of the Punjab,* Bombay, 1965.

________, "Role of Panjab Legislature in the Freedom Struggle", New Delhi.

Raut, S.K., "RSS: A Proto Fascist Organisation", *Secular Democracy,* New Delhi, November-December 1979.

Ray, Santimoy, *Freedom Movement and Indian Muslims,* New Delhi, 1979.

Reeves, P.D., "Changing Patterns of Political Alignment in the General Elections to the United Provinces Legislative Assembly, 1937 and 1946", *Modern Asian Studies,* Cambridge, Vol. 5, No. 2, 1971.

Report of the Bengal Provincial Banking Enquiry Committee 1929-30, Vol. I. Calcutta, 1930.

Report of Indian Statutory Commission, London, 1930.

Reports of the Joint Select Committee on Indian Constitutional Reforms, London, 1933.

Report of the Kanpur Riots Enquiry Committee, published as *Roots of Communal Politics,* edited by Barrier, N. Gerald, New Delhi, 1976.

Report on Indian Constitutional Reforms, Calcutta, 1918.

Robinson, Francis, *Separatism Among Indian Muslims: The Politics of the United Provinces' Muslims, 1860-1923,* Delhi, 1975.

Rossi, A. (Angelo Tasca), *The Rise of Italian Fascism 1918-1922,* New York, 1976, reprint of 1936 edition.

Saberwal, Satish, "Elements of Communalism", *Mainstream,* New Delhi, Vol. XIX, Nos. 29-30, 21 and 28 March 1981.

Sarkar, Sumit, *The Swadeshi Movement in Bengal 1903-1908,* New Delhi, 1973.

Sarkar, Tanika, "The First Phase of Civil Disobedience in Bengal, 1930-1" *The Indian Historical Review,* Delhi, Vol. IV, No, 1, July 1977.

________, "Communal Riots in Bengal", in *Communal and Pan-Islamic Trends in Colonial India,* edited by Hasan, Mushirul, New Delhi, 1981.

Savarkar, V.D., *The Indian War of Independence 1857,* New Delhi, 1970 edition.

________, *Hindutva,* Poona, 1949 reprint, first published in 1923.

________, *Hindu Sanghatan,* Bombay, 1940.

________, *Hindu Rashtra Darshan — A Collection of the Presidential Speeches,* Bombay, 1949.

Sayeed, Khalid B., *Pakistan—The Formative Phase 1857-1948,* London, 1968.

Seal, Anil, *The Emergence of Indian Nationalism,* Cambridge, 1968.

Shah, C. G., *Marxism Gandhism Stalinism,* Bombay, 1963.

Shakir, Moin, *Khilafat to Partition,* New Delhi, 1970.

Sharma, R.S., "Historiography of Ancient Indian Polity up to 1930", in his *Aspects of Political Ideas and Institutions in Ancient India,* Delhi, 1968, revised edition.

Sharma, Urmila, "Social and Economic Aspects of Separatism in the Panjab 1849-1947", unpublished M. Phil. dissertation, Department of History,, Guru Nanak Dev University, Amritsar, 1979.

Shraddhananda, Swami, *Hindu Sangathan,* Delhi, 1926.

Singh, Anita I., "Nehru and the Communal Problem 1936-1939", unpublished M. Phil. dissertation, Centre for Historical Studies, Jawaharlal Nehru University, New Delhi, 1976.

Singh, Kirpal (ed.), "Sardar Bahadur Mehtab Singh's Report on Rawalpindi Riots—1926", *The Punjab Past and Present,* Patiala, Vol. XV, Part II, October 1981.

Sinha, H.N., *Rise of the Peshwas,* Allahabad, 1954.

Sinha, N.K., *The Economic History of Bengal,* Calcutta, Vol. I, 1961 edition, Vol. II, 1968 reprint.

Sinha, Sasadhar, *Indian Independence in Perspective,* Bombay, 1964.

Smith, William Cantwell, *Modern Islam in India,* Lahore, 1963 reprint from 1946 edition.

Srinivas, M.N., *Social Change in Modern India,* New Delhi, 1966.

Strachey, John, *India,* London, 1893.

Suleri, Z.A., *My Leader,* third edition, 1946.

Talbot, I.A., "The 1946 Punjab Elections", *Modern Asian Studies,* Cambridge, Vol. 14, No. 1, 1980.

Thapar, Romila, Mukhia, Harbans and Chandra, Bipan, *Communalism and the Writing of Indian History,* New Delhi, second edition, 1977.

Thapar, Romila, "Interpretations of Ancient Indian History", in her *Ancient Indian Social History,* New Delhi, 1978.

________, *Past and Prejudice,* New Delhi, 1975.

Thomas, Antony, "Lord Linlithgow and the League", unpublished paper, Centre for Historical Studies, Jawaharlal Nehru University, New Delhi, 1979.

Thompson, E.P., *The Making of the English Working Class,* Penguin Books, 1978 reprint.

________, "An Open Letter to Leszek Kolakowski", *Socialist Register 1973,* London, 1974.

Thursby, G.R., *Hindu-Muslim Relations in British India,* Leiden, 1975.

Tomlinson, B.R., *The Indian National Congress and the Raj, 1929-1942,* London, 1976.

Trotsky, Leon, *The Struggle Against Fascism in Germany,* New York, 1972.

Vajda, Mihaly, *Fascism as a Mass Movement,* London, 1976.

Vidyalankar, A.N., *National Integration and Teaching of History,* New Delhi, no date.

Wasti, S.R., *Lord Minto and the Indian National Movement,* Oxford, 1964.

Zaidi, Z.H., "Aspects of the Development of Muslim League Policy, 1937-47", in *The Partition of India,* edited by Philips, C. H. and Wainright, M.D., London, 1970.

Zakaria, Rafiq, *Rise of Muslims in Indian Politics,* Bombay, 1971 edition.

Zetland, Lord, *Essayez: Memoirs of Lawrence, Second Marquess of Zetland,* London, 1956.

________, *Zetland Papers,* Nehru Memorial Museum and Library, New Delhi.

Index